MW01093354

WHY THE CHURCH OF THE
NAZARENE
SHOULD BE FULLY
LGBTQ+
AFFIRMING

THOMAS JAY OORD and
ALEXA OORD, editors

Paperback ISBN 978-1-948609-94-4
Hardcover ISBN 978-1-948609-96-8
Ebook ISBN 978-1-948609-95-1

Printed in the United States of America

Library of Congress Cataloguing-in-Publication Data

Why the Church of the Nazarene Should Be Fully LGBTQ+ Affirming / Thomas Jay Oord and Alexa Oord, eds.

Table of Contents

PART II: ALLY NARRATIVES

Table of Contents

PART III: SCHOLARLY PERSPECTIVES

APPENDIX

Introduction

The essays in this book were written in response to an invitation. We (Tom and Alexa) invited people to contribute to a book we would title, "Why the Church of the Nazarene Should be Fully LGBTQ+ Affirming." You're reading that book.

Despite the shared theme, the essays published here are diverse. Some are written by queer people, and they narrate portions of their life journeys. Those narratives often include struggles and the eventual affirmation of their LGBTQ+ identities and experiences as healthy rather than sinful. Many felt persecuted by people and the culture of the Church of the Nazarene, so they left the denomination. They did not feel loved. Other queer people remain but feel marginalized, shamed, and traumatized.

Some essay writers are parents, siblings, or allies of LGBTQ+ people. Most who become fully affirming do so because of close relationships with queer loved ones. Some parents, for instance, felt compelled to rethink their views on LGBTQ+ matters after their children "came out" or identified as non-heteronormative. Many reevaluated what it means to live as healthy people in healthy societies. They now believe God loves and affirms queer people.

Some contributors to this book are pastors, scholars, or leaders in the church. They believe the denomination needs to change its views on human sexuality and the way it treats those who support queer people. Some of these writers call for honest conversations, including impunity for those who think current Manual statements fail to reflect well the love of Jesus.[1] In other essays, scholars explain why scripture, theology, and history support a fully affirming LGBTQ+ position.

---

1. The call for safe and irenic discussion of LGBTQ issues is also present among Church of the Nazarene clergy. See the doctoral work of Reg Watson on this matter (R. G. Watson, *Nazarene Clergy Responses to Homosexuality and Interactions with LGBT People* [Doctoral dissertation, Regent University, 2015]). See also Bruce Barnard's research and preliminary writing in preparation for dissertation work, "You're Losing Us - The LGBTQ Community and the Church of the Nazarene."

By "fully affirming," contributors *don't* mean "anything goes" sexually. After all, "not everything is beneficial," to quote the Apostle Paul (1 Cor. 10:23). Some sexual activity—homosexual and heterosexual—isn't healthy, and life-long partnerships in marriage have immense value. They mean they fully affirm people with LGBTQ+ identities, orientations, and desires. The denomination's current statement on human sexuality does not reflect well the love Jesus calls his followers to express.

Although this book has more than 90 contributors, one may think a tiny percentage of Nazarenes want change. But there are good reasons to believe hundreds of thousands in the denomination agree with the book's contributors, and that number rises daily. A 2007 Pew poll showed that 31% of Americans who identify with the Church of the Nazarene thought society should accept homosexuality. That percentage jumped to 40% by 2014.[2] We suspect the percentage is higher today.

A Barna Report indicates that 46% of Christians under the age of 40 want laws to protect Same-Sex Marriage and LGBTQ+ rights.[3] Two major takeaways from that Barna survey are 1) American Christians increasingly accept LGBTQ+ people and their healthy sexual behavior, and 2) younger American Christians are more accepting of queer people than older Americans.

Young people are leaving the Church of the Nazarene. Many believe the denomination's views on human sexuality do not reflect the love of God. A 2008 poll of twenty religious groups said the holiness tradition—of which the Church of the Nazarene is the largest denomination—is the *worst* of all religious groups at retaining their young people. Only 32% of Nazarene youth remain.[4] A similar poll in 2015 showed no change in this rate of exit.[5]

The Church of the Nazarene is global, of course, and while the USA segment is the strongest financially, it represents a fairly small in membership percentage overall. Our experience among European Nazarenes, however, is that the majority are more progressive on LGBTQ+ issues than American Nazarenes. But African

---

2. See https://www.pewresearch.org/fact-tank/2015/12/18/most-u-s-christian-groups-grow-more-accepting-of-homosexuality/

3. See https://www.barna.com/research/americas-change-of-mind-on-same-sex-marriage-and-lgbtq-rights/

4. See http://thomasjayoord.com/index.php/blog/archives/atheists_only_slightly_worse_at_retaining_children_than_holiness_folk

5. See https://www.pewforum.org/2015/05/12/chapter-2-religious-switching-and-intermarriage/pr_15-05-12_rls_chapter2-04/

and Latin-American Nazarenes are less progressive on this issue, and less progressive on other issues, such as women in leadership and modesty in dress.

These essays also tell a story. It's a narrative about how a marginalized group has been mistreated and denied full acceptance. That story points to a loving and accepting God who calls us all to love and accept queer people. A peculiarly loving God loves peculiar people of all varieties and wants us to do the same. This love means full acceptance of LGBTQ+ people, their identities, orientations, and healthy sexual expressions.

As editors, we hope these essays foster that acceptance. We believe the Church of the Nazarene has something positive to offer the world. But the heart of the denomination's message—love—has been muted and muffled by its statements about LGBTQ+ people.

In the spirit of spurring "one another to love and good deeds," as the writer of Hebrews puts it (10:24), we offer this book.

—Thomas Jay Oord and Alexa Oord

A few words about language and about mental health...

We and many of our contributors use the term "queer" throughout this book, both as a synonym for "LGBTQ+" and as a transformative lens for rethinking power and relationships. However, some members of the LGBTQ+ community don't identify with "queer"—its history as a hateful slur may still be too painful. We embrace the term "queer" while leaving space for those who prefer other terms, an expansive approach embodied in the "+" in "LGBTQ+ affirming."

For some, the terms "queer," "gay," "heteronormative," "trans," and more are confusing. This is understandable. The labels we use to describe the diverse people and issues are in flux. That's the nature of language and labels: they change. But the change has been especially great in this area, as researchers work to better understand what many have kept hidden. To help readers, we've offered a short glossary of terms at the conclusion of the book.

Christians and the church have sometimes been the most unloving to LGBTQ+ people. And often this has led to mental health issues, among other negative outcomes. We know that reading some of these essays will be triggering for queer people and their allies who endure trauma related to abuse. Consequently, we've provide a short list of counseling and therapy resources to consult.

PART I

Queer Voices

Because I Want My Children to Live

TARYN EUDALY

The Church of the Nazarene is not a safe place for children.

I have always known I wanted children. It was a soul-deep, logically fueled desire that I simply could not ignore. After two miscarriages, one of which landed me in the hospital, nine months of anxiety and prayers, and twelve hours of labor, I held my first child in my arms. From the moment I laid my hand on their sweet head, I knew. I knew that I would give my last breath to protect this gift. And when children 2 and 3 were born, I knew that no one could come between them and me, that my fierce love would always choose their well-being.

It was a similar reaction when I found my place in the Church of the Nazarene. 23 years old and feeling the call to ministry, I had no church home. I found the local Church of the Nazarene via Google, and when I read the Statement of Faith, I saw the bones of my own salvation story written out. I exclaimed in recognition, "That's it! That's what happened to me!" When we attended our first service, the Holy Spirit said "stay." And so, we did.

We stayed through those miscarriages and through the births of our next two children. We stayed through my local licensing and district licensing. We stayed through my ordination interviews and service. We stayed through move after move, deployments and retirement. But I can no longer stay. Because I want my kids to live.

It is well documented that the suicide rates for LGBTQ+ (queer) identifying children are significantly higher than for other children and youth. Similarly, we know having just one affirming and accepting adult or community can decrease the risk of suicide and the rates of feeling suicidal or considering suicide. There are stacks of evidence that queer children and youth are more likely to be queer in families with other queer members. Given how many queer clergy, queer members, and church members with queer family are in the Church of the Nazarene, statistically, every Church of the Nazarene is likely to have at least one queer person, probably a child or young adult, who is likely to consider suicide while attending that church.

It might even be one of my kids, because I am one of those queer clergy. Being married to a man for 16 years made it easy to be queer in the Church of the Nazarene. No one ever questioned me, no one ever worried about me, and our polity said that my own attractions were not a sin. So, I was happy to stay in the Church that educated me, taught me, and affirmed my call. I was delighted to be a part of the Nazarene family.

But as my children got older and I began to learn about the likelihood that one of them could be queer, and I began to learn about the risks of religious trauma and spiritual abuse for queer children, my perspective shifted. I began to look at our church through the eyes of someone who had no protective cover of a "normal" marriage, and what I saw terrified and saddened me. Church members prayed for their gay children to be delivered from the clutches of evil. Not even from romantic or sexual relationships, but just from the attractions they felt. Church Board members would espouse the evils of homosexuality, decry the brokenness of being transgender, and pray against the devil's own work in the minds of queer folks. I was told by a District Superintendent that I could never out my queerness to church members. All of these were fully against our own Manual but accepted and encouraged by leadership, and they still defended their position using the Manual's statement on human sexuality. Then I saw how unsafe and unstable it is for our queer and questioning kids to be in the Church of the Nazarene.

Still, I chose to stay. I love my mother church, and I love my brothers and sisters in faith. We often disagree, but that is how iron sharpens iron. I have been fully willing to be confined by the doctrines I agreed to when I made my ordination vows. I have been fully willing to be quiet about parts of who I am. I have been fully capable of facing the onslaught of unintentionally hateful talk around people like me. I have gently preached the gospel of love to the same folks who would swear I have the Devil in me because of things I can't control (despite prayers and tears and struggles for years). I made this choice, over and over, because the Holy Spirit once told me to stay and never told me to leave. I had no problem submitting myself to the risks and pains of being queer in a non-affirming denomination when the Spirit called me to do it. But that is a choice I can only make for me. I have no right to decide to place my children in such dangerous environments.

It does not matter if my children identify as queer. What matters is that I would never know. For as long as I pastor a church that does not accept all of them, that will not love all of them, that speaks out against a hidden part of themselves, then they will never disclose such a thing to me. If my children cannot feel safe in the arms of the church I serve, how could they feel safe with me? If my children cannot feel safe in the arms of the Church, how can they ever trust the God whose name we claim?

It only takes one affirming place for a child to feel safe and loved for who they are. It only takes one adult who affirms their gender and sexuality to prevent suicide. It only takes one place where they will not be bullied or shamed for them to believe they can have a good life full of love and hope. And I want to be that person, that place. I want the Church to be that place. I want all children—mine and yours and the ones I'll never know—to know that the Church of the Nazarene is a place so in tune with the love of the Triune God that they boldly declare "let the little children come to me." Without qualifiers. Without disclaimers. Without spiritual violence.

So, I am leaving the Church of the Nazarene. Because it is not, and never has been, a safe place for me. Because it is not, and never has been, a loving place for all children. Because I am deeply pro-life. Because I believe in a God who does not hate. Because I believe that love covers a multitude of sins.

I am leaving the Church of the Nazarene because I want my children to live.

Taryn Eudaly is, at the time of writing, an ordained Elder in the Church of the Nazarene. She is a graduate of Portland Seminary (George Fox University) with a focused interest on the feminine roots of Holiness Churches in the 20th century. She lives in Portland, OR, with her three children and a hoard of coffee.

Scandalous Woman

KARA HUDSON

The Nazarene Church turns its back on its own children to remain comfortable.

"When you are having a hard time, *smile*! In seven minutes, you will actually begin to feel happy."

My beloved missionary uncle gave us this premarital advice in our only meeting before the wedding. At 21 years old, I was marrying a much older man in less than six months from our first date. His loving advice works for the occasional stressor, but was insufficient to help me manage this relationship.

After 15 years of marriage, I found myself walking down a long hallway to the nurse's station at the psychiatric hospital. For months, I had been separated from my husband, but in the same home. I could no longer pretend my Wife Role. When my children were not in my care, my depression was so deep that I was sleeping 22 hours a day. My concerned friend called my mother. Mom asked her to take me to my doctor. My doctor referred me to this mental hospital.

I knew my life would not ever return to normal. I wouldn't survive it. But, I didn't know *how* to follow this forbidden, necessary path so I could survive being Me. I was in shock.

This is my story.

My Nazarene Credentials

I came into the world with strong Nazarene credentials. I was born in Central America. My parents were Nazarene missionaries. My "relatives" were other missionaries and their families. I considered them aunts, uncles, grandparents, and cousins. We were moved to a different country every single four-year term, with a furlough in the United States between each. That was ten international moves by the age of 17.

I still have a cartoon I drew in my youth of my missionary uncle who was in charge of missionary assignments. He was sitting at his desk in Kansas City with a chess board of Missionary Roles in front of him. My family members were the chess pieces. My chess piece wept as he moved it.

Both my parents graduated from a Nazarene college and were ordained elders in the Church of the Nazarene. My mother graduated from Nazarene Theological Seminary.

At age five, I was saved in my Nazarene church in Central America. I said the Jesus Prayer wholeheartedly on my knees *again* at age seven in a Nazarene house church in another war-torn country. I had to make sure the first time wasn't just a dream. I didn't want to accidentally go to hell.

I was baptized by my dad at age ten in the same war-torn country. I learned from the wars that life is short and people are precious. I lived each day as if it were my last—because it could be. I was entirely sanctified in a Nazarene revival in a South American country at age eleven. I truly wanted God to know I was committed. I loved people with all my heart.

I came to the United States and graduated from a Nazarene university with honors. I participated in Nazarene college missions trips to three countries, often in the role of translator.

I went to Nazarene Theological Seminary where I found myself to *be* a credential for unmarried future Nazarene ministers. Future male ministers needed a wife to be able to get a church.

I fell into a relationship with someone who seemed as disinterested in me as I was in the meat market at the seminary. I got my M-R-S degree and fell into the Wife Role. Soon after getting his Wife Credential, my husband had a church and was ordained an elder in the Church of the Nazarene.

I stated to numerous people that this felt like an arranged marriage by God. I hadn't ever felt enamored by *anybody* the way I saw my friends besotted over the years.

Despite my husband leaving the pulpit after two ministries, I remained active in my local church as a Nazarene youth leader. I was on the Nazarene church board. I led a Nazarene women's retreat and about a dozen Nazarene inner healing retreats over the weekends. I was a small group leader for my Nazarene church. I loved people!

The Scandal

One friendship deepened. I fought the feeling for over a year. There was no kissing nor undressing. Yet, my heart beat faster when she was near. I hung on her every word. I found myself able to love her more deeply than I had loved anybody in my entire life. I didn't have any words to describe this experience because at age 36,

I simply had no other similar experience. And, she was a woman, so I considered her a "good friend".

It took over a year for my being to realize that I was in a state of such *cognitive dissonance* that there was no returning from it. My mind, heart, body, and spirit were not in agreement. Peace would mean all of me would have to align. I didn't know *how* to find peace. I didn't understand what was happening.

I was finally able to tell this to my counselor at the psychiatric hospital. She reflected those words back to me. And, she used the "L" word—Lesbian. I was shocked because I had not considered that I might be *That*. It was a distant word that was on TV, or used derogatorily by "good evangelical people". *Lesbian* was a label used to identify "sinful, depraved people".

It had never dawned on me that feeling attraction to someone was a natural part of being human. And until now, I had never experienced attraction to anybody that involved a physical, emotional, and spiritual response to said person. Not once.

I felt the curtain draw back in this very dark life that I had intended to sleep through. Sunshine filled my being, and I was able to see *myself* clearly. I was being introduced to my True Self—for the first time in my life.

This counselor did not judge me. She just saw me.

The bell rang gloriously and my life finally made sense. If I was to survive, I could not close the curtain again. I could no longer be a Nazarene chess piece—whether as Wife, Pianist, Church Board Member, or Missionary Kid. From this day forth, I would need to be Me. Just me.

I needed to do this right, for the sake of my three small children. I felt protective and longed for them to feel free to *be*. I was grateful I was going through this experience for *them*.

I told my supportive friend of my conversation with the counselor, and about the window of sunshine. I told her I did not expect this to be reciprocal. I just needed to be honest about what was happening to me.

She was in shock because I had named it. She grew up judging that lesbian label, too. Over time, she recognized her own denial about herself as well. She chose to accept our relationship fully. I'm so glad. I have never needed the seven-minute smile to fool me into feeling happy with her or be at peace in the relationship.

The Next Step

After my hospitalization, the first thing I did was to research what the Bible actually says about me. I knew this was Nature, not Nurture. And, I couldn't wrap my head around why a loving God would create me and then forbid me from having a natural physical response within a truly healthy relationship.

I found the seven Clobber Verses. It's literally how it feels when the Bible is used to bash someone over the head with judgment. It was not difficult to explore the Bible verses about homosexual people in their original languages. They have entirely different meanings! I realized "good Christian people" aren't doing their biblical research.

I learned that there is much literature demonstrating there have been lesbian, gay, bisexual, and transgender people in every culture of every time on every continent since history was first recorded. There is death for those from rejecting cultures. And, individuals thrive in cultures that do not reject them. That rejection is what leads to self-destruction. Without it, individuals are just as healthy as anyone else.

My pastor wanted to be supportive, but was unsure what the denomination required of him in my situation. I arranged for him to meet with a missionary uncle who could speak for the Nazarene denomination. Together, we learned that I was "allowed" to sit in the audience and worship in my local church. But, my active loving service to others was no longer admissible by the Nazarene denomination.

Just like that.

The Right Amount of Rejection

It seemed the goal of my former church friends is what mine would have been, if I were in their shoes. They were seeking the right amount of biblically sanctioned rejection. I wasn't planning to leave my church. So, over the course of the next six years, I recognized various categories of rejection. I still experience some after 15 years.

Shunning: I walk by those who once were good friends, smile and say "hello". They literally look straight through me as though I don't exist. It is so shocking I have to laugh.

Gossiping: Others are determined to love me "in Jesus' name". Their exaggerated smiles show everyone how loving they can be to this scandalous woman. Yet, I am aware of the incessant demonizing chatter about me to anyone that will listen. These may be cloaked as "prayer requests". Social media has made this explosive. This choice is particularly painful for me.

Disappearing: There were those who vanished so quickly it was like magic. Poof! Gone. At least these folks were honest.

Intervening: Less than 48 hours after being discharged from the hospital, a few of my former friends wanted to follow Matthew 18:16 and have an intervention. They never asked "Are you ok?" or "What happened?". I was just beginning to be able to get out of bed every day. But, they wanted me to get back in line asap.

Evangelizing: "I believe in the Bible" might be the start of it. "But, I love you *anyway*."

So, a judgmental relationship with me is evidence of their "generosity"? Do they not realize that I can have a very thoughtful, well-researched discussion with them about their Bible verses? I am still Me, even though I am gay. When I hear this, I have to sigh.

In fact, people who have rejected me have never asked me *one question* about my experience. I am no longer a valid human. I wear a Scarlet Letter "L" in sharpie on my forehead. It is the *only* part of me that some "good church people" can see.

These responses are all forms of Social Rejection. Research demonstrates that when people are socially rejected for their sexual orientation or gender identity, their rates of suicidality, addiction, self-harm, and high-risk behaviors are disproportionately higher—particularly when "conversion therapy" has been provided.

I understand why.

Of Chess and Love

The Nazarene chess game requires a performance-oriented God that judges, rejects, and sacrifices its own. The Elders don't want to look up from their "righteous pursuits" to truly see and love their own children.

The Children of the Church have been forsaken. They are the ones who know what love is, and what it is *not*.

Love means each person has value. Love means we don't judge people because they are left-handed (10% of the population), Black (12.3% of the U.S.), or gay (10% of the population). Love means left-handed people aren't forced to write with the wrong hand, as when my left-handed grandmother was a child.

Love listens and learns from others. Love means one's heart, mind, body, and spirit are in agreement. Love is a big breath of clean air.

Love *is* acceptance. It is a cup of coffee, a smile, an embrace, or a "Tell me your story." It's not complicated.

Life is short. People are precious.

It's time to burn the chess board.

Kara Hudson has been a Licensed Clinical Professional Counselor for a community mental health agency in Nampa, Idaho since 2013. Kara is the Lead Clinician for the Intensive Outpatient Program for high-risk adults and adolescents. Kara and her wife celebrate 15 joyful years together this year. They have two adult children and one teenager still at home.

Just As I Am

NANCY R. KELSO

A faith closed to the conclusions of science is suffocating our LGBTQ+ children.

I often tell people that had I been coming of age in today's world, I would have known I was gay when I was 12. Walking home from school one warm September afternoon, I was talking about a girl one grade ahead of me.

"Kristi Green this and Kristi Green that. You talk about her like she's your boyfriend or something." Those words, spoken to me by my sister, immediately filled me with shame and panic. *Was that what I sounded like? What was wrong with me? What did she see in me? How can I hide?*

I was a devoted, born again, saved and sanctified Nazarene. Third generation in fact. All in the same church. My grandmothers on both sides were my Sunday School teachers. My father was the music leader. Missionary society presidents, board members, Assembly delegates—my family was part of the core of my home congregation. I made my first appearance at church when I was six days old and attended every Sunday service, Wednesday prayer meeting, and twice a year revival meeting for the next 18 years of my life. I had bona fides.

I chose a local Christian high school because I was serious about my faith and wanted teachers who would be mentors for me not only academically, athletically, and socially, but also spiritually. If there was a way to cultivate my relationship with Jesus, I was sure to be sincerely engaged.

When I elected to attend college, the same rationale won out. I opted for a Nazarene school so that I would be surrounded by others who loved the Lord and enjoyed serving Him. That's why I was so surprised when late one night in the fall of my freshman year while chatting away with a fellow dorm mate, I kissed her. It felt like something out of left field; it also felt true and right in the moment.

My college years were full of personal turmoil. I was faced with the fact that I was most attracted to my girl friends, yet I knew this was forbidden and displeased God. Over and over, I repented, resolved not to give in to sin, and fell into the same situation. Once. Twice. Three times. All with Nazarene girls who had denominational pedigrees similar to mine.

I tried to live a straight life. I had boyfriends. I prayed. I pleaded. The attractions never left. I was told that I had lesbian demons, that I was broken, that I was sinful, that I was selfish, that I was, most certainly, sexually abused. Because, what else could explain this attraction to women?

I tried a different Nazarene college for a fresh start. And by Christmas, I was knee deep in my same old patterns. There were tears. Sobbing. Gut-wrenching sobbing with pleading prayers. "I don't want to be this way. Please, God help me." I hated this thing inside me. "Like a dog returns to its vomit," I used to say quoting Proverbs, "I return to my sin." No matter the approach, I could not escape myself.

Sublimation is one of the classic defense mechanisms. It is the directing of unwanted energies toward good things. The next twenty years of my life qualify as a case study in sublimation. I was utterly devoted to Christ and His cause. I attended seminary. I entered a pastoral internship program. I went overseas to do mission work. I was a leader. Everyone who knew me would say that I was an example of Christ's love and light. I helped plant a church. I lead worship and small groups. I got married. I had a son. I became a staff pastor at my home church. It was all real. I was real. I was thoroughly committed to Jesus.

In those days I would say that I managed my sexuality. "We can't help who we are attracted to," I used to say, "but we can choose what we do about it." I had been a celibate single person for twelve years before I met my husband. We had as good a marriage that a straight man and a lesbian can create together. He was my best friend. We had just celebrated our tenth anniversary, yet my desire to be with a woman was still there, as strong as ever. I was depressed. I wanted to die.

It had been thirty years since I first felt the shame of being clocked by my sister, and after all of it, I knew that I was gay. Nothing had changed my core longing. For so long I believed that if I gave into my homosexual desires, I would have to turn my back on God. But something had shifted in my understanding of God's infinite love. Maybe instead of wanting me to live as a heterosexual, it was more important to God that I live as my true self. Maybe my sexuality wasn't evil, warped, broken, or forbidden. Maybe it was good. Maybe I could embrace myself fully as God's child without having to sever a core component of myself.

My story can be heard in the stories of thousands of others. Our lives and our experiences are not tales of rebellious sinners turning our backs on God, but stories of sincere, mature, devoted followers of Jesus. What do we, the Church of the Nazarene, do with this lived experience of thousands of born again, sold out Christians who could not and cannot rid themselves of their homosexual attractions?

If we are not offered acceptance and blessing, do we, the believers who are homosexual, leave the Church of the Nazarene to find more accepting denominations? Do we run away and live our lives far from the communities where we were raised, isolating ourselves from the support systems our hetero friends and couples maintain? Do we live double lives as church going hetero couples on the outside, while indulging our core need for intimacy with same-sex partners on the side? To date, these are the experiences I have seen in my gay friends and family—leaving, hiding, lying.

How will the Church of the Nazarene respond? Do we continue to respond with a message of turn from it or burn for it? Do we at best offer some compassion and community for the LGBTQ people who remain single and celibate? Is it enough to say, "The Bible says one man and one woman for life. Period. End of discussion"? Does that simple summary align with the complex and varied sexuality that is evident in our world? Is there room for us to consider what the realm of medicine and social sciences have come to understand about human sexuality?

In the 1970s, the medical community officially dismissed the idea that homosexuality is an illness. For years, social science research has indicated that human sexuality is formed through a complex interplay of biological conditions. Both communities have concluded that homosexuality is a normal, albeit less common, expression of human sexuality and that sexual attraction is best understood to be a continuum - some exclusively attracted to the opposite sex, some exclusively to the same sex, and many people along the spectrum in between, experiencing both.

Today there is no reputable professional medical or social scientific organization that considers homosexuality as anything less than normal. Furthermore, and this is equally important to consider, these same organizations denounce all reparative therapies as injurious to LGBTQ+ individuals. Sexuality is hardwired into us in the same manner as left-handedness or redheadedness and cannot be changed.

I am a product of Christian education—Mennonite high school, Nazarene colleges, Evangelical and Nazarene seminaries. For my entire life it has been my understanding that science and faith are never mutually exclusive. Faith in God and biblical Christianity must always encompass truth wherever it is found.

If scientific conclusions conflict with some details of our faith, we must look again at our religious beliefs. Perhaps they need to widen, to open, to shift, to become less restrictive and more gracious. In all of my years in Christian education, I never once felt that my faith was so weak and rigid that it could not expand to encompass the findings of science.

Gay and lesbian children will keep coming into this world, and they will keep being born and raised in the Church of the Nazarene. I tell my story for them. As my sexuality unfolded, it filled my mind and heart with panic, fear, self-loathing, disgust, shame, sadness, frustration, loneliness, hopelessness, and despair. I carried that weight for thirty years before I finally laid it down at the feet of religion and trusted that the God of Love made me who I am—and I am good.

It is my hope that the Church of the Nazarene will make space for blessing, including, and affirming people who are gay. The body of Christ will be more whole and healthy for it.

Nancy R. Kelso has spent her life serving youth and young adults as a coach, teacher, pastor, and school counselor. She earned her Bachelor of Arts in English at Olivet Nazarene University and her Master of Arts in Counseling Psychology at Trinity Evangelical Divinity School.

Why Can't the Nazarenes I Know Be More Like the Knitters I Know?

NAOMI MACKEY

The first group of people I came out to was my knitting and spinning group. They are just what you would expect from a secular group that meets at the local senior center—a group of elderly women and men who enjoy knitting, crocheting and spinning wool into yarn. Most of them were in their seventh or eighth decade of life. They enjoyed vigorous debates about ranking their favorite types of animal fiber (mine are yak, silk, camel and washable wool) as well as the relative merits of cable stitches versus bobbles. (Cables are much, much more interesting!) At 35, I was the youngest member of the group by decades. But for me, the most important characteristic they all shared was that none of them attended the Church of the Nazarene.

The Church of the Nazarene has a long history of pursuing holiness of heart and life. This pursuit manifests itself in many ways, but always encourages one to get closer to God through knowing oneself better and therefore knowing what God desires of us. Belonging to the community of faith is very important to the Nazarene tradition, and as church members we even sing regularly about how happy we are to be part of the family of God.

Being Nazarene is in my blood. I remember as a small child sitting in the pews of our tiny church as my mother and grandmother tried to control my fidgeting, a church that was almost within spitting distance of an older Nazarene church my great grandparents had attended. When I was eleven, the Church of the Nazarene saved my life. Literally. A wise Sunday School teacher realized that the questions I was asking about salvation, death and heaven indicated something more than just the usual tween curiosity on the finer points of basic theology. She told my mother she was concerned about my mental health and worried that I might be suicidal. She was correct, and her timely intervention kept me from killing myself.

No matter which individual church body I attended, these people were my tribe. They surrounded me with support through some of the most difficult times in my life—poverty, my lifelong struggles with mental health, moving to four different states in the span of two years—and I knew I could count on them to love me for who I was. Within limits.

I realized that the Nazarene community would be very displeased if they knew my deepest secret. I, a thirty-something mother of two small children who had been married for a decade, was attracted to women. The more I pursued understanding the will of God in my life and understanding myself better, the more obvious this fact became. And that understanding has allowed me to better understand my status as a beloved daughter of God who pursues holiness in her life and spiritual practices.

Whether this revelation made me qualify as a lesbian woman or as a bisexual person mattered far less to me than the certain knowledge that my church community would react badly to it. Over the next five years, they proved this beyond a shadow of a doubt. My husband's co-lead pastor sat me down and tried to talk me out of my newfound self-knowledge by explaining that I was faithfully married to a man and therefore could not possibly be attracted to women.

Even worse, a common reaction was embodied by a dear friend, a lifelong Nazarene. When I came out to her, she responded with stunned silence, followed by exclaiming "I'm sorry you feel that way!" She then explained that she did not know what to say. I told her that I was hoping for a response that was some variation on the theme that we would be able to continue our two decades of friendship. I sincerely hoped she would eventually be able to acknowledge that this was not some sudden change in who I was as a person so much as a gradual revelation of a part of my personality that I had previously kept hidden.

"I'm not sure I can do that!" she stammered. We have not spoken since, as though my knowledge of myself somehow impacted her personal pursuit of holiness.

Unfortunately, the same denomination that saved my life has also crushed large parts of my personhood as I have struggled to belong to it. The same people who embodied God's love to me throughout my battles with depression, suicidality and a few nervous breakdowns have been the vessel for some of the most hateful, ugly words about God that I have ever heard. They have told me that my salvation is endangered by the very fabric of my existence. That the person I am at my deepest core is "depraved," "immoral," "sinful by nature," and in the words of more than one church-goer, "just plain wrong!" They have wielded the Bible like a weapon—tirelessly aimed at the most sensitive parts of my being—so often that I find very little joy in reading it.

And my knitting group? They interrupted their debate on the merits of acrylic yarn versus wool yarn (acrylic yarn is fantastic for baby items!) to voice unanimous acceptance of my announcement. Several of them gave me bear hugs and one exclaimed "I'm so happy you found the courage to tell us who you are!"

If only I could find that same love and support in the family of God.

Naomi Mackey *is a psychiatric nurse who graduated from Northwest Nazarene University. In her free time she loves to work with yarn in all its many forms. She lives in the Pacific Northwest with her husband and children.*

The Grace of Coming Out

ERIN MOORMAN

*The Church of the Nazarene must reevaluate what we mean when
we claim to offer grace to the queer community.*

I am asexual. I do not experience sexual attraction toward anyone.
I didn't discover this fact about myself until I was middle-aged and had been married for almost 20 years.

Despite what you might assume, it's not surprising that I spent over 42 years thinking I was heterosexual even though I'm not. I wasn't familiar with the word *asexual* until the year prior to my realization. It wasn't a thing that existed in my worldview. It's not that it was false; it just "wasn't." I knew I wasn't gay, I knew I wasn't bi, I knew I wasn't trans. Therefore, I was clearly straight. There was no reason for me to think anything else or even to ask if there *was* anything else. Especially since everything about my life is so hetero-normative: I'm romantically attracted to the opposite sex (i.e., *hetero-romantic*), I'm aesthetically attracted to the opposite sex, I enjoy physical touch, and I'm sex-favorable (i.e., open to engaging in sexual activity).

I had no reason to presume anything other than a heterosexual identity. Any frustrations I have had in my various romantic and sexual experiences all had "normal," heterosexual explanations. Questioning my orientation wasn't on my radar.

I learned the word *asexual* when some people I know informed me that they are asexual. Wanting to understand their general life experiences a little better, I picked up an introductory book to learn more. However, I found the book frustrating. It took me a while to get through it because I kept getting confused about why the author would describe something as *asexual* that I considered to be part of my "normal," *heterosexual* experience. I took a break from reading it, but when I picked it up again it finally kind of clicked: *What if I'm not confused because they're defining heterosexual experiences as asexual? Rather, what if I'm confused because I think my experiences are heterosexual experiences when they're not?*

I rarely have moments where a thought makes it necessary for me to find a place to be alone and sit, but that was one of them. I took the time to reflect on various romantic and sexual experiences I've had and realized that they made more sense when I viewed them through an asexual lens. After that, reading the rest of the book was much easier, as well as enlightening.

If I hadn't read that introductory book (*The Invisible Orientation: An Introduction to Asexuality* by Julie Sondra Decker, for those who might be interested), I would probably still assume I am heterosexual. Frankly, my life would be much the same. For the most part, nothing's changed. I haven't changed. In regard to my attractions, I've always been who I am now and who I am now has always been Me. I simply didn't know that who I am isn't heterosexual. My life remains very hetero-normative; and for all intents and purposes, my life is a very "straight" life.

The few things that have changed, however, have been *extremely* positive and life-giving.

My husband and I have always had a wonderful relationship. He is my closest friend. He is my accountability partner. I'm the same for him. Like all couples, we do occasionally argue and we've had some rough times. Yet even in those rough times, we've leaned on each other and determined to grow together.

As good as my relationship with my husband was before I came out, though, it actually got better after. It enabled us to be honest about things that we weren't even aware we weren't being honest about. Not because we weren't striving to be honest, but because we didn't realize that we weren't speaking from the same experiences. After I came out, our new understanding enabled us to finally cross bridges that had seemed impassable before.

We finally understood that "problems" which we had previously chalked up to differences between men and women or differences in personality, *weren't* that. We had more accurate information when certain discussions would come up and things just made more sense. I realized that I didn't have to feel guilty about certain desires (or lack of them). Because I had been unable to see and love myself for who I am, my husband—through no fault of his own—had also been unable to see and love me for who I am. But after coming out, we experienced a restoration of relationship that we hadn't even known we needed. It was a gift and a blessing.

In her book, *Queering Wesley, Queering the Church*, Nazarene author Keegan Osinski compares *coming out* to an experience of God's grace. I've been a Christian for 39 years and I know what it's like to experience God's grace. I can confirm that coming out was truly a moment of grace. Just coming out to myself and knowing who I am, was a moment of grace. Coming out to my husband and his acceptance of my identity was a moment of grace. The grace of coming out truly was a part of being healed and redeemed, even in a lifelong believer like me.

The Nazarene Manual's Statement on Human Sexuality and Marriage says, "We recognize the shared responsibility of the body of Christ to be a welcoming, forgiving, and loving community where hospitality, encouragement, transformation, and accountability are available to all."

This picture of a welcoming, loving community which is accountable to one another so that we all may experience transformation in Christ, describes an intimate community; but intimacy requires truth. You cannot create strong, intimate relationships with people who are told to ignore what they feel or to hide the truth of who they are. When distance is created between us and *ourselves* by pretending to be something we are not, it is also created between us and other people. I know this because my husband and I experienced this distance, unknowingly. The Church of the Nazarene should not create this distance intentionally.

True transformation and accountability—true discipleship and fellowship—is only possible when people are honest: with themselves, with Christ, and with the people they are in relationship with. If distance exists between us and other Christians, then fellowship and accountability cannot exist. If fellowship and accountability cannot exist, how can we expect discipleship to be possible? How can we expect a relationship with Christ to grow and mature? A person who is forced to live in the closet is denied that fullness of life we say God offers.

For a queer person, the "perfect love required to live a whole and healthy life cannot be achieved without coming out" (Osinksi p.23) because "[h]onest assessment of oneself is necessary for transformation" (p.21). If a person is allowed to be honest about who they are, authentic and intimate relationships become possible—not only with other people but also with Christ.

The transformation and accountability the Manual calls the body of Christ to offer will only be possible in Nazarene communities if queer people are extended the grace to simply come out and be honest about who they are. To *publicly* identify in Nazarene settings as their true orientation and gender identity; and given the grace to follow how the Spirit guides them in their lives, including with romantic same-sex relationships. Christ will always let us be honest with him in a safe way. True fellowship requires the same.

If we're not willing to allow LGBTQIA+ people to identify as queer, then we cannot claim to offer them grace. It is therefore vital that the Church of the Nazarene reevaluates what we mean when we claim to offer grace to queer folk. We must stop teaching them that they need to hide who they are. We must assure queer people that God loves them just as they are and that they are made in His image just like anyone else. We must demonstrate that we trust the Holy Spirit to work in their life the way the Spirit chooses whether or not it fits into our own experiences and expectations.

I experienced a new fullness of life and grace within my marriage when I came out because my husband accepted me for who I am and allowed the truth of my orientation to guide our relationship going forward. Let the Church of the Nazarene offer the same acceptance to the queer community. Let us not deny them the grace and intimacy which we have already received ourselves.

Erin Moorman is a lifelong Christian who has been taught and mentored in the Church of the Nazarene for over twenty years. Many years of prayerful thought and study convicted her that Nazarenes need to become safe people for the LGBTQIA+ community. A former district-licensed Nazarene pastor, she surrendered her license after God directed her to be affirming of same-sex marriage, a position which is not currently in line with the Manual.

The Rejected Calling

JENNIFER CROWDER NORICKS

I said I would serve the Church of the Nazarene as long as she would have me. And I did.

To a great extent, I am who I am because of the Church of the Nazarene. I grew up there. I come from a family of church musicians. We were the "Sunday Morning, Sunday Night, Wednesday Night" variety. My family has actively served in our local church from the time I can remember. I attended Caravan and participated in Bible quizzing. I was saved at church camp when I was seven years old, sanctified while praying in my bedroom at age 19. I'm a graduate of Olivet Nazarene University.

I've had some questions, though. My gay uncle was spurned by his Nazarene church as a young adult in the 1960s. He spent much of his life being angry, rejecting God and remaining distant from our family. When I was a teenager, he had a spiritual transformation. He returned to God and repaired relations with our family. I remember him walking around the house listening to gospel music on his Walkman (Hey, it was the 1980s!) I would hear him singing praises to Jesus while he folded his laundry or rocked on the porch swing. The scars of emotional and spiritual abuse were still apparent, but there was also a joy that was new. One thing that *didn't* change: He never stopped being gay. He was in a relationship with a man until the day he died at age 77.

It didn't make sense. The things I was being taught about homosexuality at church didn't jibe with what I saw in my uncle. What I was told about scripture didn't line up with my experience. So I set out to learn, investigate, watch, pray about, listen to and study everything I could about the LGBTQ+ community. I became friends with LGBTQ+ people. I listened to their stories. I wept with them over rejection from family, alienation from their church, and prejudice from their community.

During my long quest, two significant readings came to my attention:

The first was a book by Rev. Dr. Jack Rogers called *Jesus, the Bible, and Homosexuality: Explode the Myths, Heal the Church.* In the preface, Rogers, a retired

Presbyterian minister and academic, reveals his long-held opposition to the ordination of gays and lesbians. Then, during his compulsory participation in a denominational task force, he began deeply researching the origins of the Church's teachings on homosexuality. What he found (bias in Church history and incorrectly interpreted biblical passages, to name a few) caused him to change his position. The information in Rogers's book was quite convincing, but I was still unsure.

The second came to me while I participated in a Bible study on the book of Acts. Specifically, Acts chapters 10 and 11 went to work on me. It's the story of Peter's vision, Cornelius's conversion and baptism, and the early Church's acceptance of Gentiles into the church. "Don't call anything impure that God has made clean" (Acts 10:15, 11:9) convicted my heart. I knew my uncle had been made clean. I had since met other gay Christians whose lives also bore good fruit. Clearly, God had made them clean.

I read the scriptures on sexuality over and over again. I asked God to help me understand whatever he wanted me to know about those verses. I read more books and commentaries. I listened to podcasts. I prayed more. My quest lasted for two decades. I slowly came to the conclusion that the Church of the Nazarene had not done its due diligence before developing its stance on same-sex relationships.

I continued, however, to serve the denomination as a layperson. Throughout my adult life, I had a vague sense that God was calling me to do *something*. Drawn to the aspects of Christian service and justice, I earned a master's degree in Social Work. My husband, our two small children, and I left our established Nazarene church in 2010 to help plant a Nazarene church in our neighborhood. I served there as worship leader and a children's ministry leader.

In 2018, at the age of 45, I knew without a doubt that God was calling me to be a shepherd, minister, and advocate for LGBTQ+ people and their families. I attended a Nazarene conference on organic ministry which inspired me to start a local chapter of PFLAG (a support and advocacy group for LGBTQ+ individuals and their families.) It was a way to connect with the community I was called to serve. I received my local minister's license, enrolled in the Course of Study, and wrote a detailed outline that I felt captured what God was calling me to do. The top of my outline read:

Long-Term Goal: Become an expert resource for the Church of the Nazarene on LGBTQ+ care and inclusion

As my classmates became aware of my ministry, I began getting confidential phone calls and emails. Youth pastors wanted to know how to love and support their LGBTQ+ teens. Pastors' kids confided in me. One mom said, "Thank you for talking to my daughter. You're the first person to give her any hope." Several families at my church came to PFLAG meetings. One dad said, "You really helped me be able to show love to my transgender son.

One member of the Board of Ministry encouraged me to lean into my calling, saying, "Your ministry is so badly needed." Another member said that my stories had encouraged her to talk more openly with people in her community who were dealing with LGBTQ+ family members.

I eventually became a bi-vocational district licensed minister, simultaneously serving my church as Worship Pastor while working as a licensed mental health therapist with LGBTQ+ clientele. I finally recognized and acknowledged my own bisexuality, which changed nothing on paper (I'm still happily, monogamously married to my husband of 22 years) but increased my efficacy in ministry. I adopted a statement from paragraph 33 of the Nazarene Manual as the vision & mission statement for my ministry: "We recognize the shared responsibility of the body of Christ to be a welcoming, forgiving, and loving community where hospitality, encouragement, transformation and accountability are available to all." I strove to help establish such community.

Throughout that time, I followed the church's rules. I yielded to the authority of the denomination while hoping and praying that the human sexuality portion in the Manual's Covenant of Christian Conduct (CoCC) would be reevaluated (which typically happens with all passages in the CoCC. That's how the paragraph forbidding movie attendance was removed and the paragraph on dancing was modified.) I grieved the fact that the church used one approach toward scripture to justify ordaining women, but a different approach to justify the exclusion of LGBTQ+ people. I prayed that hearts would be broken for all the generations of LGBTQ+ people who had been forgotten by the church, from my Baby Boomer uncle all the way to the youthful Gen Zers of today.

I was fiercely protective of my lead pastor and the work she was doing in our local church. When she started getting phone calls about me, I offered to leave, lest her career or our congregation be harmed. Apparently, I was making some Nazarenes nervous. People on the district messaged the District Superintendent about my work. A larger church on our district was going to pay for our small church's roof repairs. When they learned that PFLAG met in our building, they reneged. (It's worth noting that our congregation, various scouting groups, neighborhood athletic groups, the community Easter egg hunt, and an active food pantry ministry also met and operated under that roof. But contempt for the sad, frightened, and lonely LGBTQ+ families caused the larger church to withhold their charitable contribution.)

One of my mentors cautioned me to "be wise as a serpent, gentle as a dove." I certainly tried. I tried not to be too outspoken, lest I upset more Nazarenes and cause trouble for my pastor. I tried to faithfully, authentically serve the people to whom I'd been called. I was trying to do ministry with one hand tied behind my back and it became exhausting.

I met with my newly elected D.S., wanting to know whether I had his support. I did not. He and his assistant didn't want to hear the stories of lives that God had touched through this ministry. Instead, they wanted reassurance that I was in complete agreement with the denomination's stance on sexuality, and they encouraged me to cut ties with PFLAG. I briefly thought about resigning my board position with PFLAG, but God reminded me that my involvement there was part of my organic ministry. It was time to choose: Let go of the institution so I could freely love people, or serve an institution that couldn't even see it was spiritually abusing people.

I prayed for discernment. I had said I would serve the Church of the Nazarene as long as she would have me. I would have continued walking through those minefields because I love the denomination that raised me. But they didn't seem to want my service. They weren't making a place for me to live out my calling. I was reminded of this statement by Pete Enns:

> "…if after a time you are sensing that you do not belong, that *you are a problem to be corrected rather than a valued member of the community,* maybe God is calling you elsewhere…One thing is certain: if you stay where you are without any change at all, the pressure to either conform or keep quiet will work in you like a slow-acting poison." (emphasis mine)

I realized that, while I wanted to help the church live up to her calling and become the best version of herself, I was viewed as A Problem. The Company Men who were charged with keeping everything in order weren't interested in my expertise, my experience, my ideas, or the work I was called to do.

So I left. In my resignation letter, I told the D.S. I hoped he would still consider me a resource for LGBTQ+ families in the church. Then I walked out of my Nazarene church for the last time—the church I had helped to plant eleven years earlier—stopping at the door to symbolically kick the dust off my shoes.

I went to a United Methodist Church and spent several months ugly crying in my pew. God eventually gave me the green light to open dialog with the UMC about pursuing ordination there. Door after door began to open. Various people in the congregation have reached out to me to talk about their LGBTQ+ family members. My new pastor has called me twice this past week, looking to consult on several micro and macro issues concerning LGBTQ+ people in our community.

I asked my husband, "Why do you think he keeps calling me? Do you think he's testing my fitness for ministry?"

My husband replied, "No, I think he trusts you and values your input."

It may take me a while to get used to that.

The ministry handcuffs are off. The experience, education, gifts and calling God entrusted to me are being put to use. I am beyond grateful.

But the Church of the Nazarene has utterly failed to fulfill the Great Commission for an entire people group. There is a better way. God has called and prepared some of us to help. Will the church hear the cries of our hearts? Will she humble herself to follow the leading of the Spirit? If she is to survive, she must.

> "I would have given [the Church] my head, my hand, my heart. She would not have them. She did not know what to do with them…She gave me [no] work to do for her…"   —Florence Nightingale

Jennifer Crowder Noricks, MSW, LMSW is a mental health therapist. She is a candidate in the MAPT (Master of Arts in Practical Theology) degree program at Methodist Theological School in Ohio and aspires to ordination as a deacon in the United Methodist Church. She lives in Livonia, MI with her husband and two teenage children.

Unconditionally Me

MINDY OLDENKAMP

*One woman's story of the pursuit of unconditional love,
community, and authenticity.*

I grew up in a family where two truths were woven into the core of my being: love was something given to everyone, and we were Nazarene.

My very earliest memories include a ridiculous excitement for the Sunday school lessons that incorporated flannelgraphs, my mom teaching me that "Jesus loves the little children, all the little children of the world," and the overwhelming sense that everyone at church was my family. To be fair, I am from a very small Oregon coast town, and I am, in fact, related to a ridiculously high percentage of the folks who live there. But the connections that existed within that community fostered a belief that within the walls of the church, we were all loved, plain and simple.

And it was with that basic foundation of love and the Nazarene church that I charged into the world, fairly confident I was a "normal" child. I come from some seriously strong genes, and I looked and acted just like everyone else around me. I was a poster child for OldenKamp cloning—we all learned the same Bible verses, got the same hugs from all the church grandmas.

When I was five, we left the family dairy farm in Oregon, and settled into Mangum Hall, a freshman boys' dormitory on the campus of Northwest Nazarene College. This, of course, was drastically different from what I had known before. But I could still happily play with my Barbies and my Legos, so by all definitions me, and my little life, were still normal. I just now had a few hundred siblings at my disposal. It certainly didn't occur to me that not everyone my age commandeered the lobby television and forced 18- and 19-year-old boys to watch Sesame Street. I didn't question it at all. Though the "walls" looked very different living on the college campus, the powerful sense of a loving community where I was undoubtedly accepted without question prevailed. There was a great deal of love here amongst my Nazarene family.

But as I began to knock on the door of adolescence, my perception of normal began to change. We moved from dorm life to an actual house, and I started to notice little ways that I just didn't quite fit in. I now had neighborhood kids to compare myself to, and I was starting to realize not everything was steeped in a simple love. Growing up, I tried hard to be the good little church girl—memorizing Bible verses, and clinging to the happiness I felt as a beloved child of God. But as I got older, I found myself developing a hard-core determination for lying in bed on a Sunday morning, willing myself to ignore the desperate cries from my bladder, eyes glued to the clock. I knew that if the clock reached 9:30 and no one had moved in the house, we in no way had enough time to eat, shower and make it to church on time.

It wasn't that I didn't like church. It was that I HATED dresses. I knew, as a girl, I was supposed to love dresses, and, more importantly, I was most definitely supposed to wear them to church. Every Sunday school lesson handout showed boys in ties and girls in ruffly dresses. But I hated everything about that: the tights, the shiny shoes, the pink ribbons, having to sit properly. And I definitely noticed the looks when I didn't conform to the dress rule. This was my first sign that my "normal" might not actually match everyone else's. Girls just didn't wear pants to church. That wasn't proper, and I saw the looks between the grandmas who had once hugged me so tightly. Good church girls dressed the part.

Joining the youth group in high school was a double-edged sword: full of an overwhelming desire to hold so tightly to the love and acceptance I'd been raised in, but finding that at odds with who I was becoming. I could be me, or I could be a part of the church group; but more and more, I was discovering I couldn't be both. I started cramming little secrets of myself away where no one would see them. Hiding myself in a closet, if you will.

I experienced gnarly waves of self-doubt and judgment. Everyone in youth group was only jamming out to Christian music. I still preferred Michael Jackson to Michael W. Smith and Steve Miller to Stephen Curtis Chapman. I couldn't just toss them. So I hid them—literally, behind Point of Grace and Newsboys. And figuratively, in my increasingly crowded closet.

Things only worsened when I discovered I had opinions. FemiNazi, liberal, and the dreaded "Democrat" became names flung at me. As I learned what I stood for, I came to understand those ideas may be directly opposite of people around me. I took those beliefs and shoved them in the closet too.

When I once again returned to the campus of NNC for my own college experience, I found myself one of the few who didn't date, and didn't leave with a ring on my finger. When my friends were finding husbands, I was shoving my insecurities deeper into my figurative closet. No one needed to know my desperate fear of being alone, or that exactly none of the boys on campus seemed a good fit. I continued to hide the things about myself that would make others uncomfortable, that would keep me from that church love connection.

I fought, desperately, to conform. I deeply craved to be the model person I felt like I was somehow supposed to be. I got married to a long-haired hippie boy I convinced myself was "the one". And then I found myself putting our issues in my closet too.

"It's okay you can't picture yourself having kids with him…"

"It's okay that this just doesn't feel right, you're married…"

I was absolutely still that little girl in the awkward dresses looking for those open armed hugs, but I was standing in front of a closet full of hidden truths. I could belong if I just did all the right things.

In the depths of my marriage's worst moments, I called my parents. My dad gave me words of wisdom I have carried in my heart ever since. He simply explained that it was better to be on my own than in a bad relationship, and better to be true to who I was than compromise who I was supposed to be.

For the first time in my adult life, I took a hard look at who I was, who I was supposed to be, and at all the fabulous things hanging in my emotional closet. When I went to shove "divorced" in with all the rest, it just didn't quite fit. Instead, things started tumbling out all over.

I started doing things that defined me and began to feel that familiar sense of love. That acceptance I'd been wrapped in as a small child was starting to return. I slowly began to free myself from the deep obsession with other people's thoughts about me. I found a small Nazarene church that met in a junior high gym and practiced Christ's love. I even registered as a Democrat. But there was more in the closet.

I had to admit I was gay.

So I leaned into love—the simple love I'd been taught from the beginning. I found love for my *real* self. I gave myself the grace I'd heard preached from the pulpit. I was, and am, still a beloved child of God. I felt myself flourishing, and I found joy in ways I hadn't in years.

And then I fell in love.

I met Louise, the incredible woman who would become my wife, mother to the amazing child who would become my step-daughter, and without hesitation, invited them to church with me. I wanted nothing more than for them both to feel the sense of community and family that still ran through my core. That Christ-like love was as intrinsically a part of me as anything else. I wanted my daughter to grow up knowing just how loved she was; I wanted her to have the same structure of loving God, our neighbors, and serving them through that love. I was beyond excited to share a larger sense of family with my partner, to experience and practice the intentional, unconditional love of Christ in a way that felt so completely authentic for the first time in my life.

In the beginning, it was a palpable realization of the church family I'd long craved. As the years went by, we offered ourselves openly, plugged in and became members. We helped with set-up and tear-down, and we helped with construction when the church finally found a permanent home. We saw our kiddo be loved on and find her own gang of hug-giving church grandmas. We served communion, tithed, and collected offerings, and were the welcoming faces greeting folks Sunday mornings. I no longer hid under the covers, waiting for it to be too late to make it on time—I was now the one making sure my entire little family was up and ready to be wrapped in Christ's love. When the call was put out for Sunday school teachers, I was incredibly happy to step up, and cherished the time spent loving the smallest members of our church family. It was everything about the Nazarene church I love so deeply.

Around the same time, Louise and I were finally able to legally recognize our relationship, and we announced our engagement. It was with this public shift, this out loud declaration of our true selves, that we started to experience cracks in the love we'd be experiencing in the church. Unlike the other couples in the congregation, our upcoming union wasn't announced. As we made plans for our wedding, it was explained to us that none of our pastoral staff would be able to conduct our ceremony. And in another heart-breaking blow, I was asked to take a break from teaching Sunday school while the church board considered me.

Suddenly, a single aspect of the person I had grown to be was the only thing that could define me within the church. The hurt, the removal of love, was beyond devastating. My value as a member of the church was being weighed purely on the nature of my sexuality, a part of the person I am just like my eye color or height. I looked around at my fellow congregation members and tried to understand why one part of me, a child created in the image of God, could be so offensive. It didn't impact how I loved others. It did not impact how I served God. Yet somehow, it directly impacted how *I* could be loved.

I began to see the church family I'd loved so deeply crumble around me, and leave my little family unit very separated from our church community. I wasn't different at all; it was merely the way in which my church family could see me that had changed.

The sense of loss and grief I've felt in the years since this split has been deep and painful. I *miss* my church, and it is a sadness I still carry. I have loved the Nazarene church since I was born; it is a beautiful and mission-minded church founded on loving its community.

I have loved my church family with a sense of unconditional patience and hope; I still do. I pray for the day that Christ's love as shared by countless Nazarene preachers and illustrated in the beautiful Bible passages that shaped my Christianity and my faith will be allowed to rise above politics and policy. Let unconditional love be practiced not with an "I love you, *but…*" sort of mentality, but rather with the open arms Jesus showed the least of any of us.

Mindy OldenKamp *grew up in the Nazarene church, and continues to actively pursue and practice unconditional love. She is co-founder of a local non-profit providing a safe space for LGBTQ+ youth in her hometown of Nampa, Idaho, where she lives with her wife, Louise, and daughter, Cale.*

Liberation Toward a Fresh and Faithful Nazarene Theology

KEEGAN OSINSKI

Being open and affirming of LGBTQ+ people opens up the possibility for a more vibrant and robust theology that is both faithful to the Wesleyan tradition and speaks from and to the lives of queer Christians.

Since its origins in the Azusa Street revivals and on Skid Row, the Church of the Nazarene has always prioritized theology and practice that centers care and liberation of the poor and the marginalized. The earliest Nazarenes welcomed and lived in solidarity with the addicted, the homeless, and others who had been scorned and discarded by society. The church has leaned into the teachings of Jesus and of John Wesley to build a community marked by the holiness that is perfect love of God and neighbor. Much of the Covenant of Christian Character stemmed from considerations of how to best love each other as siblings in God's family. This central ethos does not preclude the affirmation and inclusion of LGBTQ+ people. In fact, it requires it.

One benefit of such affirmation and inclusion is it opens a way for the development of a queer Wesleyan theology. Queer theology is a way of thinking about God and faith that brings to the fore questions about how we experience the divine as embodied creatures with the socially constructed trappings of gender and sexuality. It helps us talk about desire, uncertainty, pleasure, ambiguity, relationality, autonomy, and power. It helps us interrogate, critique, and process the messy actualities of life instead of building up aspirational orthodoxies that not only have no basis in our current reality but also are actively harmful.

To have a queer theology that is explicitly and self-consciously Wesleyan means we can take the insights from both queer theology and the Wesleyan tradition and see how they might interact to speak both from and to our specific ecclesial context. However, because the Wesleyan denominations, including the

Church of the Nazarene, have heretofore ignored (at best) or attacked (at worst) the lives and work of queer congregants, ministers, and theologians in their midst, such a theology has been slow to emerge.

One of the best models for developing a fresh but faithful constructive theology is Nazarene theologian Mildred Bangs Wynkoop.

With her 1972 book *A Theology of Love*, Wynkoop undertook to shift the Wesleyan, and especially the Nazarene, conversation about holiness from individual pietistic purity to a relational-ethical morality based on love. The basis of this "new" hermeneutic was actually a resourcement, a return to Wesley's work itself, and an interpretation of that work in light of the contemporary and historical theological questions that always led back to love. "Wesley's thought," Wynkoop said, "is like a great rotunda with archway entrances all around it. No matter which one is entered, it always leads to the central Hall of Love." Ultimately, she reframed the traditional thinking of Wesleyan doctrines, arguing that "rather than Wesley representing a theology of holiness it would be more faithful to his major emphasis to call it a theology of love." This change in thought opened up a whole new stream of Wesleyan-Nazarene theology that focused on relational, communal, social holiness and the lived-out ethical engagement that Wesley saw as the true embodiment of the Christian life.

In what remains of this chapter, I will take a figurative page out of Wynkoop's book, and explore the well-known Wesleyan doctrine of prevenient grace, reframing it in a contemporary context that has acceptance of queer life as its central impetus and celebration of queer love as its key touchstone. Thinking along these lines should result in an introduction to what could be a faithful queer Wesleyan theology, whose focus is, as ever, the corresponding outward activity of perfect love of God and neighbor.

Affirmation as a Prevenient Grace

Wesleyans believe in the doctrine of *prevenient grace*, that is, a grace poured out by God on all people, without exception, that precedes and enables any response of conversion, repentance, or holy works. In the Nazarene Manual, it is asserted in the seventh Article of Faith: "We believe that the grace of God through Jesus Christ is freely bestowed upon all people, enabling all who will to turn from sin to righteousness, believe on Jesus Christ for pardon and cleansing from sin, and follow good works pleasing and acceptable in His sight." Similarly, in the United Methodist Church's Book of Discipline, it is defined as "the divine love that surrounds all humanity and precedes any and all of our conscious impulses. This grace prompts our first wish to please God, our first glimmer of understanding concerning God's will, and our 'first slight transient conviction' of having sinned against God. God's grace also awakens in us an earnest longing for deliverance from sin and death and moves us toward repentance and faith."

What's more, this prevenient grace is experienced by way of what Wesley called the *means of grace*, or the practices in which Christians participate that function as a conduit of God's grace, which is always already at hand. In other words, God's grace is always before us, and we can see and receive it in our lives in a variety of activities.

What I want to suggest is that the Church's being open and affirming to the lives of LGBTQ+ people can be a means of grace. This act can be proof positive of God's love, surrounding LGBTQ+ people, freely bestowed, and open to any and all response. Just like God's prevenient grace, an open and affirming position holds arms outstretched and says, "I love you, no matter what." Just like God's prevenient grace, it takes seriously individuals' freedom to respond, in any way or not at all. It is not coercive. It is not manipulative. It is a love that accepts fully and seeks toward righteousness.

The first of John Wesley's General Rules for the Christian life was "Do no harm." It is clear, as demonstrated in much social scientific research, that non-affirming churches are indeed harmful to LGBTQ+ people, especially youths.[1] They directly contribute to homelessness, physical abuse, and myriad negative mental health outcomes. Wesleyan churches like the Church of the Nazarene have a clear injunction against such harm. They also have easy doctrinal support for its opposite. To do good, in this case, is to become explicitly affirming of LGBTQ+ life and love in both word and deed. To support the spiritual and material growth and flourishing of LGBTQ+ people is to care for the poor and marginalized in the way the Church of the Nazarene has throughout its history; in the way Wesley promoted in his holiness evangelism; and in the way Jesus Christ modeled in his life on earth and in his continued sustenance of the Church through the Holy Spirit.

Just as Mildred Bangs Wynkoop rethought Wesleyan theology in terms of her own 1970s context, we now can rethink it in ours. That means opening up to the holy possibilities that arise when we welcome into our communities LGBTQ+ people and their lives and loves and ways of considering the divine. A reframe and application of Wesley's prevenient grace as LGBTQ+ affirmation shows both how

---

1. See, for example, Eric M. Rodriguez, "At the Intersection of Church and Gay: A Review of the Psychological Research on Gay and Lesbian Christians," *Journal of Homosexuality* 57, no. 1 (December 31, 2009): 5—38, https://doi.org/10.1080/00918360903445806.

this kind of recontextualization can be faithful to the Wesleyan doctrine and how the doctrine itself can be hospitable toward queer people.

The Church has a responsibility to respond and adapt to the reality and needs of the marginalized, just as Jesus addressed those he encountered in his ministry. True acceptance and affirmation in the Church of the Nazarene will result in the encouragement and flourishing of queer Nazarenes to live into *both* of those identities, and the result will be a fuller, more complete church that will reap the benefits—one of which being a robust, thoughtful, and faithful queer Wesleyan theology that helps us consider our tradition in new ways.

Keegan Osinski *is the librarian for Theology and Ethics at Vanderbilt University Divinity Library and the author of* Queering Wesley, Queering the Church. *She is a member of the Church of the Nazarene.*

An Open Letter to My Church Family

BETHANY RAYA

An open letter of how one Christian lesbian has used the Word to fully embrace herself, and her challenge to the Church of the Nazarene.

My Church Family,

I write this letter, not with the intent to change anyone's mind or convictions, but to share my story, and if sharing my story challenges the views you hold then please honor them and grapple with them. Question if your views still serve you or if you are holding onto them because they are familiar and offer some sense of comfort. In writing this letter, I simply hope that by sharing my story future generations do not have to deal with the same struggles that I have endured. I hope you can read this letter from a place of curiosity and open-mindedness.

I have chosen to write this in two parts: first sharing my story, and second discussing a few of the verses in the Bible that refer to homosexuality. From an early age, I came to love God and had the desire to learn more, draw closer, and do His work—that always felt natural to me, and it still does. As time passed, I learned more about the God of love, mercy, and grace. A God who is constantly chasing after us, a God who loves us just as we are, not as who we can be. A God who wants to be with us, to create with us, to engage with us, walk with us, and guide us. A God who is above all things wants to reside with us!

For seventeen years, I sat in the pews of my church three times a week, forging a relationship with this God, volunteering to help in my church, taking on leadership roles, praying with others, giving tithes and offering, and overall being part of the community. Over time, I started to hear about the evilness, damnation, and wrongdoings of a certain group of people. This didn't sit well with me, because how could a God of love, mercy, and grace look down or damn a group of people simply because they love someone of the same sex? These two versions of God did not seem to be the same. And to further complicate things, *I* was in this group of people—the people who loved someone of the same sex.

From the age of about 11, I realized that my attraction was towards women. I had no attraction towards men, and it actually rather repulsed me (I imagine it's the same for heterosexual people when they think of being with someone of the same sex). I tried to be with men, which came from a sense of expectation from society, family, and religion. With each heterosexual experience, I found that I had to force myself. Furthermore, I was lying, putting up a front, deceiving and hurting another person: myself. Ultimately, I was trying to be something that felt foreign and unnatural to me. Worst of all, in trying to be something that was against my design, it felt like I was lying to God. I even tried to "pray the gay away," and when that didn't work, I tried to "pray the gay away" again. But never did my attraction towards women dissipate.

There was a time that I made the difficult decision to leave the church—because why should I be part of a community that hated me? But never did I stop engaging with God. Then there came a point in my life where I was done lying to myself and done staying away from the house of God. So I started researching what the Bible actually says about homosexuality. Because again, the two versions of God did not seem to go together—how can something that came natural to me be a sin? I read multiple books, talked to pastors, prayed, and grappled with what I had been taught, only to discover that what we think the Bible is saying goes deeper than we imagine.

The book *Unclobber* by Colby Martin was recommended to me while I was in the midst of my journey. From Martin, I learned that there are a total of 31,102 verses in the Bible, and only six discuss homosexuality. (Also, the word homosexual never appeared in the Bible until 1946, more about that below). Here is a brief summary of some of the passages that mention homosexuality and some of the explanations Martin provides that have helped me come to peace with who I am:

Sodom and Gomorrah- Genesis 19:4-5

"4 Before they had gone to bed, all the men from every part of the city of Sodom—both young and old—surrounded the house."

The storyteller points out that *every* man in the city shows up at Lot's house. This should rule out that the story is about sex-sex attraction, as it simply cannot be the case that *every* man in the city from old to young is gay.

"5 They called to Lot, "Where are the men who came to you tonight? Bring them out to us so that we can have sex with them.""

Consent is not on the mob's mind; rather they want to do something *to* the men. In other words, they want to gang rape the men. This was how dominance is demonstrated in the ancient world (and very much today), and its use strips others of power. These verses are not about homoerotic desire, but rather about dishonoring the other and stripping them of their masculinity and thereby their humanity.

To ask Genesis to weigh in on the question of the biblical posture toward same-sex attraction or the sinfulness of a loving, committed same-sex relationship is to ask questions it does not and cannot answer. Further, Ezekiel 16:49-50 states, *"Now this was the sin of your sister Sodom, she and her daughters were arrogant, over-fed and unconcerned they did not help the poor and needy. They were haughty and did detestable things before me. Therefore I did away with them as you have seen."* As far as Ezekiel sees it, Sodom and Gomorrah was not about homosexuality.

Leviticus 18:22; 1 Corinthians 6:9

Leviticus 18:22 (English version): "Man shall not lie with man, for it is an abomination."

1 Corinthians 6:9 "Or do you not know that the unrighteous will not inherit the kingdom of God? Do not be deceived: neither the sexually immoral, nor idolaters, nor adulterers, nor men who practice homosexuality."

The Greek word "arsenokoitai" is used in Leviticus 18:22 and 1 Corinthians 6:9. This word was not translated to mean "homosexual" until 1946, when the Germans wanted to mass produce the Bible but did not have enough money. So the American Bible company Biblia paid for the project and influenced the decision, resulting in the word "homosexual" entering the German Bible for the first time in history, and then later in the English Bible. The German, Swedish and Norwegian versions of Leviticus 18:22 state, *"Man shall not lie with young boys as he does with a woman, for it is an abomination."* "Homosexual" replaced "those that lie with young boys."

Romans 1:26-27

"For this reason God gave them up to dishonorable passions. For their women exchanged natural relations for those that are contrary to nature; and the men likewise gave up natural relations with women and were consumed with passion for one another, men committing shameless acts with men and receiving in themselves the due penalty for their error."

The word translated as "dishonorable" is the Greek word for *atimia*. If something is *atima* it is about bringing dishonor to a person or family. To commit *atimia* was to engage in a behavior that had no value and would bring shame, it was a violation of the cultural customs of the day. Paul demonstrated how Gentiles were engaged in acts that clearly went against Jewish cultural traditions.

The word "shameless" is the Greek word *aschemosune,* and it describes behavior that is unseemly or indecent. The situation being described here is one where men, being overtaken by their passions, engage in same-sex acts that were possibly performed in public spaces or in conjunction with pagan idol worship.

When verses 26 and 27 are taken together, what emerges is a picture of Gentiles who have rejected God, turned toward idolatry, and were given over to distorted sexual practices that offend and are contrary to Jewish purity laws and cleanliness customs. The shameless acts were done as a result of men being consumed with passion. In other words, they were not acting out of a place of love and mutuality, but out of a desire for excess. This passage conveys the feelings the Jews had about culturally offensive sex acts.

———

So after grappling for years, researching, praying, and just downright calling on God, I can finally say that I am at peace with who I am and at peace with God! The most repeated phrase in the Bible is "fear not." As Martin says, "When we feel that something we are hearing doesn't resonate with the God of love, we must raise our hands. Especially if our hands shake with fear. Apathy and passivity are the opposite of love. When we stay silent, we are making a big bold decision. We are casting a loud vote for the status quo. It is a vote for fear over love. And the only thing necessary for the triumph of discrimination in the Christian faith is for doubtful Christians to stay quiet."

So today, I ask you, my church family, will you continue to stay silent and be comfortable or will you join hands with your LGBT brothers and sisters and fully welcome us into the Church of the Nazarene?

With love,

Bethany

Bethany Raya is a graduate student studying human resource development and is a university scholarship administrator. She has earned her undergraduate degree in sociology and a minor in gender studies. Raya has held numerous leadership positions in the church youth ministries and has co-founded a local non-profit aiming to create a safe place for LGBT kids in the Treasure Valley.

The Parable of Y2K

DANIEL RODRIGUEZ SCHLORFF

A proud pansexual pastor (formerly Nazarene) considers
similarities between Y2K hysteria and wanting gays to go to hell.

It's December 31, 1999, and all the Valparaiso Nazarene youth group alumni are gathered around a bonfire. Everyone except me. I was actually sitting at my computer to watch the Y2K catastrophe occur while my friends who went off-region to attend places like Mount Vernon and SNU were back in town. So, it's odd that I wasn't at this bonfire. But I was preoccupied. You see, my college girlfriend had just broken up with me a week prior, and all I could think about was Ryan back at Olivet. But it can't be. I mean, the Bible clearly says bad things about gays in the Bible, right? My longing for Ryan, who barely knew I existed, felt as natural as anything else I knew to be natural. So, naturally, I wondered whether Paul was right when he said that men having desire for other men is unnatural. I was a 19-year-old virgin trying to take every thought captive, yet I couldn't stop it. The thoughts just kept coming. Granted, I was a Nazarene, so these thoughts were rated PG, but they were juxtaposed by the teachings of hellfire and damnation for those who dwell on sin. Finally, right before midnight, I worked up the nerve to ask God the thing I hadn't wanted to know: "God, am I gay?" As I sat next to my computer, I pleaded with God not to let me be gay, because I didn't want to go to hell. Twenty-three years later, I still feel the weight of that moment of realization when God laid on my heart that he would not take this cup from me.

As it turned out, Y2K was a non-event. We can all laugh about that now, but when Visa and MasterCard were worried that their computers would erase all the debt from their books simply because their computers simply weren't advanced enough to account for a minor coding issue, then it became everyone's problem. People were backing up their computers on an endless stream of floppy disks, only to be told that the files on those floppy disks probably could not be retrieved by computers since they were all going to crash, anyway. Some predicted Y2K would surely usher in wars and pestilence and the great tribulation and the second coming. While others simply went to bonfires.

When the modern reader thinks back to Y2K and all the misguided warnings about Armageddon, I cannot help but draw a comparison to those who read the Bible in English paraphrase. They actually believe they have a supernatural source of authority that gives them license to castigate others—based solely on their own flawed theology, based on their flawed English paraphrase Bibles. But I was one of them. As a Nazarene, I was a religious zealot. Have you seen those "Jesus is the reason for the season" bumper stickers? I turned up the dial. As a high school student, I had a poster on my locker that had written on it, "Burn, Santa, burn! Burn, bunny, burn!" And, to my shame, I was a holy terror on the National Day of Silence, while some high school peers bravely lived their truth. I must have made their coming out hell.

Hell can be pretty brutal. I know, I lived it when I first came out. Even though I had many friends at Olivet, and I traveled on a ministry team called The Olivetians, I somehow got unfriended by most of my Nazarene friends on MySpace and on Facebook following graduation. My three college roommates were best men at each other's weddings, and I wasn't even invited. I was feeling true loneliness. Perhaps it was the same loneliness I made others feel in high school. I considered how evil ("moral") I had been in the name of God (my own will).

I was realizing the true meaning of "Thou shalt not take the name of the Lord thy God in vain." It was not about using the name of God as a curse word, though that's a common misinterpretation. It has more to do with putting your own agenda forward as if it is for God. People who say "God damn it" are not in violation of this commandment. Rather, the crusades and the inquisition are clear violations of this commandment. In the same way, when I was tormenting fellow high school students on the National Day of Silence, I was subverting God's will for my own. I mistook my own cause for the cause of the Lord. And, not unlike Saul of Tarsus, scales fell from my eyes.

As it turns out, the six clobber passages (that is, the six passages of the Bible that are often cited as proof-text to support anti-gay political views) don't mean what fundamentalists say it means. And, to superimpose fundamentalist interpretation over and above the teachings of Jesus is tantamount to taking the name of the Lord in vain. And the irony is, it's all like running software on pre-Y2K computer systems. Like Plato's allegory of the shadow figures in the cave, basing theology and social teachings on flawed biblical interpretation will have one take on deeply and sincerely held religious beliefs that, in actuality, have nothing to do with God at all. They are but shadows.

In closing, I'd like to plug biblical scholarship. Tools like historical and cultural criticism of the Bible would go a long way in helping people understand the complexities of the six clobber passages. In 1980, John Boswell became the first scholar that I'm aware of that took a look at the clobber passages and applied all manner of hermeneutical tools to them. Without his book, *Christianity, Social Tolerance, and Homosexuality*, I might not be here today. In my darkest hours, when I could not see past the loneliness and pain of coming out, John Boswell's scholarship helped me truly understand how I was made in the image and likeness of God—not "even though" I'm pansexual but "because of" my sexuality.

I'm glad I didn't go to that bonfire. If I had, I might not have properly dealt with my interest in Ryan, the guy I wished would notice me. Pleading with God not to go to hell was perhaps the only way this Nazarene zealot could have scales fall from his eyes. Upgrading pre-Y2K computers, so to speak, is the only way other Nazarene zealots have any chance of awakening to the beauty of God's creation. We need to witness and celebrate, not just affirm or accept, the fact that God made me, a pansexual pastor, in his image and likeness.

The Reverend Dr. Daniel Rodriguez Schlorff, a former Nazarene minister, now serves Third Congregational Church in Middletown, CT as Senior Minister. After Olivet, he then studied at the University of Chicago Divinity School through Meadville/Lombard, earned a second master's degree at Hartford Seminary, and later completed the Doctor of Ministry and Certificate of Sexuality and Religion at Pacific School of Religion.

Were You Wrong?

JAN SHANNON

*Was the Church of the Nazarene wrong when they said the Holy
Spirit was working through gay people?*

The Holy Spirit is working through millions of individuals in the Church of
the Nazarene. Through the work of pastors, music ministers, missionaries and
Sunday school superintendents, including those of us in the LGBTQ (Lesbian,
Gay, Bisexual, Transgender, Queer) community, these dedicated leaders have allowed the Holy Spirit to work through them changing lives, saving souls, and
redeeming the lost to new life in Christ. These leaders are calling for true holiness
by encouraging disciples to move from salvation to sanctification—to giving up
their wants and desires and submitting their life and will to the infilling of the
Holy Spirit. It was this zeal for holiness and personal piety that drew me to the
Nazarenes, and I believe it's this same zeal for holiness that brings up the issue of
homosexuality in the church. I believe the Church of the Nazarene truly desires
to be led by the Holy Spirit, and I know there are LGBTQ leaders in the Church
of the Nazarene. I want to see this denomination flourish and grow by allowing
the Holy Spirit to continue to work through LGBTQ people of faith within this
denomination.

Preaching and teaching are the cornerstones of Nazarene life and worship. The
Manual of the Church of the Nazarene is very clear on the calling of ministers.
"When the church, illuminated by the Holy Spirit, recognizes such a divine call,
the church endorses and assists the individual's entry into a lifetime of ministry."
Throughout the global church, dozens of schools and seminaries call and instruct
the next generation of Nazarene pastors. The Course of Study was created to assist
people who could not afford to go to seminary to train as a pastor. I was one of them.

If statistics are true, upwards of 10% of the leadership in the Church of the
Nazarene are part of the LGBTQ community, and the Holy Spirit is working
through us just as the Holy Spirit is working through straight folks. It is only when
we come out and admit that we are gay, (or bisexual, lesbian, etc.) that we are told

we do not have the Spirit of God working through us but are damned to Hell for being gay. How is it possible that one minute we were "full of the Spirit" and had a "divine call" and the next minute we weren't? Were we called to a "lifetime of ministry" or was the Church *not* "illuminated by the Holy Spirit" when it said we had the "gifts and graces for ministry"? Which is it?

I was called, felt the tug on my heart to serve the Lord as a minister of the gospel, when I was 14 years old. I again felt called as a married woman with kids in 2001, and this call was affirmed by my pastor, the church board, and the local licensing committee. Based on the recommendation of my head pastor, the support of several elders in the church, and by vote of the church board, I was granted a local license and began serving in my church as a minister. A year later, I was given a district license, because my year as a locally licensed minister confirmed for the district committee that I possessed the gifts and graces for ministry. I preached, led women's retreats, worked as interim youth leader, and entered the Course of Study towards ordination as an elder. Many of the older members of my church had never been in favor of women as preachers, but they said they saw "the Hand of God" on my life, and they "could not deny the fruit that God produced" through my preaching and teaching.

Though we were without a youth pastor for a year, our youth group continued to grow and flourish under my leadership. I baptized eight children during my ministry, offered communion numerous times, and performed two weddings including pre-marital counseling, all with the blessing of the Church. Today, over 20 years later, I have had many people tell me that their Christian life is stronger and closer to Christ because of my guidance in a Bible study or sermon. One of my greatest blessings was the moment a young lesbian woman told me that the only reason she was still a Christian was because I had taught her that God loves everyone so God must love her too. She pursues a life dedicated to living out the love of God for everyone, helping her peers see that life is better with God in it. And God wrought all of this work through me while I was in an illicit homosexual relationship.

I am not so special—I am just a normal, sinful, striving Christian gal. It is only because of the power of God, working through me in the person of the Holy Spirit, that has led those people to Christ. It is the Spirit of God which changes hearts and lives and convicts people of sin and of righteousness. If God is working through me, even as a practicing homosexual, then the Holy Spirit must not be bound to only heterosexual ministers. God can work through gay people too.

My story is not abnormal. Many gay Christians have served in both the Church of the Nazarene and other denominations, and their ministry and giftedness was affirmed until the day they came out as gay.

Music is often the vehicle that the Spirit uses to speak the message of God to the hearts of His children. Christian singers and songwriters have been gifted to create and perform worship songs that carry God's gospel of love to congregations all over the world. Music has always been a major part of Christian life, and many gifted Christian artists are gay.

Ray Boltz, whose songs and videos won thousands of souls to Christ, is gay. He always knew that he was gay, and yet God was able to work through him to produce good fruit in changed hearts and lives. I remember Sunday evening services watching Ray Boltz videos like "I Pledge Allegiance to the Lamb" and "The Anchor Holds." And how many hundreds of retirement services have used "Thank You for Giving to the Lord" and brought the entire congregation to tears as they celebrated the lives of service to God's work? Truly, "Thank You" by itself speaks volumes about Boltz's belief in dedicating our lives to God's service. Ray Boltz, both as a man with a wife and children and now as an out gay man, has dedicated his life to spreading the gospel of Jesus Christ. God's Spirit has worked and is working through Ray Boltz, a gay man.

The Manual states that "a person's homosexual or bisexual attraction may have complex and differing origins" and the Manual also states that the "human race is created in Godlikeness." Both these statements are true at the same time. The God Who Creates created us all, straight and gay alike, and all are equally capable of being filled by the Holy Spirit and gifted and used for God's purpose in redeeming the world.

So, were you wrong? Was the Church wrong when it said Ray Boltz' music was a vehicle for the Holy Spirit to reach tens of thousands for Christ? No, you weren't wrong.

Was the Church of the Nazarene wrong when it said I was filled with the Holy Spirit and that God was working through me to bring people to Christ? No, the Church wasn't wrong.

I implore the Church of the Nazarene to earnestly seek God's heart on this issue and see the truth that God can and does work through both straight and gay people to bring about the will of God.

Jan Shannon *earned BAs in Humanities and Women and Gender Studies with a minor in Religion from Eastern Washington University, and a Master of Divinity from Iliff School of Theology. Shannon writes for Spokane FāVS, a local religion news website, preaches and leads Bible study, and speaks publicly on the intersection of faith and life as a gay woman.*

Wrestling with God

BRANDON SMEE

Being gay in a church that didn't accept me led to years of wrestling with God, but when God spoke a blessing in the midst of the struggle, everything began to change.

I.

I lingered after the church service while the evening sun set, my heart pounding and the rest of me coldly electrified. My steps were heavy walking to the empty fellowship hall where my youth pastor had agreed to meet. I had to tell someone the truth. I believed it had to be her—not a friend or a family member, but someone who could speak God's will for me. So I sat down across from the pastor, took a deep breath and began to speak.

I have heard that some children have a sense of their queerness at as young as four or five years old. I was around that age when I first attended church. My devout grandparents, who were missionaries with World Mission, dressed me in a suit and whisked me to College Church of the Nazarene in the suburbs of Kansas City, for a wet Sunday service during which they fittingly sang "Holy Spirit Rain Down." There I sat amazed amid the luminous stained glass, the endless rows of pews, and the glowing red carpet. Yet what captured me most was the sermon. The pastor's text was Genesis 32:22-32, Jacob wrestling with God. As Jacob struggles, the man (God in disguise) strikes Jacob's hip and it pops out of joint, or in the pastor's telling, the divine touch instantly saps his muscles of their strength. All the awful tangibility of God struck upon my young mind: God was one who could touch me, a God with whom I could struggle.

Years later at thirteen, I had begun occasionally attending a Nazarene church for myself, attending the youth group. I was shy, awkward, and didn't feel like I fit with other boys. Peers bullied me at school for seeming "gay." I felt alone. Yet it happened that one night at youth group an intern from the Nazarene seminary was sharing a message. I don't remember what he preached. But what happened when he read from scripture, Luke 5:1-11, where Jesus calls Peter with the miraculous catch of fish, I cannot forget. There is a moment after Peter and his partners pull the fish into the boat when Peter falls at Jesus's knees and confesses his brokenness. In that moment, I too was Peter kneeling before Jesus. I sensed his presence there with me, calling me to follow and to fish for people. In my loneliness, Jesus had noticed me, and in him God had come near to me, even close enough to touch me. That evening, I told my parents everything had changed. I signed up for the summer mission trip. Less than six months later, I was baptized. Through the reading of scripture, God had touched me.

I found that in reading God's Word, the church finds its power, even frightful power. The Church of the Nazarene confesses belief in the plenary inspiration of scripture, holding that it "inerrantly reveal[s] the will of God concerning us and our salvation." Scripture began my searching and introduced me to Christ, and in the provision of the Spirit it had fed my growth toward Christlikeness. In other hands, I would discover, it could sow destruction. In political policies that disadvantaged people who didn't fit our definition of pure, in how peers in school treated people who seemed queer, in the words spoken in the church's Manual, its Sunday Schools, and its pulpits, scripture's breaking and shattering power thundered all around.

And it thundered in me. Though scripture had revealed my salvation, there was another truth within me revealing itself in my being. It began to appear in the sidelong glances that seemed to catch me by surprise, at the novel, organic stirrings in my heart, and the fearful sense that who I was becoming was not in my control. I tried to block it all away. I took refuge in my belief in God to shield myself from my feelings. I poured through my ESV Study Bible to figure out what these things meant before the Lord. I pleaded; I bargained; I struggled. When I could no longer plausibly deny it, I lay awake at night pondering my course. I could not leave my faith. I could not surrender the convictions I had gained from reading scripture within the life of my church. So, I let what the church had taught me thus far instruct me.

I sent a text to my youth pastor, we met in the fellowship hall, and I told her I was gay. Her eyes grew wide. It struck me that perhaps her training at the local Nazarene university had not prepared her for this. Reaching for something familiar, she encouraged me to pray Psalm 51. A psalm of repentance, for sinners. "My sin is always before you; against you and you only have I sinned," the psalmist says. When I got home, I hid my face from my eyes in the bathroom mirror, and I prayed the psalm, hoping that it would make my queerness go away. I prayed it again, until it felt like it was taunting me. My attraction to other men did not change, and I grew more alone and desperate. In youth group, it seemed every joke was a gay joke. But the adults weren't laughing. A family member was recruited to counsel me out of homosexuality. One youth sponsor reminisced about the days when gays were beat up in schools. Another man was kicked out of the church when he revealed he had a partner. In our hands, scripture cut deep.

I felt my space in the church shrinking. Being gay was enough to disqualify me, to mark me as a sinner. So I begged God that I could be entirely sanctified, that all my sin would be stricken from my heart and soul, that I could draw close again to the intimacy of the Jesus who came and blessed me. I wanted to dwell in that intimacy. But I was stuck attempting to brace myself against the rising tide of my sexuality, and Christ seemed far off.

II.

In Genesis 32:22-32, Jacob wrestles God for a blessing. There is a pattern of struggle and grace in the Christian life. The Nazarene tradition holds that entire consecration precedes the "fullness of the blessing" or entire sanctification. All of us must become God's so we can experience all of God, and for this reason we wrestle. We wrestle with our sin, with our ignorance, with our rebellion. God confronts us with all our untruth, that by our lived faith we might overcome it. Yet, for this queer Christian, the struggle for holiness grew twisted. I went into the valley. I turned my strength, my mind, and my faith against myself, until the labor of consecration turned into rejecting who I was, apologizing for my pain, and straining to pull myself from the "depths of perversion" where my sexuality placed me. I have heard stories of queer souls being recast into straightness, "success stories." I have never met one in real life. In my experience, queerness is virulent in the human spirit; even when paved over it still sends its green tendrils through the cracks. Some know this and keep LGBTQ+ people from ministry altogether. When I was last a member of a Nazarene church, the Manual barred anyone who had ever done a homosexual act from ministry. Yet, in my eyes, entire sanctification held out the hope that if I could just purify myself enough, God would wipe away my sin nature and the stain of my sexuality. So I wrestled with God through the night, waiting for the fullness of the blessing.

In fact it was late at night when God next confronted me like Jacob. I couldn't sleep so I stayed awake praying, trying to drag myself through the spiritual sludge that had built up over years of struggling with my sexuality, when I realized something. In all my years of striving, I had only ever confessed my sexuality to God as a sin—I had never shared it with my creator, I had never come out. With trepidation,

I lifted my heart to the Almighty. I took a deep breath and began to speak: "God, I'm gay." And I heard the Lord say, "You can be as gay as you need to be with me."

A bit of light dawned on the horizon. A bit of wonder. For the first time, I heard an affirmation that who I was could be a site of acceptance instead of shame. God touched me and it changed me; God spoke and gave the blessing of release. Try as I might, I could not stay the same. By steps, I began to trust God more with my identity, as the One Who Is began to show me who I am. And the Holy One opened up the scripture to me, to read in ways that I had never read before. In one instance, while reading Genesis 1:27, "Male and female he made them" God's Spirit turned me to what was not said, the absence of boundaries and boxes around "male" and "female" allowing people just to be. God opened up this and other passages. And in all this I was growing in accepting the self God had created me to be. The Lord had come to set me free, and only by living in this freedom would I find the fullness of the blessing.

In some sense, we wrestle with God all our lives, working out our salvation with fear and trembling. But at times the struggle opens up and we receive a blessing. Like Jacob, we see God and live, and I came to see where God was working in my life. I slowly came to accept my sexuality. One wrestling match with God yielded a benediction. Not unlike entire sanctification, my growth in grace did not end there. Instead it began anew with power and bold confidence. The hand of God was moving all along, through my experiences in the Church of the Nazarene where I received my knowledge of God and of Christ's love for me, my baptism, my call to serve God's people, and beyond it. Jesus Christ was in all of it.

Even so, there were times when the church and I struggled. When I needed Psalm 139, "I am fearfully and wonderfully made," it gave me Psalm 51, "For I know my transgressions, and my sin is always before you." It tried to excise the unwanted parts of my soul. It was never just the actions of one person in the church. I found myself amid a whole system in which the church read scripture upside down and ended up aligning its action with the world instead of God. It aligned itself with the world because it saw me bullied for being queer, and agreed I was disordered. It saw me alone and treated my "sin" as a special kind of iniquity. It saw me struggling to live out God's call in purity and holiness, and added burdens to me that it was unwilling to move. Yet Jesus loved me in my rejection, stayed with me in my loneliness, and wrung a blessing out of my pain. In my shame, Jesus delivered me.

Like Jacob, I have seen God through the struggle and lived. I first wrestled with Jesus in the Church of the Nazarene, and that is the space that raised me. In Jacob's story we see that God is still wrestling with the church, offering it a blessing if it holds on to the end. In its wrestling, it may find itself changed. In its struggle, it may come to behold God and the people whom God has called blessed. I can only hope that the blessing God has given to me would be multiplied in the lives of others.

Brandon Smee *is a Clinical Pastoral Education Resident at the University of Kansas Hospital. A graduate of Princeton Theological Seminary and a Kansas City native, Brandon is in the ordination process in the Episcopal Church.*

Shutting Out Sparrows

PAIGE TILDEN

Christ preached acceptance. Do you?

The life of an intersex person has always been hard, both historically and in the modern day. While the term intersex is a modern expression, the historical expression of the term was that of the eunuch, specifically those born as one, called "eunuch of the sun." Since our more modern medicine has ways to "help"—and by help what is meant is forcibly conform an infant's body to a standard male/female binary without any consent or discussion with the child, then denying it happened—the stigma as well as awareness of this diversity in our species has been slowly getting erased. Yet we see in scripture that eunuchs are welcomed and encouraged to be a part of the faith community. We see this example of acceptance not only from the well-known story with Philip and the eunuch, but also in Matthew 19, where Jesus said those who are born as eunuchs (today we are called intersex people), those who were made eunuchs, and those who chose to live that way for the Kingdom were explicitly told they are welcome.

When I was not even one year old, I was subjected to one of the surgeries that many like me have listed in our medical history simply as a minor reconstruction—when they are often actually much larger procedures. We in the Western world often are appalled that other cultures will mutilate genitals, but unnecessary surgeries on infants happen approximately five times a day here in the United States alone. After the butchering of these genitals has been completed, the person's medical history can sometimes be entirely scrubbed from medical logs to ensure a desired heteronormativity in which the child would be raised.

Following my procedure, I was raised, named, and otherwise treated as a typical male child. My female skeletal structure, however, was evident, regardless of any kind of upbringing. Often, especially when called from behind, my entire life has been filled with people confused as to whether they were looking at a male or female body. While others in my situation would likely be upset that it happened so often, I just preferred to accept it, make a joke, and move on. Little did I know that my body was actually *both* male and female, and that is what people saw.

As I hit my mid-twenties, my life changed. My body suddenly started a second puberty, and I began to display all the traditional signs of puberty again—but it was a female development this time. When the dots all finally connected, I felt as if my entire life made sense, and it came in a wave of understanding. I had questioned so many things about my life, mindset, body, hobbies, relationships, all of it. Everything came into a brand new level of appreciation and understanding when I accepted that I was now actually, at least in part, female as well as male. I discovered that while in utero, my paternal twin and I fused into one body, sharing both male and female parts. Medically, I am a mosaic or chimera of male and female chromosomes in a single human body.

My expectation when I was accepting the truth of my very existence was that my path was not going to be one of ease or joy. But in addition to that, I found struggle and rejection from many of the people I had called friends. My choice seemed to be to either accept the ways God had made me (and which finally made sense to me by a scientific explanation by my doctor), or to reject the ways God had made me, and the plans God had for my life inherent in its creation. This was a difficult choice to make in many ways, but I reasoned if my struggle and pain were to lead even one more person to Christ, then I would obediently bear the burden. In comparison to what others suffer for their faith, surely the loss of a few relationships would be bearable in the greater scheme of things. I was willing to accept that loss for the sake of the Kingdom.

Sadly, the place of least acceptance of my newfound circumstances was my then church home. With a resolve to bear my cross with purpose, I knew what I needed to do. I came prepared with scripture, research, and a heart focused on how I could use my story to reach others for Christ. But the well had been tainted long before I was even able to share my story to my church family. Many in that church, including the pastor, were gossiping behind my back—spreading lies that I was a trans person instead of asking me the truth directly. While being trans should *also* be wholly accepted in our faith practices, there is a significant stigma against it, and to say I was trans was an inaccurate portrayal of my reality. Neither being intersex or trans are choices, but it seems inconceivable to tell someone who has not initiated any medical sex change procedures and who has begun to menstruate that they are making a sinful choice to accept their body the way God had made them.

When I had formally decided that it was no longer time to attend a church regularly, I had also come to the realization that many who had chosen to pastor were no longer seeking out God's will. Instead they were focused on maintaining organizational viability, protecting their own interests and life, and most of all, pleasing a congregation's whims over sticking to scriptural truth. This realization was assuredly signed, sealed, and delivered to my wife and me when our pastor told us, "I would rather deny your child a dedication than risk my job security." Someone this focused on themselves stands against the very principles that Christ embodied. Just past the more often quoted line of Matthew 10:29-31, which says God cares for "even the sparrows" but cares very much more for people, there is much graver warning from Jesus that was ignored in this case, and that warning applies to all who exclude anyone who is a gender or sexual minority.

In Matthew 18, Christ very explicitly states that it would be better for people to drown themselves with a large stone tied around their necks than for them to cause someone else to stumble in their faith. The sheer shock value of this statement coming out of Jesus' mouth should be enough of a warning for those in pastoral leadership. Ending your own life, in the eyes of the one who was sent to sacrifice His life for ours, is better than pushing someone away from their faith. Yet this is what the church does to so many people who are part of the gender and sexual minority community! Are we not all made in His image? Whether it is the belief in an erroneous translation of the scripture, disapproval of anyone who isn't like themselves, or simply the inability to adjust their worldview because they are so rooted in the history and traditions they have, they are sinning. They sin not only against God's creation, but against God Himself by saying that something He made is not good enough to be loved, or even accepted in a place dedicated to His worship. How audacious has the church become to ignore such an important instruction from Him whom we follow!

Christ came to Earth to give all of humanity the fullest extent of love and grace that we can ever experience. Someday, when we leave this existence and move to the next, and we see God face to face, we are all going to be held to account for that which we did here to those around us. We know that one day Christ will return and be seated on a throne too glorious for us to behold. All will bend the knee and we will be separated like a shepherd separates their sheep and goats. There we will be told, regardless of how we are sorted, that whatever we did (or did not do) for the least of those around us, we did also to the King of Kings. How can anyone expect to be allowed into the kingdom of heaven when they shut the door on the faces of others? You won't. How can we focus on the principles of tithing and cleanliness but be so blind to the more important ideas of justice, mercy, and faithfulness? It is a sign we have a plank in our eye.

All have sinned. All fall short. None of us are righteous. To tell someone that they cannot be righteous enough to be in the church because of their life circumstances is pure hypocrisy, because nobody was, is, or ever will be righteous enough, except Jesus. This is why we are told not to judge. Whenever we are looking for sin, real or perceived, in any person's life on this planet, we will always find something, both in others and in ourselves. If we dare to think that we will not have the same measure applied to us that we used to judge others, then we truly have failed to understand the purpose of the Gospel. Christ called the "sinners" of His time on Earth to prove that anyone could follow Him, not just the Pharisees who made a point of showing how righteous they were. Let us also then focus on letting all of God's creation worship without obstruction. I fear if we don't, we'll find ourselves too easily entangled between the planks we ignore and the stones we're told to tie around our necks.

Paige Tilden *is a mother of two, a graduate from Northwest Nazarene University, and is involved in advocacy work for the intersex community.*

A Place at the Table

ALLISON NICOLE TUCKER

An ex-Nazarene professor and pastor's daughter explains the ways in which the church failed to love her as Christ would.

I was three when I first visited Eastern Nazarene College's campus. I only know this because of a picture I've seen where I am standing next to my father on the front lawn. I'm so small I barely come up to his knees, but my smile is massive and I'm sporting a tiny ENC t-shirt. ENC t-shirts, although of a much larger size, still make up a substantial part of my wardrobe today, but wearing them is a little more painful. From the first visit until today, ENC has been a fixture in my life. As a pastor's kid in the Eastern region, I always knew I was heading there for college. I was an early decision applicant in my junior year of high school and the second I graduated, I was Boston bound and never looked back.

My ENC story is one of heartbreak because it was first one of love. I fell blindly head over heels for ENC as soon as I arrived. I loved the Boston area and the arboretum campus. There really is something magical about Quincy in the Fall. I buried myself in the theatre department, involving myself in every production, and overloading my schedule with classes that I excelled in. I made friends immediately who I clicked with and a few who I love dearly to this day. As a fourth generation Nazarene and a pastor's kid, ENC was surely the place for me. Until it wasn't. Looking back, the writing was always on the wall, but I couldn't see it initially.

I do remember some early red flags. There were many on-campus clubs, but no LGBTQ+ clubs. Even my rural conservative high school in Virginia had a gay-straight alliance club. There were married dorms for students, but only if they were heterosexual couples. The lifestyle manual outright forbade students from being in homosexual relationships. So did the faculty manual for that matter, but I wouldn't learn that for several years. If you did end up in a homosexual relationship, you would suddenly lose certain on-campus privileges such as access to jobs or ministry opportunities. When abuse was reported by homosexual students, it was less likely to be taken seriously. If you had asked me when I was a college student how I identified, I would have said "straight" without the blink of an eye. But when I came out to my closest friends at the time, they almost all told me they already knew.

My queerness has been a fight from the very beginning—a fight first and foremost with myself. I grew up steeped in Nazarene culture, and part of that was "knowing" that being gay was a choice that led to eternal punishment. It was wicked in a way that other sins weren't. I didn't know how to accept myself as gay because in my understanding, that would threaten my eternal salvation. I can't begin to explain how terrifying that is to try to understand as a child. The Nazarene doctrine in its current form regarding the LGBTQ+ community is what fostered my internalized homophobia, which then turned inward on my own queer expression, and eventually led to extreme self-hatred, anxiety, and depression.

My entire identity growing up was rooted in my Christian faith. I loved being a pastor's kid, went to all the services, retreats, Bible studies, classes, and more. When I realized that another important aspect of my identity was seemingly in stark contrast to that faith which defined me, I felt my whole selfhood split in two. It was tragically painful and still is. I couldn't understand how a loving and consensual relationship with another human could so deeply threaten my internal devotion to God so far as to condemn me to eternal suffering. But whenever I brought this conflict to a pastor, they affirmed the Nazarene position, simultaneously disaffirming my identity. And so, further into the closet I went as a child and teenager.

During my time at ENC, I realized that alongside my greatest passion in life, theatre, was another huge passion: education. I knew immediately that I needed to teach at ENC. Many people who have listened to my story have wanted to know why I bothered fighting to stay at ENC when I clearly wasn't wanted there by the leadership. I understand this question. ENC is, of course, bound to the Nazarene statement of faith, and they did find out about my sexual orientation early on in my employment as a professor. I took great care to hide my relationship from the public eye. For years my partner and I would never hold hands outside of the house. We drove out of the city we live in to go grocery shopping or to have dinner at a restaurant. I have never publicly shared the beautiful pictures from my wedding. So many of my friends and family members were not invited to the small ceremony for fear of rumors spreading. Even still, I had relatives, friends, community members, ENC students, alumni, and faculty members report me to ENC. I was always on borrowed time on the staff at ENC, which was made clear to me by administration several times over the past few years. I was not "mission fit." But in my mind, I was exactly what ENC students needed. So, I stayed for as long as I could.

I have spent much time over the years thinking about how differently things would have been for me if I had grown up with even one example of a queer Christian adult in my life. I knew I had the potential to be that queer Christian adult for ENC students, but the personal cost was dear. When you have fought internally to accept yourself and take pride in your orientation and relationship but cannot tell anyone, it takes a toll on you. The day I came out to my parents was one of the worst days of my life. A close second was the day I had to sit in a small office with members of ENC's administration being forced to lie about my orientation and relationship to save my job. I struggled to always work as hard as possible—hoping my hard work would prove my worth. In the end, it did not.

I might spend the rest of my life trying to heal from my time on staff at ENC and with what coming out in a Christian community has done to me emotionally. The Nazarene denomination shattered my relationship with myself, almost stole my will to live, and damaged my ability to see myself as a deserving child of God. I am still working to heal my relationship with God and relearn what that relationship actually means for me. This shouldn't be the case for the next generation of queer Christian kids growing up. No one should be forced to choose between their relationship with God and a healthy relationship with themselves. Imagine a world where young queer kids go to a Nazarene college and are met by faculty and staff members like them who can guide them into finding their faith path as they grow into adulthood.

Perhaps you're reading this and you are queer and Christian, or ex-Christian or unsure, I see you. I have been where you are. Or perhaps you are in support of the Nazarene denomination's stance on the LQBTQ+ "issue." I implore you to consider the long-term damage that is being done to the least of these around you. Please bring the doctrine of holiness back into the conversation. That is what was always missing in my treatment at ENC: humanity as viewed by a loving God.

I was treated as a problem to be solved or a dirty secret to hide away quietly. My hard work, my Christian ministry, my sacrifice, my love for the students, my humanity—none of that was factored in. Please, look at your queer siblings as the full, beautiful, capable, talented, loving, unique, complex humans that they are. I fear the alternative is a Nazarene church that continues to bleed those of us who weren't given a place at the table.

Allison Nicole Tucker is a professional theatre artist and filmmaker in the greater Boston area. She is the owner and executive director of South Shore School of Theatre in Quincy, MA and works with a variety of film companies in the New England area. Allison has degrees in theatre arts from Eastern Nazarene College and Emerson University and is working on her PhD at Lesley University in Cambridge.

The Biggest Loser

DEVON VAN ESSEN

The Church of the Nazarene is missing out on all the gifts that queer people have to offer.

As an English professor for twelve years at a Nazarene university, I had the privilege to witness thousands of bright, creative, interesting students enter my classroom. I discussed literature with them, read their essays, and met with them in my office. Outside of class, I attended their performances, cheered their softball games, visited their art exhibits and debates, and passed by as they talked, laughed, and flirted in the halls. What a blessing to share in some small part of their lives.

They were the children of Nazarene pastors, district superintendents, and congregants, many from the cradle. They were also young people from a variety of other denominational or religious backgrounds or from no religious background. I too was one of those students once, having been raised Free Methodist, then educated in a private Christian high school before coming to this Nazarene university. For whatever reason, we had all ended up here, experiencing a Nazarene education, Nazarene chapels, and the potential for each of us to become lifelong members of the Church of the Nazarene.

Some of these students were also gay, bisexual, transgender, or otherwise part of the LGBTQ+ community. As I got to know each of my classes and helped them get to know me, often a moment would arrive when a student would choose to come out and reveal themselves in the truth of their identity. Rarely was it a direct face-to-face conversation. Sometimes it was in an essay. Sometimes an email. Sometimes simply an object, like a sticker or piece of jewelry subtly displayed. Often it was covert, introduced as an innocuous question to test the waters or spoken in coded language. *IYKYK (if you know, you know)*, as the kids say.

Nearly all these queer students were closeted to some degree at this Nazarene university; they did not experience it as a safe place to be fully themselves. I could empathize—I was also a closeted queer person as their professor. I also felt profoundly unsafe and unable to bring my full self to work every day.

What does it mean to be closeted? Being closeted means your relationships are—must be—cautious, stymied, stunted. It means holding yourself back out of fear of betrayal and rejection. It means cloistering your heart and building thick walls around it. It means rejecting yourself first so that others won't have the chance to.

Coming out is the opposite. It is an act of profound courage and vulnerability, a self-revealing that is as beautiful as it is fragile. Because I knew the bravery it took for these students to offer me some glimpse into their truth, I treated their coming out moments as sacred, as occasions for care and thanks and celebration. Holy, in its deepest etymological meaning: whole, sound, and well.

Once they knew they were accepted and loved as queer, I witnessed students transform from cautious and withdrawn to enthusiastic and engaged. In a word, they blossomed, as individuals and as students. They asked for extra reading. They sent me creative pieces of writing that I had not assigned. They stayed after class to talk. They spoke up in class with amazing insights. Not only did I have the profound privilege to witness this blossoming, but their classroom community did as well. Instead of a withdrawn, fearful classmate, other students benefited from a classmate who felt able to bring their confident, joyful self into that learning space. In occasional cases where there were multiple LGBTQ+ students (who were usually already friends, since we tend to find each other and flock together), the class became a festive, creative flourishing that bloomed into something far beyond my own ability to create as a professor alone. What a blessing.

And this—this is why the Church of the Nazarene should fully affirm LGBTQ+ people with no reservations: because the church is missing out on the queer community, queer creativity, and queer joy that appear when LGBTQ+ people feel safe and welcome to bring their full selves into your church.

You should do it for selfish reasons, apart from all the moral, ethical, and biblical arguments that also support this move. You should do it because you are missing the party.

Now make no mistake, for many of these students, our conversations after their coming out were not all unicorns and rainbows. Often they shared deep pain, hurt, and experiences of rejection, bullying, sometimes cruelty at the hands of Christians. Some of them had stopped attending church or found services painful when they did attend. Nearly all of them were counting the days until they could leave the university and the Nazarene church—or all church—behind altogether. Not because they didn't want to be there, but because they knew they were not wanted. Not truly. Not if they embraced who they were.

Unlike their peers, they knew they would never benefit from or contribute to the networks of graduates, alumni, and church members in their future careers and community service. They would not be hired or ordained. Whatever they may accomplish down the road, they would not be brought back to be awarded, honored, or feted as successful model alumni by a proud alma mater. Not if they transitioned. Not if they married a partner of the same gender. Not even if they ever simply dared to live publicly in their authentic identity.

And so far, they are correct. The Nazarene Church and its universities have cast out some of their most luminous souls—not always overtly, but effectively all the same—by making it poisonous for them to stay.

I wish I could tell the stories here of specific young people I remember: those who went on to create beautiful poetry and films, earn graduate degrees and found organizations, fall in love and have children, explore their gender and illuminate the world, all after leaving the Nazarene Church behind. I would also have to tell you about those I know who floundered, those left bruised and broken by the rejection and trauma visited on them by the Nazarene Church, those who felt abandoned by God, who never fully recovered. I want you to hear their stories so you can imagine what might have been, if only they had been embraced and loved from the beginning. But their narratives are their own.

I can only tell my own story. I came to understand my queer identity in my early twenties—and then repressed that knowledge for a decade until the secret began to destroy my body from the inside. As I slowly began to come out to my Christian friends and family, I found freedom, but also more pain as I lost friends—some of whom simply disappeared, some who made assumptions and snap judgments about my "lifestyle," and some who claimed to love me but refused to stand beside me when it might cost them something.

And through it all was the certain knowledge that coming out fully would mean the end of a vocation I loved and felt called to, the end of my important work creating safe spaces for queer students on campus, and the end of my own place in a community I had contributed to for twelve years. The prospect broke my heart.

I stayed for too long, as so many of us do, by convincing myself that the acceptance and affirmation of a few individuals on campus would make up for institutional repression and silence from the rest of my community. I was wrong. Similarly, many people believe that if the Church is just "nicer" to LGBTQ+ people—less overtly hateful, less outwardly judgmental—then LGBTQ+ people ought to feel safe and welcome, even if we aren't allowed to fall in love, marry, transition, or hold leadership positions. It's a trap, and we queer Christians are no longer falling for it.

When I finally left, I heard one comment over and over, from sympathetic colleagues, administrators, and students: "What a loss for the university!" And they were right, more so than they knew.

Every year that goes by without LGBTQ-affirming doctrine and praxis, Nazarene universities and churches lose. They lose bright, brilliant minds that would have enriched their faculties, pulpits, and Sunday schools. They lose creative, talented spirits that would have brought music, art, and drama into their worship spaces. They lose the full potential of the LGBTQ+ members who exist in their churches and schools but cannot flourish. They lose the alchemy of queer magic and joy that appears when LGBTQ+ people are fully loved, fully valued, fully empowered. They lose brothers, sisters, and nonbinary siblings; leaders, friends, and confidants, who would have taught *them* how to love, how to find their courage, and how to be a truly *holy* community.

Devon Van Essen *(she/her) is an alumna and former professor of a Nazarene university. She now teaches English and Composition at Treasure Valley Community College and lives in Idaho.*

Around the Table, An Offering of Sorts

ROSE

Queer folk have long been pushed away from a seat at the table in the Nazarene Church. Isn't it time we start building a better table?

I have long labored and lamented over this paper, groaning under the effort as it came to be born in this world. It is a creation that has fought hard to be here, clawed its way through doubt and shame, and has come out a little worse for the wear. And, I suppose, like most creations, it comes to the world flawed and wanting for love. And so. Here we stand. Together. You and me. (I hope) hand in hand as we gaze down at this little piece of work that represents a conversation just as fragile and vulnerable to hurt as another sort of newborn creation. Let us treat it (and one another) most tenderly.

When I was a kid, I did all those things that a young girl is meant to do— watched the latest Disney Channel Original Movies, took part in hair braiding trains, gossiped about the latest boy crushes—but I was never a "girly" sort of girl. Even at a young age, I felt like an imposter, somehow. And I knew, from a young age, that my sense of belonging relied upon my ability to perform. And, so, I performed. I hoped, I prayed that this was somehow youthful error, that perhaps I was a late bloomer of sorts and that, with age, those feelings I was meant to have for boys, those girly clothes, and ways of being that I was meant to enjoy would come along. But bloom I did not. While girls were turning into women around me, I grew up like a dandelion—a weed, peculiar and pretty in its own ways, but decidedly out of place in the garden. Neither did I fit in with the boys. When I would try to tag along when the youth group guys would go off to chop wood with their axes or build the fire, they'd look at me like a sort of hanger-on, confused as to why I wanted to be in *their* group, while the other girls were hanging out inside, cooking the meals and chatting away. Now, this is not to say that all guys enjoy outdoorsy stuff or that all girls are lovers of housework (ha!). But if you grew up in a church like mine, certain gender stereotypes were reinforced, whether explicitly or otherwise, and I tended to fit into a decidedly masculine category.

Or, more accurately, I *didn't* fit. My sort of awkwardness was never the endearing type, and I bumbled my way through those teenage years more haphazardly than most. I had this foreboding sense that something was "off" about me, different in that unspoken way. Because, while there are many topics kept "hush-hush" in the church, being gay is one of the biggest. There's no roadmap for someone experiencing struggles or questions around their sexuality. No God to turn to when (according to the church) the God that they've been taught to love *hates* homosexuality. And, while church and church camps were the very places that I began to believe in love (and in my own lovability), there was this new love growing up inside of me that I could never speak of. One I hated. One that threatened my very place in the community. And so, I learned to turn that hate inward. While I will not go into the particulars, the story of my reckoning with myself is not one unfamiliar for many within the queer community. Years of rejection and isolation from our formational communities have often been the source of behaviors harmful to ourselves, as we try to cope with new realities of being unwanted, by God, by good Church folk, by our families. It is a way of living and being that teaches us that we are *unworthy* of being loved. Unworthy of a place to belong. Unworthy of being invited to a place at the table.

It's funny. I've often prided myself on being a somewhat "mild" gay—what with my fondness for gentle television like *Little House on the Prairie* and *Full House*, my embarrassingly early bedtime, and my equally embarrassing catchphrases like "oh my Lanta" and "bad Larry." I've often tried to settle the nerves of those around me who might reject me by saying, "Oh no, I'm not *that* kind of gay. I'm like the least offensive queer." And, while it's always delivered with a tilted head and a crooked smile, it reveals a deeper feeling of this need to apologize for myself and my kin who identify in the LGBTQIA+ community. I think I felt, in some way, that I could (and should) "make up" for my queerness by being mild-mannered and gently tempered. But the truth was, so very many of my Nazarene family had already disowned me, sometimes before they'd even met me. This, again, is not an unfamiliar tale. So many of us, disowned by our own families, face(d) a double rejection from the family of God, leading precious many to leave the faith altogether.

As I imagine many readers might know, the Nazarene Manual's official stance on human sexuality reads in this way:

"The Church of the Nazarene believes that every man or woman should be treated with *dignity*, *grace*, and *holy love*, *whatever their sexual orientation* (emphasis added). However, we continue to firmly hold the position that the homosexual lifestyle is sinful and is contrary to the scriptures."

While the stance offers a perhaps hopeful look into the posture with which one is to receive an individual ("whatever their sexual orientation"), the gap between the theoretical and lived practice is a devastating one. So often, queer folk are not only not invited to the table; they are effectively banned from it, with a posture that expresses, rather than holy love, a message of "you are not welcome here," and "you do not and will not ever belong." So often, the message is that "you need to get your junk together, then we can talk." So, we try to crawl up underneath that metaphorical table, to gather from those comfortably seated the crumbs of love and acceptance and abundance, but there is never enough. When shame forces you from the table, you are left with two choices, to remain in famine, or to build a new table. Now this explanation of mine is not meant to be an indictment that raises up shame, but rather one that extinguishes it—in the bodies of those who have done harm and in the bodies of those who have been the victims or recipients of harm. It is meant, rather, to be an invitation into something new. Something we *can* co-create. So, if you will allow, let us imagine together a new table.

Perhaps, before we go there though, let me say this. For many who have walked with me, they will notice my step into a new sort of season, as I've decided to live within the doctrinal expectations of the Nazarene faith. This choice comes with great sacrifice—of personal identity and potential for intimate love. The cost of one living outside of one's authentic self is a steep one. And it is my belief that the communities that I find myself in are disadvantaged, as they rarely get to meet the gentler, more earnest parts of myself that are more deeply revealed when I am living into the whole of my being. I do not take this step lightly. I *do* feel as if there is something profoundly dear and worth fighting for in our shared Nazarene tradition. I wish to remain here, to find a home here, if you will have me. And so I find myself willing to enter the gaps of the in-between, of not knowing quite what it is that God has for me, but hoping that, in my commitments to living the life expected of me, I might find a way to belong. Please hear me when I name—this is not prescriptive. Or, I do not expect another human to make the same decisions, to the denial of their self, uniquely and wonderfully made as they are.

But, dear church, what I *am* asking—humbly—is that you meet my kin and me here, in the gaps created within the broken spaces of our theology. Where the seats of the table are left unfilled, cold, and deserted, because there are those for whom welcome is not promised. Or for whom the meal being offered is laced with the poison of conditional love, that those who are craving to receive it must mend something within themselves before they are deemed worthy of a place at the table. We need a different sort of table altogether. We need, you and I, to build something new. It is not work we can do alone. I do not believe that we are *meant* to do it alone, estranged from one another. When there is no more room, we build a bigger table; we snuggle up our chairs closer together and gather up more chairs around. We grab our tools, hoist up our trousers, and we get to work.

Let me say it in a different sort of way. I have joked and named myself to be an inoffensive queer. But oh, what a bland and boring table it would be with all of us "inoffensives" gathered up around it. Drowning in our own politeness and respectability. The problem is not with "offensiveness," but rather that queer folk have been told, for far too long, that they must conform themselves to some unfair, unjust standard of "normalcy" just to be invited to sit at the table. What did our early church look like? Give me color. Give me expression and flamboyancy, give me troublemakers and peacemakers, give me holy rollers and grungy outcasts, give me the meek and the bold, give me the incarcerated and sick, the healing and the hurting. Show me the "least" of these, and I will show you my Jesus. What a table that would be.

This last portion of the essay has called for a biographic of sorts for the author. The author for this piece would prefer to remain in anonymity and asks that you honor that hope. If you are a human who knows "Rose" in the world, please tenderly hold that wish for privacy in more public spaces, and allow the author's words, rather than lists of achievements and personality indicators, to speak for themselves.

Queer for Life, Nazarene No More

ELIZABETH WREN MCNALLY

The church of the Nazarene taught me that abusing children is acceptable and lying to members is expected, but it is not okay to be queer. God doesn't accept queers, but he forgives liars and pedophiles.

The question of whether any church should change their stance on how they should treat a person—let alone a mass group of people—is just such a quandary for me. We are a human race, and it's beyond my comprehension why this is such an issue. Isn't the Bible very specific that God is the only one who should judge, and that we are supposed to treat others as we want to be treated?

I was raised in a Nazarene household, and there has never been a time in my life that I didn't know I was a lesbian. Of course, I never knew what the word lesbian meant, or that it was even a word—that it existed. I never realized I had an identifiable word for my sexuality. I never came out. I don't think people should come out. I think people should just be who they are and not have to answer to anyone.

I was raised in a very strict household that was dominated by a woman who could gaslight anyone that wasn't on her side or anyone that she deemed to challenge her; the threats and her wrath haunt me every day.

I love being a girl. In the dead of winter with the worst blizzard, I would still wear a dress and *loved* having a good handbag of some sort. I was in love with my Barbies, collected shoes, collected bags, and was always drawn to women. Being around men would make my skin crawl.

I have extended family in the church. Cousins who were missionaries, an uncle is a pastor, a step-dad and multiple family members who were elders—it was who we were. Nazarene. No drinking alcohol, potlucks on Sundays, Caravans on Wednesdays, Sunday school before Church, camps and NYC. There was church at least three times a week. During the summer there was Church softball, summer camp, mission trips, fundraising for programs and so much more.

The problem I am having is that I was raised in such an abusive home that I have blacked out almost all of my childhood. I was raised by a mother and stepdad who were kicked out of the church for their pedophilic behavior with the youth of the church. Nobody talks about it. Nobody saw the signs in me—and if they did, nobody interjected their Holy Christian self to save me. To be clear, I am not a lesbian because of how I was raised. I am a lesbian because I am sexually attracted only to women. I have always been a lesbian; my point in sharing how I was raised is that the Nazarene church picks and chooses who they condemn, and they cover up so much scandal. The church punishes people and judges them for who they are as humans. They are not inclusive.

A man of God, an Elder, coming into my bedroom, rubbing my head, putting his hands where they said in school no one should put their hands and to tell a trusted adult. But if you can't trust the people In your house who take you to church three times a week, who can you trust?

I remember being told that being gay is against God. I didn't know what "gay" was. Of course, I was also making out with girls at Church Camp and losing my virginity to a pastor's daughter. GAH—it was amazing! I was in heaven at church camp.

I remember all the double standards. No drinking, but there was a hidden fridge in my mother's closet with alcohol. I never was able to determine if that was because she was going against the church or because my stepdad was a convicted felon on parole and not allowed to drink.

Now, as an adult, I have identified what queer is—that I am for fact a lesbian and am very happily married to a woman. I have not had a relationship with my mother or step-dad for over five years—and life is perfect. I am an embarrassment to the majority of the family because I am a lesbian; their Nazarene background has opted to condemn me, not embrace me. They have taught me that *Jesus* may forgive my sins, but *they* will not.

When people, Christian or not, question me as an adult and my walk with Christ, my answer is simple: "My walk with God is mine and mine alone. He knows my heart and my path. If he wants me to feel guilty or that I am a sinner, he will—but see, *I* don't feel like I am sinning. I don't feel bad. I don't feel like I need to repent. And if I was living in a not Christlike way, I would feel I need to repent."

Let me just say that I don't know why they aren't affirming to everyone. Why does it matter? Why does anyone care where someone else's heart is? Why is it okay for my parents to abuse me and other children in the church, but it's not okay for me to love another woman? Why does a convicted felon who created hundreds of victims get to be an Elder in the Church, but the girl who attends Sunday School, Jr. Church, Sunday night service and Caravans doesn't get to kiss a girl?

The first girl I did kiss was a pastor's daughter—at church camp. It didn't feel wrong. We kissed everywhere—in the kitchen, in the dorms, in Ruth, in Mary, in Margaret (cabins at camp). We kissed in Church, we held hands in church, we prayed at the altar in church. It never felt wrong. It felt wrong when a family member told me I was an embarrassment. It felt wrong when my church family condemned my life choices. God didn't make me feel wrong, people did—like when my grandmother, a devout Nazarene, didn't want me and my wife to enter her house. I wonder how she feels about my cousin, who is a lesbian.

Why would the Church not allow its members to be happy, loved, and filled with joy? If I was created in the likeness of Christ, didn't he make me this way? I didn't choose to love her, to love all the girls—why was it wrong for me to tell a girl I loved her, but it wasn't wrong for liars to be members of the Church?

Alcohol was hidden in our house. The past of my family members was hidden, and when it was told, it was told wrong. It was told as a testimony—to gain trust, to gain love, to gain admirers. The truth was never told.

The Church of the Nazarene should become affirming to the queer community. The Church needs to do better by the communities they are located in, to stop spreading hate. I am currently in my fifth year of working through the traumas that I have endured at the hands of the Nazarene Church. The depths of despair I have been at—my lowest lows in life are at the hands of the Nazarene Church. There are times in my life that the Church of the Nazarene would be the reason for my death.

I learned to lie at Church. I learned to judge people at Church. All of it for Church. I learned that Church didn't want me to be real. I learned that the people in church wanted to hide the truth. The Church is cloaked in lies, secrets, and judgment. I tried to tell people what was happening at home, but it fell on deaf ears. No one wanted to believe me, no one wanted to help me, and no one was there to help me simply *just be me*. There was no one like me in my hometown church. I submitted to what the Church wanted me to be and not what I was or who I am.

I spent the ages 3 to 16 growing up in the Nazarene Church, and all I saw were individuals who are not authentic. My experience is that the Nazarene Church is for people who want to judge others who don't believe in the same things, and who want to put people down—to step on them and emotionally damage people. Church wasn't for helping people. Church wasn't for love. It was for telling you that you aren't living the correct way. That you are on a path to hell. That the One true God above would damn me to hell for loving women. But God didn't make me feel that way—church members did.

If I was created in His likeness, didn't he know he created me like this? Having to separate the church from the house I grew up in is hard. Our life was consumed by Church and I didn't know where one ended and the next started. Everything revolved around Church. I grew up in a house where we didn't say I love you. We didn't hug. We didn't extend joy and kindness or even support. I don't recall a single school event that my family attended.

I don't understand why any church wouldn't just accept everyone. Why does it matter? Make it make sense. Why do these religions claim to be Christ-like and yet don't support everyone? What is wrong with them? Why do they care what sex we are, who we love, who we want to marry… What does any of that matter? It's not for us as people to judge or determine the fate of others.

I will end with this: the number one place that I have been rejected from for being queer is the Church of The Nazarene. The only people who have made me feel unloved because I am queer are members of the Church of the Nazarene. But their God does not condemn people to eternal damnation for being queer. Their God loves me and my wife.

Elizabeth Wren McNally is living her best life in Key West as a probation agent and married to her soul mate Monica. She graduated from the University of Wisconsin and has two adult children living in Wisconsin. She is a survivor.

Just As I Am?

MARVA WEIGELT

Unless you have walked this road, you cannot possibly imagine.
Yet I dare you to try.

When I was asked about contributing to this project, my initial instinct was a clear "no." I've labored many years to get to a place of relative understanding with my family and have no wish to jeopardize or harm that hard-won harmony in any way.

I was delayed in recognizing this automatic reluctance as a deeply conditioned survival response, an instinct to shield others from uncomfortable truths and to protect my family's image rather than considering broader implications.

There's a greater reason to speak than simply to tell my own story. I happen to know firsthand that Nazarene youth still attempt to end their lives due to being met with judgment and condemnation instead of being embraced as rarer-than-usual expressions of Divine diversity. If my risk to be honest and vulnerable might potentially reduce future harm, I am willing.

As a cradle-roll Nazarene born to parents who met at Northwest Nazarene College, arriving while my dad was a student at Nazarene Theological Seminary, and growing up as a double PK—a pastor and theology professor's kid—I was indelibly signed from birth with the signature Wesleyan-Holiness doctrine and spirit of the Church of the Nazarene in the 1960s and '70s. All four grandparents and two step-grandparents were Nazarenes, and my younger brother is a Nazarene pastor—a multi-generational legacy.

At 12, I took the Pastor's Class and became a member of College Church of the Nazarene in Nampa, Idaho, although I was already deeply involved with church life, twice on Sunday and every Wednesday night, not to mention Vacation Bible School, youth choir, bell choir, Bible quizzing, and Caravans (I can still recite my Silver Moon Maiden pledge from first grade, which seems ironic in light of the fact it ended up being impossible for me to "live straight and true.")

I was an earnest young Jesus-follower who was also innately curious and intro-spective, a spiritually minded and mystically hearted person, who struggled at times with puzzling contradiction and sometimes bewildering incongruence among be-lief, word and action. This included an emphasis on image management which was so clear an expectation that Sunday School teachers sometimes reminded me of my extra-big responsibility for setting a good example because of my father's position, a caution which still echoes fifty-some years later, I must admit.

At about the time I joined the church, I began quietly noticing ways in which I was different from my family, a developmentally appropriate task at that age. In addition to natural variation in personality and temperament, gift and talent, per-spective and interest, I began observing that my draw toward romantic attractions was also a point of dissimilarity. Although my affections felt deeply and sweetly natural to me, I became vaguely and then increasingly aware of my uniqueness in family, church, and community in an era with a notable scarcity of open conver-sation and supportive context on matters of human sexuality, especially within the church.

When I entered Northwest Nazarene College as a psychology major in 1976—with a desire to become a counselor in a large church because of my frustrations with existing support resources—I had no idea the one still-hidden difference that distinguished me from the majority of my classmates had been removed two years earlier from the American Psychiatric Association's Diagnostic & Statistical Manual of Mental Disorders. "Homosexuality" was no longer classified as a "sexual deviation" or disorder by the time I was 15.

Sadly, over twenty painful years elapsed before this good news reached my ears, and only then because a skilled therapist helped me understand from an ob-jective standpoint that while I was suffering from a number of valid psychological maladies in response to stress and trauma, my sexual identity was a non-issue—a wholly natural expression of my selfhood.

To be clear, I did not feel innately distressed by my divergence from the norm, only discomfited by the obvious need to cloak my authentic self in exchange for belonging. For a variety of reasons which I would not understand for decades, I was suffering the effects of a complex response to childhood adversity.

Although some have misguidedly attributed my queerness to early trauma, I can say with deep certainty at 64, and as a mental health care provider, that my sexual identity was not a choice, a rebellion, or a response to losing my mom at age 3, but simply a natural part of my inborn genetics and brain wiring. This unfortunately became in turn a cause for further alienation, judgment and harm due to the Church of the Nazarene's policy that I, simply by being myself, was an abomination against God.

Through some strange grace, I have always at a core level sensed myself to be a wonderfully made creation with a deep spiritual calling. Despite issues with depression, addiction, suicidal despair, and shame (well into my late 30s), these symptoms were not caused by my sexual identity, but to a significant extent by how misunderstood and rejected I felt in my most fundamental supporting milieu of family and church.

Once I accepted, understood and more fully became my truest self, the symptoms gradually abated, and as I asked my dad to consider in a pivotal dialogue, "If I am an abomination against God, explain to me how I have grown up to be the most peaceful person I know."

I disaffiliated with the church in 1979, at the age of 20, and have now lived much more of my life outside than within its influence, which might make you wonder why my voice is here in this particular collection.

Activism on my own behalf is not a natural inclination, especially on this highly charged and controversial topic. With family and friends I have been inclined toward a gentle, incremental, and relational approach to fostering deeper understanding, but I felt a seismic shift when my young nephew began examining his relationship with the church in light of his own queerness, as did another extended family member with aspirations to ministry, after painful experiences with his family and a Nazarene college.

Suddenly, in a new light with the next generation, I feel a greater urgency as a queer elder to advocate more boldly for LGBTQIA+ inclusion and celebration at the denominational level, knowing from direct experience that continued discrimination causes untold harm to God's beloved creations and to confused families uncomfortably forced to choose between love's deepest, open-hearted knowing and what the Code of Conduct claims about their children.

As I close, it seems important to invite consideration of a significant qualitative difference I've repeatedly experienced. I automatically default to an instinctive wariness, self-consciousness, and self-censorship in the presence of people I know to be dedicated to upholding a denominational position which condemns and excludes me, despite their evident love and longing to be in unconditional and unburdened relationship with me.

By contrast, I experience comfort and freedom to bring my most authentic self into encounters with people who are unhindered in truly celebrating me just as I am. In particular, it has been enormously healing to provide peer support services to clergy from other Christian denominations who unstintingly accept and trust me as a confidante and spiritual equal.

In such a benevolently welcoming embrace, I feel historic hurt and confusion dissolving in the gentle solvent of Love, and in my mind and heart there is no question which quality of engagement most effectively sparks a holy Christ-light and kindles true spiritual kinship.

The Rest of the Story...

After preparing and sharing with trusted reviewers a draft of what you've just read, I curiously circled back to confront current and historical Code of Conduct statements and related documents. Without warning, the force of the condemnatory language swept me away under a tsunami of all-too-familiar toxic shame and grief and into what I recognize belatedly as an intense post-traumatic stress flashback. I wondered why I had ever been born or why I was still alive.

To confront the possibility that family members, childhood friends, and college classmates perceive me in so dim and slanted a light was horrifying at a gut level, and I realized as never before what a state of denial I've needed to maintain over the last half-century in order to hold onto my sense of self in the presence of those who embrace this distorted and damning view of my fundamental personhood.

Earlier in my life I responded to similarly overwhelming trauma responses with instinctive self-destructiveness, turning the external judgments inward, and thus exponentially deepening the harm, simply because I lacked adequate maturity, support and resources to do otherwise.

Even now, in my 60s, with all my years of therapy, my ongoing spiritual journey, and my mental health training and peer support practice experience, I struggled mightily this week to keep from drowning in despair that all this work has not been enough to protect me from a stunning loss of equilibrium and perspective.

As I reached for life-giving support and stabilization from some of the many understanding allies in my life, I felt overwhelming gratitude and a renewed determination to share my story, despite my deepened grief and heightened sense of caution.

While treading these troubled waters in the aftermath of my traumatic flashback, I felt the need to pause from the intensity of trying to find words. I found myself standing reflectively in front of my second-story window on a dismal mid-winter's day, looking out for perspective at a small community in the heart of America which has unexpectedly helped me heal simply by seeing, loving, and celebrating me just as I am.

A favorite hymn came spontaneously to mind, and from deep within arose the urge to affirm aloud in song what I have proven to myself repeatedly in the face of trauma and adversity. Even when sorrows like sea billows roll, it is indeed well with my soul, despite what anyone else might assume.

Unless you have walked this or a similar road, you cannot possibly imagine, yet I dare you to try. I invite your compassionate curiosity. I challenge you to consider that despite the church's historically dim and incomplete understanding of this issue, there is more to know about Divine creativity.

Imagine with me that when this mistaken assumption is corrected, suddenly we are free to stop wondering who's at fault. I weep to think of the opening, pardoning, cleansing, and relief that might become possible for my beloved dad and me before he dies.

If you are still on the fence, I ask you to simply sense the quality of Love I offer. Somehow, against the odds, I managed to grow up without reliable mirrors to accurately and lovingly reflect my rare self back to me. I miraculously lived long enough to find havens of reason, grace, and acceptance where I was seen as a delightfully creative interpretation of what it means to be made in God's image, instead of a perverse miscreation or wayward deviant.

After decades of mental, emotional and spiritual healing, I finally found my mission and ministry offering compassionate and non-judgmental listening to support others in finding their own path to wholeness. I wish I had some kind of count of how many times I've said, after an hour of holy, open-hearted listening, "I know why I was born." That in itself is a miracle for someone who often felt like a mistake when seen through the eyes of those who believed what the church espoused. Divine grace abounds despite human obstacles and limits in understanding. I am living proof.

My calling from birth seems well-encapsulated in the Hebrew phrase *Tikkun Olam*—the repair of the world—at both the mystical and practical level, starting from peace within and rippling outward far beyond what I can see or measure, and although that calling has sometimes been far from clear to me in the midst of obscuring human judgment and alienation, from a very young age I have been graced with face to face glimpses of a higher truth, and in that I rest just as I am.

Marva Weigelt is a Certified Peer Specialist at Insight in Newton, Kansas. She is actively pursuing uncovery from beneath complicated layers of childhood grief and trauma while using her adversity-born ingenuity, healing, empathy and self-invention stories to inspire others. Marva is a persistent idealist who believes that grace, hope and transformation can totally knock your socks off at any age.

A Gay Daughter and her Pastor Father: An Interview

ALLISON TUCKER AND TRACY TUCKER

Estrangement hits home in a clash between understanding and dogma.

Moderator: As part of the book titled *Why the Church of the Nazarene Should Be Fully LGBTQ+ Affirming*, we are interviewing two of the contributors to this project. Allison Tucker is a professional theatre artist and filmmaker in the Boston area, and her father, Tracy Tucker, a Nazarene elder with 30 years of full-time service in the Church of the Nazarene. For the past 7 years, Tracy has served full time as a Hospice Chaplain.

Welcome to our discussion. I know both of you have already written essays for this project but because of your unique connection to the topic we have decided to capture your story. Jumping right in: Allison, I understand you had some hidden feelings that surfaced during a visit with your parents several years ago. You came out as gay. Growing up in a Nazarene parsonage, that must have generated some interesting dynamics for you and some stressful and even fearful feelings about how your family might accept this news.

Let's start with how you would characterize your relationship with your dad growing up?

Allison: My dad was always my best friend and a superhero in my eyes. I wanted to be exactly like him. I remember when I was twelve watching him pour me my first cup of hot black coffee and quickly swallowing it down with a grimace, determined to love it because he did. My favorite pastime was bringing him a new theological or ethical question and soaking up every word. The best compliment you could give me as a kid was that I was just like my dad. Actually, that is still one of my favorite compliments.

Tracy: And I must tell you that while I dearly love and am proud of both of my daughters, Allison did tend to follow more closely to my routines and various roles in ministry.

Moderator: That's a wonderful picture of your relationship. What was your personal tension with the church and/or each other, and when did you first start feeling it?

Tracy: I was involved in a couple different arenas of training for ministry students through online teaching and a District Training Center for the district where I served. Most of what the curriculum prescribed was fairly basic and didn't generate much of a tension, but some of it did. I have quite a number of memory snippets of doubt about what I was teaching. I wasn't sure how I felt about some of what I was saying to the students. I don't think that is unusual or even a bad thing. I hope I'm never fully satisfied with what I believe about God in particular and everything else in general. But it was the confusing message about divine love as it is expressed to all humanity—all humanity.

I sometimes felt as though the underlying message of what I was teaching promoted an us/them distinction: like the *saved* and the *unsaved*, or *Christians* versus *non-Christians*. For me this felt too subjective, and it didn't gel with my understanding of God's lovingkindness. And eventually it felt as though our goal was to evangelize all those whose view of God didn't line up with ours.

In a group conversation some years ago with church leaders, it was clearly stated that should a gay couple begin to attend services at a local Nazarene Church and openly express their gayness, it would be the pastor's responsibility to have an honest conversation with them about that "lifestyle choice." At the same time it became obvious that we might not extend the same level of judgment to heterosexual couples who would be openly engaged in premarital sexual relationships.

The challenge for me was to reconcile this commitment to correcting the failings of others in such a random and unloving fashion. Regardless how I felt, right or wrong, about homosexuality, the judgment itself is what I struggled with. Then when Allison came out, that tension for me really escalated.

Allison: A critical moment in my life was when I was thirteen and I first realized I disagreed with my dad on something. I can still remember that feeling in the pit of my stomach like the wind had been knocked out of me. We were sitting in the car going through a Dunkin drive-thru and I mentioned that a close friend of mine at the time had confided in me that he was gay. I "knew" that being gay was both a choice and a sin, but that conflicted with what I knew about my friend. He wasn't making a choice to exist, honestly, and he was a good person, so things didn't add up. I brought this conversation to my dad like usual and when he reinforced the Nazarene church's belief system, I felt something within me tense up. I knew that wasn't true for me, but I also didn't know how to disagree with him.

I couldn't separate my relationship with my dad at the time from my relationship with the Church because my dad was the church for me. He was my pastor and my theologian. I trusted him implicitly with my physical and spiritual life. That made my impending conflict with the Church particularly tricky.

Moderator: Allison, it's obvious this experience has truly cost you something. For either of you, how did being a part of the Church of the Nazarene contribute to your conflict? What were the biggest barriers?

Allison: I felt like the Church of the Nazarene took my dad from me. When I came out to him, I needed him to see ME. But I felt like he could only see the sin as defined by the Church of the Nazarene.

Tracy: Well, there have been several significant barriers for me. But I need to first qualify what I mean by that. I am not establishing blame or pointing a finger; I am responsible for how I respond and how I interpret my surroundings. Having stated that, I also know that context is everything. Growing up in a conservative setting in a southern state, I inherited the best of teachings on what it means to love God. The accompanying legalism and fundamentalist influences, however, have made it difficult to find space for spiritual growth that challenges some of the Nazarene norms. Especially conversations around sensitive topics such as alternative lifestyles and gender leanings are often less of a conversation and more of an argument. There just doesn't seem to be enough grace for an intelligent and open dialog.

Then, of course, I have to always remember that I am ordained in this church that I love and have been educated through (TNU, NTS) and have served full time for 30 years. I have always considered myself a "team-player." Taking a stand with my daughter that many in my denomination feel threatened by, creates a tension within me that I don't always know how to address.

Allison: It took me a while to see this conflict from my dad's perspective. I saw the Church of the Nazarene turn its back on me when I was met with blatant hostility at ENC and when I saw other members of the LGBTQ+ community openly persecuted in the church. I was used to living in that position. However, I realized that for my dad, taking this stand would be his first experience being at odds with his faith. I was even more angry with the Church of the Nazarene that they put him in this position of having to choose between his church and his daughter.

Moderator: I hope you are finding a pathway to some level of peace in this. What has the healing process for you looked like?

Allison: The healing process was a seemingly endless series of the most difficult conversations of my life. It didn't help that we lived so far apart. We both had to dig in with both hands and embrace the discomfort of the situation. I remember several conversations early on where I sobbed the entire time. More than once when I hung up, I had to consider whether I could keep investing in this process with him. I wanted to be patient, but it was so emotionally taxing to have to defend my reality over and over. I think what gave me the most strength was focusing on empathy. I knew how far into Nazarene thought he was. I had been there, too. It has taken me so many years to unlearn the hatred I felt towards myself because of my orientation. How could I expect him to unlearn that programming overnight? I focused my attention on what it must be like for a man who lived his life devoted to Nazarene thought, rather than what it would be like for him as a father. That was helpful for sustaining our continued conversations. They didn't get easier for a while, but they were so worth it in the end.

Tracy: For me the first step was to recognize that my passion for my daughters is far more of a priority than loyalty to a religious system. Once I drew that conclusion, I was then forced into a process of exploring other ways of identifying and talking about the real issue. I guess it's kind of like "necessity is the mother of invention." It wasn't until I realized that I had no idea how I felt about what it means for someone to be gay, that I finally explored that matter in any real depth. I had read certain places in the Bible that seem at first blush to speak to homosexuality, and I have read what other people believe and even what the denominational leadership has written, but I had never entered the dialog myself. Now I have been compelled to immerse myself in it.

But really, the healing has taken place because of the very difficult and painful hard work of staying in dialog with Allison, in fact with both of my daughters.

Moderator: You used the word "painful." In what sense do you mean?

Tracy: After Allison came out, we couldn't talk for a while. It wasn't about being angry. I'm sure my response wasn't helpful and she was more than a little wounded. But the real pain, at least for me, was the separation. We had always been able to talk with each other. I think we both felt the relationship was worth the effort. But it didn't happen without a lot of work and tears.

Allison: More than once I have referred to that time of separation as the most painful time of my life. I have always known my dad was just a text or a phone call away, and when I needed him most, he felt impossibly far away. I don't think I left my bed for a month. I knew coming out would be incredibly difficult, and it was, but afterwards I desperately wanted my dad. Instead, every time I called or answered the phone I was speaking with Pastor Tracy or Counselor Tracy, not my dad. That was difficult. I kept pushing with the hope that I would reach my dad. I could hear the pain in his voice, and I could hear him struggling so hard to make sense of everything, but I just wanted to be held and loved.

Moderator: What would either or both of you do differently?

Tracy: I'm not really sure how to answer that question. This was actually like a perfect storm for me. It caught me by surprise, yet it was inevitable. The convergence of doctrine that I was committed to, along with Allison's new awareness as she revealed it to me, and then the social pressure of having to own this new reality in the marketplace. And with social media being what it is… need I say more? Perhaps I simply need to respond to the question with, "What I would do differently would be to create safe space early on that promotes open dialog regardless of the content of the dialog." I don't think such conversations were restricted, but I didn't do a good enough job of promoting them. Instead, I think I encouraged an authoritarian view of God and the church. And I think this same lack of dialog exists in many church settings.

Allison: I don't think I could have done anything differently. Coming out is an extremely personal journey, and I did the best that I could in my circumstances. So many young people in my situation don't, and they haven't made it out alive. I am keenly aware that I am lucky. When I didn't feel the love and support of my family in the way I felt I needed, I was still surrounded by chosen family who held me together. Not everyone has that support.

Moderator: Looking forward, what are you most afraid of or most concerned about?

Tracy: So it's confession time. And I have to confess that I like to be liked. I am a bit traumatized as I respond to your questions knowing that they will likely be published and I will likely face some difficult feedback or backlash.

Allison: I would like to think I'm through the worst of it. My worst fears have been realized already. I've lost jobs, friends, and family members…and I survived. I suppose I fear for the future of the church but it's more of a passive fear for me at this point. It's difficult to think about the mission of a church that I gave my heart and soul to for most of my life, only to have that church turn its back on me. At this point I'm waiting to see if they make what I see to be the only ethical decision in this matter.

Tracy: Actually, my real fear is that other families will face this same conflict and not survive. I am so fortunate to have such a great relationship with my girls that we can sludge through our challenges and pull back together. Not every Nazarene or even Christian home can boast that. It seems to me that it's the responsibility of our Church to promote and facilitate healthy and open conversations on the questions, fears, biases, feelings, possibilities and attitudes, helpful and hurtful on the matter of embracing members of the LGBTQ+ community, especially within our own families.

Allison Nicole Tucker is a professional theatre artist and filmmaker in the greater Boston area. She is the owner and executive director of South Shore School of Theatre in Quincy, MA and works with a variety of film companies in the New England area. Allison has degrees in theatre arts from Eastern Nazarene College and Emerson University and is working on her PhD at Lesley University in Cambridge.

Tracy L. Tucker is a Senior Chaplain for Community Hospice and Palliative Care in Jacksonville Florida, following 30 years in fulltime parish ministry. He earned his MDiv from Nazarene Theological Seminary and is currently working on his DTM through Northwind Theological Seminary. Tracy is a Board Certified Chaplain through the Association of Professional Chaplains (APC) and has a Certification in Thanatology through the Association for Death Education and Counseling (ADEC).

PART II

Ally Narratives

Naming Someone: A Love Story

JENNIFER R. JENSEN

*We named our children before we were dating; then our adult
child changed the name we chose.*

It was a warm summer day. The man I would someday marry rode in the passenger seat, the boy I was currently dating was driving. I sat in the back seat leaning forward so we could all hear each other. We had been on an excursion together somewhere, maybe the beach, maybe a park. We were headed home, and as we drove down the semi-country road, I piped up with a new conversation topic.

"If I ever have kids, I want to name my son Christopher Michael," I said, hoping to impress the driver, Michael. He grunted, and continued driving.

"Oh," Tom, my future husband replied, "what would you name a girl?"

"I think Lynaela Katheryn, after my mom and because I invented Lynaela," I said.

"I've always wanted to name a daughter after my mom," Tom said.

"What's her name?" I asked

"Shelby," he said. "She was born in Alabama at home. My grandpa had to walk to the county seat to register her birth. He claimed he forgot whatever my grandma wanted to name her, so he named her Shelby" He laughed at that and I smiled back. "My grandma was mad, but I've always liked it. Even though it is supposed to be a boy's name," he added.

"Oooh—I might steal that—Shelby Kathryn-lynae sounds so cool!"

And just like that—my future husband and I named our future, entirely hypothetical, probably going to be born with other people, children. It was actually a prophetic glimpse of him as a parent that made me decide to marry him, but that's a story for another day. Our firstborn was a son, named Christopher (but not Michael!) and five years later, while we were awaiting our second, we weren't sure of the sex, but we did know that if they were a girl, their name was already decided: Shelby Kathryn-lynae. Tom's mother was very excited when our child, assigned female at birth, was born.

As is normal for everyone, both of our children had some challenges growing up. Some of which we didn't know about, others we experienced together as a family. Tom wound up having some serious chronic illness, and ultimately needed multiple surgeries culminating in a double below the knee amputation; we lost our home when our youngest was a junior in high school to a hundred years flood; they experienced significant mental illness during their college years, resulting in multiple hospitalizations for medication modifications and therapeutic and behavioral counseling. As a family, all of these experiences were daunting and hard, but as my husband recently said to me, we haven't really had hard times as long as we've had each other. I know that sounds kind of sappy, but it really is our story. We've had fights and arguments and other kinds of normal tensions and issues. But we have always found our way back to loving one another and being stronger together.

In December of 2021, my husband's mother, our child's namesake, passed away.

In February of 2022, our youngest child came out to us as non-binary with pronouns of they/them/their. Although it was somewhat of a surprise, it also wasn't. I had often suspected they were trans, although I had sort of a "traditional" intuition—I thought they were a trans male person. Initially, because I think they were trying to take it slow for us (their parents), they did not mention a name change. I was relieved, because, well, it seemed like their name was a big part of our love story and I didn't want to lose that. I was worried that my husband would be devastated, after all, it was his mother—and although their relationship was often strained (even to the end, but again a different story for another time), he loved her.

By March, my child had decided to change their name. They had their own strained relationship with the grandmother that made them not want to keep a name associated with her, but they also thought something else would feel more like them. The name they initially chose was connected to another difficulty for my husband, which meant he really struggled. There were some words, some explanations, some tears. Ultimately, our child found the perfect name for them. They kept their middle name, but reimagined their first name to work for them.

Today, it is their birthday, nearly a year after they came out to me, and a month and a half since they legally changed their name. In the last year, I have watched them bloom and blossom into who they were always supposed to be. And as my husband and I have walked through this with them, we have both been able to see past the little story of how we picked our children's names before they were born, before we were even technically a couple, to the wonder and beauty of a created person becoming who they were meant to be. It's no longer just my story, or his story, but it is bigger and the expansion includes more than we could have thought possible way back when.

In honor of their birthday, I reimagined Psalm 139: 13-16 as a song acknowledging their uniqueness but also their being made, still, in the image of God, the creative Maker whose love and intention for us are also much bigger than the story we keep for ourselves.

> You created me.
> You molded & shaped & crafted
> my pieces & parts
> You infused me with your goodness
> with kindness and strength.
> I praise you for making me in this way,
> for you only make good people
> created in your image
> built with love
> forged in the furnaces of the ultimate Maker.
> As you watch me
> grow to who you have set me free to be
> launched from the womb of my parent,
> I can feel your knowing smile
> wash over my spirit
> I hear you call me by my name
> and whisper beloved you are mine.

Rev. Jennifer R. Jensen (she/her) *is an ordained elder in the Church of the Nazarene. She serves as an associate pastor on the Northwest Indiana district and bi-vocationally, works as a consultant for computer software. She has a business degree from Olivet Nazarene University and a Master of Education. She loves Jesus, her husband, her children, and her grandchildren.*

Damn Time

S. VONDALE ALLEN

*You may think you have heard it said, "homosexuality is an
abomination," but I believe experience is calling us to look
more closely. May we come to lead with love. May the stance
of the Church of the Nazarene become one that is governed by
"What does love look like in this situation?"*

Playing in the surf one day, my husband and I, with our daughters, were standing in the ocean with our backs to the waves, allowing them to catch us off
guard. We were deep enough in the water to keep our footing, but the waves were
strong enough to cause our daughters to stumble a bit if we did not keep a good
grip on them. Some of the waves would hit us harder than others and we were
having quite a few belly-laughs, when occasionally a stronger wave would sweep
their feet out from under them. They were in no danger, as we had a tight grip on
them, but for a second or two, there was the slightest bit of uncertainty—and then
their little giggles would tumble out from deep inside, as we held them tightly.
Distracted by our fun, we were caught off-guard when unexpectedly, a much larger
wave rolled over us. This massive wave rolled my husband and me, with both our
girls in tow, tumbling us over, rolling us in the rocks and broken shell bits. I held
on to my daughter desperately, unable to figure out which way was up as the waves
kept coming. Every time I thought I knew where to plant my feet, another wave
would roll over us and I had to try again to get my bearings. Even the smaller
waves, hitting before we could get our feet planted on solid ground, had enough
force to once again send us under, gasping for breath.

Recent life circumstances have brought this memory to the surface. A new
kind of wave, unseen and unexpected, has rolled over, toppled, tumbled, pulled
me under, dashed me against all manner of debris, lurking under the surface of my
life. Though not certain, I had some awareness of something pulling at me from
within, and at times I sensed there was something under the surface of my life. The

magnitude of damage and change that could be brought about so quickly, simply from the tumble I have taken, was unimaginable. Once again, I am hanging on with a tight grip, this time for my life, and life as I have known it, is gone.

As a young girl, I dreamed of growing up to be a mom and wife with a man to take care of me. Secondary to that, I dreamed of devoting my life to ministry. Being raised Southern Baptist, becoming a missionary was the only option I could fathom. As a junior in high school, I met the young man whom I felt Jesus had brought my way to live out this dream with. He was a good Christian boy, Nazarene, and a fabulous singer. He had a mesmerizing voice, and he could access this gift in a way that would fill the altars, no sermon needed. After our first date I knew I wanted to marry him. We dated, and while still in high school, began to work together in youth ministry. My dream of being a wife and mother were right in front of me and held the added potential for a life of ministry together. As we continued to date, I sensed there was something prohibiting us from continuing our relationship to the next step. I brushed the feeling aside until one night, while hugging me tightly, he said he needed to talk to me and expressed his fear that he would never get to hug me like that again after our talk. A week later, my future husband shared with me his same-sex attraction.

We discussed the issue with our pastors who advised us to get married soon, which, along with enough faith and prayer, would "fix" him. We married quickly and set off on our way to Wesley Bible College, discovering seven weeks into our marriage that we were expecting. After the birth of our first daughter, we left college, but still poured ourselves into ministry, him as a song leader and me as a children's teacher. Two daughters and five years into our marriage, my husband became the worship leader at a 400+ congregation and I eventually took the lead of a thriving small group. Desperate to figure out what Jesus wanted to do with my life, I envied our best friend and associate pastor's job, prompting a tearful argument with God about why he placed such things in my heart when, as a woman, I was not allowed to do that job. I told my husband often, "If I were a man, I'd be a preacher." Eventually we landed in his home church, a Nazarene church, with him in the role of worship leader, where he cautioned me to be careful about saying I wanted to be a preacher because the Nazarenes would "hold me to it." My world was shaken. I had never known that was even a remote possibility.

Over the years, occasionally with cause, I would ask my husband if the same-sex attraction was ever an issue (which we had promised to "figure out," if it ever was) and he always assured me it was not. Though I had reasonable doubts, struggling with lack of intimacy and depression, I trusted that Jesus had indeed "fixed" him.

Fast Forward

After 20 years of waiting, in 2013, I began to pursue ordination in the Church of the Nazarene. With my district license, in January of 2017, I accepted my first, and last, senior pastor position. I was ordained in June of 2018. In December of that same year my husband was "outed" to me. When confronted, my husband "introduced himself" to me again, reaching out his hand to shake mine with, "Hi my name is _____ and I am bisexual. It's nice to meet you." I reached out, shook his hand, saying, "It's about damn time."

In the years leading up to this moment, I had sat by my husband through three different incidents where he literally almost died. Every health problem could be linked directly to stress. Diagnosed with sarcoidosis, an immune condition exacerbated by stress, which had shut down the electrical system in his heart, my husband had to get a pacemaker at the age of 45, just four months after introducing himself to me as bisexual.

I understand now that my now former husband is gay. Intoxication, at a moderate level, continues to be the most reliable source of relief I can find for the shock of reality that is my life. I am writing my story to express the belief to the Church of the Nazarene that it is about "damn time" the Church of the Nazarene embrace our LGBTQ+ brothers and sisters. No one could have prayed more, believed more, given themselves to the work of Jesus more, or tried harder to keep their family intact. Jesus, and the Church of the Nazarene was our life. My husband and I were best friends, devoted to our family, in Church, in therapy, and we prayed and believed in the power of the Holy Spirit. Jesus did not "fix" my husband because he did not need fixing. There is no need for faith to fix the beautiful creation that he was born as. Some people will say we did not believe enough or pray enough, but I am writing to implore anyone who will to understand, no one chooses this life. My husband tried everything, sacrificing his health, almost to death, to deny being the person he is. We tried to "pray the gay away," got married, had a wonderful family, gave faithfully in tithes and effort, for 25 years. None of this changed the person my husband was genuinely created to be. It did almost kill us both, because of the despair we both experienced from trying to deny reality.

The Fallout

I have no career because the District's concern was optics, over our well-being. The choices I had, though unspoken, were obvious. I could have divorced my husband immediately, making the reason why known, in order to have my name and my divorce cleared, or my husband could continue to deny reality. I knew pretending was killing him, and me. These were slow deaths, but they were deaths, nonetheless. I had the choice to "throw him under the bus" or give up my credentials. This would mean that I had "wasted" five years with nothing to show for it. At 19 I had done what I was "supposed" to do. I got married, had a family, served Jesus, and the promise was, everything will be okay. Not so! In our case, rather than being concerned with optics or causing more harm to this beautiful, created being, I believe I chose love. I stayed with my husband, trying to honor the promise to "figure it out."

As a pastor, I taught the study "Kingdom Culture" written by Tara Beth Leach, a Nazarene. In Jesus' Sermon on the Mount, what I saw overwhelmingly was Jesus saying, "You have heard it said, but I say.…" What I believe Jesus taught here was the difference in the "spirit of the law" and "the letter of the law." Jesus repeatedly showed us that the spirit of the law over-rules the letter of the law. Jesus taught us to ask the question "What does love look like *in this situation*?" Jesus defied the letter of the law when love looks more like the spirit of the law. Every time.

Statistics overwhelmingly show that people are dying because of stances like that of the Church of the Nazarene, often referred to as the "side B" stance that says, a person may be born this way, but they cannot live this way. My now former husband has been suicidal multiple times because of the despair he felt because, even after 25 years of devoting himself to the Church and Jesus, he was ashamed that Jesus had not "fixed" him. Currently, I am working multiple jobs. I am exhausted, and have no future security. I have been diagnosed with PTSD and fear becoming an alcoholic because that is the only thing that alleviates the incessant chatter in my brain, trying to make sense of this madness. I struggle with depression and anxiety. I am on my own to make sense of this mess that the church pushed us into. I have been suicidal and still struggle, sometimes thinking, "I don't want to be here." Our family gave everything we had to the Church of the Nazarene and Jesus, and here we are. My ex-husband is still gay, and I struggle to take care of myself, with nothing to show for the years invested.

When taking classes to become a pastor, I learned about Wesley's quadrilateral, which in simple terms says our thoughts about God are formed from four different aspects. Those aspects being scripture, reason, tradition, and experience. I was taught that these four elements form our thoughts about God and that, if at any point, it seems like one of these aspects says something vastly different than the other three, then it begs us to re-examine what the other aspects are telling us. The conundrum is to figure out where we have erred. In my experience, the stance of the Church of the Nazarene, concerning homosexuality, predominantly influenced by scriptural interpretation, reason, and tradition, but overlooks the role of experience, which continues to show us something vastly different than what we have believed from the other three aspects.

I believe the Church of the Nazarene must stop participating in this slow death of its people. Our stance leads people into a life of confusion where, after having tried everything—prayer, fasting, tithing, getting married, having a family—believing that Jesus will fix them, and then Jesus does not do so. This cannot help but create a sense that something must be drastically wrong with them, when truthfully, there is nothing wrong with them or their faith, their prayer life, their service, their tithing, their love for God, themselves, or other people, whomever it is they love. Our teaching on this issue is killing people. It is damn time we stop this madness.

S. Vondale Allen is a former ordained elder in the Church of the Nazarene, having served six years as an associate and senior pastor on the Georgia District. S. Vondale has worked with an organization that provides housing for homeless LGBTQ+ youth and is currently ordained by the Universal Life Church and continues to seek ways to spread light and love in the lives of people with whom she connects.

Who Should Be Part of the Church's Story?

DEANNA L. ANDREE

The church has traditionally sought to exclude LGBTQIA+ people, but when Christians take the time to apply what they know about the nature of God to relationships with LGBTQIA+ people, it becomes obvious that the church's position has missed the mark.

I love stories. Stories help me to "get it." I love meeting people. I love hearing their stories. History is a series of stories. The Bible is full of stories. It was not a hard decision to decide to cross the country to attend Eastern Nazarene College to study history. I wanted to expand my perspectives and experiences. I especially loved studying church history. The blending of theological ideas and the history of Christianity was fascinating—and liberating. It led to the assurance that my mind and intellect are a part of God's creative process and just as much a part of my spiritual life as the traditions I grew up in. Essentially, the Holy Spirit uses my mind to convict and teach me as much as other traditionally-accepted modes of communication and learning. God expects us to think. That is the perspective I bring to the issue of including LGBTQIA+ people fully in the Church of the Nazarene.

Growing up in the Nazarene Church, the common teaching was that homosexuality was a sin. (We can get into details about how "that manual" words this now, but we all know that we were taught to "not approve.") I *never* liked this. I really, REALLY did not like it. But we were given specific verses that we were told were explicit, accurate translations condemning homosexuality and taught to hang all of our understanding on those few words without considering the context or the cultural influences. We didn't do a lot of reading for the big picture. We weren't told to think through the stories. (I have since seen how problematic this is.) But the bigger issue is how very *off* that whole position felt all along. It felt so very wrong. There was no place for LGBTQIA+ people in the church. That was inconsistent with the God that loved me. It was inconsistent with the God who had reached me when I was in some dark places as a little girl, with some dark stories to tell. It FELT wrong. It was wrong. Yet, I remained perplexed. As I grew, I stayed away from the conversation. I chose to not ever tell my friends "what the church or the Bible said" about who belonged there and to focus on other things about the church instead. I didn't think it was a loving act to exclude people. I chose to be friends with those who wanted to be my friend as well, and if we clicked, that was it. That was all that mattered.

Later in life, my dear friend Andrew[1] was a dedicated and inspiring Christian. He was one of those people who you could not wait to be around. He made you feel special. He made you feel like you were the only person in the world that he wanted to be spending time with during his time with you. Oh, he was funny. I loved to sing with him. He played the role of God in a musical once and he portrayed love in such a moving way. His off-stage life was fully committed to Christ. He sought after righteousness, humbled himself at the altar, searched for God's will and did everything the Nazarene church prescribed. Yet, he was always left feeling like he was not pure, not holy, not saved, and that he would never obtain the grace that should have been freely given to him for being the beautiful creation that he was. He died tragically young, without knowing that perfect peace, love, and acceptance. Only in his death was he able to experience the welcoming into the arms of Christ that would give him that love. There is no reason the church should not have been able to show that kind of love to him during his life.

I knew then, when I loved my friend, that there was something not right about the way we interpreted scripture. I did not have the proper theological or historical training to understand where the church went wrong. I just knew it was wrong. I did, somehow, know that full acceptance was the only way to love my friend. That was the Holy Spirit. The Holy Spirit was asking me to think beyond narrow interpretations of scripture to see that all are accepted in God's kingdom.

I am not going to get into any theological arguments about how the scripture has been twisted or misinterpreted to be biased against the LGBTQIA+ community, or how the historical church has used its powers to deceive and hurt the powerless. Many other scholars have shown this argument eloquently. Nor am I going to try to explain how the scientific community has shown that sexuality is a spectrum occurring in nature far beyond the simplicity of male and female, as I am not even remotely qualified to do such things. I am qualified to say that I have been affirmed more and more that all people—no matter where they are on the sexual spectrum—are exactly how they are supposed to be in the eyes of God. Even more

---

1. Name changed because I cannot ask permission to use his name.

importantly, all people are created to be with others. We are designed for relationship. It is not loving to deny anybody the right to love and be loved, commune with others or have intimate loyalty with a life partner. I do not believe that God wants us to isolate others because we do not understand their experiences.

Through the years, I have been fortunate to meet members of the LGBTQIA+ community who have shared their stories with me. I am grateful that they have been willing to once again open their hearts and share with me the ways that the church and Christians have hurt them. There are many that manage to hang onto their faith, despite their painful experiences. They find faith communities where they are welcome. Some spirits are not so enduring. The pain that Christians cause is too much to bear. These testimonies have won my complete support and affirmation.

A friend shared the following story with me. About five years ago, the 8th-grade daughter of some of her friends (let's call them the Millers) came to her parents and said, "I don't know how else to say this. I basically think that I am a dude." That began their family's transgender journey. The Millers took their daughter to therapy and went as a family. They read books and articles. They prayed. They cried. They prayed some more. They had many conversations as a family. The Millers wanted to be supportive and do what was best for their child. The mother told the friend, "I am not going to lose my kid!" Because the stakes are high in this type of situation. The rate of suicide for transgender kids is terrifying. So they accepted that their daughter wanted—needed—to live as their son. The mother told of the joy she saw when they let their now son buy clothes in the young men's department and to get a short haircut. Their child changed his name and his pronouns. They decided to switch him to another school district when he started high school because it would be easier for kids to accept this new version of him. The other major choice they felt they HAD to make was to leave the Nazarene church. The Millers were lifelong Christians and had been heavily involved in their local Nazarene church. But they knew that it was no longer a place that was safe or healthy for their child or their family. They had to leave to protect their child from toxic adults who felt it okay to question their parenting and to breach appropriate boundaries by verbally challenging and attacking their child directly.

The culture of the Nazarene church offered no grace, no compassion, no love for a family that was working through emotional issues they never dreamed they would face. THAT is what happens when the church refuses to be inclusive, when the church holds tightly to its prejudices and hatred—yes, hatred—of LGBTQIA+ issues. The result is the church hurts LGBTQIA+ people, even young people and children, and thinks it is ok to do so. The idea of "love the sinner, hate the sin" needs to be thrown away and forgotten. There is no sin. "Just love them and let the Lord sort them out?" No, there is nothing to sort out regarding sexual sin. Complete acceptance is the only appropriate choice. Inclusiveness is about using our hearts and minds to understand and apply the nature of God. The nature of God is love.

I now have two teenagers who have asked their parents not to attend a church that does not completely accept and affirm LGBTQIA+ people. They cannot justify being a part of a community who does not accept all of God's creation as they were intended to be. We wanted that church to be the Church of the Nazarene. But it is not. LGBTQIA+ people are part of God's story, too. It is time for the church to love and include all people, just as Christ does.

Deanna Andree *is a graduate of Eastern Nazarene College with a bachelor's degree in History, and James Madison University with a Master of Education. She is a teacher in Manchester, New Hampshire, who works with wonderfully challenging middle school students. Deanna is married to Jonathan and they have two teenagers with far superior tastes in music than their parents. Deanna enjoys playing and singing in her women's ukulele band for enjoyment and stress relief.*

Our Father, Who Art In?

JUSTIN BARKSDALE

There has never been a time when our LGBTQIA+ brothers and sisters have not been part of the family of God.

It was one of the worst sermons I've ever heard. There was no central text anchoring the message. No clear narrative emerged to carry the listener forward. Lacking in both content and style, the sermon fell flat. All of it just felt wrong coming out of his mouth.

That was the worst part: it was coming out of *his* mouth.

A few years ago, a stranger reached out to me on social media. She'd been adopted as a child and had reason to believe that my deceased father might also be hers. Initially I hesitated to answer her request to help confirm her hunch. My dad passed away over two decades prior, leaving a sterling legacy as a husband, father, and pastor. Suddenly all of that could be at risk if I opened myself to the possibility of my father having another child.

After prayer and heartfelt conversations with my mother, siblings, and wife, I consented to help this mysterious stranger find resolution. I couldn't deny someone an opportunity to discover their true identity. Weeks later, a DNA test confirmed what had been sleuthed out from family stories and deep dives on the internet. I suddenly had a new sister.

After the initial shock of learning that my dad had unknowingly fathered a child while serving in the military prior to meeting my mother, I had to decide how to respond to my new sister, Marie. We debriefed as a family and it became clear that our best response would be unconditional love. We chose to affirm that Marie was part of our family and to open our hearts to her.

We collected old family pictures into a shared digital file so that Marie could get acquainted with dad. The photos, artwork, and stories began to allow my sister to meet our dad decades after he passed away. My aunt found one of dad's early pieces of art and mailed it to Kansas so that Marie and her husband and kids could enjoy a tangible piece of Dad's creativity.

It was therapeutic to recall so many good things about my dad's life, and it was emotional to share those sacred moments with my newfound sister. I was deeply moved by my second-hand experience of her finding connection, a deeper sense of meaning, and a broader group of people to whom she belonged.

It was all so beautiful, but there was one thing still missing. The mementos only revealed so much. A picture may be worth a thousand words, but all of those words lack one thing. The sound of our dad's voice remained a mystery to Marie.

We never owned a video camera and Dad passed away in 1995, well before technology made it easy to capture life's moments, so there were no videos to be found. Our only hope was to find an old audio cassette tape from when dad preached in the church where he had served. Sure enough, mom sifted through enough dusty boxes to find a recording of Dad's last sermon, delivered shortly before his passing.

A hodgepodge of old and new technology was gathered from Goodwill and Amazon to digitize the last audio recording of our father. As I was assembling all of the equipment I reflected on how I grew up hearing my dad preach and had been inspired to become a preacher as well. His style, mannerisms, and delivery had been a model for me. I thought back to my college classes on biblical interpretation, hermeneutics, and theology and how they further shaped my preaching after my dad passed away. It dawned on me that I had now been preaching for nearly twenty years and I was eager to be transported back to where my own journey had begun. I was ready to hear my dad preach again and to share not just his voice, but his words with Marie.

This is why it was such a major disappointment to hear such a lousy sermon. Our father finally spoke from beyond the grave and meandered aimlessly for thirty minutes. Not exactly the introduction I had hoped to offer Marie.

For a brief moment I considered not sharing the sermon at all. It would be so much easier to just not acknowledge the outdated, clumsy message. But I knew that Marie deserved to hear his voice and that she couldn't experience his voice apart from hearing these words.

The file was uploaded. Marie loved it. She listened to it over and over. Marie shared how it helped put some missing pieces of her puzzle into place. I had opened my heart and shared with Marie everything that could be shared. She was affirmed as unconditionally part of the family.

In time, Marie asked questions about Dad's sermon. What kind of Bible did he use? What's a good way to begin reading the Bible? These questions opened up an opportunity to do a joint Bible-reading program with the help of an app. Each day we would read a selected passage and had the opportunity to share insights with each other.

Eventually life caught up to us and the Bible-reading program lapsed. Initially, I felt some guilt. How could I let my dad down like this? It had been a meaningful way to connect with Marie, and I let it fade.

My guilt lifted when I realized that our early Bible study conversations had established a foundation that was now much more personal. The texts and phone calls continue and are more organic. We have created a real relationship.

Our authentic relationship allows me to be honest about how I cringed at hearing our dad's words, but melted at the sound of his voice. Our relationship leaves room for us to receive our father's words differently and yet remain equally enamored with his voice. It's not his words, but rather his voice that connects us.

The timbre of his voice comes through when we share moments together. It becomes embodied every time Marie shares a corny joke that he would've loved. When we first connected on an internet video call, our dad's voice was rejoicing through happy tears right along with us. We embody his voice best by loving each other as family.

Our dad has said everything he's going to say. There are no more words, only his voice. I can appreciate even his clunky sermon when I tune into his voice. When I hear it, I remember being loved by him. It is the love that I received that calls me to love in the same way. I don't recall much of the exact words our father said, but I do remember how he lived and how he loved. His voice echoes every time I connect with Marie. His voice calls me to embrace and wholeheartedly affirm her as my sister.

On a cold February Sunday, our father's voice resounded loudly. It started with a gasp of surprise. I stepped into my office to prepare for a worship service and was startled to see Marie! She had covertly flown in from Kansas and was now before me. No longer a mysterious stranger, I suddenly knew her as a tangible expression of the life and heart of our father. My gasp quickly gave way to sobs of joy as Marie and I embraced as sister and brother. Two pieces of our father's heart were united. Our hearts were full, the pieces of the puzzle were in place, and our father's voice had led us to this holy moment. His legacy was being enriched and expanded by Marie joining the family.

I can't minimize the weeks that we shared our Bible-reading regimen. It was special. But the full depth of our relationship doesn't rest on us reading the Bible the same way or agreeing in its application. Thankfully, we are called together as family not simply because the words of scripture lead us to do so. Better yet, we are family because the voice that gives breath and life to the words of scripture calls us to be united.

Sometimes our father's wry sense of humor finds expression in my thoughts. When I begin the Lord's Prayer, I pause to humorously wonder who I'm addressing as I say, "Our Father, who art in heaven." Is it my heavenly Father, or my earthly fa- ther who resides in heaven? Of course I'm praying to God, but it also helps me to re- member who my father was and how he shapes my understanding of God as Father.

Because Jim Barksdale embodied love and grace, it feels natural for his chil- dren to embrace one another with love and grace as well. His voice, which we longed to hear, calls us to nothing less.

There are thousands more siblings, born from above, who desperately need to hear our heavenly Father's voice and to be fully welcomed as family.

The Church of the Nazarene has orphaned brothers and sisters who are listen- ing and longing. Our LGBTQIA+ sisters and brothers are listening to our words. What are they hearing us say about them? Is there room in the family for them? Do they fit into the stories? Are they welcomed fully? Might our Father's legacy be enriched and expanded by their inclusion? Do our words accurately embody the voice of our Father?

Our LGBTQIA+ siblings are longing to be accepted unconditionally. I've learned this by listening to them. I've heard Rachael, who is gifted with a soft heart and a sharp mind and yet would not be welcomed in church leadership because of her sexual orientation. This dear sister loves Jesus and His church, but is not finding a home in the Church of the Nazarene because her divine gifts and graces of ministry are met with deaf ears.

I've listened to Cortney, who is in a loving, monogamous, flourishing roman- tic relationship, but cannot hear that this is blessed by our Father because of her partner's gender. This cherished one loves God and loves her partner but is not finding a home in the Church of the Nazarene because our love for her finds its limit precisely where her love begins.

These are honest-to-God siblings. As I've listened to their voices, I've come to realize that we share the same Father. Their words clearly echo our Father's voice. They enact justice, love mercy, and walk humbly with our God. I can extend my hand to them and embody John Wesley's plea, "If thine heart is as my heart, if thou lovest God and all mankind, I ask no more: give me thine hand."

What's the alternative? Shall I stand outside while the Father throws a party for my siblings? Can I impose limits on the Father's love? Will I stand silent while brothers and sisters are denied their place in the family? Will I let discomfort and aversion for risk keep me from publicly embracing my precious kin? Shall I fall into what the prophet Ezekiel called the sin of Sodom: being proud, having plenty, enjoying peace and not helping those in need?

Or will I hear the Father's voice naming who's in the family? Can I honestly believe that Jesus fully reveals the heart of the Father; that he fulfills the law and sums it up with a simple invitation to love God and love each other? Will I submit to the Spirit in order to discern how to best love my siblings?

Hear this: there has never been a time that Marie and I weren't brother and sister, bound by the shared blood of our father. There was just a period of time when we didn't yet know it. There has never been a time when our LGBTQIA+ siblings haven't been part of the family of God, bound by the blood of Jesus. There's just a period of time when we haven't yet known it to be true. It's time for the Church of the Nazarene to listen to the voice of our Father and welcome our siblings fully into the family.

Justin Barksdale has served as a pastor in the Wesleyan-Holiness tradition since 2002. He earned his MA from Northwest Nazarene University. He resides in Western Washington with his wife and three children.

Bodies are Holy—
Even Transgender Bodies

TYLER BRINKMAN

Transgender people prove the holiness of human bodies.

I grew up in the Church of the Nazarene. I'm one of those fifth generation, cradle-to-grave Nazarenes. The Church of the Nazarene is the soil in which my faith took root. I was nurtured by our theology of holiness and our fervent proclamation of the radical optimism of grace. I am comforted by our hymnody—who doesn't love a good, vigorous rendition of "Holiness Unto the Lord"?

My whole life I knew I wanted to go to Olivet Nazarene University. I remember bringing the university catalog to my free reading time back in elementary school. I'd pour over the mission statement and values, course descriptions, and even the rather boring descriptions of administrative policies. In 2007, I finally began at Olivet as a student, and it felt amazing. Three years later, I graduated with a bachelor's degree in religious studies. My time as a religion major was a literal Godsend, and I still frequently reflect on the insights my professors shared and the love they expressed through their lectures, discussions, and one-on-one conversations.

Then in 2020, about 2 months after my son was born, I resigned my membership and ministerial credentials. It was extremely difficult to give up on being ordained in my home church. That decision to give up my license was not impulsive, and a long time coming, but it was still something that I could never envision until the previous few years. I thought I could stick it out with the Church of the Nazarene, even if I would never really fit in all that much. It turns out that I was wrong—it was too much. The birth of my son was the straw that broke the camel's back. I never wanted him to grow up in a church where he might feel "less than."

There were some seismic personal and theological shifts in the ten years between graduating Olivet and resigning my credentials, but perhaps the biggest difference is my conviction that people's physical bodies are holy and sacred. This belief is not a departure from the Church of the Nazarene's historic teaching; it is a continuation of it. One of the most important books ever written by any Nazarene is Mildred Bangs Wynkoop's *A Theology of Love*. This is a book that nearly every Nazarene pastor will have read or at least be familiar with. Wynkoop was a professor at Trevecca, but her influence and respect goes much further than the city limits of Nashville. Indeed, Nazarene Theological Seminary named their Center for Women's Leadership after her.

In *A Theology of Love*, Wynkoop explains how the Bible consistently connects human souls with human bodies. The idea that our souls take priority over human bodies stems from Greek paganism rather than anything in the Bible. This is one of Wynkoop's starting points in how she thinks about holiness, which she argues is love. It is not an abstract love though; holiness is a love for a whole person—their heart, soul, mind, and body. This kind of love is transformative; it releases people from the bondage of sin and liberates them to love and holiness. This is the radical optimism of grace proclaimed by holiness folk.

But why in the world do I bring up a 50-year-old theology book that does not mention LGBTQ+ people at all? It's because bodies matter. They are holy and sacred. Lots of other contributors to this volume will have talked about gay, lesbian, and bisexual people. I want to focus on transgender people. Trans people experience much higher rates of suicide, homelessness, and being victims of sexual assault and murder. These are not the results of gender dysphoria, which is the sense that they are born into the wrong sex. Many people never feel at home in their bodies, and many people never feel at home in their relationships with their neighbors, coworkers, families, and spouses. It is a feeling of broken relationship with one's self and with others. I think this is similar to the kind of lack of love Wynkoop talks about. The "closet" is a place of isolation, shame, and death.

The only consistently effective therapy and treatment for gender dysphoria is transitioning and strong social support from the other people in their lives. The support and affirmation from their loved ones is essential. In embracing themselves, they lose the life they once knew. They risk being abandoned by their loved ones, homelessness and poverty, physical and sexual violence, and even murder. Few people embody the gospel truth that a person must "lose their life in order to find it." If sin leads to death, and holy love leads to life—then we must look at what actually keeps people alive. Transgender people affirming themselves and receiving affirmation from others keeps them alive. From this, we can see this kind of support is the very embodiment of love. And love *is* holiness.

Tyler Brinkman *is currently married, with one son. They live in Milwaukee and attend a United Methodist Church in their neighborhood.*

Sheep Go To Heaven

JOSH "CATFISH" CARPENTER

The LGBTQ+ population is marginalized by religion worldwide. We can begin healing this relationship after the church becomes openly affirming.

I was born and raised in the Nazarene church. I became a member in 1994 and I left in 2018. I was an active, participating, and (when I could) voting teen and adult member. I attended just about every local and district Nazarene church event and service until I was about 17. I went on Nazarene mission trips, attended NYC in 1996, played on the special music and offertory rotation, served at community dinners, nearly earned my district license, preached sermons, laid hands in prayer—all in the Church of the Nazarene.

After graduating high school, I went on to play football at MidAmerica Nazarene University. I finished high school with a 1.8 GPA and struggled with undiagnosed depression, ADHD, low self-esteem, and an anxiety disorder. I had no chance of graduating college my first time around. It would be a decade later, at Miami of Ohio, that I would finally earn the 4-year degree I'd been striving for all my life. So far, I'm the only one in my family to do so.

Studying for my degree in history at Miami taught me a lot about how to evaluate historical sources. Historical events can't be recreated, carbon-copied, or tested like science does with the physical world. So historians use a system called the historical method that works to open up the truthfulness of the past.

The method uses science to draw logical conclusions about past events. It consults the archaeological record. One of the ways we know what happened at Pompeii is because so much of the event is frozen in time—bodies, buildings, even marketing content. The method also calls for historians to compare and contrast as many sources they can gather on whatever historical event they're studying. So if Nation A writes on a clay tablet saying they decimated Army B in battle, a good historian asks, what other sources cover the event and what do they say? Comparing and contrasting multiple accounts of an event helps historians figure out biases. It also provides crucial context to what is found in the archaeological record.

Historians are also taught to examine a text according to its genre. For example, the classic novel *Watership Down* isn't history. It's a work of fiction that's centered on a story about a community of rabbits. A historian can see past the fiction. They identify the micro-stories and allegory in the book that can be used to draw some pretty powerful parallels between community ethics and the real world.

Over the years, I've spent a lot of time trying to figure out what a historically accurate bible says about gender, marriage, and sexuality. During that time, I learned that what the Church of the Nazarene taught me about biblical truth as a young'un' was quite different from the truths that were being revealed to me as an older college student.

For example, I learned that the story of Adam and Eve more than likely has nothing to do with the doctrine of original sin. In fact, the doctrine that we were born sinful is strictly a Christian doctrine. It didn't even exist when the book of Genesis came into existence. Historically speaking, the story of Adam and Eve is about how important fertility and procreation are to the continued existence of an ancient nomadic tribe.

If you think about it, fertility is pretty important to sustaining the gardens, flocks, and population of a nomadic tribe like the Israelites. From the fertility of their gardens' soils to the fertility of the people in the tribe, the ability for everything to reproduce is the absolute key to their existence as a religion and race.

So it shouldn't be surprising to find out how deeply woven polygamy is into their laws and culture. It only takes one man to impregnate multiple women and grow the group on an exponential level. In the Old Testament men were allowed to bed or be bedded by just about anyone, as long as it ended up in procreation. For example, Lot's daughters had his children without his knowledge, and King Solomon was conceived illegitimately. Yet, both of their bloodlines were blessed by God to continue.

The few times that the New Testament mentions marriage, the husband is allowed sexual access to both his wife and slaves. Jesus taught that the only family we have are the people who do the will of the Father. Mark 12:25 comes right out and says that there is no marriage in the Kingdom of Heaven. And Paul urges people to become celibate and completely devoted to spreading the gospel. It would be centuries after Jesus' death that the politics of Rome would introduce the concept of a traditional marriage and marriage laws to the church.

I don't think I'm the only person who sees inconsistencies in the Nazarene church's stance on affirming same-sex marriages. Gender, sexuality, and biological sex all differ from each other and are very complex. They can't just be boiled down into simple orthodoxy, or annexed away from the church's mission or history. The LGBTQ+ already have a history in the church, they just don't have a voice.

In 2016 I went to Iraqi Kurdistan on a peace delegation. While I was there, our group heard stories from many in the LGBTQ+ community, and the difficulties they faced living in fear that someone would find out who they truly are.

Many LGBTQ+ folks are told that God completely rejects them. They have problems getting jobs and securing income. Their financial dependency leads them to be even more susceptible to abuse. They're kicked out of schools because they dress too masculine or feminine, denying them basic education, adding more to their plight.

Gay men live with a death wish if they're found out. They are often publicly beaten, some die. Lesbians are also shamed and beaten, and are restricted from participating in certain religious practices. Because of all of these factors, many of the individuals in the Iraqi-Kurdistan LGBTQ+ community are deathly afraid of their family's reactions if they come out. And I think this fear is shared by many of the folks throughout the LGBTQ+ community in the United States.

Some of the similarities might surprise you. Low income LGBTQ+ folks in the US are often up against impossible odds. They still face many barriers in the US medical and mental health fields. There are not only shortages in the medical and mental health labor markets, but there's always a chance that your therapist isn't LGBTQ+ affirming.

LGBTQ+ youth in the US become homeless at a disproportionate rate. The vast majority of it is due to family rejection, and the aftermath of being a child that's forcibly removed from their home. I imagine it's one of the reasons why they're more likely to leave home underage. After that they usually live in transitional housing or on the streets. Homelessness at a young age doesn't just crumble your financial future. It breaks you psychologically, and will stay with you your whole life.

The end of Matthew 25 literally defines how we all will be judged, "For I was hungry and you gave me something to eat, I was thirsty and you gave me something to drink, I was a stranger and you invited me in, I needed clothes and you clothed me, I was sick and you looked after me, I was in prison and you came to visit me.'"

My experience befriending, serving, and advocating for the worldwide LGBTQ+ community has taught me that at some point, most become detached from the people and place of church. But they continue to seek God. They want a safe place to sing, raise their hands in praise, fellowship, get married, raise Godly families, and serve their community. The Church of the Nazarene has the resources to greatly help the LGBTQ+ community worldwide. Becoming a fully affirming church would not just help validate the lives of the folks in the LGBTQ+ community. It would start the healing process between the church and a community that they've long ignored.

Josh "Catfish" Carpenter *is an Americana performing artist, writer, and historian. He earned his bachelor's degree in history and economics at Miami University (Ohio) in 2011.*

Following Our Attractions

TERRY CLEES

The very things that attracted many to the Church of the Nazarene should be the very things that allow us to lean into the LGBTQ community with open arms.

The first idea that attracted me to the Church of the Nazarene was that I believed their theology was progressive and not rooted in dogmatic fundamentalism. I believed this to be the case in part because of the denomination being on the forefront of allowing women to be members of the clergy. From the founding of the denomination, Nazarenes have affirmed women and men as being "equally called" to ministry and historically all ministry positions have been open to both women and men, including the position of ordained elder. This was not the case for many denominations when the infant Church of the Nazarene began ordaining women in 1908. In fact, it was considered heretical and went against the teachings of the Bible according to many of the denominations at the time.

Why did the Church of the Nazarene go against the flow of traditional churches at the time and seemingly turn their backs on the "proof texts" that were recited against women in ministry? I believe the answer is twofold. First of all, there was experience. Phineas Breese had experienced the power of strong women throughout his life. He was witness to their outstanding preaching and exceptional leadership. He wrote about Amanda Berry Smith, an African-American evangelist: "She preached one Sabbath afternoon, as I never heard her preach before, in strains of holy eloquence and unction…The Lord opened heaven on the people in mighty tides of glory." Secondly was an examination of the text in question and the determination that it was for a specific time and place and not something to make a dogmatic statement of for the ages.

The second idea that attracted me to the Church of the Nazarene was that I believed their theology to be dynamic. The denomination was not afraid to make changes to their theology and the wording of their Manual. The Hiram F. Reynolds

Institute research group and the Board of General Superintendent Thought Partners were recent think tanks put together to help guide the Church of the Nazarene to be pragmatic, mission focused, and futuristic in thinking. Dr. Thomas Noble, when writing on the Nazarene Theological Stance, says, "To be 'conservative' in theology therefore does not mean to embrace right-wing politics (although some of us may wish to do so). It means rather to accept the necessity of this legitimate kind of doctrinal development. The world does not stand still and so our presentation of the gospel (including 'holiness by grace') must adapt to cultural change through the decades."

"Change" is a word largely feared by the religious right. To them "change" means you must have been wrong the first time and therefore slaps biblical infallibility right out of the equation. The Church of the Nazarene, however, is not afraid to admit, in light of recent textual and historical criticism and scientific discovery, that they could have been wrong. There are plenty of examples in the history of the denomination's Manual of change in an effort to get key ideas right and be more culturally relevant.

Therefore, in light of my two biggest attractions to the Church of the Nazarene, I believe it is time to open our arms wide to the LGBTQ community.

I met Joshua at the gym. I had an inkling right away that he was a gay man—even though he persistently denied it, until we became good friends after working out at the same time for several weeks. We eventually became workout partners, and he became friends with my wife and children. It was only natural, considering I was a pastor at the small local Church of the Nazarene, that I would invite him to come to the place of worship where I pastored. Reluctantly, he finally agreed. The congregation accepted him and loved him. He became a pillar of the church and helped in many different ways. When it came time for Vacation Bible School, I thought he would be an excellent team leader. I took the recommendation before the church board and they absolutely agreed.

Vacation Bible School came and went with great success. Children learned about God's love and forgiveness and had fun doing so. Although, a regular family with three children was surprisingly absent. They also were missing from Sunday morning services the next couple of weeks. It was not long before I heard from the powers that be that there was some concern that I had let a gay person work with our children. Apparently, this family went to the much larger Church of the Nazarene on the other side of town and complained about who I was letting work with our children. My heart broke.

Joshua was kind and compassionate. He loved Jesus and he loved others. He, despite being busy at work, made time to serve the Lord. He gave faithfully. He was a model Christian, but the denomination saw him as an abomination because he had spent his whole life attracted to members of the same sex. Here was a faithful child of God that my denomination, built on holy love, rejected from being a member and insulted by their wording in the Manual. Experience told me he was worthy, just as it had told Phineas Bresee that women, despite the proof texts, were worthy some one hundred years prior.

I decided to use the latest textual and historical criticism and the latest scientific research to see if perhaps the denomination that I loved was wrong about their strong stance against what we now define as same-sex attraction.

There is not nearly enough space in a short essay to do justice in presenting why one proof text is misleading, much less the four or five long standing arguments against homosexuality. I will simply conclude that I was shocked at the number of resources that made very strong arguments that condemning homosexuality and even calling it an abomination was misleading at best. It seems that the word "homosexuality" became a blanket word to describe abusive relationships, pederasty, and out of control sexuality. It absolutely does not appear that the biblical authors were ever referring to same-sex attraction between two adults.

In my studies, I found that many of the preconceived ideas about homosexuality are just not true. One of the long-standing mantras is that being gay is a choice. In my friendship with Joshua, I met and became friends with many people in the LGBTQ community. In every one of those friendships, I concluded that the person was not gay by choice, but it was simply who they were and what their attraction was. They were attracted to the same sex in the same way that I am attracted to the opposite sex. They could no more be straight than I could be gay. I looked into the science of it and discovered the overwhelming research evidence that that sexual orientation is likely caused, in part, by biological factors that start before birth. I also discovered that trying to "turn" someone from their sexual orientation is a dangerous and destructive practice.

The more research I did, the more I became convinced that ostracizing a people group based on five or six biblical texts that could have multiple interpretations was not right. I added in that it was not a choice for the individuals but who they were; and I felt the need to repent for every way I had ever expressed prejudice behaviors based on someone's sexual orientation. In a denomination based on holy love, how could we ever see a people group who many love the Lord as an abomination? Have we allowed holy judgment into our hearts because holy love has proven too difficult?

It is time to right the ship and admit we were wrong. It is time to love one another just as Christ has loved us (John 13:34).

Dr. Terry Clees *has several degrees including a Master of Divinity degree from Northwest Nazarene University and a Doctor of Ministry degree from George Fox University. He currently works as a bereavement coordinator where he has seen daily the destructive nature of unreconciled relationships due to sexual orientation.*

From Skepticism to Joy

MARISSA COBLENTZ

In Acts 11, early church leaders move from skeptical critics to joyful recipients of God's work; can we follow that example today?

Turn in your Bible with me to Acts chapter 11.

In Acts 10, we read about Peter's visit to the home of Cornelius culminating in Cornelius—a Gentile—and his household receiving the gift of the Holy Spirit. Picking up in Acts 11, Peter is criticized by the circumcised believers for going to the home of a Gentile and eating with him.

What happens when a well-respected leader in the church is seen fraternizing with "unclean" people? Maybe there is some criticism. Maybe we demand an explanation. Maybe we respond like these established leaders of the early church in Jerusalem.

How did Peter respond? He told the story of his experience. In fact, the author of Acts takes the time to re-tell the whole story, even though we just read it in the previous chapter. What happened in these two chapters is a Big Deal! Welcoming Gentiles meant redefining how Jewish Christians read the Old Testament. It meant taking love of enemies to a whole new level. And it meant opening the door to a huge unknown presence. Who would Cornelius bring with him into the church? What impact would Gentile believers have on this fledgling movement?

When Peter finished sharing the story of his vision from heaven and subsequent visit to Cornelius, how did the Jewish leaders respond?

Let's pause here because this is important.

If you were sitting in Jerusalem in the first century, how would you respond to Peter's story?

I am not surprised by the initial criticism of Peter and would not have been surprised if he received more questions. Questions like, "Why would you go without first consulting us and making sure that we were all of one mind?" "Are you sure that what you saw was really a vision from God?" "That's great that you all had a good experience, but will it stick?" "How can we maintain our holy witness to the world if we let unclean people in?"

If you read on in Acts 11, you will not see any of those questions. In fact, reading this chapter is one of the most surprising stories in scripture to me. After Peter shared his testimony, the believers in Jerusalem rejoiced! They moved shockingly quickly from skepticism to joy. At first they did not understand what had happened in Caesarea, but as soon as Peter shared what God had done for Cornelius, they understood that the miraculous gift of God's Holy Spirit had been poured out upon them just as it had been in the upper room.

What did it take to change their minds about the inclusion of Gentiles in this early Christian movement?

Surprisingly little.

Two visions. One sanctified household. One testimony.

The church would never be the same.

When the Spirit is at work, it is not uncommon to see this joyful celebration of God's work. When we have seen miracles, we live in expectancy of more miracles. Where will God show up next? We are quick to notice, quick to rejoice. There is a sense that everything is going to be okay and we can trust each other and God.

I love that.

We spend so much time worried and anxious—that there won't be enough, that God won't be enough. We second-guess ourselves and each other. Our hands go from open and welcoming to closed and tight. Our hearts harden. We have been hurt in the past, and we don't want to be made fools again. We will be more careful, we will love less freely and trust less wholly. We will build more walls around our hearts to protect them. We may find less joy, but it is worth the sacrifice to feel less pain.

What happened when Peter told the leaders in Jerusalem about his vision and subsequent experience with Cornelius? They rejoiced! In fact, the Jewish leaders in that moment effectively handed the church over to the Gentiles. There were no restrictions on what position Gentile believers could hold. Sunday School teacher, choir director, NMI president, youth leader, usher, district superintendent, general superintendent.

As the story progresses in the book of Acts, it is staggering to see how quickly the leaders in Jerusalem resolved the questions that arose surrounding the inclusion of Gentiles in the days to come. Peter opened the door. Paul brought more clarity. But the openness with which the Gentile believers were welcomed is truly one of the greatest miracles in the Early Church.

I want to be careful in how we think and talk about this story. In our tradition, sometimes we spend too much time looking for a "second Pentecost." Pentecost was a one-time thing, and this incredible pouring out of the Holy Spirit is not something to spend all our time searching for. But we do have a strong history of embracing the radical inclusivity of God.

In our tradition, we take a bold stance regarding women in leadership. Unlike so many of the most dominant and vocal theological traditions in America today, we have NO restrictions on what position women can hold in our denomination. That same list of positions is open to women: Sunday School teacher, choir director, NMI president, youth leader, usher, district superintendent, general superintendent. Historically, we share a similar experience with the leaders in Jerusalem. Over a hundred years ago, male leaders of the Holiness Movement in America looked around and saw the Spirit at work in the lives of women. Women teaching, preaching, praying, and leading. Like the leaders in Jerusalem, these early Holiness people didn't worry about losing power or reputation; they just rejoiced at what God was doing in the world. They responded with an attitude similar to Peter's: "If God gave them the same gift he gave us who believed in the Lord Jesus Christ, who was I think that I could stand in God's way?"

It is hard to comprehend in today's culture how truly radical it was for early twentieth century holiness leaders to entrust the leadership of our fledgling movement to women—in a world where women were not even allowed to vote, let alone lead the church!

The Church of the Nazarene today, once again, has the opportunity to act with boldness and trust. People are coming to us with their stories of God's Spirit at work in the lives of those some of us might call "unclean." Maybe we initially respond with criticism. "How could you go into that person's house and eat with them?" How will we respond when we hear the answer to that question? How will we respond when we hear stories of God's Spirit at work in the lives of those we might consider outsiders?

Maybe you don't know a gay person whose life demonstrates the presence of the Holy Spirit, but maybe your daughter does and she wants to tell you about that person so you can rejoice together.

Maybe you haven't seen a vision for how the church could possibly maintain its identity of purity and fidelity to the faith of those who came before us while welcoming gay, trans, and queer youth, couples, and families of all types, but maybe someone sitting in the next pew over has seen the vision and is just dying to share what they see God already doing in your congregation.

How will you respond? To your daughter, your friend, your neighbor, your youth leader, choir director, even lead pastor when they say, "I think maybe God is at work in the lives of people we thought could never get in, people we thought would always be outsiders."

Will you receive that person's testimony with joy? Will you welcome the "wideness of God's mercy"? Will you marvel at how the Spirit blows? Will you welcome those people who have an incredible testimony of the Spirit at work in their lives and tentatively share their story with you?

What would it take to change your mind?

I hope no more and no less than it took for the leaders in Jerusalem to accept YOU, to welcome YOU into THEIR church. As Paul wrote in Ephesians, "You who once were far away have been brought near by the blood of Christ." That Early Church decision is why we have access to salvation today.

May we follow the example of those early pioneers trying to figure out what in the world God was up to. May we go looking with joyful eagerness for the next new place God will pour out his Spirit, and even if it is the last place we expected to find it, may we eagerly embrace the beautiful, transforming, joyous creative work of the Spirit in the world today.

Marissa Coblentz is an ordained minister in the Church of the Nazarene who is currently working as an engineer in the public sector. She and her husband and three children reside in Southern Indiana.

To Love or Not to Love:
That is the Nazarene Question

GLORIA M. COFFIN

*I have something to say about God and loving our neighbors
as ourselves. Actually, it's about God and every act of
every day we live.*

As a child, I learned the Ten Commandments and thought most of them were going to be quite easy to obey. There were times when a bad word, missing church, and showing disrespect for my parents were tempting, but murder, infidelity, and stealing were not. I did not pray to idols, lie, or want my neighbors' belongings. On occasion I would have appreciated similar items as those of the little girl around the corner, but I didn't really want hers. Although your challenges may have been different from mine, you probably get my point. The Ten Commandments were rules I thought I understood, most of which I felt comfortable following.

As a young adult, I learned the relationship process in the commandments: the first four about my connection to God and the last six about my interaction with people around me. Gradually I began to recognize the direction they gave me for living in a complicated world, guidance for walking with God to do no harm as I walked with my peers. Today, I wonder how our world would change if we carefully followed the intent of the Ten Commandments.

The Christian religion believes God came to live among us as Jesus Christ. He followed the Ten Commandments hoping we would learn the difference they make. When asked to choose the most important commandment, Jesus spoke a mouthful, "Love God with all you are," adding the second greatest was, "Love your neighbor as yourself." Then Jesus threw in the corker, "Everything else depends on these two commandments."

The first four commandments lead me to love God with all I am, and the last six direct me to love my neighbor as myself. It makes me wonder how our world would change if we carefully followed the greatest commandment and the second, which, as Jesus may have cheekily explained, is so much like it.

When I run into my friends, we catch up, sympathizing with one another's challenges and enjoying each other's blessings. Occasionally I want to pinch myself. Some have lives very much the same as mine, yet significantly different. How can I be comfortable sharing the details of theirs? The answer is simple. We are friends. They listen to me. They care about my life. The greatest commandment led me to an inner love for God who clearly loves everyone regardless of the variables. The second greatest commandment taught me to treat them as I treat myself.

There is no "if, but, or unless" clause in that commandment. It doesn't describe my neighbor as one who only hangs out in the kind of places where I go, who uses pronouns the way I do, or whose clothes match a special dress code for the public bathroom. It does not say I can only treat neighbors as I treat myself if they follow the Bible as I interpret it. It does not even tell me to exclude neighbors from activities I enjoy when the neighbors go home at night to families unlike mine.

The second greatest commandment says to love my neighbor as myself, nothing more, nothing less. It does not tell me to differentiate, "Oh, I love my neighbor, but I hate what my neighbor does." It tells me to love my neighbor as I love myself, period. Over time, America has tried to grow into that commandment. Many have stopped treating women and children and people of color as if they deserve less than we do. We seem determined to love our neighbor.

Except when our neighbor is gay or lesbian, transgender or queer.

The list is much longer. It identifies neighbors we don't want to sit beside in our favorite pew or kneel with when praying for hurting family members. Sometimes our church doesn't think we should share communion with them. If these thoughts bring tears to my eyes, I wonder how the loving creator reacts to it.

No wonder we are in chaos, fighting needless battles and struggling to survive horrible evils. Unspeakable atrocities leave behind damaged children, abused spouses, and broken marriages, but we reject harmless individuals who are from loving families, and those who are in committed relationships because we don't understand their sexual attractions or their gender differences. In this one case, our LGBTQ+ neighbors, we believe God calls us to stand as judge and jury. In my Bible, Jesus himself says that's God's job. Jesus' job was to love.

When we have the chance in our church to welcome, support, affirm, and love all neighbors as we love ourselves, why should we not choose to reflect the commandment so like the first and greatest? If we cannot do that in our church the way we can do it everywhere else, how can we love God with all we are when we are there?

If our church rejects us because we will not be silent, is she really the church we thought she was? Worse yet, if we want our church to accept us so much we decide not to treat LGBTQ+ neighbors the way we want to be treated, what will we have done to the reflection of God?

Gloria Coffin is an inner-city hospital call chaplain with a passion for staff support as well as patient/family care. She is an ordained elder with a BA in Psychology/Counseling Major.

I'll Love You...IF

JAMES E. COPPLE

Judgment and condemnation emerges from isolation and ignorance and understanding and empathy come from proximity.

My stepson Steven enrolled at Eastern Nazarene College as a freshman. Steven grew up as a member of the Church of Jesus Christ of Latter Day Saints—the Mormons. He was a young man struggling with his sexual orientation. We thought ENC would be a safe place to secure his degree in an environment that had a history of tolerating diversity. I attended ENC in the 60s, where I was a conscientious objector, a civil rights activist, and a strong proponent for social justice. I later taught at ENC and found it to be an institution that truly promoted a liberal arts education. I believed ENC would be a safe place for Steven to sort out his values and his faith.

In his sophomore year, after coming out, he was attending one of the required chapels at ENC. ENC scheduled an evangelist as a speaker. A woman evangelist—Steven was intrigued. At the end of her sermon she held an altar call. In her prayer for people to come forward, she used, and I paraphrase, language that suggested there were people who might need healing because they were confused about their sexual orientation. Her prayer was essentially a homophobic diatribe equating homosexuality to a disease. Steven was hurt and angered. He got up and walked out of the chapel. Steven later met with the chaplain and told him how hurt he was by her message. The chaplain asked, "What was wrong?" Steven responded, in the spirit of John 9, "I was once blind and now I see—and she just condemned my testimony and my identity."

At the end of his sophomore year, Steven left ENC. His roommate his sophomore year would pray nightly for Steven. His prayers focused on his sexual orientation and the fact that Steven was a Mormon. Knowing of Steven's sexual orientation, an enlightened RA gave Steven a private room. Still, it was simply too much. The intolerance, the bigotry, and the ignorance of both students and faculty forced him to leave and attend a public university in the DC area. To be clear,

Steven would find no spiritual home with the Mormons or the Nazarenes. Today, he is a follower of Jesus Christ and a ship in search of a welcoming port.

While we continue our debates about scripture, theology, and practice, there is a movement to create proximity and facilitate a conversation that generates understanding. *The 1908 Project* seeks conversation and dialogue around these critical issues. Yet, leadership in the denomination rests on dogmatic platitudes and pronouncements and consequently is driving people out of the Church.

Historically, in this country and others, proximity—the act of actually seeing, hearing, and listening to others—might be a path for changing policy and practice. It is when we isolate ourselves in the echo chambers of our ideologies that we fail to see the person or the family. Passing resolutions affirming our love for one another is aspirational but it does not get us to inclusion. When families see one of their children or a parent "come out" and express their desire to be affirmed for their identity, prejudices and biases cave and "otherness" disappears.

We must move beyond our fears, our need to proof-text our biases, or cling to social and political biases that force an "otherness" in our relationships. This should be the goal of every loving, believing person of faith. The values we hold on to in order to justify exclusion will crumble in the face of love, understanding, and empathy.

Proximity creates an environment where people can dialogue, explore each other's differences, and create a space for transparency and change. The refusal to discuss these issues suggests leaders live in fear, take authoritarian approaches to protect their positions, and finally hide behind their titles versus serving the gospel.

There are things we can do to encourage proximity and tolerance through listening and seeking understanding.

1. Seek out organizations and individuals who represent the LGBTQIA+ community. Meet them on their terms and on their turf.
2. Familiarize yourself with the terms or language of gay culture.
3. Invite members of the gay community to your congregation and maybe have them speak in your Sunday School classes. Have an honest and open dialogue about their life. Assure them that the church is a safe place for these conversations.
4. Research the literature on the biological/genetic predisposition of queerness.
5. Reflect on and challenge the stereotypes developed by the evangelical church regarding homosexuality.
6. Find ways to stand with the gay community when they are forced to respond to homophobic attacks.

7. Quite simply, get to know and come alongside people working through their sexual identification.
8. Challenge authority that may simply dismiss gay and lesbian individuals as an aberration or as sinners.
9. Whenever possible, bring light to the discussion and avoid the bitter and harsh attacks that keep us in the dark.
10. Invite conversations around the issues of sexuality, the struggle of transitioning and begin those conversations by listening.

Several years ago, while working overseas, a group of us were standing in a parking lot of a Nazarene Mission Compound. A missionary went off on one of those all too familiar diatribes about gay people. She was speaking specifically about President Obama and his advocacy for inclusion. Her language was harsh, vile, and degrading. I stood there for a few moments wondering if I should say something or just leave it alone. Finally, she referred to the LGBTQIA+ community as a community of "f*gs." I stopped her, and finally and simply said, "You are speaking about my son. And, frankly, I can't imagine Jesus ever calling my son a f*g." Later I would ask if she had ever known or been in conversation with people of a different sexual orientation. Her answer, with bowed head and a degree of shame, "No, I haven't and maybe I should."

That day she began a journey that would change her life. She sought to create proximity and to gain an understanding of the people she was condemning.

That is all we can ask for—is to seek understanding, build relationships and begin seeing as Jesus sees, hearing as Jesus hears, and doing as Jesus would do. Seek Justice, Love Mercy and walk humbly before your God. Leaders who fear proximity or a conversation on this issue—are not leaders but Pharisees wrapped in a cloak of cowardice. We must and can do better.

James E. Copple is the founder of The 1908 Project, an effort to promote dialogue and conversation around difficult issues in the Church of the Nazarene. Copple is a graduate of Eastern Nazarene College, Nazarene Theological Seminary, and did doctoral work in history at Boston College and The Johns Hopkins University. He is the founding principal of Strategic Applications International (SAI) and the current Executive Director of ACT NOW, a national movement to create dialogue between Police and Local Communities.

The Spirit Transforms

KATIE A. DONALDSON

The Church of the Nazarene must stop hurting people due to poor theology and irresponsible scriptural interpretation. May they return to being the loving, holy people God has called them to be.

"What is love? / Baby, don't hurt me / Don't hurt me / No more." Haddaway's famous song lyrics may be about unrequited romantic love, yet the sentiment holds true in multiple situations—like how a religious denomination also holds power in demonstrating what love is. "What is LOVE?" is central for Nazarene theology. Mildred Bangs Wynkoop's foundational book, *A Theology of Love: The Dynamic of Wesleyanism*, answers that question by saying that true holiness is essentially relational; being a holy people means being in loving relationships.

For the Church of the Nazarene, "What is LOVE?" is a crucial question when considering the relationship with the LGBTQ+ community. As a Wesleyan denomination, prioritizing loving relationships within the context of pursuing holiness, the Church of the Nazarene should be courageous enough to consider how the Church is transformed by the Spirit into a deeper understanding of God's love for all people. This is a means of grace that takes shape through our study of Jesus' teachings of loving God and neighbor, as well as the communal practice of pursuing justice and ending oppression and discrimination. If the Church of the Nazarene were to truly love as Christ did, it would become fully LGBTQ+ affirming: saying clearly that everyone is a child of God and everybody plays a role in the mission of God.

Yet, even with a foundational theology of love, we get stuck on the scripture references that apparently call same-sex relationships sinful. We get manipulated by poor translations of scripture that use the term *homosexual* instead of *pedophile*. Or we end up using stories about cities being brought to the ground due to rape culture as an example of why same-sex relationships are a distortion of how God planned humanity's sexuality. But, as Wesleyans, we can say that the Spirit has the power to move and assist in our understanding of all things. We all need to consider how the love toward God and neighbor should have a larger role in the denomination's relationship with the LGBTQ+ community. If we claim to be a denomination with a theology of love, then we must use this lens in our engagement with the LGBTQ+ community. Because for the Church of the Nazarene to write into polity things that imply it is acceptable to say things like we love you *but*—insert things like, "we hate the sin," "just want the best for you," "don't want you going against God's plan of one man with one woman,"—is gas-lighting people who trust the polity of the church to be Wesleyan. But when we start to limit the possibility of love, we put the movement of the Spirit into a box and become stagnant in a world that so desperately needs the all-inclusive, unconditional, magnificent love and acceptance of God.

In scripture, love is described as a beautiful gift, freely given by God to all. Love is to be an example for all humanity's relational structures—relationship with God, with each other, and with creation. The Creator's love can only do this through humanity's willingness to be transformed. This is the holy work of sanctification, becoming more Christ-like. Whenever we consider Christ-likeness, we should look at his words here on earth, take into account who he was speaking to, and what culture was surrounding him. Just like how Christ's teaching helped the Spirit widen the Jewish understanding of covenantal love, we too can allow our stance on sexuality and marriage to not be shrunk to an exclusively heterosexual perspective, but allow covenant-love to be the focal point.

Covenant-love is presented throughout Scripture as God's original relational desire. It is part of the *shalom* of God—*shalom* being the peace, the rightness, the goodness that was always meant to be. We see this love between the first humans and the Lord; they lived in full connection without shame. The covenant-love that the Lord constantly asks humanity to strive towards. To not be looking for self-worth through people's opinions; rather, to find our self-worth and purpose solely in the steadfast loving relationship with God. It is this concept of steadfastness that deems God's love as unique and something to desire. Steadfast means it will not waver, it will always be. It is not ever because of what we do, but rather how much we are loved by the Creator. This love is what is covenantal. It is a promise that the love will always remain. All relationships aim for this because it is full acceptance. This is the love God has for us, we are immeasurably loved because we all are children of God. There is no 'but' or 'except' to that statement. God's steadfast-covenantal-love is the *shalom* all humanity is searching for. This is the love the church is called to be sharing with all the world. The love that is constant no matter what. Church membership is a welcome into community, a corporate relationship. Marriage is known as an example of God's covenantal love between two people, and gender does not play a role in that. It is the heart and the steadfast relational example that matters. And it is with this understanding we see that gender does not limit God's example of love. Therefore, in regard to both membership to the church and within a marriage, covenantal-love is the key and not gender. We should not limit God's love, rather let it expand its acceptance.

The Church of the Nazarene should be an affirming church because, as Wesleyans, we believe the Spirit shapes us and can even help us enter the process of reconciliation when we have been wrong. The church can focus on the love of God and neighbor, without limiting where that love can flourish or who can love whom. May we live into this beautifully written statement from the Church of the Nazarene's covenant on human sexuality and marriage:

The Church of the Nazarene views human sexuality as one expression of the holiness and beauty that God the Creator intended. Because all humans are beings created in the image of God, they are of inestimable value and worth. As a result we believe that human sexuality is meant to include more than the sensual experience, and is a gift of God designed to reflect the whole of our physical and relational createdness. (31, Manual 2017—2021)

May we let love be love, and allow covenant-love to shape us. May we stop hurting people due to poor theology and irresponsible scriptural interpretation. May we be the loving, holy people God has called us to be.

Katie A. Donaldson is the pastor at Fallbrook United Methodist Church. It is because of her Master's of Divinity and emphasis in cross-cultural ministry from Nazarene Theological Seminary and years of practical ministry experience that she enjoys sharing God's hospitality. She loves connecting to the surrounding community of the church while building relationships inside.

Judging the Fruit

BUFFY FLEECE

The Church of the Nazarene's fruit produced by our attitude toward the LGBTQ+ community is rotten; it is time to examine ourselves.

In the mid 90s, there was a popular band named Creed. Scott Stapp, the lead singer, was raised in a Christian home. Creed's lyrics and videos had images that alluded to the Christian faith. I was a student at Mount Vernon Nazarene University at the time, and everyone wanted to know if this was a Christian band. If they were, it would be acceptable to be a fan. I read articles about them. I watched VH1's *Behind the Music* on Creed. They never gave a clear answer. I sought advice from my brother-in-law, a pastor, and he gave me that sage Christian perspective, "Look at the fruit."

Judging things, people, music, movies, or events based on "their fruit" is the most common advice I have received from Christian leaders and mentors. In other words, we are examining what people are producing with their lives, actions, and even music. I imagine that we are looking for the fruit of the Spirit. "But the fruit of the Spirit is love, joy, peace, forbearance, kindness, goodness, faithfulness, gentleness and self-control. Against such things there is no law" (Galatians 5:22-23). This seems to be a good measuring tool to decide what is good, and the church is quick to judge others by this standard. However, it is not a standard that we often hold ourselves accountable to.

Throughout the 90's, the Church of the Nazarene's Manual statement on same-sex relationships was, "Homosexuality is one means by which human sexuality is perverted. We recognize the depth of the perversion that leads to homosexual acts but affirm the biblical position that such acts are sinful and subject to the wrath of God." We justified our actions toward the LGBTQ+ community with that statement. We mocked artists like Elton John. We deemed the AIDS epidemic as God's judgment against gay men. We promoted stereotypes that reflected the worst aspects of the LGBTQ+ community as the norm, not the exception. We coined the phrases "gay agenda" and "gay lifestyle." We promoted toxic gender roles in order to avoid the appearance of evil. We did all of this in the name of God while pretending we were producing good fruit.

As a middle school teacher, I help lead the "Signs of Suicide" program every year. Without fail, the majority of students that reach out for help are emerging LGBTQ+ students. These children are beginning to understand who they are, and they are afraid. They fear rejection, judgment, bullying and worse from family, friends, and their faith. Recent studies by The Trevor Project showed us that LGBTQ+ students are twice as likely to have experienced bullying, twice as likely to become addicted to drugs or alcohol, and three times more likely to lack a trusted adult. They are at a substantially greater risk of depression and suicide. Yet we sit back in our pews and pretend that our years of hateful rhetoric, disastrous promotion of conversion therapy, and our blatant rejection of our LGBTQ+ children have nothing to do with these numbers. We think we are giving them love and fail to acknowledge our rotten fruit.

I have two queer children; my youngest has only recently come out. As a pastor myself, my children coming out as queer has been a difficult path to navigate. The church tells me my daughter Annie cannot have a girlfriend and say she loves Jesus. She says she can. She says she loves God, has said the sinner's prayer, has been baptized, and feels a call to preach. So, who is right, Annie or the church? Well, let us examine the fruit. Her girlfriend is the kind of person you hope your child hangs out with. She is kind and considerate. She challenges my daughter to be more conscious of other people and their feelings. They build each other up and speak words of hope when the stress of school and being a teenager has them down. When they are together, they share joy and laughter. In the past eight months they have been dating, my daughter has become more open to discussing the church and God. Her faith has grown deeper. I asked her if she wanted to leave the Church of the Nazarene. She gave me a firm no, replying, "Mom, other kids like me need a safe place. You can be that. You can love LGBTQ+ people in the church so they know that God loves them too." So, does that fit the criteria of good fruit—love, joy, peace, patience, kindness, goodness, faithfulness, self-control? It is significantly healthier than many of the heterosexual relationships I have witnessed in church youth groups.

My four children have grown up in a different world than me. They are sensitive to the unnecessary labels we have given that cause division and xenophobia. More than that, they desire to live without the labels that society uses to make sense of the world. My daughter does not want to be labeled gay, bisexual or straight; she does not want the box that labels place her in. She just wants to be seen as Annie. She is not "my gay child;" she is my child. My second oldest is not "my non-binary child;" they are just my child. There is so much more to them than their sexuality or their gender. They are a smart, kind, funny, and talented human. They love hiking, swimming, softball, and music. They are a whole person.

Many of my friends that are gay are in long-term monogamous relationships. Many of them are married with children. They are not the embodiment of the weird gay caricatures that I grew up with in the 90's. They are just normal people, with normal jobs, and normal families. They are not my gay friends; they are just my friends. They are nurturing parents, excellent teachers, loving partners, and supportive friends. Many times, they are the safe space the church has not been, giving me room to process my own hurt without judgment.

When these friends come to church with me and enter a loving relationship with the Creator, what will our response be as the church? Will we refuse to recognize them as a family? Will we require that they separate? How will their kids react to that? Will they be open to a religion that is responsible for their family breaking up? The world is changing, and the church cannot ignore the changing dynamics.

I do not ask for reflection and change just because it would be convenient for my family; I ask because there is a population of people whose lives literally depend on us getting this right. Our ability to question long held religious beliefs is part of who we are. It is why I, as a woman, can be a pastor. At some point, men in power judged the fruit of women preaching and decided that they could not deny the good fruit. That led to a reversal in policies held by churches for centuries. As a female pastor, I owe it to my LGBTQ+ friends to use my voice to raise the same concern—there is undeniably good fruit from the ministry of our LGBTQ+ Christian brothers and sisters. It is time to reexamine our long-held beliefs.

Buffy Fleece is a bi-vocational pastor in Columbus, OH. During the day she is a middle school Spanish teacher in Columbus City Schools. She has a BA in Spanish Education from Mount Vernon Nazarene University and a MDiv from Nazarene Theological Seminary.

Why Don't You Just Leave?

JR. FORASTEROS

When I came out as a queer-affirming pastor, I was asked, "Why don't you just leave the denomination?" But I'm affirming because I'm Nazarene, not despite it.

It wasn't long after I had first announced publicly that I'm an LGBTQ+ affirming pastor that my District Superintendent texted, asking if we could meet. I grinned; I had known this was coming when I posted. He had been contacted by the General Superintendent who oversaw our district and instructed to listen to the podcast episode I had posted. He was told to inquire as to why, if I disagreed with our denominational position, I didn't hand in my credentials and seek out an affirming denomination.

It's a fair question, and one I've been asked by a number of individuals in the last few years. The Church of the Nazarene is openly homophobic; why *would* an affirming pastor remain in the denomination? Aren't I violating my ordination oaths by staying?

In short, no.

I wasn't raised Nazarene—I grew up Southern Baptist (and was originally ordained in the SBC). I came to the Church of the Nazarene by choice, after leaving the SBC over disputes about penal substitutionary atonement and ordination of women. I chose to be Nazarene, and I'm a Nazarene with the zeal of a convert.

As I was considering my new denomination, I couldn't escape the so-called 'Special Rules' (cue dramatic music drop). As a long-time movie buff and critic, the idea that I might not be allowed to go to the movies (or the circus!) was troublesome; the prohibition against dancing—against which I have a genetic predisposition—less so. But still—the Baptists are famously a people of no creed—all their rules are unspoken. The idea that we Nazarenes have a stated list of rules was fascinating to me. I had to know more.

I dove into the Manual to discover we have two separate documents—the

Articles of Faith and the Special Rules, which are now called the Code of Christian Conduct. The difference between the two lists was immediately clear, as was the wisdom behind having two distinct documents.

The Articles of Faith are our timeless doctrines—belief in the Trinity, the Second Coming, Entire Sanctification. These are our creed, the hallmarks of Nazarenes across time and cultures. As such, they change very little from manual to manual, with the majority of the changes being to update language.

The Special Rules, on the other hand, change every assembly. And they're reactive—we didn't have a special rule on the sanctity of life until the first manual published after Roe v Wade. We're allowed to go see movies now (and the circus!). Even dancing is mostly fine. And of course there's the big debate about this section of our manual becoming regional.

All of this points to a reality that's been baked into our denomination since the beginning: the Special Rules/Code of Conduct interpret the Articles of Faith. The *good* thing about the articles of faith being so broad is that they're timeless. They *don't* change from year to year. We're *always* going to believe in the Trinity and anticipate Jesus' Second Coming.

The drawback, though, is that they're abstract. What does it *mean* that we believe in the Trinity? How does our eschatological hope shape our present moment? This is a particular problem for a Holiness people who believe deeply that the Holy Spirit is living and active in our present moment. We *should* look different in tangible, noticeable ways from the world around us.

The Special Rules are our way of feeling out what those tangible differences might look like. They're applied holiness.

But culture isn't static; it's constantly shifting—not just from year to year, but as we move around the globe, through a country or even within a city. This means that what holiness looks like, what holiness *requires* of us is going to look different for different churches in different places and at different times. It's messy. It's complex and complicated.

And that's why our manual is designed to be updated. It's why the Special Rules are constantly changing—because *we're* changing them. We recognize that, while the Articles of Faith are mostly static, the Code of Conduct/Special Rules are mostly in flux. They're *supposed to be*. It's not a bug; it's a feature.

By virtue of the fact that our Special Rules are culturally contingent, we're essentially guaranteed to get them wrong. They're likely to be out of date by the time the latest edition of the Manual has been updated, printed and delivered to our churches in the wake of the latest General Assembly.

As such, to insist on strict adherence to the Special Rules is ludicrous. They're not a document that was designed with such in mind. They're the beginning of a conversation—what holiness looks like in our time and place—not the end of one. And by virtue of the fact that we're collectively working out our salvation, we're going to get it wrong sometimes. Again, that's not the worst thing; with appropriate humility, it's not even a *bad* thing. Imagine that we, as a denomination, model a radical commitment to live out our holy calling publicly, mess and all.

And while it should go without saying that we as Nazarenes are not required to agree with the Special Rules, certain reactionary groups in our denomination are working to require just that. But if we're never allowed to disagree with the Special Rules, then how could we possibly ever change them? If disagreeing with the Special Rules was grounds for revoking ordination, then surely anyone who's ever authored such a change should be brought up on charges. Obviously, such an idea is ludicrous, and those who insist on mindless adherence to the Special Rules either fail to understand what this document is or are pursuing a decidedly unholy agenda by working to make our denomination's governing documents something they're literally (and literarily) not designed to be.

Which brings me back to my public stance for LGBTQ+ affirmation: yes, our statement on human sexuality is homophobic. But that statement is in our Special Rules. In other words, those who authored this statement (and who voted it into our Manual), believe that a homophobic stance on queer identity is the most faithful way to embody holiness in this time and place.

I deeply disagree with these siblings. I believe that God created, calls, and honors queer individuals. I believe that a faithfully Wesleyan holiness church will be queer (in that we reject whole-heartedly and full-throatedly the cis-heteronormative patriarchy in our churches and in our world). I believe that, to be consistent with our Articles of Faith, the Church of the Nazarene must be fully LGBTQ+ affirming.

We're disagreeing about polity, and I believe those who are 'Side B'/non-affirming/homophobic are committing the same kind of sin as our Baptist siblings who deny God's call on women to preach and pastor. It's the same kind of sin as the preachers who used the Bible to uphold chattel slavery in the US as God's will for America.

I love the Church of the Nazarene too much to pretend this issue doesn't matter. And I love my queer siblings and neighbors too much to pretend this issue isn't urgent.

I'm affirming *because* I'm Nazarene; not despite it. And I'm not going anywhere.

jr. forasteros lives in Dallas, TX with his wife, Amanda. He pastors Catalyst Church and is the author of Empathy for the Devil *from IVP. He is a columnist at* Sojourners *and writes about horror for TOR.com. He plans to die historic on the Fury Road, but until then, he's probably either preaching or announcing roller derby.*

What the Denomination Said When I Asked if I Could Include LGTBQ+ People

JONATHAN J. FOSTER

I will never forget how uncomfortable *I was as the church deemed me "out of alignment" for expressing my concerns about their (our) posture toward LGTBQ+ human beings. But even more compelling, I will never forget how* comfortable *I was with Jesus. In the end, the hardest/easiest decision I ever made was to follow Jesus rather than the church.*

I want to tell you a little story. It's a story about what The Church of the Nazarene said in the last few moments of my denominational life. 2019.

The outset of Holy Week.

The outset of a week we reflect upon the unjust scapegoating of our Lord.

The outset of the rest of my life.

I sat with three men representing my denomination: a fellow pastor, a District Superintendent, and a General Superintendent. Decent people. I have no need to suggest anything otherwise. I didn't know them well, but they probably loved God as best as they knew how, fasted and prayed, gave of their time and money, and maybe even recycled.

Was it a heresy trial? I don't know. Come to think of it, I doubt the word trial was used, and given the pleasantries exchanged, I'm not sure the word feels appropriate. I mean, imagine Galileo, Giordano Bruno, or Martin Luther getting a handshake from the powers that be right before being arrested, burned, or excommunicated. (And imagine putting myself in the same paragraph as Galileo, Bruno, or Luther). Hmm, maybe we'll call it a conversation. Yes, a heresy conversation. A kinder, gentler kind of trial. No need for stoking fires around stakes; let's do this in a more civilized way.

Our "heresy conversation" centered around my approach to matters regarding LGTBQ+ human beings. Specifically, I had asked our district for permission to treat these people with respect such that they would be welcomed and included in my church. Even more, that we gain clarity around the issues present before we assume such human beings as reprobate.

I wasn't demanding answers. I was asking for space to walk with people, to not single them out, not suggest that their issues were different than anyone's issues, and to walk with them in the midst of questions. Questions they have. *Questions we all have.*

For example, when a baby is born with unformed reproductive organs or is intersex, how would the denomination have me support the parents? As that child grows into a teen and adult, what is the expectation? What if, despite being raised as a man, they realize, years later, that they are a woman? What if this person, whom the church has always known as a man, begins to have affection for other men? What if this person feels a calling to serve on the church board? What does the denomination expect of the pastor in this situation?

Or how would the denomination like me to reference someone with an X and Y chromosome but who also has ovaries and not testicles? What if this person is experiencing frustration about their sexuality? What if we don't know this person's biological or physical makeup? How would we even gain such information? What if someone comes to me, expressing gender dysphoria? What exactly should I ask before I agree to baptize, bring into membership, or allow them to teach?

Or what's the proper response to a young lady who, after disclosing stories of being abused by her father, stepfather, then a high school boy, rushes to tell me that she found a girl in college whom she feels safe with and loves? Does the denomination expect me to suggest that the only way for her to experience romantic love is to place herself back in a heterosexual and unsafe relationship?

I had already brought several of these questions to my district superintendent. Again, he was a kind man, but someone who, by his own admission, wasn't prepared to have nuanced discussions around sexuality. I don't say this to cast doubt upon this individual's integrity or lack of mental capacity—though I certainly hope to cast doubt upon the integrity of a system that promotes such people to the role of a superintendent. Pastors desperately need more than someone whose only recourse is to point to static, black-and-white words in a manual. Pastors need a mentor to join them in a dynamic, flesh-colored world.

My questions that I'd like to think were formulated with an awareness of human complexity, were met with one of two simplistic responses:

1. Are you in or out?
2. You are not in alignment with the theology of The Church of the Nazarene.

My response to the coercion of the first question went something like... Wait. *What?* I'm "in." For good or for bad, I've been "in" my whole life. I'm a third-generation Nazarene pastor; someone who has done all the camps, retreats, colleges, seminaries, and ordinations; someone whose every memory in one way or the other was colored Nazarene. There's no reason for me to be out now. Why would you resort to requesting blind allegiance in matters so complex?

My response to the theological pronouncement went something like... Wait. *What?* Are you sure? Can you tell me more about our theology? Does it speak to everything? Do we have the definitive truth? Even if we had the definitive truth in this area, why would we treat these human beings any differently than anyone else? And, given that Jesus was nothing less than inclusive with people from all walks of life, would he have been in alignment with our theology? How do I stay in alignment but treat those outside heterosexual norms in a gracious way? By the way, who created heterosexual norms? Did non-heterosexuals have a say? Does the Bible speak infallibly to this issue? Are there any gray areas in the Bible? Is our theology 100% clear on all matters concerning sexuality, and if so, *why is there such widespread disagreement?*

My D.S. could not answer my questions. Our conversations usually ended with a smile, a shaking head, and a request to reconnect at a later date. This back and forth continued for a few months, all of which led up to the "heresy conversation" and the church's remarkable confession.

So, there we were. In the board room. Around the board table. The denomination growing bored of me and the entire conversation.

"You know this issue isn't going away, right? Are you sure you want to take this kind of stance?"

These are our rules; every organization has rules.

"True, but we're an organization that rallies around Jesus, someone who died because the religious people wouldn't rethink their rules."

That's not us though. We can rethink our rules. It would just have to go through the proper channels with the proper committees.

"You want me to form a committee and wait until the next district assembly to make a motion that certain wording in our manual be edited? Even if there *was* approval for this idea, we'd have to wait three more years for the general assembly. And even if by some miracle it passed, it would still take months or years for the vocabulary to be ironed out. Meanwhile, what would you have me do with friends who are carrying the shame of our religious system because they identify as gay? When they disclose suicidal thoughts, what would you suggest? Should I let them know that in four to six years, the church will have some sexuality statements completed, and then they'll know what to do? When the religious people dragged the woman 'caught in adultery' to Jesus, *did he form a committee?*"

No, but he did tell her not to sin.

"Do you think the moral of that story has to do with us telling people they are sinning? Or does the moral have to do with us organizing our practices around scapegoating?"

Sure, scapegoating is wrong, but the Bible is pretty clear about homosexuality.

"The Bible is clear? Really? Do you know what Jesus said about the eunuch? Are you sure we know exactly what the four passages (out of 31,000 verses in the Bible) that mention homosexuality are saying?"

I'm sighing as I retell the story thinking about how much I sighed when I was in the story. I imagined the gentiles in the 1st century making their case to be accepted by Jews, the African slaves in the 19th century trying to change the attitude of white southerners, or the women in the 20th century trying to reason with men about their right to vote. But apparently, none of those sitting around the board table with me that day were thinking of such things.

The more I attempted to move the conversation away from "individual personal sin" and into "denominational systemic sin," the more the discussion bogged down. It just went 'round and 'round… like being on a merry-go-round… like a dog chasing its tail… like a dog chasing its tail on a merry-go-round.

Finally, the General sat up and tapped both hands on the table. "Jonathan," he said with no shortage of conviction, "if you want me to say that I don't know how to answer every question you have raised or that the church cannot definitively interpret all these issues… then yes, I will say that: I don't know."

As a matter of fact, that's *exactly* what I wanted. I wanted him, the two others, the district, the North American region, and the entire global denomination to say what everyone already knew: No one has exact answers to anything, least of all to every question dealing with sexuality.

"Great," I responded, "so we are all in agreement: *We don't know.* Therefore, our default position could be love. We could create spaces where people are welcomed and loved irrespective of who they are and what they are going through." I leaned back in my chair and said, "I think our work here is done."

In the wake of my admittedly somewhat sarcastic but no less truthful attempt to make a point, an uneasy silence filled the room. It was interrupted only by fingers tapping, seats shifting, and my future compressing. Surely, they sensed grace when they admitted to not having answers, right? Surely, they wouldn't force me, my young church, with all of its LGTBQ+ loving parishioners, out, right? Surely, they knew the table was big enough for everyone, right?

Alas, institutional thinking is formidable. To build upon Upton Sinclair, getting an organization to change its mind is impossible, especially when so much rides on an organization's *not* changing its mind. You've probably already guessed the ending. The D.S. turned to me and said, "Jonathan, you are out of alignment with the theology of the Church of the Nazarene."

It was a remarkable confession The Church of the Nazarene made in the last moments of my denominational life. They told me that I was out of alignment with a theology *that they did not understand.*

What absurdity!

Confused people telling someone that they are too confused to belong?

Uncertain theologians being so certain about getting rid of someone?

Purveyors of grace lacking the grace to allow a pastor to build a gracious community?

I will never forget that moment; how uncomfortable I was with the church, but strangely, how comfortable I was with Jesus. What could I do? Ultimately, I had to agree. I *was* out of alignment with that kind of theology. What a sham(e). What a power-loving-religious-sham(e) I experienced in 2019.

The outset of Holy Week.

The outset of a week we reflect upon the unjust scapegoating of our Lord.

The outset of the rest of my life.

Jonathan J. Foster *is the author of* Questions About Sexuality that Got Me Uninvited from My Denomination *and other books including his doctoral dissertation through Northwind Theological Seminary entitled* Theology of Consent: Mimetic Theory in an Open and Relational Universe. *Learn more at jonathanfosteronline.com.*

They Are Not Hurting Anyone, We Are Hurting Them

KEN GARNER

After wrestling, studying, meeting, praying with, fearing, and listening to LGBTQ people, I realized they are not hurting anyone. We are hurting them. And we are the Church.

I'm not attempting to be the expert in the field of gender and sexual orientation. I grapple, research, and try to understand people that until recently I said that I love, but I really condemned and feared them. Yes, feared. As I wrestled with LGBTQ people and what I thought the Bible said, a friend said to me, "What are you afraid of? They are not hurting you. They are not hurting anyone." Their words prodded and haunted me while I wrestled with LGBTQ people and God. Were they hurting anyone?

Think About It

"I've read the Bible and I'm doomed. But this is who I am, and if God cannot accept me for who I am, then I am doomed." A person I love very much said this to me at a local diner one day. A small fundamentalist Baptist church accepted and loved this man and his partner. He attended regularly and served in that church for decades. But on that day, he still felt doomed. After grappling for 30 years and trying to make homosexuality the 'abomination' that it was supposed to be, here sat a person I loved. Here sat a person who loved God. Here sat a person who loved others and did not hurt them. Here sat a person who felt he was beyond God's love according to modern scripture interpretation. During our ongoing conversations, I realized that something was just not right in how we were treating LGBTQ people. Something needed to change.

When websites popped into existence, I started reading biblical arguments against and for homosexuality. I remember commenting to my wife over a decade ago, "I wish even one group against homosexuality could produce a biblical study

as competent and convincing as the sites that were pro homosexuality." That statement stuck with me and motivated me to dive deeper into this 'issue.' I continued
running into my fear of homosexuality. What if the teaching I had accepted was
not really biblical? Fear caused me to treat LGTBQ people like issues. But were
they hurting anyone?

Can being LGBTQ be 'healed', converted, denied, or cast out of a person?
Therapies, casting out demons of homosexuality, and denial overwhelmingly do
not help an LGBTQ person become straight. They overwhelmingly cause emotional and social distress that hurts families and often ends in depression, suicide,
and more. Do the research. Better yet, talk to LGBTQ people. If you have nothing
to fear, then listen to them. If you are fearful of affirming queer people, face that
fear and listen to them.

"What are you afraid of? They are not hurting anyone."

Getting to Know LGBTQ People

'There is no substitute for experience' rings true. I decided to continue researching
but also to talk to people instead of hypothetically talking about LGBTQ people
like they were issues.

Meeting LGBTQ people changed everything for me. I continue to meet
LGBTQ people. I no longer talk about them generically. I cannot talk about
scripture without people coming to mind. They have names, faces, hopes, dreams,
hurts, and personalities like me and everyone else. They are friends and family.
They are peers in ministry. People. They are not any more or less deviant than
the rest of the population. But I, we, are afraid of them. I see and hear fear in the
comments, discussions, jokes, and ostracization of LGBTQ people. But their lives
impact me.

I watch the fear and agony, not just frustration, but agony that LGBTQ people live with. They are shamed. They are ridiculed. They are denied positions they
are the most qualified to hold. They tried for all they were worth to be 'straight'
and to fit in. One man told us that he begged God every day to take it away but
God never had....and never did. That man died alone and ashamed, isolating himself from his best friends. I witnessed incredibly talented and compassionate people
denied acceptance, ministry positions, fulfillment, respect, and love because they
could not exorcize, sanctify, eradicate, or reprogram who they were. Their constant
fear and agony troubles me.

I tried to help queer people heal from their hurts and "go straight." I thought
they must have been abused as a child, or maybe just neglected. Something had to
have happened, right? Wrong. Not every abused, neglected, or humiliated kid ends

up gay or promiscuous or any other thing. So, I stopped trying to 'fix' LGBTQ people. Then I started 'seeing' LGBTQ people.

When I gave up trying to fix LGBTQ people, I started to see LGBTQ for who they really are. For decades, I thought they were hiding from their hurts and true selves. Then I saw differently. A loved one who is gay told me, "Kenny, do you really think I had a choice, that I chose this life? Do you really think I chose to live this difficult of a life? Look at my life. It was not a choice. It is who I am."

LGBTQ people define courage. Do you really think a teenager is going to come out as gay and take all the peer abuse for the fun of it? Not the ones I'm meeting. They know they cannot hope to be what everyone wants them to be, so queer people decide to just say, "Here I am. I'm LGBTQ. I can't do anything about it. If you don't like it, I can't do anything about that either. Now let's get it over with and get on with life." They choose to be courageously authentic because they were dying trying to be anyone else.

They are self-aware. Really. I'm not sure why, but queer people know themselves as well or better than I know myself. They wrestle, compare, read, study, and do whatever they need to do, but they come to grips with who they are. By the time a person comes out, they have done so much self-work that I find them incredibly self-aware and refreshing to be around.

"What are you afraid of? They are not hurting anyone."

The Bible Tells Me So
Again, I go back to an early fear and feeling that I had about Bible studies for and against homosexuality. The pro-homosexuality studies always seemed more logical, more in depth, and more honest. So I started doing my own research and continue today. I am not going to walk through every Bible passage that deals with sexuality. However, I do want to share a few things that led me to seeing and reading these scriptures with a new understanding.

Ultimately, I do not believe that scripture deals with our concept or definition of homosexuality. It does not prohibit or endorse homosexuality. Here are three realizations that opened my eyes and heart to new understanding:

- The etymology of the words 'homosexual' and 'homosexuality'.
- Not one scripture deals with our concept or definition of homosexuality. Instead they deal with the different problems of power, extramarital sex, predators, and sexual abuse.
- Scripture shows a tradition of adapting and changing from generation to generation to love and to include people.

In biblical history, the term 'homosexuality' was not a known term or concept. English translations that use the words 'homosexual' or 'homosexuality' are inaccurate. They project our modern concept of homosexuality back into a history that viewed sex and sexuality differently. The words 'homosexual' or 'homosexuality' were not coined until the mid to late 1800's. After that, in 1946, English translators exchanged words like 'fornication', 'sexual immorality', or 'perversion' for homosexual and homosexuality. But our concept of homosexuality does not translate to the problems that the scriptures were talking about with those words. Scripture never talked about our concept of homosexuality. It never talked about two men or two women being attracted to one another, being in love with one another, and being in a marriage relationship. If scripture did not talk about our concept of homosexuality, what was it talking about?

Scripture references deal with sexual perversion. You might say, "Yes, like homosexuality." But no, they never talked about homosexuality. Scripture never says to deny two people of the same sex the possibility of marriage or to permit it. Men used sex to overpower and dominate over each other, boys, conquered enemies, subordinates, and women. Men often dealt in perverted sex for power, domination, self-gratification, temple prostitution and money. The passages of scripture that we use to clobber and shame LGBTQ people really do not address LGBTQ people. They address different situations and the problems of greed and power. They address people who are hurting other people. LGBTQ people are not hurting anyone. I could go on, but I started to realize that scripture was not dealing with our concept of homosexuality and LGBTQ people in 2021.

"What are you afraid of? They are not hurting anyone."

The Church

In my relationships and conversations with LGBTQ people, the Church of Jesus Christ saddens me the most. Of the LGBTQ people I know, the worst abuse and rejection comes from those growing up in Christian families and churches. And I mean real abuse! It breaks my heart to see and feel the damage caused by people carrying Bibles and spouting off a few half verses crammed full of their own fear. And I confess, I championed the company line many times. Forgive my fear. As a youth pastor, I met LGBTQ teenagers. I remember one young man who was a great guy and a good athlete. We were goofing around in the gym sometime after this young man "came out." It broke my heart to see the other guys in the gym. They were his friends until he came out. No matter how open this young man was, they would not pass him the ball. What were they afraid of? Was something going to rub off or would he take it wrong if someone passed the ball to him? Broke my heart. I knew something was wrong. What scares us about LGBTQ people?

Scripture and history demonstrate a tradition of applying scripture to the changing culture. Each new generation in scripture was tasked with applying God's love and image to their generation. Someone said scripture was not meant to be the last word but the first word. We have a tradition of evaluating and applying the love of God and the image of God in each person to each new generation. Change is not bad. Everything that grows changes. Changing just to change is not wise. But learning, loving, and changing shows maturity, humility and wisdom.

"What are you afraid of? They are not hurting you. They are not hurting anyone."

Experience matters. Some people tell me I only affirm LGBTQ people because I have family members and friends who are LGBTQ. On one hand, no. Believe me or not, but no. On the other, you bet your eternal life on it. Experience matters. And meeting and knowing people matters. If you do not know a LGBTQ person, you should not judge them. Experience matters because it becomes tradition. It becomes how we read scripture. We cannot read scripture outside of tradition. Everything filters through experience whether we want to admit it or not. My experiences lead me to affirm LGBTQ people.

"What are you afraid of? They are not hurting you. They are not hurting anyone." We are hurting them and we need to stop.

Ken Garner grew up in the Church of the Nazarene. He was educated in Nazarene universities and served as an ordained Elder in the Church of the Nazarene until April 1, 2022. He was a Youth Pastor, Executive Pastor, and Lead Pastor. Now he and his wife, Teresa Beth (Ulmet) Garner, live in Ohio and try to love more with less fear as they connect with spiritual wanderers through their venture, Love More Less Fear, LLC, lovemorelessfear.com, and their podcast.

The End of the Othering

KARL GIBERSON

*Nazarene refusal to affirm the LGBTQ+ community is
unscientific, based on eccentric biblical interpretation, motivated
by homophobic instincts, and destructive of families. It's immoral.*

New Year's weekend in 2018 was bitterly cold—the kind of winter that motivates song lyrics about "ground as hard as iron, water like a stone." My wife and I were enjoying the weekend at our lake house in central Massachusetts. Some friends who had planned to join us got sick and canceled at the last minute, so we were alone.

My daughter called on Saturday. The car driven by some friends of hers, traveling to New Jersey with their new baby, had broken down not far from us and could we possibly help out? The seasonal symbolism of the request was not lost on me, and I was soon in my car, going to pick them up. Both were former students of mine at Eastern Nazarene College, varsity athletes, and friends of my daughter.

They spent the weekend with us, enjoying our woodstove, hot meals, warm beds, and the quietude of a snow-covered lake in winter; they were attentive to their new baby boy who, oblivious to his circumstances as loved babies always are, slept and ate; smiled and cried; and, as babies are wont to do, messed his diaper a few times.

A few days later, their car repaired, our holiday visitors headed home to New Jersey.

It was a memorable New Year's weekend in several ways. Certainly it felt wonderful to have provided comfort for a family in troubled circumstances. But my winter visitors did far more for me than I did for them. They showed me, up close and personal, with all the profound emotional depth needed, just how wonderful—and completely normal—a same-sex couple raising a little boy could be. Bethany and Brittany brought to life—*embodied* would be a better word—an abstraction that I had only embraced intellectually.

It was, for me, the terminus of a long journey I call the "End of the Othering."

I grew up in a small rural village in New Brunswick, Canada. My father was a pastor in a "Bible Belt" demographic. There were, of course, no gay people in our village, or the next village, or any other village, to the best of my knowledge. Gay people existed only as the "other"—debauched, sinful reprobates who had no business mingling in polite society. We spoke of gays only as slurred abstractions—"you homo" was an epithet of last resort after milder insults had been exhausted.

I was convinced that homosexuality was both a terrible sin and a profound sickness, condemned by the Bible, unnatural, a perverted and indecent choice, made only by wicked people

I enrolled at Eastern Nazarene College in 1975, never having encountered (to my knowledge) a member of the gay community. Gays remained "the other." I graduated four years later, having made many wonderful friends at college—none of them gay of course. Or so I thought…

All this changed in 1980 when I received a brief message from Kevin, the first and one of the best friends I made in college. The message, printed in tiny letters on the flap of a birthday card, was "I am gay and living in San Diego with a lover. Any questions, call me." The short humorously tiny message hit me with an out-sized force that I can still recall, decades later. Kevin was gay. But Kevin was not "the other." He was my *friend*. I had stayed at his house and he had made the long journey to Canada to stay at mine. While at ENC we had studied together, shared a hundred pizzas and even sneaked off to a seedy theater to watch our first porn movie. He was "us," not "them."

Kevin gave me the first face of the LGBTQ community. It was that of a friend.

The fiction that gays are perverted outsiders crumbles when you discover that someone you respect, love and value and think of as "us" is gay. The tiny message on the flap of that envelope pried open my tightly closed mind and started me on a life-long quest to accept, to understand, and to embrace the LGBTQ community.

My journey parallels that of the American scientific and liberal culture but, alas, not that of the evangelical community that has lagged far behind, having decided that this is a hill to die on. I watched as a veritable mountain of evidence from the natural and social sciences destroyed dangerous misconceptions about the nature of same-sex attraction. Unfortunately, evangelicals—especially Nazarenes—rejected the science and instead nurtured a culture of fear and hatred that has driven millions of young people away from the church, splitting families, and pushing many to suicide.

These changes have all happened in my lifetime. In the years before I went to college, the American Psychological Association considered homosexuality to be a mental disorder—something to be "cured" or "controlled." Evangelicals agreed but enlarged it to be a morally perverted lifestyle *choice*, condemned in the Bible, personally destructive, socially corrosive—and only addressed through spiritual transformation. The Nazarene manual reflected such views by labeling homosexuality an "abomination," the strongest language used to describe any of the many things condemned in the Nazarene guide to faith and practice.

Such attitudes had for centuries amplified prejudices so that the LGBTQ community had been effectively—and often legally—"othered." As people began to "come out," they found themselves ostracized into a small subculture with its own bars, magazines, movie theaters, neighborhoods, and so on.

Kevin forced me to confront my own prejudices as I began to engage the LGBTQ question. It was a fascinating journey and to this day I remain astonished at how clueless we all were just a few decades ago.

In the past half century, scientific studies have demolished the notion that homosexuality is a *choice* that can be reversed with determined lifestyle changes. The evidence clearly indicates that adolescents *discover* they are gay; they do not *choose* to be gay. Tragically, evangelicals rejected this science and offered psychologically destructive "pray away the gay" conversion therapies. Young people, alarmed to discover they were gay, were told they had a spiritual problem and getting right with God was the only way to fix things. My friend Kevin had transferred from ENC to another college seeking such a cure. The damage done by these "conversion therapies" was so great that many of the programs—Exodus, Love in Action, Evergreen International, Living Waters, Love Won Out—voluntarily closed up. Many of their leaders apologized for the damage they did to the people in their programs—damage that included a significant increase in consideration of suicide. Progressive states made such therapies illegal.

The "pray away the gay" programs—and the vacuous science and theology on which they are based—are so abusive and harmful that I am ashamed that I was ever a part of a religious tradition that endorsed them.

Evangelicals have long been inclined to defend the Bible against perceived threats from science, as we have seen on questions related to evolution, the age of the earth, and the Big Bang Theory—the cultural battles I engaged professionally. Many evangelicals, including biblically trained scholars that I respect and know as friends, are convinced the Bible condemns the LGBTQ lifestyle. But there is far less here than most people think. The description of same-sex activity as an "abomination," for example, comes from Leviticus and is simply one of countless obscure rules that nobody takes seriously any longer—like not eating shellfish, making clothes from different materials, getting tattoos, or "cutting the hair at the sides of your head." One has to wonder why the same-sex taboo is so important, in contrast to the peculiar—and ignored—injunctions in adjacent verses. A careful reading of *all* the biblical texts, in fact, provides no basis to reject same-sex relationships between two free adults that love each other—unless the Levitical code is read with an eccentric selectivity and the other passages are distorted. The biblical injunctions are against rape, temple prostitution, and pederasty, but never once against same-sex marriage. Jesus, of course, said nothing on the subject.

I won't labor this point, as there are other essays in this volume that will engage these issues. Suffice to say, in the absence of a deep ingrained prejudice, there is only a weak case that the Bible condemns same-sex activity. Unfortunately, many of us *do* have such a deeply ingrained prejudice. It's called *homophobia* and manifests itself as a visceral objection to same-sex attraction; it's so powerful that many people are quick to compare same-sex activity to having sex with animals—an incredibly offensive and absurd analogy. (A student who made this comparison in my class at Eastern Nazarene College was almost assaulted by his more tolerant classmates.) Homophobia is a poorly understood but widespread instinctual human prejudice, like fear of snakes, or a deference to tall people. Billions of people, in fact, live under political regimes—many of them completely outside the Christian Tradition—with aggressive anti-LGBTQ laws that are not based in any way on the Bible.

After decades of exploration, I am convinced that evangelicals have been misled by their homophobic impulses. Deeply rooted prejudices, often invisible to us, create a *confirmation bias* that shapes what we see and don't see in the world. We end up concluding that things must be so because we *want* them to be so, not because the evidence points in that direction. This is how we read the Bible, glossing over the teachings on shellfish and sideburns while exclaiming "See! Homosexuality is an abomination! The Bible says so!"

The true abomination in this discussion is the way that evangelicals have treated the LGBTQ community. I was powerfully reminded of this—and my shameful role in it—when I received a message from a former ENC student, who had struggled in college with his sexual orientation. In his message he gave me the time and the day of when he had scheduled his suicide. As a last effort to "cure" himself of his homosexuality—as my friend Kevin had tried to do—he was attending yet another "pray away the gay" conversion weekend. If the conversion failed this time—as it had so many others—he planned to end his life on the Monday evening after he returned to his dorm room at ENC.

As I read his chilling words a wave of shame rolled over me, for I knew I had been complicit as a part of the culture of misunderstanding, prejudice, and hatred that had brought him to this decision. ENC professors were expected to stand clearly in condemnation of the LGBTQ community. Failing to do so could result in getting fired—as happened to one of my closest faculty friends and a very popular professor. To protect my job, which I loved, I was silent. My students—alone, afraid, and in need of compassion—were wrestling with terrible choices. I let them down. I was timid, self-serving. And I'm sorry.

Both of the young women who came to my house on that cold New Year's weekend were lifelong Nazarenes. Both were estranged from their parents when they "came out." One remains so, her faithful Nazarene parents unable to accept their daughter as a happily married lesbian who has given birth via IVF to two wonderful grandchildren. As I watch this family develop, I am struck by how wholesome and thoroughly *normal* it is. Two parents in love with and faithful to each other, raising two healthy happy children. And research shows that children raised in such families grow up to be kinder, less aggressive, and more tolerant than their peers raised in "traditional" families. Why can we not embrace this? How can we continue to pass such hostile judgments on those of us who find themselves with non-traditional attractions?

It is time to end the othering.

Karl Giberson has held faculty positions at Eastern Nazarene College, Gordon College, and Stonehill College. He is a leading scholar of science and religion, having published 11 books (several translated into other languages) and hundreds of articles. He has spoken widely at the Vatican, Oxford University, London's Thomas More Center, and at venues in Brazil, Spain, the Canary Islands, and all over the United States.

Be Careful Who You Choose to Exclude, They Might be Someone You Love

MURPHY L. GILL

The Nazarene Church chooses to view some difficult issues with grace, liberty and charity, but with regard to full LGBTQ+ inclusion, she refuses to offer the same grace, liberty and charity.

"Oh, if I told them, I'd never have a bed or be welcome at home ever again." Every time I think of that moment, I find those words continue to hold open a deep and still-fresh wound in the most sensitive parts of my spirit even to this day. That wound initially signaled to me that there was something fundamentally wrong in some aspect of what I was taught to believe about LGBTQ+ people, which I had blindly reasserted at every opportunity. I was convinced in that moment that this precious young woman, a lesbian and a Christian was not the one inflicting the wound, but rather that it was the continuing work of the Holy Spirit in my own spirit, journey and life. I am still as certain of this today as I was that day.

By all accounts, I was a good Nazarene pastor doing what I was supposed to do. I was a lifelong Nazarene, born to parents who met at a Nazarene college. I grew up being active in my local Nazarene church, my youth group, and in district NYI events. As a teenager I felt a clear calling to go into full-time pastoral ministry. I then followed that call into my own Nazarene College experience and then into full time ministry. For the next 3 decades I walked that narrow path and rarely, if ever, questioned things I now realize I should have. But events in the year or so leading up to the moment back in that little Michigan coffee shop began to cause me to question deeply. I began to seriously consider that just maybe there really is an infinitely bigger, vastly more loving, and actually grace-filled God out there, and they are nothing like the one I had been working to follow for over 30 years.

This essay is about why I believe that the Church of the Nazarene, whose culture and ethos were all I ever knew growing up and whose people and community

I love, ought to become fully LGBTQ+ affirming. My take on this subject is both experientially and theologically based. As a lifelong Nazarene and a long-time Nazarene pastor, I understand the core and foundational history that went into forming the Church I loved for so long. I understand that the formational days were days of significant compromise between the various contributing church groups who were seeking to become the Church of the Nazarene. That is a beautiful thing, compromise. Being willing to truly listen to the viewpoints of others, and to ultimately believe that even though we disagree on some things which are important to us, they can still be followers of the same Christ which we follow. We can all live and work and breathe and serve and love under the same big tent, as we say.

All my life I have heard Nazarene clergy and lay leaders alike quote a line that is often incorrectly attributed to the Nazarene theological patriarch John Wesley: *"In essentials, unity; in non-essentials, liberty; and, in all things, charity."* But that sentiment is rarely lived out within the Church of the Nazarene. If it were truly embodied in practice, this "issue" and many other "non-essential" things wouldn't be the litmus test of whether someone can be in the club or not, or whether a minister who holds this view is allowed to serve in the Church. It would simply be another one of the multiplicity of things we intentionally choose to offer liberty and charity for. Certainly, there are other "issues" we find in scripture which have much clearer and stronger admonitions against them which the Church of the Nazarene has chosen to offer liberty and charity for, such as divorce or women serving in ministry and leading men. We also allow for differences in belief concerning other non-essential things like evolution, atonement theory, creation care, or even baptism.

The Church has chosen to view these issues through a lens of liberty and charity, which it certainly ought to. She has chosen to use a lens that takes into account the core Wesleyan interpretive tenants of tradition, reason, experience and scripture in order to choose not to view these issues as deal breakers. However, with regard to the issue of full LGBTQ+ inclusion in the life and work of the Church, She has refused to give the same kind of grace, liberty and charity. She has instead chosen to view the countless millions of LGBTQ+ people as beyond the grace and acceptance of the Church simply because of six passages of scripture that are in no way relevant to the idea or concept of monogamous, covenantal, same-gender relationships and love. This idea was an idea for which the writers of those six passages which the Church consistently uses to bludgeon those in the LGBTQ+ community, could never have even conceived of. None of those six passages were written with a truly loving relationship between two humans who love and care for one another but happen to be of the same gender, in mind.

Having served in countless pastoral counseling roles in the LGBTQ+ community here in Nashville since leaving my Nazarene pulpit in 2018, I am still shocked
by the sheer number of these precious LGBTQ+ humans who have been devastated by the rejection of the Church. Even more stunning are the number of them
who are pastor's kids and staff pastor's kids. The story I referenced at the outset of
this paper was the first of countless times I have sat and listened to the wounded
but still beating heart of a precious LGBTQ+ person. In this case, it was also the
first time to hear a (PK) pastor's kids' story. But the story for me, really began much
earlier than that day.

My part of the story began in the fall of 2015. In September of that year,
the world finally began to watch what was being called the Syrian Refugee Crisis.
Bashar Al-Assad was massacring his own people. The ensuing exodus was massive as
millions fled their own country while millions more were slaughtered in the streets.
Then one day, it happened. A photo began to circulate of a little three-year-old boy,
named Alan, who was lying face-down on a beach on the coast of Greece, dead.
His face became the face of the atrocities being carried out on innocents in Syria.
I remember how horrible it was to see that sight, but what followed was equally
as horrible. There was a great cry from many in our country for America to begin
taking many more of the refugees in as the European countries were simply overwhelmed. The position of our political leaders recited on the evening news was that
we couldn't take in many more of these refugees because there *might* be "terrorists"
that could sneak in and hurt us. That was shocking enough, but then came the
response by the Church, which was... nothing.

The Church went right along with the politicians. It was okay with the response of not taking in strangers and aliens who were being slaughtered in their
own country because there might be a bad guy who sneaks in. My mind immediately rejected that idea because—as a good pastor ought to say—that is the exact
opposite of what Jesus would say or do. It was wrong. And a thread began to be
pulled out of this mosaic tapestry that had been woven throughout my whole
life. I began to ask myself, "if the Church could be so desperately wrong about
something that should be so simple to respond to, what other things is it wrong
about that need to be dealt with?" I was pastoring a small Nazarene congregation
in southern Michigan at the time, and my preaching became more focused on
the idea of Social Holiness. John Wesley explained it like this *"The gospel of Christ
knows of no religion, but social; no holiness but social holiness."*

I am a pretty social person, and I thrive working around people. So, my practice was to not work on sermon prep or other study at the church itself. I wanted
to be around people and sense their energy and creativity, so I would generally take

my computer and my other materials to the local Starbucks. I became very familiar with all the staff and the regulars, so much so that they began to refer to me as the pastor of the chapel at St. Arbucks. They would often come and chat with me during their breaks in a sort of informal counseling session. I even did weddings and baby dedications for some of them. I soon learned that many of the staff at the coffee shop were members of the LGBTQ+ community, and some of them were also Christian. Of course, in the Nazarene world, those two things, Christian and gay weren't supposed to be a thing that could exist. But there it was right in front of my face, and all of a sudden, I had found another thread to tug at.

One day, while working on an upcoming sermon at the coffee shop, one of the baristas, a precious young woman, who I knew to be both a lesbian and a Christian came and sat at my table as she had done many times before. We chatted for a while, and then without thinking too much about it, I asked about her relationship with her parents and how they took it when she told them she was gay. I knew from our previous conversations that her dad pastored a small independent Baptist church a couple of hours away and I was curious how they were handling the situation. Her response, which you have already read at the beginning of this paper, was stunning. It was a response that I have now heard more times than I wish to recount from other traumatized young LGBTQ+ people, but that was my first time hearing it; it was real, and it was raw. She said "Oh, if I told them, I'd never have a bed or be welcome at home ever again", and that broke me. I sat at that table, and I cried. I cried for her, and simultaneously my anger boiled toward her parents.

But soon, I began to come to the realization that while her parents were indeed to blame for the truly un-Christlike environment they had fostered in their home (so much so that the very identity, heart, and soul of their precious daughter had to be kept hidden from them), it dawned on me that the fault truly lies at the feet of the Church. The Church was ultimately to blame. The Evangelical Church's choice to not look at full LGBTQ+ affirmation and inclusion with the same grace, liberty, and charity that they choose to look at other "issues" is fundamentally the root of all the trauma inflicted on so many in the LGBTQ+ community.

The question of LGBTQ+ full inclusion and affirmation is certainly not easy, nor without its unknowables. But for many Christian denominations and their theologians, it's not an issue to argue over. It is, as Wesley would say, a non-essential. But unfortunately for denominations like the Church of the Nazarene, many have dug their heels in and have refused to even give an ear to the matter. To these I say: please—on behalf of the children, grandchildren, and future members of the Church who come to the realization that they are gay and don't know who will accept them—take a moment to reconsider this issue now rather than later. Remember that the person you choose to exclude and reject just might turn out to be someone you love, and who loves you.

Murphy Gill *is a realtor in Nashville, TN and serves on the pastoral staff at GracePointe Church. He is a 1988 graduate of Trevecca Nazarene University and was an ordained Nazarene elder until 2018. Murphy and his wife Michelle spent over 30 years in full-time ministry in the Church of the Nazarene and now work to advocate on behalf of the LGBTQ+ community.*

Hey, Nazarenes! Why Can't Everyone Be in Your Big Tent?

MICHELLE GILL

For a denomination that proclaims the Holy Spirit moves among them, there doesn't seem to be room for the revelation of the Holy Spirt to queer Christians and their allies.

Why should the Church of the Nazarene become fully LGBTQ+ affirming? Let's start with the Manual Statement 31 on Marriage and Human Sexuality. "As the global church receives and ministers to the people of our world, the faithful outworking of these statements as congregations is complex and must be navigated with care, humility, courage and discernment." That is a worthy goal. It is not, however, the reality of the Church of the Nazarene.

Despite beginning with the statement that we are all created in God's image, the statement goes on to say that LGBTQ+ people are marred or broken. It does not just come right out with that, but it prefaces its condemnation of LGBTQ+ relationships with a discussion about how sin entered the world, and the world is fallen. Being queer is not a choice. Who would choose to be marginalized by society and especially the church? If you take the time to talk to a queer person, they will tell you they have known they were different from early childhood. It may have taken them a while to determine how it is they were different, but they have always felt it. Different does not mean broken, though. I have heard many say that people are gay because they were somehow parented errantly or abused by their parents or other adults. But many queer people had perfectly safe, normal, happy childhoods. They are not broken. The fact is they were born queer. It is not a trauma or mistake. It just is how they were made. Rachel Held Evans wrote, "These people were not 'broken.' Far from being 'unnatural,' homosexuality has been widely documented in the animal kingdom, and far from being a product of American culture, variations in gender and sexuality have been observed in hundreds of cultures around the world from those that embrace variance in gender and sexuality (like the Navajo, or the Bugis of Indonesia), to those that make them punishable by death."

When you look at the diversity of God's creation, how do you put humans into a binary and not a spectrum? Again, quoting Evans, "I affirm LGBTQ+ people because they are human beings, created in the image of God. I affirm their sexual orientations and gender identities because they reflect the diversity of God's creation, where little fits into rigid binary categories."

One of the more distressing parts of this statement on human sexuality is the complete omission of transgender people. It is tantamount to erasing their existence. It is an incredible oversight. Trans people exist and want to worship the God that created them, yet no guidance is offered by the denomination on how to treat them and interact with them. It is as though they do not exist. Thankfully, there are no directives to restrict them from participation and membership, but there is also no directive to love and accept them. Given the treatment of trans people by society in general and by conservatives, especially in recent days, this is an egregious omission.

The statement indicates that being homosexual is not in and of itself a sin and on this I agree with the church. I find it unfathomable that God would declare this to be a sin knowing full well that people are born this way. It is just part of who they are. There are six verses that reference same-sex relations. There are no verses that reference loving committed same gender relationships, which is the subject at hand. The verses refer to violent rape for purposes of humiliation of military conquests or to assert alpha masculinity. Some of these verses are about pederasty or using slaves for sexual gratification. Others reference people who were not drawn to the same gender, none the less participating in these relations. The word homosexual did not appear in translations until 1946. A letter has been discovered pointing out the error. Because of what appears to be an administrative oversight, not malicious intent, the error was not corrected. The rest, I am sad to say, is history.

I know that it is easy enough for the theological gatekeepers of the church to understand and see that there is disparity in the hermeneutic applied to matters of LGBTQ+ inclusion and affirmation. I am an accountant, who is a pastor's wife and I figured it out. I do still consider my husband to be a pastor because God called him and ordained him. He is no longer a Nazarene pastor because he saw the disparity. More than just seeing the failure to apply consistent hermeneutics, he saw the damage being done to the LGBTQ+ community. I was admittedly shocked when he told me that his change in understanding of these scriptures was a deal breaker and he would have to resign and surrender his credentials. The Church of the Nazarene sanctions a variety of beliefs about creation and evolution, atonement theory, military service (contentious objection to military service) and infant baptism. However, the tent is not big enough for varying views on LGBTQ+ inclusion and affirmation.

The current non-affirming position of the Church of the Nazarene does not stand up to the Wesleyan Quadrilateral. The four sources of the Wesleyan Quadrilateral are scripture, tradition, reason, and Christian experience. As already stated, the scripture references to LGBTQ+ relationships are scant and flimsy at best. There are six verses and Jesus never mentioned it. Those verses are about pederasty, sexual excess, and violence. A little cursory research into the historical context will uncover at the least doubts about these verses addressing loving LGBTQ+ relationships. As mentioned earlier, research has uncovered an error in the translation and combination of the two Greek words arsenokoitai and malakos into one word, homosexual. Letters between a seminarian and the team leader of the 1946 RSV translation team, Dr. Weigle, have been uncovered. The seminarian drew attention to the error and Dr. Weigle agreed with him. There is no evidence the mistranslation was maliciously left in the 1946 RSV. But it appeared in print errantly, none the less. There is enough doubt surrounding the context and translation of the scriptures to give pause to condemning these people based on this evidence.

The second leg of the quadrilateral is tradition. According to The Reformation Project, church tradition does not address same-sex relationships. For reference, Christian tradition held that the earth was the center of the universe for the first 1600 years, until it was proven that it was not. Christians today have more information about homosexuality than our church mothers and fathers. The most interesting information the Reformation Project offers us is that before the 20th century, there were no writings or tradition concerning LGBTQ+ people. There was no tradition of requiring lifelong celibacy for LGBTQ+ people.

Reason is the next leg of the quadrilateral. What kind of loving God would declare a group of people sinful or condemn them to a life of loneliness and celibacy? Nowhere in scripture does God command celibacy. Love the sinner, hate the sin defies reason. It is also a soul crushing and traumatic way to treat a human created in God's image. Reason also beckons us to look at the issues of translation and context. Ignoring this body of evidence is not the care, humility, courage, and discernment that the statement calls for.

Christian experience is the last leg of the quadrilateral. There are queer Christians, full stop. Their experience is real, whether the Church of the Nazarene recognizes it or not. Since we left the Church of the Nazarene and became affirming,

I have come to know many LGBTQ+ people. The grace that they exhibit in the face of belittling, shaming, and othering at the hands of "church people" is inspirational. I have become involved with a group of women called the Mama Bears. We go to events and give out free mom hugs. It is quite an experience to hug someone who has been deprived of a mother's love. I have gotten to know may gay young people whose parents have turned their backs on their children when they came out to them. I met Kelsey though Mama Bears. Her parents first tried to change her and then rejected her when she could not change who she was. They simply told her that their faith informed them that she was hell bound and they felt the best way to deal with her was to cut her off. That message came from the pulpit. She started writing a blog to process what she was going through. I learned so much from this young woman about grace and kindness. Although her parents turned their backs on her, she continued to love them and try to understand them. She continued to try to repair the breach. Her story is a happier story than most. She and her mom have recently been talking and are trying to reestablish their relationship. Not all stories end so happily. My friend Daniel, whose family has also abandoned him, is alone in this world because of who he is attracted to.

Still discussing experience, let's discuss what the experience of LGBTQ+ people have with the church. They hear themselves condemned from the pulpit and from their youth pastors. They are told by the church that they are broken and falling in love with someone is sin for them. According to the Trevor Project, nearly half of all LBTBQ+ youth have seriously considered suicide. Is the Church of the Nazarene fine with that? According to the Reformation Project, LGBTQ+ youth are twice as likely to attempt suicide if their parents pressure them to change their orientation. They are three times as likely to attempt suicide if they are encouraged to change their orientation by religious leaders. In addition to telling people they are bent and broken and very likely hell bound, the church has imposed the burden of celibacy on them if they are to have any chance of escaping eternal damnation. Is not the mission of the church to promote human flourishing? This non-affirming stance is the opposite of that. It is a spiritual and sometimes a physical death sentence. Let me again emphasize that this is not navigating the issue with care, humility, courage, and discernment.

The church must revisit this subject with the humility to consider that we have not gotten it right. The writings of Mildred Bangs Wynkoop and J.K Grider point the church toward love and affirmation. There are many reasons the church should reconsider its position and contrary to popular argument none of those reasons are because the Bible expressly prohibits same-sex marriage or because the church is "caving" into cultural pressure. It is not because the church has changed a position. You need look no further than prohibitions on jewelry or makeup. Or divorce. There was a time that divorce was acceptable only in cases of "biblical grounds" (adultery).

There was a time when even if a pastor's spouse were to commit adultery and divorce that pastor, they would still have to step down from leadership and surrender their credentials. Today, there are current District Superintendents that have suffered a divorce. Now the church evaluates these issues on a case-by-case basis. There are board members in most Nazarene Churches that have experienced a divorce and have remarried. They may or may not have biblical grounds for divorce. Did the church abandon scripture or simply take note that their former hardline position on divorce was harmful both to those dealing with that reality and the church herself, by disqualifying qualified, gifted ministers? I am sure some church historian could educate me further on the whys, but the fact is that divorce is no longer dealt with in the same way by the Church of the Nazarene.

On a final note, the Church of the Nazarene is actively doing harm to LGBTQ+ people with this non-affirming position. The church is pushing away some of its best and brightest pastors and candidates for ordination by making this a litmus test for service. It is time to take a long hard look at this and start making amends.

Michelle Gill is a former lifelong Nazarene. She graduated from Trevecca Nazarene University with a B.S. in Accounting. She is married to another TNU grad, Murphy, who was a pastor in the Church of the Nazarene for more than 30 years. Michelle is an advocate for LGBTQ+ community and is a member of the Mama Bears organization.

"But the Bible Says" Is Not Enough

RANDALL HARTMAN

*When the Church of the Nazarene returns to its Wesleyan roots,
they will move toward full LGBTQ+ inclusion.*

As a retired elder in the Church of the Nazarene, I have given my life to the church. I attended my first Nazarene church service when I was three days old. I graduated from two Nazarene institutions of higher learning. I served as District Secretary on two districts. I pastored Nazarene churches for 35 years. The Nazarene world has been my life, my family, my passion. But in the fall of 2021, everything changed.

The subject of LGBTQ+ full inclusion into the Church of the Nazarene began to capture my attention. Even though I have no immediate family members who are part of the queer community, I decided to explore the subject. I read books, studied biblical passages, and prayed. I became convinced God fully embraced members of the gay community. As members of this community grew in their faith, I saw no problem with them joining the church and serving in leadership.

I wrote a 500 word article about my change of mind and posted it on my personal website. I then posted the link on Facebook. I thought, "What harm could there be in expressing my opinion? Who would care?" As an unassigned elder at the end of my career, I thought it safe to publicly share my change of mind. After sharing the article, my District Superintendent contacted me to clarify my position. We met and had a civil conversation about what the Bible says regarding the LGBTQ+ community. At the end of our discussion he told me to not post anything else about the subject on social media.

After careful consideration, I wrote the District Superintendent to let him know God was giving me the green light to continue sharing my articles on social media. He responded by requesting another meeting.

In this meeting, he and a member of the District Advisory Board had several forms that I could choose to sign which would remove my ministerial credentials.

He encouraged me several times to "recant" my position and if I did, everything would be fine. But if I didn't, he would do what he needed to do. I refused to sign any document and stood by my new position. Several weeks later, I received a certified letter informing me that formal charges had been filed against me and there would be a trial.

Within a month I walked into a meeting room to undergo a trial. The purpose was to strip me of my ordination credentials because I had published my article and refused to recant. In the middle of the room my peers sat at tables pushed together to form one massive table. These included pastors with whom I had served side by side with across the years on the Michigan District. They had transitioned from colleagues into jurors.

It was surreal to hear formal charges read against me and to have "evidence" presented proving why my ministerial credentials should be revoked. The Judicial Manual of the Church of the Nazarene requires a unanimous verdict. At the end of the trial, they failed to reach a unanimous verdict and I retained my ministerial credentials.

People attempting to discredit my new position often comment, "But the Bible says…." This is followed with a short list of verses that suggest the condemnation of homosexuality. Those against full inclusion of the LGBTQ+ into the Church of the Nazarene point to these verses as though they end the discussion.

But wait. There's more.

The "Bible says" lots of things that we conveniently ignore:

- The Bible says that if you have a flat nose or broken hand you cannot approach the altar with an offering. (Lev. 21:18-21)
- The Bible says if two men are fighting and a wife defends her husband but accidentally touches the privates of the other man, her hand should be cut off. (Deuteronomy 25:11-12)
- The Bible says that if a person is born out of wedlock they cannot enter church. (Deuteronomy 23:2)

If you've read the Bible with care you know it says many things that we ignore or explain away. As you read the above examples you might have said to yourself, "Well, that's the Old Testament."

But there are New Testament verses that we also ignore. An important example is Paul's injunction against women speaking in church. (1 Corinthians 14:34) This is not something implied in the text. It is clear. Verse 34 even restates the teaching to emphasize the prohibition. The Bible says women "are not permitted to speak." Why does the Church of the Nazarene allow women ministers? (Just to be clear, I'm happy we have women ministers in the church!)

Do you see the point I'm making? In these examples the thoughtful person says, "But there are things to consider such as context and culture." Exactly. Why are we reluctant to apply this same logic to the few passages used to vilify members of the queer community? If we look at 1 Corinthians 14:34 and say, "This is not what the Bible means for us today" why can't we do that for verses suggesting homosexuality is a sin? It isn't enough to glance at a Bible verse that touches on the subject of homosexuality and conclude it is a sin.

Without guidance, the temptation to embrace only the Bible truths that we agree with is overwhelming. This willy-nilly approach to living out biblical truth leads us down a road of confusion.

This is why Wesleyan theologians point to the Wesleyan Quadrilateral as a guide to understand the Bible and live out its truths. This framework teaches us to view the Bible through the filters of tradition, reason, and experience. If you remember geometry class, you will recall that a quadrilateral is a shape composed of four different sides. Each side can be of different lengths. Wesleyans believe the Bible is the longest leg, the most important in the quadrilateral and is supported by the other three legs. When we proclaim "the Bible says," we must not ignore tradition, reason, and experience. All sides of the quadrilateral impact our understanding of the biblical text.

As an example, think about applying the quadrilateral to slavery. The Bible embraces slavery. It even gives advice on how to treat slaves. Historically the church pointed to the Bible as justification for owning slaves. Do you see the absurdity looking at Bible verses about slavery and simply saying, "But the Bible allows slavery"? Why did the church change from pro-slavery to anti-slavery? It's because they considered the "reason" leg of the quadrilateral. They recognized, contrary to what the Bible says, it made no sense that God would favor slavery.

In the same way, as we try to understand the Bible we must allow ourselves to ask questions such as:

- Does it make sense that God would condemn the entire LGBTQ+ community because of who they love?
- Can a God of love hate the love between two people because they are of the same gender?
- Should the church exclude from membership a married same-sex couple who testify to being Christ-followers?
- Does God demand LGBTQ+ people must never experience a sexual relationship even though married?

It is not enough to say, "But the Bible says." That phrase should not end the discussion. On the contrary, it invites a discussion!

The road toward change begins when we return to our Wesleyan roots and allow freedom to question and debate. Attempts by the leadership in the Church of the Nazarene to silence discussion about LGBTQ+ inclusion are futile. The discussion is already happening. People and pastors like me are realizing the love of God is far bigger than we once believed.

No amount of denominational huffing and puffing is going to put out the growing flame of understanding the breadth and depth of God's love.

Randall Hartman is a retired ordained elder in the Church of the Nazarene. He has a B.S. from Olivet Nazarene University, a Master of Divinity from Nazarene Theological Seminary and a Doctor of Ministry from Grace Theological Seminary. As a lead pastor he has 35 years of experience. In the last six years served as a long-term interim pastor in seven crisis churches leading them to wholeness. He currently posts his writings on randallhartman.com

Please Just Love

JESSICA HIATT

The failure of the Christian church to place radical love above doctrine, radical acceptance above condemnation, and radical hospitality above exclusion is causing spiritual harm and agony in the lives of LGBTQIA+ believers.

He was dying. The cancer had taken over his body and ravaged it. No chemotherapy, radiation, or surgery was going to help. The fight was over and it was time to concentrate on the quality of the little time he had left. Family and friends gathered around the hospital bedside, telling stories, laughing and crying in turn. He had his favorite blanket, his own pajamas. His requests for prime rib and home-brewed beer were fulfilled. It was going to be a good death, peaceful and reconciled, surrounded by love. Then he asked for a priest to come and give the sacrament of The Anointing of the Sick. The priest refused. Why? Because the patient was gay, and had been married to his husband for 35 years, and would not, could not, confess this as sin.

I'm a hospital chaplain, and these are lightly fictionalized accounts of real patient encounters. None of them are unusual, though the specific details change. The institutional church is causing hopelessness and despair in its refusal to accept LGBTQIA+ people, and I hear their stories.

This gay man dying of cancer came in to the emergency room because of uncontrolled pain and was admitted. I had been able to visit, establish a relationship of trust, and provide support to him and his husband as they navigated the maze of decisions that happen at the end of life. At the bedside I was privileged to get to know this devoted and delightful couple. They told me stories of meeting and falling in love, of good and bad times, of their unique struggles as a gay couple.

When we were alone, the patient talked to me about realizing he was gay, and the process of coming to terms with that and then coming out to his conservative Catholic family. The patient was baptized and confirmed in the Catholic church, and his faith in God and hope for eternal life through Jesus had not changed, even as he spent his life living with the burden of knowing the church thought he was sinning and going to hell by being true to himself. He had a deep faith, and an inner hope of God's unconditional love. He wasn't afraid of dying, and like many non-practicing Catholics, still held the rituals of the church in high regard.

When I called the local parish to request that a priest come to the hospital to give the sacrament, I mentioned the specific situation. In the past, priests and pastors of other denominations had come to the bedside, and when face to face with a same-sex couple, had devastated and traumatized the patient by condemning them for their "sin" of loving another human who happened to be of the same sex, and by refusing them the comfort of sacrament or blessing when the patient had hours or days to live. My experience had taught me to be wary, as causing more suffering and anguish at the end of life is not my practice.

This man died without knowing the peace and comfort that his faith was meant to bring. He died feeling condemned. He died questioning whether God loved him. And he was not alone. The failure of the Christian church to place radical love above doctrine, radical acceptance above condemnation, and radical hospitality above exclusion is causing spiritual harm and agony in the lives of LGBTQIA+ believers.

I deal with suicide in my work with The Trevor Project, and at the hospital. A transgender patient and their story has stuck with me, still bringing me heartache as I am writing this. He was a teenager, and from a charismatic and conservative Christian home. His parents rejected his identity, refusing to use his chosen name and pronouns. The church's pastor and elders had been involved, laying on hands, anointing with oil, praying for this "demon" to leave this young person. It drove him to hang himself in an unsuccessful effort to kill himself, and he ended up in the hospital waiting for a bed at an inpatient psychiatric facility, all for being true to who he was, and trying to grow into who he was created to be.

During my conversations with him and his family, I heard the breaking heart of a child simply needing to be loved, and the steadfast and dogmatic following of doctrine of parents convinced their child was possessed. The church was at the forefront of this. When faith is foundational to the building of a life, it is extremely difficult to question when that questioning is met with fury and rejection. If the parents accepted this child as he was, the church would abandon them as well. They had been plainly told this, I learned this through conversation. The parents were also hurting because of the inability of the church to love and accept differences. To that end they kept using their child's dead name (the name the child had moved past) instead of using the chosen name, and using she/her pronouns instead of the chosen he/him. In the room with this teen and his parents, every time they used his deadname, he visibly flinched and became smaller, collapsing further into misery. This was not the unconditional love of God, and the false authority of the church was behind it.

A middle aged woman asked to visit with a chaplain during her hospital stay. After establishing rapport with her, it quickly became clear she was carrying a heavy burden and had a need to tell her story. She was cautious in the beginning, asking about my own faith background and beliefs. As the tale unfolded, I understood why. As a young person, she realized that she was sexually attracted to other girls, and enjoyed making love with other girls. She had approached her youth pastor to talk about it. She had grown up in this church, and felt safe and supported in her relationship with Jesus and her faith community. Her childhood and teen years had been full of Vacation Bible Schools, Sunday school, summer church camp, even a mission trip overseas.

Spilling out her confusion to the youth pastor, she told me, felt like a safe and trusted space. The youth pastor listened to her, and advised that these feelings were best tucked away, they were not pleasing to God, they were of Satan. The sexual encounters were abhorrent and disgusting. She was told to marry young, have plenty of sex, and trust in the Lord to bring sexual desire for her husband. This is what she did, or tried to do.

Now a couple of decades later, she absolutely knew she was living a lie. While she loved her husband and children, she was miserable. She had met a woman and had been in a relationship with her for some time. The illness that led to her hospital stay had made her realize that life is short and not guaranteed. She was ready to live into her own wholeness and be who she was created to be, but because of the youth pastor's counsel, she had years of denying her true self to overcome. Because of the youth pastor's counsel she was going to emotionally hurt and damage her husband and children. This upheaval, angst, and suffering would not have been there had the church shown acceptance and love of her true self.

These stories, and many others, in tandem with my own reading of scripture and study, have brought me to the conclusion that the organization that claims to follow the teachings of Christ, otherwise known as the church, simply is not showing Jesus' love to those in the LGBTQIA+ community. The refusal to be open and affirming is not bringing people into a relationship with Jesus and setting them on the journey to being whole and fully human. Instead the refusal is placing doctrine, condemnation, and exclusion above love, acceptance, and hospitality. This needs to change.

Jessica Hiatt (she, her, hers) is a Humanist Chaplain for a large healthcare system, providing emotional and spiritual support to patients, their families, and staff. She received her MDiv from Northwest Nazarene University, and completed her Clinical Pastoral Education in Idaho. Jessica is a Court Appointed Special Advocate for children in foster care, and works with The Trevor Project. She is married with three grown children and lives in Oregon.

An Open Letter to the Church of the Nazarene, My Denominational "Mama"

LIBBY TEDDER HUGUS

In this parable of an open letter, I use an analogy to imagine the Church of the Nazarene as "Mama"—the denominational mother who nourished, loved, educated and blessed me into my adult life. She is also the "Mama" I have had to disassociate myself from in my personal pursuit of the practice faith and vocational ministry.

Dear Mama,

In your womb I was tucked safely in the dark cave of your body while God delighted in knitting me together neuron by nerve by cell. God entrusted me to you, knowing the wisdom of your parenting would lead me in the way I should go.

At my birth you smiled into my eyes, soothed my aching cries, told me I was beloved and oh-so-wanted. You whispered that you would do everything in your power to teach me about God's love. Soon thereafter you dedicated me to God's good provision, witnessed by the congregation. While I belonged to you, I belonged to something much, much bigger.

At your breast I found comfort and nourishment. I listened to you hum praise choruses and faith hymns, handed to you by your Mama and her Mama before her. I knew how much I was loved. You delighted to see me unfold as a human created in God's good and loving image.

At your feet I played and absorbed the traditions of your living, breathing faith system—rooted in years of tradition and fueled by fervent generations of resilient others longing for God's nearness. Wide-eyed and tender hearted, I trusted you and I trusted them.

At your table I was fed the Bread of Life, watered from the well that never runs dry. I was assured of my belovedness. I was challenged to understand belovedness as my birthright, as an open invitation to other hungry humans to belong and to be saved from a life separated from love. You asked me to spread the delicious bread crumbs everywhere I went.

In your baptismal fount, I was buried to my separate ways and raised into the living flow of God's communion; committed to being transformed in the Image of Love.

Beside you I observed and grew. I imitated you as you aimed to imitate God. I took wobbly steps in faith, influenced by those entrusted to teach. I was surrounded by Sunday School teachers and children's pastors and Caravans facilitators and preachers and choirs of the faithful singing those same choruses and hymns. Sundays, Wednesdays, revivals, camps, retreats, district and general assemblies, quizzing, year after year I learned to practice faith.

At your altars I wept in earnest pursuit of knowing God, making choices to follow wholeheartedly. I repented sincerely when I found myself separated from God's love.

From your womb, God and I communed. I knew God and God knew me. You introduced me to God's story. It was as wonderful as you taught me—and more so.

I began to think for myself, as little and curious, through the pure idealism of youth. I sincerely wanted to make sense of God's story, our story. You taught me that the founder of our faith tradition, the Reverend John Wesley, wanted us to filter our expression of faith through a "quadrilateral" (such a nerdy term, Mama) of reason, tradition, experience and scripture. Together we contrasted what you modeled to me with what I was experiencing as a human in the world.

Before entering high school, at an altar at National Youth Conference, I said "yes" to God's call to vocational ministry. I committed my trajectory to serving God within your system. It felt scary and big, but also felt freeing and joyful. I took sincere responsibility to inherit the Nazarene mantle.

But, Mama, through a teensy crack at the edges of how I understood and experienced you, dissonance seeped in. Not all denominations were like you. Not all Christians gathered for worship like you or organized or believed or required adherence to your social standards. Something about the version of the story you told me was… off. The mental models and my bodily experiences were not integrating.

Like all healthy adolescents, I questioned you. There were ways your faith practice was hyper-individualized; too caught up in the idea of holiness rather than the practice of love. Mama, I think you lost sight of Wesley's admonition that there can be no salvation until the *whole* is saved. You chose to love your polity, theology, politics and manual more than your neighbor. The focus of Jesus' greatest commandment got fuzzy. You claimed we were "called unto holiness" and set apart. But set apart from what and to what purpose? You invested so much energy protecting "us" rather than earnestly seeking the nourishment of the whole, especially those who pulled up a chair to the table looking starkly different than you.

Perhaps this "whack-a-mole" dynamic was my first clue. If there are too many "others" or enemies to be afraid of, maybe it's time to rethink who the enemy actually is. Afterall, there is no fear in love.

I felt especially uncomfortable about the strict rules you established around human sexuality. I had friends who did not fit the mold you prescribed as "holy enough." They were queer—all colors of the rainbow—and they were beautiful. They were not defiled, impure, or disgusting; they were hungry seekers of the Bread of Life too, thirsty for the water that will never run dry. They were imaginative and hospitable and justice seekers, just like us.

There was a distinct code switch I perceived between what you claimed and how you acted, and like an ear worm it began to eat its way through my identification as Nazarene. You trained me up in the way I should go, but the tracks were no longer parallel with my experience and reasoning of who and how God loves. The God who communed with me also delighted in queer community.

There simply is no "us and them" around God's table. The distinction doesn't exist. You were behaving like we had to hoard the bread crumbs from the hungry.

The tracks you were chugging along were rigid, prideful, and fearful. You invested so much energy proving yours were the only tracks God's holiness could ride. It's as if you came to trust your beliefs and assumptions about God more than God. You'd forced God into your image and couldn't trust the living love behind your assumptions. Do you see the dissonance? You don't referee holiness, Mama. God does. And God's love is boundless.

Why would the love and belonging applied to me at my birth not apply to my queer siblings? It is not for you to say whose DNA, sexual identity and gender expression is in or out. In God's love, there simply is no in and out—unless we choose to separate ourselves from it. Remember? The image? We're all created in it. Every single human you disagree with or refuse to understand is created in the same image. I am dearly wanted by God and so is every queer human.

We choose separation from God's love when our actions block participation with that love, not because of who we love or how we express our humanity. We choose that separation when we claim we're more inside the circle of love than our neighbor.

Off those harsh tracks, I began to pioneer a new path in embodying the faith you handed to me. There is a wide mercy beyond all expectation. There is a fierce inner wisdom connected to my very good body and my very good sexuality and all the other good bodies and sexualities represented under the rainbow.

While I belonged to you, I belonged to something much, much bigger. I learned to trust this belonging when your version of truth played referee to who is inbounds and who is not. You claimed I was pushing too close to the boundaries Mama, and there are no boundaries. We're all radically loved—including queer humans.

It was exhausting to reconcile the dissonance between your way of being in the world, and my new awareness beyond limiting assumptions and fears. I wanted to stay in the shelter of our familiar home. I wanted to advocate for the changes I had tasted as the wild mercy of inclusion. But you simply could not listen. Pride and fear and rigidity kept you from being willing to hear me share about what I had discovered about God's wide love.

I had to part ways with you to stay true to God and pursue my life's calling in vocational ministry. Dissonance management no longer served my participation in the disciple-making mission. It was too constrictive Mama. I had to turn in my credentials. I had to disassociate from you. I'll always be imprinted by your identity Mama, but God's full Rainbow Image is the only one I chose to mirror.

It was really painful to look you in the eyes and tell you this truth. Your eyes glistened with tears as we embraced and I turned to exit our home. Still, you've chosen not to change. I have come to terms with this. It grieves me. It makes me ache for what you have yet to experience of the Beloved—the same One who knit me together in your womb; of whom you sang over me at your breast; the One you taught me about in all those Sunday School classes, caravans, revivals, camps, District and General Assemblies, quizzing matches, late night conversations in college and strenuous courses in seminary… You've closed yourself off to an entire experience of God's delight in the array of a stunningly diverse family.

I miss you, Mama. And more than that: I ache for the fuller, wider, more hopeful and radically inclusive experience of God's love that *you* are missing. Because what you reject and exclude in your houses of worship and polity and statements of faith and Manual and polity and theology, you reject and exclude about the very same God you're aiming to honor.

Thank you Mama, for nurturing and educating me. Thank you for pointing me to the God beyond the rigid tracks you still insist on traversing. You don't have to throw it all out though, Mama, did you know that? Faith beyond Nazarene identification has the same roots, just more beautiful and juicy fruit than you have allowed yourself the pleasure of tasting.

I wonder if you'd like to explore what God is like outside your tightly clutched pearls of tradition and limiting beliefs? If you ever do, an incredibly blessed rainbow of humans will welcome you with sparkling eyes.

Come on in, the water is wide. Off the rippling tides of God's deep and bound-less love dance rainbow refractions of goodness. The queer community would love to show you just how deep and wide the currents of mercy are.

With all the love in my heart,
Libby

The Backstory to this Open Letter:

I am a former district licensed minister in the Church of the Nazarene, educated and graduated (with honors and recognized awards) from Nazarene institutions of higher learning. I was pursuing Ordination when I made the painful but liberating choice to part ways with my denominational Mama.

Now, as a Nazarene, I was as purebred as they come, inheriting a legacy from faithful Christians many of whom rooted their vocations in her soil. My family were Nazarene pastors, missionaries, church planters, professors, administrators, and a high-level denominational leader. My parents, brother, uncle and cousin, three maternal grandparents (two of whom were women), great-grandmother, and great-great grandmother are or were all ordained Nazarene ministers. Such a beautiful legacy to be gifted, especially in the rare form of *women* being validated in this calling. I loved and lead and ministered and worked for change within her bounds until I was 28.

And then I chose to leave, because I realized I could no longer belong to this particular denomination and remain true to my calling. When I used my intellect and experience to measure the matter of full queer inclusion in the body of Christ through the lens of the scriptures and tradition, my "Mama" was painfully lacking.

God's love was deeper, wider, and more colorful than her narrow aperture was asking me to perceive. God's feast was hosted around a more inclusive table than I was told to set. I chose to gather with other hungry folks 'in exile' around that table and be nourished by the merciful gospel I had come to treasure, the same one Mama taught me to seek after. I have not once regretted this choice in the decade since.

Finally, I want to offer an invitation.

For any of you seeking wider, more inclusive tables outside of Mama's walls: come join us. The exiled desert can be full of grief and loss, and it can be full of sweet nourishment and oasis. God's love is deep enough, God's table wide enough: please trust me on this.

For any of you seeking more inclusive tables within Mama's walls, consider how to organize your efforts on behalf of "the other," especially the voiceless. Does the polity, statements of faith, theology and practice of Mama's denomination integrate with a theology of love? Ask yourself: who is missing from this table? Why?

For any of you resisting the moral of the parable, that Mama's walls are keeping out those who are supposed to be invited in, please consider what you believe and have experienced about humans being created in God's Image. Is it an image of fear? An image of exclusion? An image that referees who is in and who is out? Why? Why not?

Dearly Beloved, God loved us first: let's act like it. May love always be our compass.

Libby Tedder Hugus is a reverend, coach, author & speaker. She offers her presence to the world as a spiritual midwife, wordsmith & human resonator. She believes there is always room for one more around the table: both at home and in God's family and that generous hospitality can and will heal the world. You can track her down at thetablecasper.org

Open and Affirming or
Closed and Condemning?

MONTY JACKSON

*I don't think the Nazarene church can become LGBTQ+
affirming fully. It takes a theology that sees inclusivity as a
prerequisite to the mission.*

I grew up in the Antelope Valley, a place in the high desert of Southern California. I am traditionally Seventh Day Adventist (SDA). The SDA church has over 21 million members worldwide, and in 2015 Pew research found Seventh Day Adventists to be "among the most racially and ethnically diverse American religious groups: 37% are white, while 32% are black, 15% are Hispanic, 8% are Asian and another 8% are another race or mixed race." I was baptized at age 10, and that day in Sabbath School, the teacher made a claim that touched my heart and caused my mind to question. The teacher congratulated us on our decision to be baptized and invited the other children to consider being baptized and joining the Seventh Day Adventists church.

She said those who do not accept the seventh day as the day of worship would *"bust hell wide open."* I was stunned. On the ride home in the station wagon, I asked Dad (a devoted First Elder in the SDA Church) if what my Sabbath School teacher said about people worshiping on the right day was true. Dad said yes. During the rest of the trip home, all I could think about were my friends who lived down the street from our house who I played ball with after school.

They were welcoming people. Their mom made the best lemonade and always invited us in. I questioned how a loving God could condemn these beautiful people for choosing the wrong day to honor and worship the Deity. Before reaching our driveway, in my silent monologue with God, I said, "God, if you would burn up my friends, then you can burn me up too." A god who would burn people for failing to choose and practice the Hebrew Sabbath law should be resisted. All earthlings should agree to revolt against any force or entity that thinks so little of the human.

Why I think the Church of the Nazarene should become fully LGBTQ+ affirming? Well, I'm not sure the Nazarene Church can. Before I took the call to pastor an open and affirming UCC Congregation, I sought the counsel of a friend, Rev. Scott Weiner, who asked me a simple question: *"What group of people do you want to spend your time with, people who are open and affirming or closed and condemning?"* Inclusivity is a prerequisite to the Christian mission. If the Nazarene Church adapted the label open and affirming, would the Church be more inviting for the right reason? What role does Nazarene theology play in creating the need for LGBTQ+ inclusion? How is it that those who claim prevenient grace do not assume prevenient grace for all? How can people claim a second work of grace, entire sanctification, and lack the spiritually mature act of welcome? Does Nazarene liturgy contribute to the need for being open and affirming? Is the Nazarene Church too insular?

Is this culture capable of progressing? I ask these questions because a shift to becoming an open and affirming people must be authentic, not just another church retention or numerical growth plan. What kind of work should be done before becoming this new "accepting" Nazarene Church? We know today most Americans support gay rights. Springtide survey shows that 71% of Gen-Zers care about LGBTQ+ rights. Many see evangelical Christian practices as hypocritical and harmful. The Church of the Nazarene's current sectarian views need a theological sea change and a cultural shift from a theology and theopraxis that promotes puritanical philosophy and dogma. In this religious practice, Holiness people are an exclusive club.

Before "affirming" the image of God in people who have been othered by the Christian faithful, maybe a conversation with the LGBTQ+ community should be a step in the process. How do we know if categorizing them with the gateway term "open & affirming" is not another way of Othering the splendid spectrum? The idea that a religious organization approves of a people group's humanity is problematic at best. The white American Church has a poor record of standing up for people different from them. Remember, there was a period in the south that after church service on Sunday, the "church picnic" often ended with the hanging of enslaved Black people:

> "In the "lynching era," between 1880 to 1940, white Christians lynched nearly five thousand black men and women in a manner with obvious echoes of the Roman crucifixion of Jesus. Yet these "Christians" did not see the irony or contradiction in their actions."　　—James H. Cone

Here is an example of how the Nazarene church has been welcoming. In the late '90s, I was invited by Rev. James Baughman to be the worship pastor at Lewiston First Church of the Nazarene. I accepted the offer and moved from the Antelope Valley to the beautiful Lewis Clark valley in Lewiston, Idaho. Lewiston, Idaho, and Clarkston, Washington, are divided by the lovely Snake River. Pastor Baughman's forward-thinking leadership invited an Afro-American who he thought was the right person to lead his all-white congregation in worship. On my first Sunday, before getting out of the car, my wife Patti, our children, who were toddlers at the time, and myself were greeted in the parking lot by the pastor and a couple of lay leaders. The police were there because someone shot the stained glass window out, and church leadership were concerned for our safety.

They wondered if I should lead worship that morning because there was concern that the stained glass shooting was racially motivated. Of course, that only made it clear to me that I was called to the right place at the right time. I sent my family home and led worship that morning with the covering of glory, with the fire of the spirit, and we got off to a great beginning. Together we sang a song I wrote, "Keep the Glory Down," inspired by the primary founder of the Church of the Nazarene, Phineas Bresee.

It should not take more than biblical truth to be an inclusive church. However, if it does, one of our early church fathers, St. Augustine, a Bishop in a North African town called Hippo, spoke about two books. He believed that God gave us two books that revealed God to us: first, the Book of Nature (the natural world) and second, the Book of Scripture, the Bible. These two books support one another, and Scripture and Nature reveal the splendid spectrum of God's truth. Both show God's handiwork. The saving image of God resides in all humanity. I choose to be open, affirming, and relational.

Rev. Monty Jackson, MDiv is the Pastor of Christ Church Maplewood UCC. He earned his Master of Divinity from Eden Theological Seminary. Jackson is an award-winning singer songwriter, music arranger and record producer.

Love Does No Harm

JENNIFER R. JENSEN

Reading Romans 13 as a radical call to do no harm as the holiest way of loving our neighbor.

As I write this essay that you are hopefully reading in the warm Indianapolis sunshine, it is the beginning of the liturgical new year, a chilly November day in Northwest Indiana. I read the lectionary verses this morning from the book of Romans. And while the passage today is probably not the most commonly used to denounce or exclude LGBTQIA+ Christians, in the NIV 1984, words like "orgies" and "sexual immorality" and "debauchery" are definitely bandied about as the lifestyle and behaviors of the queer community. The NIV 2011 tones it down a bit, mentioning "carousing" instead of "orgies." Verses like this in various places in scripture are pulled out of context and used as weapons against those who are faithfully following Jesus but also identifying as gay, bi, lesbian, or transgender. There are two problems: first, many in the LGBTQIA+ community are faithfully committed to a single partner and are definitely not engaging in orgies or carousing. Second, pulling verses out of context is a terrible practice that detracts from the beauty and harmony of scripture as a whole. That is certainly true of Romans 13: 11-14.

Looking just a few verses back in this chapter, Paul is writing about something different, something bigger than some classes of sin. Indeed, if you start the passage at verse 8, you can see that the essential theme in this chapter is not general sin at all, but rather, the invitation to love one another in a bigger way than ever before, so that the sins he is calling out are specifically in the context of being hurtful to one another, of being anti-love. Paul says in verse 10 that love does no harm to its neighbor. Therefore love is the fulfillment of the law. As he continues to describe love and admonish Christians to put aside deeds of darkness and put on the light of love, it is clear that his meaning is inclusive of the previous verses—behave decently, do no harm, skip the behaviors (including drunkenness, dissension, and jealousy) that so often harm us or others. The desires Paul goes on to describe in verse 14 are selfish ones, those that put us in positions to create pain and suffering and that go very much against the idea of doing no harm.

Thus, Paul is defining sinfulness this way: engaging our own desires in ways that cause hurt, pain, damage to our neighbor. Leaping ahead to a Wesleyan, perhaps specifically Nazarene even, definition of sinfulness—willful disobedience to a known law of God—it is not a significant extrapolation to suggest that we can distill sin to disobeying God by damaging someone else through our actions and enhance our understanding of holiness to its broadest definition: obeying God by loving one another and doing no harm to our neighbor. Theologically speaking, if we review scripture in its entirety these two assertions are easily identifiable as to both the character and actions of God, a useful and sound way to interpret all scripture. God is love and God calls us to love in the way that God loves.

A lot of words could be used to split hairs over whether or not LGBTQ+ individuals are born that way or choose it, whether or not there are so-called "clobber" verses and how they can be applied, whether or not being gay and living a "gay lifestyle" are two different things, and why or how that matters to the conversation of inclusion or exclusion. I am quite positive others will explore those themes and discuss the various beliefs and Bible texts to back their perspective up. But if we get our arms around this definition of holiness—obey God by loving one another and doing no harm to our neighbor—it doesn't matter what anyone believes about any of those things because harm is being done. Harm is being done in the name of the God who loves. Harm is being done by people who claim they love Jesus. Harm is being done intentionally, unintentionally, and with the full backing of an entire holiness denomination that should know better. And it must stop.

Don't worry, I heard the defensive wheels revving as soon as you read that last paragraph: "But if it's sin and we don't speak it they go to hell," and "it's not love if we are not pointing out sin," and "I've never harmed anyone in my life, and certainly not in God's name!" I understand how you could be confused. After all, the voices we've heard from the pulpit haven't always done a great job of helping us understand the reality we live in as well as they could have. The reality of our Christian faith is that we have a long historical precedent of doing harm in the name of God: pastors advocating slavery, Christians participating in passing along misinformation related to Muslims, holiness churches supporting misogynist and racist practices, including funding Ku Klux Klan chapters around the US. Of course, these are all separate and distinct from the issue at hand, but certainly, this is a small list of recent past acts undertaken in the name of Jesus and perpetuating harm to individuals that we should, as Christ-followers, consider our neighbors.

And as for you harming the LGBTQ+ community? I don't make accusations without receipts, so here are several examples of you, as a Christian, allowing or supporting harm to folks because their sexual preferences, orientations, and/or gender identities differed from your own, or what you believe the Bible clearly says:

1. Excluding or disavowing pastors who actively serve their community or preach the gospel from service or ministry—even when they follow celibacy mandates or rules, simply because they identify as gay, trans, or lesbian. This is a horrible exclusion, particularly for someone who is already making a sacrifice to be affiliated with a church. Worse, once they are excluded as leaders of any stripe, they are often treated poorly by their church family—who hold revocation of membership over their heads for any inkling of a relationship, but also refuse to be the community of love they need to continue a life of celibacy.

2. Refusing to acknowledge the pronouns or new name of a transgender person. This is particularly true if you are the family member of a person who identifies as gender non-conforming. This causes harm in several ways. Not only increasing the likelihood of at least a suicide attempt (42% of transgender adults in a 2016 study confessed to an attempt) it also increases the risk of drug abuse and alcoholism (26% in the same study reported this as a means to cope with transgender-related discrimination). It seems that actively participating in actions that increase the likelihood of self-harm and illicit substance dependence ought to be a no-brainer. It is not difficult to adjust to new pronouns, to new names, to new identities, and it is far easier than comforting the grieving parent of a deceased child.

3. Actively misinforming others or believing that drag queens or kings, trans people, or LGBTQIA+ people are recruiting children or grooming them or abusing them, while simultaneously rigorously ignoring sexual abuses and misdeeds occurring in a church or parachurch organization. Churches have shown themselves to be far more dangerous to children and young adults, especially when accountability is non-existent. How many churches hold up the pastor(s) as unquestionable authorities and yet rail against men dressing as women, as though makeup on a man is more scary than unbridled power? The truth is that the performers at a drag show are far less dangerous than the Christians who bomb power plants or shoot unarmed attendees at those shows. The constant errant narrative of "grooming" by LGBTQIA+ people is hurting not only the

LGBTQIA+ community, but children who are being harmed by others, and those who believe the falsehoods and take other lives in an effort to "save the children."

4. Opposing adoption or foster parenting by LGBTQIA+ parents. Although same-sex couples are legally able to adopt in all 50 states, faith-based agencies will still deny or obstruct adoptions or foster care by gay or lesbian couples. This is harmful, again, to children. In Kansas where foster care is run by contractors statewide, agencies are permitted to refuse LGBTQIA+ couples to foster, if doing so conflicts with their religious beliefs. This is in a state that has had children sleeping in agency offices. It seems counter intuitive to think that a child is better off sleeping under someone's desk versus in a bed, simply because the potential parents are the same gender.

5. Dead-naming a trans person or deliberately using the wrong pronouns. Doing this is an intentionally hurtful thing and respecting pronouns and names is the bare minimum of not doing harm. It is not unprecedented nor is it unbiblical: Jacob became Israel in Genesis, which was representative of an entire nation. I don't think God would have thought it was hard to call them by the right name, nor do I think God appreciates you dead-naming a trans person as a way of proving your rightness. It's harmful and not loving.

If you review the short list I have provided and determine that in the interest of being a Jesus follower, it is far more important to be judgmental about the sinfulness of homosexuality than to consider the harmfulness of these behaviors, I wonder who it is that you do follow, because it isn't Jesus. Jesus told everyone not to harm children. Jesus also admonished the disciples about criticizing someone who was healing in Jesus name but not part of their group. Scripture tells us that God hates lying, and in Acts we see the Holy Spirit moving particularly against those who lie in conjunction with their faith. When we see God giving us instruction, so explicitly, against things that actively harm others and then we do things that actively harm others, we are not serving the Church or following God or being Christlike—indeed, we are being anti-Christ.

I am of the opinion that, in accordance with the already issued statement of the Church of the Nazarene, being LGBTQIA+ is not a sin. Identifying as having a particular sexual desire, as ascribing to a non-binary or transgender identity is also not a sin, as for the most part these are cultural and not sexual constructs. Where they are sexual constructs (i.e. someone is undergoing gender-affirming medical care), they are still not a sin. Indeed, the acceptance of the eunuch in Acts for baptism seems to be a pretty clear indication that gender is a non-issue for Christ followers. And when we look at where there is harm being done, we have to ask are the LGBTQIA+ individuals the ones who are being unloving? Are they the ones excluding others? Are they the ones who are rejecting and judging? To that end, if we return to my original assertion that being holy has a broad definition—obeying God by loving one another and doing no harm to our neighbor—then the only way to be holy is to be 100% affirming. Because at the moment, we are the ones, as supposed entirely sanctified Christians, who are doing the most harm.

I am an ordained elder in the Church of the Nazarene, and I know full well what I risk, just by writing this essay. Losing my credential will be disheartening, but the day was coming when I would have to turn it in voluntarily, because the Holy Spirit continues to whisper that holding it is doing harm, because silence is acceptance.

I have an obligation to love first, to stand for a holiness doctrine that does no harm and loves my neighbor: my lesbian neighbor, my gay neighbor, my bi neighbor, my trans neighbor, my queer neighbor, my intersex neighbor, my asexual neighbor. My neighbor. Because love does no harm to a neighbor.

Rev. Jennifer R. Jensen *is an ordained elder in the Church of the Nazarene. She serves as an associate pastor on the Northwest Indiana district and bi-vocationally, works as a consultant for computer software. She has a business degree from Olivet Nazarene University and a Master of Education.*

The Gospel According to Footloose

JEFF KEONI LANE

A truly loving Nazarene ethic isn't about purity or polity but it is about particularity. In every new age the Church of the Nazarene should be known as the people who make room for the marginalized in society and those people today are our LGBTQ family and friends.

Years ago I was heading from the airport to a conference with a fellow Nazarene pastor when our cab driver asked "What is a Nazarene?" I deferred to my friend who, to my surprise, began to explain how our identity follows from the Nazarite purity vows, committing to practices like abstaining from alcohol. As I listened I realized they had a very different perspective about the ethic at the core of what it means to be a "Nazarene."

I think everything you need to know about Nazarene ethics you can learn from watching movies from 1984.

If you mention ethics and the Bible, people usually start by talking about the explicit imperatives like the "Thou shalt nots" of the Decalogue and to a lesser extent various constraints like prohibitions against eating pelican. The commands to not steal, or lie or covet the objects or relationships of a neighbor are generally held to always be good form and good for shaping communities.

Failing to live up to these principles generally wears away at the strength of a society. If a colleague has a penchant for poaching, you might be less inclined to leave your lunch in the office fridge. If someone is known to be violent or untrustworthy, they will probably have trouble finding a roommate who doesn't feel the need to sleep with one eye open.

Viewing ethics as principles to be obeyed or embodied reminds me of the 1984 film Gremlins, in which a young adult is gifted an unusual creature at Christmas. At the outset we see that there are three simple rules to caring for this exotic pet, and if they are adhered to then life will continue normally. But if you end up exposing them to light, or dousing them in water, or God forbid feeding them after midnight, then your whole town will end up in disaster. Being sure to obey these rules is the difference between living with a cute and furry animal or a mischievous monster.

From Gremlins we might learn that many of the commands or rules in the Bible we view as principles demonstrate the sacred and stabilizing significance that authority and identity can play in a community or a relationship. For example, in the early days of Hebrew covenants, God commanded the people who identified as part of the covenant made with Abraham to be circumcised. This was a specific physical sign that a male belonged to the Israelites. Sometimes ethics and belonging are simply just that clear cut.

Living by a series of ethical laws is definitely illustrative of my experience in the Church of the Nazarene since childhood, though the litmus test has changed from time to time. In my experience the rules that judged whether someone "belonged" have ranged from how many weekly services they attended, whether you had been divorced, whether they drank alcohol or even who they voted for in the last election. But today more than any, the ethical test at the heart of our community's conversation is your willingness to extend a full welcome to our many brothers and sisters, sons and daughters who are a part of the LGBTQ community.

In the late Spring of 2004, I was called to a meeting of Nazarene pastors to consider a public response to the recent Massachusetts Supreme Judicial Court ruling essentially legalizing same-sex marriage in the state. That day there were a number of ideas floated on the table from educational support to churches to full page ads in opposition to the decision. In the end we decided to table it and never ended up creating any real response. But looking back on that day I realized the spirit of the proposals themselves were in line with this Nazarene ethic that we are protectors of a certain set of rules and identities similar to the Nazarite vows of purity.

In the film Ghostbusters, in the opening foray into busting ghosts, Egon, one of the proton pack-wearing protagonists, admonishes them to never "cross the streams". This is their Nazarite moment. But later in the climax of the film Egon suggests that crossing the streams might be their only hope, thus saving all of humanity from interdimensional oppression.

Watching Ghostbusters teaches us that some laws and absolutes occasionally cannot be applied universally and absolutely, no matter how much those rules may have girded your identity in the past. The practice of "descending into the particulars" was made a part of the tradition of those who study the Christian scriptures by among others the Jesuits who understood that in certain situations these laws could not be applied unilaterally.

For example take the biblical law "thou shalt not steal." Generally speaking I think we would all agree that stealing is amoral. But what about for someone who is starving? What if your children are starving?

When I was in high school I stole a hubcap from a tire to replace one my friend had lost while we were joyriding in his father's van. I don't recollect for a moment even thinking about the ethical nature of doing it. I simply saw a similar van in our school parking lot and walked over and popped it off. It wasn't until I realized it was the school's culinary arts van and the head chef was outside watching me pop it off on his smoke break that I began to realize the wrongness of my actions. (Don't worry, after I outran the chef and got away from school for an hour, I ended up returning it.) But in that case I think it's pretty clear I was in the wrong. The law of "thou shalt not steal" holds.

But imagine you are faced with the dilemma like the nuns in the end of the Sound of Music trying to help the Von Trapps escape the Nazis by confiscating their carburetors. In that case you might descend into the particulars and find a different answer.

Similarly, in the historic cases of usury or equivocation we recognize that sometimes situations call us to reimagine our ethical application of what may have seen as easily applicable admonishments. Sometimes situations call us to reconsider the sanctity of our standards.

Growing up in a "Nazarene" church but not necessarily a "Nazarene" home allowed me to see some of the principles of the denomination with more clarity. There were certainly principles that existed in both worlds like avoiding killing, stealing and the like. But the strict prohibitions against movies, alcohol, dancing or sports on Sundays weren't really absolutes outside Sunday and Wednesday services. In that way the Nazarene ethic was less about owning these absolutes and more about avoiding "their" observation.

I remember seeing a Nazarene administrator joyfully "dancing" around at a college event who immediately got defensive and angry when they realized it was being filmed. I remember traveling for a Nazarene trip and the fear that some of the members felt that it might be discovered that we had gone to see a movie. Thankfully much of those Nazarite ways are in our past. There are times that the Church of the Nazarene has allowed situations to reconsider the necessity and universality of our standards, but then there are other times our reconsidcration must come from our openness to relationships.

The 1984 film Footloose is the story of an outsider, Ren McCormack, played by Kevin Bacon, who comes into town and begins questioning the limits that have been placed on them. Many of the restrictions were a reaction to some of the local kids who had died in a car crash after a night of dancing outside of town. In response the town instituted "Nazarite" like rules against dancing and certain forms of entertainment. Townsfolk are seen railing against rock music and burning books. At first Ren has trouble understanding the restrictions of the town, but eventually he begins to gain perspective about the reactionary reasoning and the rendered relationships that shape the disconnect between the town and its youth. Ren has a famous scene in which he rallies support to have a school dance that had been barred in the past. In the town meeting he even quotes scriptures in the face of the prominent town pastor.

Now I used to think that Ren's scene was a textbook case on how to use scripture adversarially, quoting passages that affirmed dancing in the Bible. It seemed only reasonable that if they were going to use religion to galvanize their position then he would weaponize the text to lay siege. But when you listen to his speech you see that Ren does not simply use scripture "against" them and their "Nazarite" tendencies but he expresses an understanding of their perspective and shows how the scriptures speak not only to a broader more nuanced vision of their rules against dancing but even more importantly the potential costs of their strained relationship with their kids.

In the newly forming church in Acts 15 a number of the church leaders are gathering to decide how to incorporate all the uncircumcised gentiles into their sect of the Abrahamic faith. If they applied the principles precisely then the process of inclusion was clear. The partakers from the party of the Pharisees in the process were seemingly fine with the price the gentiles would have to pay to receive entrance into the church. The apostles who had been traveling abroad building relationships with the greater gentile world came back; they were able to offer a report that God's Spirit was present with the Gentile believers in the same way that the Spirit was present in the fellowship of the believers in Jerusalem.

When Peter, Paul, Barnabas and James advocate for the inclusion of the gentiles they are not making an argument based on principles or a particular situational ethic, but a plea based in their perspective. They had a firsthand account of the new thing that God had been doing to broaden their circles of belonging and brought the perspective that was so sorely needed in this situation. Like many Nazarene leaders I know firsthand the many gay and transgender people who live lives full of the Spirit of God. To exclude them from full participation is not only a disservice to them but a loss to our denomination as well.

If I could go back to that cab driver and define for him what it means to be a Nazarene I would proudly tell the story that I always claimed as our identity, the passage in John 1 where Nathaniel responds to Philip "Nazareth! Can anything good come from there?" The proudest moments of being a Nazarene have been witnessing the church that welcomes and includes and stands in solidarity with those in our world who need inclusion. From abolition to women in leadership, our Wesleyan Holiness heritage comes with a long history of making room for the marginalized.

I have witnessed great moments where the Church of the Nazarene has been a force for inclusion across racial, socio-economic, gender and political differences. This is an opportunity once again for the Church of the Nazarene to rise to its mission to stand in solidarity with millions of LGBTQ family and friends and their allies and welcome them into full inclusion.

That is the Nazarene ethic of which we should all be proud.

Jeff Keoni Lane is a pastor and teacher. He earned his MDiv from Nazarene Theological Seminary and his STM from Boston University School of Theology. Lane is the co-author of The Samaritan Project *and* Theology of Luck. *He serves as a pastor at West Somerville Church of the Nazarene.*

The Earth Is Full Already!

MARSHA LYNN

Earth's human population is growing at an alarming rate.
Perhaps greater gender and sexual diversity is a natural
response to overpopulation.

In Genesis 9, after the flood waters receded, God told Noah and his family to "be fruitful and increase in number; multiply on the earth and increase upon it" (Genesis 9:7 NIV).

In November 2022, earth's estimated population surpassed eight billion people. It seems safe to say we have obeyed the command to multiply on the earth. In the part of southern Indiana, USA, where my husband and I lay claim to five acres of trees, grass, garden, and running creek water, Wikipedia tells me there are around 75 people per square mile. In contrast, the world's most densely populated cities have closer to 75,000 per square mile. That level of density is beyond my comprehension. Obviously, the people in those cities are not able to grow enough food to feed themselves. Earth is showing signs of stress from the burden of sustaining its current human population. We are full up.

One question to ask is: Will someone (Someone?) or something eventually put the brakes on? Whether one believes that God, natural evolution, civil government, or fate is responsible, it seems clear something needs to change if earth is to remain habitable for future generations. Whether it be a global pandemic, war, starvation, genocide, or some other controlling force, earth's human population growth must slow in order to thrive and leave room for other species as well as agriculture.

Along those lines, I have been pondering a "what if…" question:

What If…

What if whatever Force or force will cap earth's human population brings multiple resources to the table? Would some of those tools involve lowering the human fertility rate? Contraceptives are a start: various means to prevent human sperm from uniting with human eggs. Maybe, however, that is just one part of the solution. Maybe human sexuality needs more basic modifications: Either a lower sex drive or alternative means for sexual expression that do not lead to unplanned pregnancies.

We already seem to be seeing this sort of force at work. Fertility rates are dropping in many areas. There are multiple reasons for this. An increase in homosexuality is one. The human sex drive remains strong, but no longer automatically seeks to unite sperm with egg.

What if a growing portion of the population with same-sex attraction is a natural response to an overpopulated planet rather than sinful?

But What About the Bible?

Many people will offer Bible passages and claim that homosexual relations are obviously a sin. There are multiple possible responses to that, but for my purposes here, I will simply note that there is no reference in the Bible to anything resembling the long-term, same-sex, loving relationships we find in our society today. It isn't mentioned as a temptation or struggle for believers nor as a common practice in secular society.

Those who insist that biblical texts clearly apply to the type of committed unions between consensual adults we are seeing in the 21st century also need to consider that those words date back to a time when the world population was less than 200 million. Is it possible we are in a different age now in terms of what is good for humanity and our host planet? Do we need to be open to a new view of human sexuality and reproduction? Is God once again doing "a new thing among us" (Isaiah 43:19)?

Is Physical Diversity the Result of Sin?

In John 9, Jesus' disciples questioned him about the source of sin in a man born blind. It is easy to understand their confusion. It doesn't seem fair that a child would suffer a lifetime of blindness because one or both parents sinned. On the other hand, how can a newborn baby be guilty of sin? The part of the puzzle they did not question was that blindness was punishment for sin. Jesus' response was that neither the parents nor the child was to blame. No sin lay behind the blindness. The disciples' underlying assumption was incorrect. Much like Job's friends in the Old Testament and many others through the years, they had been taught to blame misfortune on sin, but Jesus explained that was not the case.

Today we know there are many different causes for blindness. Some people are born blind, others inherit or develop diseases of the eyes, others lose their sight due to accidents or poor choices by themselves or others. Regardless of the cause, however, blindness in itself is not a sign of moral deficiency. Nor is excellent vision a sign of moral superiority. Vision or the lack thereof is a physical attribute, not a moral issue.

Few, if any, people today associate impaired vision with sin. Those who experience such impairment may even reach the point where they do not view it as a disability. It is part of who they are, has shaped them into the person they are becoming, and is "normal" for them. Blind people often enjoy being more in touch with their other senses than other people. Perhaps that is why Jesus consistently asked people what they wanted before healing them. Were some people he encountered reluctant to leave the familiar behind? What if physical differences that seem "broken" to us, are "normal" for those experiencing them?

Being Sinister

I am left-handed. As soon as I was able to grasp objects as a baby, my mother noticed I would move anything placed in my right hand to my left. Left-handedness is not something I chose as a child. Like approximately 10% of humans, I was born that way. With enough motivation and effort, I might have been able to adjust to using my right hand for writing, eating, and shaking those baby rattles, but it certainly was not my natural inclination. As I grew, I persisted in being left-handed, despite the example of my right-handed parents, siblings, and friends.

The Latin word for right is *dexter*, as in dexterous, skilled. The Latin word for left is *sinister*, as in menacing. In many times and places favoring one's left hand has been seen as sinister. I am relieved to have never been pushed to use my "correct" (right) hand where my left was more capable. Undoubtedly, a large part of that was the full acceptance of my preference by my parents and their advocacy for me as a child. If I had run into adults who expressed disapproval of my hand preference, I would be no less left-handed, but I might deal with shame, guilt, and self-doubt, something that has never plagued me in this regard. Being left-handed is something I have long regarded as making me part of a fun subset of the population, even when inconvenient. In a group setting, I often look around to find my fellow "lefties." The 1 in 10 ratio holds pretty true. In a group of thirty, I expect to find at least two other lefties and usually do. And those people are no more or less sinister than the rest of the group. Despite what many have thought through time and space, right-handed people are not morally superior to us "sinister" left-handers. At this point in life, if I were offered a "cure" for left-handedness, I would decline. Being left-handed is normal for me and part of my identity.

Diversity

What if we could view those outside the cisgender population the way most people see left-handedness? I recently encountered a young man I first noticed several years ago when he was a student at the local high school. When he mentioned his boyfriend, I thought to myself, "He is gay! I *knew* there was something special about him!" As that thought came to me, I realized that even though I am fully heterosexual, I seem drawn to young people who fall outside the norms. I like their nonconformity and flair. They are part of a special subset of the population that appeals to me, another "club" of exceptions to the norm, like being left-handed.

Different? Yes. Sinister? Not as far as I can see. In fact, many LGBTQ people made a commitment to Christ as children and were initially devastated to discover that their developing sexuality cast any romantic interest they might have as sinful in the eyes of the church. Many continue to live as followers of Jesus Christ, despite how few churches offer them full fellowship and acceptance and how inclined many church people are to dismiss their faith as false.

Perhaps a shift in what we see as acceptable in terms of sexuality is what we need at this stage of human development. The earth is full already! Why would we insist on calling what seems to be naturally increasing within humanity in an overpopulated world sinister or evil? As I look around at creation, I see that God loves diversity. Why would sexual diversity in the human experience be different? Especially diversity that helps slow down population growth in an overpopulated world? People outside the norms have much to offer! My world is a better place because of them.

Marsha Lynn enjoyed three careers before retirement—electrical engineer, then full-time mother, and finally a public library director. She has also served in multiple areas of ministry in her local church. She first considered theological questions as a child in the Church of the Nazarene and continues to ponder them in her retirement years.

Do No Harm as a Wesleyan Ethic for Inclusion

MEGAN MADSEN, NEÉ KREBS

Exclusivist theology harms the LGBTQIA+ community; at minimum loving our neighbors means not harming them.

I used to be a Nazarene. I was even ordained as a Nazarene elder after serving the denomination faithfully for a number of years. Both my college and seminary degrees are from Nazarene institutions of higher learning. It was the denomination where my faith was nurtured, where I experienced a call to ministry and an affirmation of that call, where I learned how to be a pastor and a theologian. I used to say "our" denomination. A part of me will always grieve what I lost. But now, I am a proud United Methodist, serving on a Conference that is wholeheartedly affirming of the LGBTQIA+ community. All means all for us.

When I became a Methodist, I learned about John Wesley's Three Rules. When he founded the Methodist movement, he offered these three simple rules for being a Methodist as the only requirement. They are part and parcel to our Methodist identity. They are Do No Harm, Do Good, and Stay in Love with God.

Upon first glance, these rules seem very simple, indeed! Yet, how truly difficult they are. "Do No Harm" is not simply to avoid active harm by not murdering or not stealing. It is also to reject and dismantle systems that harm our neighbors, like racial disparities in housing, education, policing, and many other areas. Perhaps, it is to choose local produce and local farming, instead of outsourcing for a cheaper tomato. Maybe it's recycling, reducing, and reusing as a way of loving God's good creation. It is to choose the well-being of our neighbors above our own comforts, whether those neighbors are human or not. Critically, it is to refuse to harm those made in God's image simply because they are made in that image.

Likewise, "Do Good" is simple to say, yet so much more difficult to embody! This is a call to leave no good undone, as much as it is a call to actively do good in the world. One might say that the calling of Jesus to love God with all that we are and to love our neighbor aligns pretty well with the Three Rules. We cannot love our neighbors if we are harming them. We cannot love our neighbors if we are not doing good to and for them. We can only love our neighbors best when we are growing and learning on the journey of our relationship with God.

The Church of the Nazarene split out of the Methodist Church, and one of the things that was left behind in the divorce was these Three Rules. For us Methodists, these rules have become our metric for how we participate in and respond to the needs of the world.

In some ways, the Church of the Nazarene has a similar ethical standard by which it can illuminate what God has called its people to. This metric is the very name of the Church of the Nazarene. This denomination was named after Christ Jesus's hometown, Nazareth. In John 1:46, Nathanael asks if anything good can come from such a place. This is the name that the Church of the Nazarene has chosen to align itself with. Not Christ's divinity but with Christ's humble humanity. This name was chosen to call members of your denomination into an identity where followers of Jesus were always called to return to the margins of society. To be identified with those that are rejected, oppressed, and deprived. To align themselves with those in need of both compassion and justice. In Methodist terms, it is the call and commitment to Do No Harm and to Do Good by Staying in Love with God.

Reclaiming use of Wesley's Three Rules, specifically the call to Do No Harm, offers a clear path forward regarding the Church of the Nazarene's posture toward the LGBTQIA+ community. That path is full inclusion and affirmation.

In the interest of integrity, nobody familiar with the United Methodist Church can claim that we are innocent of committing this harm. This essay, however, is directed to those who continue in relationship with the Church of the Nazarene, not from a place of judgment but from one who used to count myself among you.

There are many denominations who hold the same stance as the Church of the Nazarene, which is that sexual orientation is *not* sinful but any acting on a same-sex attraction *is*. Even if the highest ideals of the Church of the Nazarene's commitment to this stance were embodied, this is a still harmful theology. And bad theology kills. This is not hypothetical or exaggeration. Harm is being done to our neighbors by non-affirming theology.

It is high time that followers of Jesus reckon with this truth—we have done untold harm to our LGBTQIA+ neighbors. We have tied weights around their feet and asked them to swim. According to Jesus, it would be better if we put those weights on our own necks (Matthew 18:6). The rates of depression, suicide attempts and completion, and many other mental illnesses skyrocket among

LGBTQIA+ people who are *not* accepted by their families and by their faith communities. The rates increase by four times compared to their peers. One of the best ways to combat depression and suicide attempts among LGBTQIA+ youth? For these children to experience acceptance and love from their families. Having *a single adult* accept and affirm them reduces the risk of suicide by 40%. This data is readily available at The Trevor Project, which provides resources and support to youth who identify as LGBTQIA+ and those who wish to support them.

As followers of Jesus who take seriously the call to Do No Harm, we have to reflect seriously and critically on this information. These numbers are staggering. The quickest way to Do Good for a young person who is LGBTQIA+ is to simply love and accept them as they are. It bears noting here that love has no asterisks. We cannot love a person and reject core aspects of their identity. Banish forever the words, "I love you, but…" Trauma and harm are being done because well-meaning followers of Jesus are rejecting our own children, siblings, parents, cousins, friends. In other words, because we have failed to love our neighbor as ourself.

The statistics mentioned above may seem distant, so I will share specific ways I have witnessed and experienced harm due to a non-affirming theology.

A curious thing started to happen as I learned more about scripture, the history of Jesus' church, and about God, I began to change my mind about things I had been taught to assume. One of these shifts took place in college. During those years, a number of my closest friends began to come out of the closet. These were peers who I knew and loved. Friends I had prayed and worshiped with. They were just as full of faith and trust in God as I was. They desired to follow Jesus as much as I did. Yet they were also gay, bi, or trans.

For years, I'd believed what I had heard, that this was a choice that only people who were against God would choose. Yet my *actual* experience with *actual* people who are LGBTQIA+ was the exact opposite of those claims. These were good people, trying their best to live as members of Christ's Kin-dom, as reflections of Jesus in the world.

I could no longer reconcile the God who Jesus described with excluding my friends and neighbors from full participation in a Christian life simply because they were LGBTQIA+. Scripture paints the picture of a God who knows us and loves us as we are. This is a God who comes to humanity in flesh, in the body of a poor person from a bad neighborhood. A colonized person living under the reign of Rome, who grew up witnessing violent oppression enacted against his own people. This Jesus is God-with-us, yet his teachings were being used to harm people made in God's image. I could reach only one conclusion—either God loved all of us, or God loved none of us. I chose to believe in God's love.

During this time, I was studying at a Nazarene university that I loved. Yet, this institution was actively harming my queer friends. They were having scholarships taken away for merely being gay, let alone actually dating someone of the same sex. Others were afraid to come out—who could afford tens of thousands of dollars a year without scholarships? There were members of the faculty being punished for not reporting these students to the administration. This is real and lifelong financial and psychological harm.

The Nazarene seminary I attended fired a gay staff member after receiving backlash from members of the Church of the Nazarene for his sexual orientation. His fireable offense? Being gay. This was admitted in legal proceedings. The courts, however, decided that it is *legal* for religious institutions to commit acts that meet the legal requirement of bigotry and prejudice if their theology justifies it. More financial and psychological harm.

How many young Nazarenes have been sent to conversion therapy? A harmful practice deemed abusive and cruel by all therapeutic bodies in the United States. How many have experienced bullying or rejection? How many have been welcomed into a church until they desire membership? How many have felt forced to pretend to be straight for years, hiding their most authentic self from the world, fearing that God will reject them in the same way as their church home?

Even being an ally to the LGBTQIA+ community is punishable in the Church of the Nazarene. Districts across the United States are targeting young clergy who hold an affirming stance. These are folks who fit the required mold—they are straight, often married in a heterosexual relationship and serving the church in sacrificial ways. Yet if this pastor tells the truth, that they support full inclusion of LGBTQIA+ people in the Church of the Nazarene, this person faces loss of ordination, district licensing, and job loss. This doesn't even speak toward the deeply painful loss of community and relationships.

Harm was being done. Harm is being done now. This is not the way of Jesus. This is not the way of the Nazarene.

You might say that I have walked in both worlds in the church—the side that does not welcome LGBTQIA+ people and a world where all really means all. Before, I used to secretly research safe places for my LGBTQIA+ colleagues to worship. Now I get to step into God's work among all people. I get to extend apology and healing and hope because our God does love queer folks, without any asterisks.

Rev. Megan Madsen, neé Krebs, *is a United Methodist elder in the Pacific Northwest Conference. She earned her bachelors from Northwest Nazarene University and her MDiv from Nazarene Theological Seminary. She was ordained in the Church of the Nazarene in 2018 and received by the UMC by Safe Harbor protocols in 2022. She lives and pastors in Spokane, Washington with her husband and two dogs.*

The Jesus Lens

LON MARSHALL

When deciding on sexuality questions, I have looked to Bible interpretation, communal discernment, personal relationships, and Jesus' example.

In 1928, the conditions were right for an alignment of church traditions around the hermeneutical concept of inerrancy: the idea that the Bible has no errors. It is written as God spoke it, and we are to take it literally. Well, most of it. This was the era of the Scopes Monkey Trial, the rise of evolution, and the scientific method. There was an "evil" development called Modernity, and these aligned churches were mounting their forces against it.

The newly formed Church of the Nazarene, just 20 years old, comprised many traditions, including people that were drawn to this alignment. At the 1928 Church of the Nazarene General Assembly, influential leaders tried to make an amendment to the scripture Article of Faith, to say that scripture is inerrant.

Enter H. Orton Wiley. He was a pastor and theologian in the early Church of the Nazarene. Actually, he was the first pastor of the church I served in right out of graduate school and freshly married. He wrote the 3 volumes of systematic theology most taught in Church of the Nazarene higher education. I still have mine.

Wiley worked behind the scenes to craft the wording of this decisive Article of Faith that would be voted on by delegates at that critical hinge in history. Some 36 years ago, I wrote a term paper about this very issue. I titled it "The Nazarene Trojan Horse." A great deal of that paper was predicated on personal interviews I had with the late Paul Bassett at Nazarene Theological Seminary.[1] There is also a small pamphlet titled "All Things Necessary to Our Salvation," by Michael Lodahl. H. Orton Wiley's critical intervention is reported there as well.

---

1. You can read it yourself: LonMarshall.com/NazTrojanHorse.pdf

Wiley decided to use the word 'plenary' as his adjective for scripture. After doing my homework, I believe this was a strategy to keep the Wesleyan-Holiness hermeneutic intact. The Nazarene Church in theory is a large tent. Space is made for a wide spectrum of theological views distinctively Wesleyan-Holiness. Plenary is just vague enough to fit into the pattern. Many of the doctrines allow for a wide understanding. Baptism can be poured, submerged, and sprinkled. There is even an allowance for infant baptism. The Second coming will happen, but not specified before, during, or after tribulation. So scripture is plenary and not inerrant.

Plenary means full, or complete. A plenary session means all the members are present. An engineering understanding of a plenary drive means it runs all the way through, and the word is primarily used in archetypes as a type of scaffolding or storyboard, later having no bearing on function.

Wiley wanted to emphasize the essential idea about a Wesleyan Holiness understanding of scripture. It contains *all things necessary to our salvation.* Everything else was up for communal discernment. Wiley shared a view with other Wesleyan scholars that inspiration of scripture was a cooperative effort of the Holy Spirit and human beings. That means he left room for mistakes, cultural influence, lost in translation, contradictions and other foibles of which we humans are capable.

I am a convinced Mennonite, but I am a cradle Nazarene. My parents decided to follow Jesus not long after they were married in 1961. It happened at an altar of prayer in Southgate Church of the Nazarene in Colorado Springs, Colorado. They committed to raise their children in a Christian home following the law of love. I'm sure I was in church days after my birth, and didn't miss a Sunday morning, night, and Wednesday night thereafter. There were revivals, church picnics, and church camp. We were embedded in this community of faith. We moved to Greeley, Colorado, when I was 7 and were part of Sunny View and First Church of the Nazarene the rest of my growing up years. Later, I attended a Nazarene university and eventually took an associate pastor calling in a Nazarene Church, which led to my ordination in the Church of the Nazarene. My children spent the early years of their lives in a Nazarene church. I was a Nazarene for 45 years of my life, and in many ways, I am still very Nazarene.

I was drawn to the Mennonites. My wife had attended a Mennonite high school and had many friends that intrigued me. I was charmed by the Peace theology, the rich hymnology, and four part harmony a cappella singing. I was fascinated with the flat polity and communal interpretation.

At the same time, I experienced a growing disenchantment with the Church of the Nazarene. Since the attack on 9/11, I didn't feel right about the vein of militarism in the church. The top down politics and individual religiosity didn't sit well with me. And the eschatology bordered on fanaticism.

H. Orton Wiley had helped make sure the Church of the Nazarene had sound theology on paper. There were good elements in the early days of the Church of the Nazarene, and there continued pockets of loving, Wesleyan-Holiness ortho-praxy (the practical living out of theology). But the fight against modernity, the ensuing rise of the evangelical right, and the culture wars had taken their toll on the Church of the Nazarene.

When we decided to leave the Church of the Nazarene to attend and later join a local church in the Mennonite Church USA denomination, our first priority was to check their faith statement and make sure they had the right understanding of homosexuality. You know, one man and one woman? This was nearly 13 years ago. We all change. Every seven years, all the cells in our bodies are new. If we change this way physically, we must change mentally, emotionally, and relationally.

My perspective has changed by new understandings of scripture, discernment with other Christians, experiences with friends and family that identify as LGBTQIA+, and what I call the Jesus lens—looking at our world through the eyes of Jesus. This includes listening to science and all the general revelation that comes when you open yourself to the leading of the Spirit of Jesus.

Communal discernment was new to me. Having been part of Mennonite Church USA for nearly 13 years, I am starting to understand it. We value all of the voices and give space for each to speak. There is prayer and looking to the leading of the Holy Spirit. Consensus decision making is the best case scenario, but sometimes voting for a majority percentage is needed. Listening to understand is sometimes all that is needed. Waiting for one's turn to talk is fertile ground for escalating polarization.

I was oblivious for much of my life. I was not aware of a gay or queer person until graduate school. I thought everyone I knew was straight. Honestly, I didn't know a Democrat until college. And even then, I thought there were only three at the university I attended.

Since then, I have met many LGBTQIA+ people. I even have some in my family. My sister in law, Nancy Kelso, got married to another woman last summer. It was my first lesbian wedding. The love of the group gathered was palpable. I was so grateful she was happy. Nancy has been so gracious with my insensitivity and entitlement over the years. She has literally loved me to life! If anyone has the Fruit of the Spirit, it is her. She has convinced me to change my mind. She was a cradle Nazarene too, and a minister in the Church of the Nazarene. She has also contributed an essay to this book. I highly recommend it.

The evangelical Christian church has also changed its mind slowly. Now it is almost status quo to accept that a person can be attracted to the same sex. It was not that way even 20 years ago. Also, "reparative" or "conversion" therapy is not seen as reputable since the dismantling of Exodus International. The acceptable perspective for non-affirming Christians is to accept the gay identity and call for celibacy.

To have a close relationship with a gay or queer person makes all the difference. When we allow ourselves to have empathy for these marginalized people, we open ourselves to a new world. We begin to imagine the part of the body of Christ they fill.

In the Mennonite Church, I have learned about the *Jesus Lens approach* to reading the Bible. It is associated with the idea that the Bible is not a flat book, meaning that every part of scripture is taken equally. There are some parts of scripture that rise above the others. Years ago, a Carmelite Catholic priest who I was seeing for spiritual direction told me that when I pray, I should look for a few words of scripture to meditate on. He said to start with the Gospels, and better yet, the actual words of Jesus. Then he said, *"Water is purest, closest to the source."*

We can also consider the amount of words that are written about a topic. For instance, the Bible says a lot about money. It also talks a great deal about the poor, the oppressed, and migrants. Paying attention to what Jesus pays attention to can be helpful in discerning how to treat LGBTQIA+ people.

There are a couple of books that have been influential in continuing to change my mind after forming close personal relationships with LGBTQIA+ people: *Romans Disarmed: Resisting Empire, Demanding Justice* (2019) by Sylvia C. Keesmaat and Brian J. Walsh, and *Disarming Scripture: Cherry-Picking Liberals, Violence-Loving Conservatives* and *Why We All Need to Learn to Read the Bible Like Jesus Did* (2014), by Derek Flood.

I want to cultivate a posture of humility. I have decided these issues are very complicated. A Wesleyan-Holiness view of scripture does leave room for the human element. We can reinterpret millennia-old texts written in dead languages, reinterpreted in other languages and meanings. And, we can change our view of the Bible like we have with slavery, divorce, corporal punishment, and women in ministry (remember orthopraxy!). At the very least, I can love my neighbor and welcome them and their gifts into God's new creation and leave the judgment to God.

Lon Marshall is a Licensed Marital and Family Therapist. He is the architect and founder of Cornerstone Brief Therapy in Coralville, Iowa. His caring methods have been recognized for their ability to bring about positive change. He has a master's degree in Counseling Psychology from the University of Missouri in Kansas City. He also is a peacemaker with his conference Mennonite Conflict Transformation team.

Saved, Sanctified... and Gay

SUSAN ADRIAN MCCLUNG

*A Christian mother's story of a gay son and a faith lost
and then found.*

"I think you have something you need to tell me."
I breathed out a weighted sigh, tried to suppress a slightly giddy smile, and waited for my son to respond to my question by telling me he was gay. Why the smile? I knew he had no clue what was coming. He couldn't imagine that he would be instantly wrapped in love and acceptance from me, his Bible believing, church going, conservative, Evangelical mother.

It was a sweet and tender moment etched in my memory now, but only because years earlier I had been presented with a choice. A choice to either stumble over the Gospel and be broken to bits or let that stone of grace fall on me and crush everything I had ever believed in. Either way I, and the theology I held onto like a golden cow, was going down. It was painful but worth it for just this moment.

My husband and I raised our children the way our parents raised us—in the living, breathing, life giving Word of God and the community of believers known as the Church of the Nazarene. Our parents lived out the true meaning of salvation as did their parents before them. We were legacy members of the Kingdom. The faith we passed on to our children was true and good. It was transformational for every generation that it touched. Eventually we moved on to a non-denominational congregation, but the truth was the same.

My children were dedicated to the Lord as babies. They attended Sunday School each week, participated in every Christmas program, memorized scripture, went to VBS in the summertime. They each professed Jesus as their Savior at a young age, were baptized in a swimming pool, and earned the highest awards in Bible Quizzing. As teens they attended youth camps and sang and played in worship bands. They prayed for the sick, witnessed to their friends, loved their neighbors—they checked every box. My son, my pride and joy, was saved, sanctified and as I suspected: gay.

Why? Why was my perfect Christian boy gay? What did I do wrong as a parent? How had I failed him? Did I pray too little? Was it public school, TV, friends? Did I love him too little or too much? Oh, why did I let him try on my high heels when he was 3! Long before our tender moment of truth, I spent many sleepless nights with these thoughts.

Contemplating these questions, along with a string of other unfortunate and puzzling events led me to that fateful night when God and I wrestled. December 2017—I woke up in the middle of the night and suddenly didn't believe in God. Not because I was angry or confused, but it was as if a switch flipped and I was now an unwilling atheist. Nothing made sense, and I felt like a fool for believing the things I did. But I also desperately wanted to return to my state of naive ignorance before the switch went haywire. For months I swirled in a tailspin of cognitive dissonance and a process that I later found out is called "deconstructing". It was unbelievably painful, but good—just like the God I didn't believe in.

Over the course of a couple of years, through good counsel and even better *counseling* with a licensed therapist, I worked my way back to God, but not the God I left. The God I left was a mere fragment of the God I was facing now. He was the same, but how I viewed Him was different; better; bigger. I became less certain of who He is but more willing to walk with Him anyway. His Word, the Bible, was the same, but now I viewed it totally different as well. It didn't feel inerrant anymore, but it became a lifeline of truth. The stone that the builders rejected was the same, but now I could stop fighting it, stumbling over it, and its grace. I let it fall on me and crush me to dust. Once again, painful, but good. God could then sprinkle me with His Holy Spirit, and mold me into a vessel that would effectively pour out the grace that Jesus bought.

And pour it out, I did! My gay son, who certainly knows the Bible better than most who use it to condemn him, could stand in the grace of Jesus, alone. He could be who he was, fearfully and wonderfully made, as a Christian gay man, and I could openly love him. It was freeing. It felt like the true Gospel. I now knew the truth and it did set me free.

I could love my other son and his female fiancé who both identify as bisexual and are proud to be a queer couple. I could love all my children's queer friends. I could just accept them and love them and tell them how much they are loved by God just as they are. I could even take it a step beyond and proclaim myself an ally to the queer community. I could fight for the rights that we expect, to be open to them as well, just like I imagine Jesus would.

When others question this "cheap grace" as it is often called, it's easy to get into a debate of nonsense. Nonsense, because I am not a theologian. I can't usually go toe to toe with those who know the Greek, and the Hebrew and spent years studying the ins and outs of the translated Bible. I'm not a Pharisee or a Sadducee. I'm just a mother, who loves God and loves her children and *has* read the Bible cover to cover over 20 times.

And in those readings, I recall Paul having to contend with the Jewish believers to bring the message of salvation through Jesus to the Gentiles. The argument against, rested on the clarity of their known scriptures in relation to the Gentiles and the Chosen people of Israel and the need for circumcision and adherence to the Law to be a true follower of Jesus. Sounds familiar. How often I hear, "But, the Bible is very clear about homosexuality!" It was also very clear about the Gentiles, until Peter saw a sheet full of unclean animals and God called them clean. Paul then carried the torch to the Gentiles, and it spread like wildfire among those that were once not God's people but now were.

God did a seemingly new thing by extending His grace to the Gentiles. In fact, His grace was always big enough. He needed the Jewish believers to see that. I wonder if His grace is still big enough to include the LGBTQIA+ community. Could He be doing a new thing now? Could He be coaxing us to join Him in welcoming in a whole new people group to His Kingdom? He has always wanted them. He has always fought for them. He just needs *us* to see it. Let's stop calling a beautiful group of people unclean!

So now, here I am, preparing for my son's wedding this Spring—my son's gay wedding. Two grooms, no Bridezilla. I'm thrilled. Most of my Christian friends, who loved me and my children through the years, will not be attending. Most of my family will not be attending. My pastor will not come. But, it's ok. I know Jesus will be there. He's the first one we invited. Maybe He'll even turn the water into wine. My husband and I will pray a blessing over the new couple and it will be wonderful.

To any parents of queer children: I give you permission to love and celebrate them, unapologetically. I give you permission to speak openly about them at church and to your Christian friends. My two boys are no longer part of a Christian community. They have been hurt too badly. I pray often for them to return. But more than that, I pray for the church to which they will return. May it be a church that truly lives out the Gospel for all people. May it be a church that embodies every tribe, every tongue, every nation. May it see the LGBTQIA+ community as a unique member of the body of Christ and let them take up their rightful place within God's glorious Kingdom. May it be home to people who have been homeless in their faith for far too long.

Susan McClung *is a mother to three grown children and a 10 year old still at home. She graduated from Southern Nazarene University in 1993 with a bachelor's degree in Nursing and from Baylor College of Medicine in 2000 with a master's degree in Midwifery. She met her husband, Dennis at SNU and will be celebrating 30 years of marriage this fall. Her father and mother were both Nazarene pastors. She currently attends a non-denominational church in Tacoma, Washington and is active in teaching children's Sunday School. She also volunteers at Carenet, a pregnancy and family resource center, by teaching a program to high schoolers about Sex Trafficking Awareness.*

The Scales Fell Off

SHEILA MEE

I have learned that however people identify themselves, the most important thing I can do is love them.

I was a missionary. One of my missionary friends once joked that in the Church of the Nazarene, "Even God wants to be one!" She was referring to the place of honor we held in the denomination. I had served in five countries in Latin America for more than twenty years. Three of these were war-torn countries. We received homage from those in the United States for serving in such places.

On furlough, every fifth year, I worked on a Master of Divinity degree at Nazarene Theological Seminary. This took three furloughs. The knowledge I gained enhanced my ministry greatly, and was life-changing in many ways. During the last year of my studies, I did an internship as a chaplain in a large hospital in Kansas City.

There was a referral to see an older gentleman, Dean, who was scheduled for a heart procedure. When I walked into his room, he was lying on the bed. Gary, a younger man, hovered beside him. When I introduced myself, Gary immediately exclaimed, "Oh, we are so glad to see you! Our pastor is out of town and we wanted someone to pray with us. Dean is having heart surgery. We know God is in control. We were both born again several years before we met and have trusted God completely. Frankly, now, we are scared."

Gary's anxiety and worry were apparent in both his speech and demeanor. Dean, lying quietly, looked exhausted and concerned. Clearly, they needed support.[1]

As Gary talked and I observed their body language toward one another, it became quite apparent that they were a couple. They were obviously devoted to each other and talking about a relationship with God in language with which I was very comfortable. Simply put, they were using my God language. I was very

---

1. For privacy reasons, names are fictitious.

conscious of their need of pastoral support. I was also aware of experiencing some strange internal upheaval that I later was able to identify as "cognitive dissonance".

My mind was telling me all the things I had been taught, especially in the church. Homosexuality is sin. These two men could not possibly be Christians. Meanwhile, my heart was saying, "These are good men who are very sincere in their faith." And my body was responding viscerally: rapid heartbeat, a churning in my stomach. As a heterosexual woman, it felt impossible to understand them. Spiritually, I felt beyond confused.

I was saved in the Church of the Nazarene at fourteen and experienced entire sanctification a couple of years later. A graduate of Southern Nazarene University, I would soon graduate from NTS. I had thorough theological training. As a devoted Nazarene missionary, I had taught theology to pastors-in-training throughout Latin America. How was it possible that a gay couple was testifying to being born again and expressing a deep dependence upon God. This could not be!

In spite of my internal upheaval, my responsibility was to provide pastoral support. I had prayer with them. They were grateful and appreciative. When I followed up the next day, I learned the procedure had gone well and they were praising God.

Following both of these encounters, I did a lot of processing with my chaplaincy supervisor. I had been thrown into what felt like an outlandish, impossible world that I had never experienced. It was traumatic, emotionally and spiritually.

To my knowledge, I had never consciously known a gay person, let alone a gay person who claimed to be Christian. Because studies show around 10 percent of the world population is gay, it is highly unlikely that I had really never known a gay person. With deep reflection, I identified several individuals I had known during my life who probably were homosexual, though not openly so.

At that point in time, I had no idea how closely queerness would affect me and my family. All I knew was something within me was shifting.

Today, as I reflect upon my experience, I have deep sense of gratitude for Dean and Gary, and to God for leading me to them. It began an awakening within me. The scales over my eyes were softening and loosening. I was beginning to see that all people are created in the divine image, not just ones who are like me. It opened me to the possibility of recognizing that all are loved by God. None are inferior or malformed or deficient.

Over the next several months it seemed I encountered gay people wherever I went. I became aware of co-workers, patients, and others who were gay. I found myself observing, wondering, and struggling with what I was discovering. The cognitive dissonance did not just disappear. Instead, it lessened more and more as I began to connect with others.

I also began pondering the innate differences that are present in all humans. Some are born with blond hair, others with black or red or brown, some straight, some curly. One man might be a gifted musician, another an excellent mechanic. Some children are petite and slender while others are stocky and sturdy. One woman is extroverted and outgoing. Another is quiet and introverted.

One innate difference that really struck me was handedness. There are five children in my family of origin. All are right-handed except me. I was born left-handed like my mother. When she went to school, she was forced to write with her right hand. She was punished when she did not. All of her life she had almost illegible handwriting, but diligently used her right hand. She did everything else with her left hand.

When I went to school, I was allowed to use my left hand but had to turn my paper the same direction as the right-handed kids. This forced my hand into an awkward position. So to this day, it looks like I am writing upside down. Others in my generation do the same thing.

I have learned that in ancient times, left-handedness was considered evil and unclean. Early Catholicism said left-handed people were of the devil. In some countries it was actually declared illegal. At the very least, people considered it to be abnormal and inferior. Fortunately, today, handedness is not the issue it once was, at least in the United States. My youngest grandson is showing signs of being left-handed, and no one views it as odd or wrong.

I was one of the estimated 10% of the population worldwide that is born left-handed. I began to ponder whether it is possible that some people are born gay or transgender or some of the other gender variations. If that is the case, how could I condemn them anymore than I could condemn myself or others for being born left-handed? As it was wrong to force my mother to unnaturally use her right hand and thus, hinder her throughout her life, was it wrong for me to insist that all other humans have the same gender expression and sexual orientation that I do?

A case in point is a young man I know. He appeared to be a girl when he was born and his mother started raising him as such. As a toddler, before he had the words, he would point to the clothes he wanted to wear...always the boyish ones. When he got old enough to help shop, he wanted to buy everything in the boys' section. He played only with what many would consider to be masculine toys. He was homeschooled the first two grades. When he went to third grade and the kids would line up after recess, he always got in the boys' line. He wore a hoody all the time and kept it pulled up over his head to hide his hair. He seemed to be sad much of the time.

When he was about 15, he finally came out. He was really a transgender man. His mom was not surprised. I was not surprised. He was immediately embraced and lovingly supported. He got the counseling and medical assistance he needed and began transitioning. Now, seven years later, he is who he was born to be: a bright, happy, growing young man. About 40% of young people like him who do not have familial support end up committing suicide. I would have been broken-hearted if this young man, incidentally my grandson, had become part of this horrific statistic.

Not surprisingly, the change in me, along with other changes I was experiencing, led me to explore whether I could, in good conscience, remain within the Church of the Nazarene. I no longer believed it was right to expect someone to change to become what someone else wants them to be. I could no longer buy into the concept, "Love the sinner, but hate the sin." Real love is about embracing people as they are, created in the divine image. I knew I certainly could not continue to serve as a missionary, teaching and preaching concepts I could no longer embrace.

The scales had fallen from my eyes and I could not put them back on.

Ultimately, I became part of a congregation that is affirming of all people. I felt grief that I could not remain in the church that had nurtured, sustained me, and provided a place of service for so many years. It breaks my heart to recognize that had I been born a lesbian or transgender woman, I never would have gotten that amazing love and support.

Some years later, my youngest daughter was finally able to embrace who she is, recognizing her sexual identity as a lesbian. I am eternally grateful I was at a place in my own spirituality where there was no question about acceptance and support. She knew that and told me without fear. She needed me to be on her side and she knew I was.

I saw her transformed from a young woman who was becoming more and more silent and withdrawn into one who blossomed and grew into the fullness of who she was born to be. It was an amazing experience. She and her partner, later wife, tried for several years to remain within the Church of the Nazarene. Their pastor did all he could to be supportive within the constraints of the church. Ultimately they, too, had to leave.

As I conclude this portion of my story, I want to say the alternative to not loving and accepting those with gender identities different from our own is death. For some, it is literal death. The suicide rate is astronomical in the LGBTQ+ community. Sometimes it is the death of relationship with the church that has been deeply wounding and rejecting. Sometimes it is the death of human relationships. I have seen families split apart because one sibling cannot accept her lesbian sister, or because parents refuse to allow their son into their home because he is gay. Fortunately, for many, it is not death of a relationship with the Divine.

Today, I have good friends of every sexual orientation, people just like me who love and live and want the same things out of life that I do. I have learned that however people identify themselves, the most important thing I can do is love them. Love means accepting who they are. I have learned that deep spirituality, whether in Christianity or in other forms, has nothing to do with sexual orientation.

I remain deeply grateful to Gary and Dean, who started me on this journey. I am also grateful for the amazing LGBTQ+ friends I have made across the years who have deeply enriched my life. Loving acceptance truly pays off.

Rev. Sheila Mee, MDiv, DMin, formerly Sheila Hudson, is a graduate of Southern Nazarene University (formerly Bethany Nazarene College) and Nazarene Theological Seminary. She holds a Doctor of Ministry from the University of Creation Spirituality. She was a Nazarene missionary for 25 years, serving in Nicaragua, El Salvador, Peru, Guatemala and Mexico. The latter half of her ministry she served as a chaplain at Children's Hospital & Medical Center in Omaha, Nebraska.

The LGBTQ+ Community as a New *Locus Theologicus*

BRIAN MEYERS

The Church of the Nazarene was not the decider of its theology, the love of God was. And if this is true, God's love extends to those who find themselves in the LGBTQIA+ community!

"In the beginning was the word, and the word was with God, and the word was God" (Jn. 1:1)

The idea of the word becoming flesh is a tangible portion of the divine touching into our brokenness. But what we do not see in the word or of the word is hate. We only see love. What if we were to take the word becoming flesh as an articulation of the love that abounds to all people, even those who are part of the LGBTQ+ community?

God's creation of humankind cannot be limited to only heterosexual people, but also to homosexual, lesbian, bisexual, transgender people, etc. God does not have anyone telling him who to create and who not to create. There is no limit in God's creation of humans.

God does not despise or condemn humans to eternal damnation because of their sexual orientation. So many religious groups condemn and want hell for all who are not heterosexual.

I believe they come to such archaic conclusions based on twisted and erroneous interpretations of the Bible, the Qur'an, or other religious texts. Much ink has been wasted by those who misinterpret what the scriptural texts were meant to say.

Many even dare to place words in God's mouth and scream, "God hates homosexuals! God condemns them to the fires of hell!" Really? Has anyone gone to hell and done a census of how many gay people are there? Of course not.

What kind of monster-god would create a lesbian and then damn her from love? I suspect homophobia gives rise to such words of condemnation, as people place words in God's mouth to justify their personal issues. How many of these pastors and lay people have unresolved sexual orientation issues themselves? How many are homophobic to hide their own struggles?

Contrary to what these false pastors preach, God reveals himself *in* and *through* each member of the LGBTQ+ community. God reveals himself to the world through the poor and the marginalized. The LGBTQ+ family is not at the margin of salvation, but at the center of it.

Jesus was born, lived, and died poor. And the message of God's love is specially for the poor and marginalized. The marginalized do not fit into the mold society wants, but they are the privileged who receive the Word of God and are invited to follow.

The marginalized are all those whom society hates or undervalues: women, minorities, the poor, the homeless, the undocumented immigrants, the mentally ill, the incarcerated, the old, the sick, and the members of the LGBTQ+ community. The LGBTQ+ community are hated because they exist and for who they are. For this precise reason, God takes them, elevates their dignity, and chooses them as the new group of people through which he makes himself present.

For theology to make sense to modern day society, it must be incarnated. Theology must be done in light of our current struggles and challenges. It must be reinterpreted according to current cultural needs and challenges. Theology is done in the streets and ghettos, with the marginalized and in the workplace—in every place God is present and in every experience.

Theology is dynamic. Those who practice this art will collect, reflect, pray, and write about how they perceive God through the lens of life struggles, challenges, dreams, hopes, frustrations, and suffering. The theology of first century Palestine—as profound and beautiful as it is—must be re-analyzed and read with the lens of the 21st century.

The same truth received in past centuries now encounters 21st century thought. And, more specifically, it encounters the LGBTQ+ community. Theology today must take the LGBTQ+ community and its concerns as a primary source, seeing through the eyes, minds, and hearts of each its members.

To use the Latin, the LGBTQ+ community is a new *locus theologicus*. This specific group is one through which God chooses to be present in the world. LGBTQ+ members use their stories and life journeys as the lens through which they understand God. God walks with them, not away from them.

God sides with victims and those who are discriminated against. God does not side with the perpetrators of evil, with those who condemn and send to hell his children because of who they are. God is also victimized whenever an LGBTQ+ person is forced to run into a closet and hide. God feels their fears, he knows their suffering. God understands the rejection by their families, churches, and society. In them, God is also rejected. God suffers whenever an LGBTQ+ member is shouted at, hit, persecuted, and killed.

Opponents of LGBTQ+ people commit great sin when they destroy God's gay, lesbian, bisexual, or trans children. Jesus taught us to love God AND to love our neighbors as ourselves. We cannot love God and hate others, whoever they may be. When "Christian" attack, hurt, and wound the LGBTQ+ community, they are not loving the neighbors as Jesus taught. I believe the Holy Spirit inspires a growing number of more men and women to speak loudly in love for the LGBTQ+ community. And the Holy Spirit cannot be muted.

History has taught us, over and over, the consequences of taking God out the picture: the crusades, the inquisition, the conquering and destruction of millions in the Americas by foreign lands, slavery, systemic murder of the African-American community, concentration camps, war, sexual abuse against minors, etc. In all these cases God's agenda has been switched for the groups' agenda. Now the LGBTQ+ community is the focus of hate.

LGBTQ+ people today shout for love and respect. Their cries for liberation have the Holy Spirit at the center. The Spirit is also active in everyone who risks life to uphold the rights and dignity of the LGBTQ+ community. In the minds, bodies, and souls of LGBTQ+ people, Jesus is once again hated, rejected, condemned, and put to death. In every homophobic shout, punch, kicking, thrown of roofs, shooting, beheading, etc., Jesus suffers.

We who are part of the LGBTQ+ community pay a price. Many of us are thought of as sinners, mentally ill, unstable, perverts, pedophiles, etc. Some of us have been murdered. Our families and communities hate who we are: effeminate, flamboyant, queer, daring, provocative, extravagant, etc. Yet, through these characteristics we live out our gifts from God.

Many of us have tried to live according to the norms of religion and society. By doing so, we only hurt ourselves. We try to act like someone we weren't. Inside us, a voice screams, wanting to be heard and eager to come out.

But just as God does not conform to the norms established by humanity, we must not stop on our journey to self-realization and fulfillment as LGBTQ+ individuals. God does not want us to be like the rest; he wants us to be ourselves, just as he made us.

I believe God is with us who are LGBTQ+. And God is for us.

Brian Meyers *is currently a Behavioral Health chaplain at Scripps Mercy Hospital in San Diego, CA. He is finishing his master's degree in Christian Ministry from PLNU in the summer of 2023. Brian has years of experience working in non-denominational and de-nominational church settings, as well as years of working alongside the LGBTQ+ movement as an ally and participating in many events in and around San Diego.*

The Spirit's Leading Me
into More Truth

RAND MICHAEL

The Spirit has surprised me, leading me into awareness,
welcoming, and supporting my LGBTQIA+ brothers and sisters.

I grew up in the Church of the Nazarene, coming into its fellowship while in elementary school. Through the Nazarene Church, I came to know Jesus as my Savior and The Spirit as my Sanctifier.

The Nazarene culture of personal testimony shaped, encouraged, inspired, and instructed me. Then came a time in my journey when I joined those who would stand and publicly share what the Lord had been doing in their lives. Ah, the internal nudging, prompting, urging, debating that I typically experienced prior to giving voice to what The Spirit had been stirring in me.

My life in Christ was Spirit-energized and shaped by people, their lives and testimonies, including the pastor's preaching, and by The Spirit through the scriptures. In my Bible, I richly underlined passages and wrote many notes.

This is my testimony about The Spirit's leading me into more truth about my LGBTQIA+ brothers and sisters.

My process with this testimony has been similar to what I experienced earlier in my life as I debated whether to stand up and publicly testify. Like then, so now: I need to honor The Spirit's Teaching-Nudging-Prompting me into more Truth.

On His last night with His disciples, Jesus declared: "When the Spirit of truth comes, he will be guiding you into all truth" (John 16:13).

Over the years, the Spirit has led me into more awareness, inclusiveness, and compassion. The Spirit's actions have surprised and challenged me...sometimes in ways that, frankly, I initially resisted. I confess that on occasion, I have been like Peter when he instantly and adamantly reacted so negatively to the vision The Spirit gave him (see Acts 10:14). However, I am also like Peter who later came to testify: "…God has shown me that I should not call anyone impure or unclean…" (Acts 10:28 TNIV).

In regard to members of the LGBTQIA+ community, The Spirit has spoken to me through the lives of six Christians, through Jesus' radical inclusion of all people, and through a deeper understanding of the God-breathed scriptures. The message through all these has been the same.

First, The Spirit has touched and challenged me boldly as I have had the privilege of engaging in deep conversation with three different committed couples. All six individuals are dedicated followers of Jesus whose couple relationships are characterized by fidelity and the fruit of The Spirit.

As I spent time with these couples and individuals, I sensed The Spirit's saying to me, "Be quiet… be receptive… and love with the love of Jesus. I have truth into which to lead you." As The Spirit nudged me, I felt torn between being cooperative with The Spirit on the one hand and resisting The Spirit's prompting on the other. I could not reconcile what I was experiencing in these couples with what I had been taught regarding same-sex relationships.

In our living room, my wife Phyllis and I conversed at length with Tim and Scott. These compassionate men were in a decades long exclusive relationship that became marriage as soon as that was possible for them.

Paige and Rebecca, in their twenties, were deeply committed to and exclusive with one another. They planned on marrying as soon as they could.

Marta, a Cuban immigrant in her 50's and a long-time educator and principal, was a student in my course on spirituality and counseling. At the end of the semester, these adult learners and I sat in a circle. They shared deeply about their spirituality and what in the course had contributed to their growing and changing.

With tears in her eyes and a quaver in her voice, Marta said, "You think I have a choice? If I had a choice, I would not choose to be lesbian!" With a sigh, she confessed how tired and offended she felt when people asked her "And what do you *choose* to identify with?" Marta continued: "I did *not* choose. My *only* choice was to finally recognize my orientation or continuing to deny it." Marta and her spouse, Patty, had been married for several years. Later, it was my privilege to meet and converse with Patty as well.

All three couples had similar core stories: that their sexual orientation is *not* a choice and that they continue to experience pain, shunning, rejection, and prejudice by some who claim to be disciples of Jesus. Yet, despite treatment by some Christians and churches, all three couples, all six people, love God and are themselves earnest believers. All six have a sense of calling and mission to minister to others. They long to be respected, embraced, and supported by the church as well as have a place of ministry in and through the church.

Through these six people and their loving, committed relationships, The Spirit was confronting me with Truth, first-hand Truth, which I had not experienced previously.

The Spirit was confronting me regarding how I am to think about and relate to people who are attracted to the same sex. The Spirit prompted me to consider my own orientation—that I did *not choose* to be heterosexual, I simply am.

Second, The Spirit was challenging me to ponder how Jesus related to marginalized and shunned people. Jesus sought them out; He welcomed and included them; He fellowshipped with them; He commissioned them to minister in His Name and on His behalf. An example of His followers replicating this radical inclusion is seen in Philip's engaging with the Ethiopian eunuch (Acts 8:26-40).

Guided by The Spirit, Luke, the human author of the Acts of the Apostles, recounted this astounding story of inclusion. The castrated African had gone to Jerusalem to worship despite his being socially despised and religiously excluded due to his race and his physical condition.

The point of the story is to clearly declare that categories which were once used to demean and exclude people—even categories which a person cannot change—are not valid in The Kingdom of God as embodied and taught by Jesus. Further, the scriptural focus of the story (Isaiah 53) is a powerful declaration of what The Suffering Servant Jesus endured on our behalf: shame and exclusion.

Luke is clear that God is behind the entire engagement between Philip and the Ethiopian eunuch. Philip was obedient to God's command to take the multiple day journey to a sparsely populated location where there would be few travelers. Odd, as Philip was having great success evangelizing in Samaria. Guided by The Spirit, Philip encountered the Ethiopian eunuch. Philip was open, receptive, and welcoming, even initiating toward the man. Philip was obedient to The Spirit; he was an ambassador of God's loving inclusion, letting go of any prior prejudices.

What The Spirit was doing in and through Philip, we see The Spirit doing years later in the life and ministry of the Apostle Paul who had been harsh of attitude and rigid in exclusion. In his various Spirit-breathed letters, Paul gives us glimpses of his own his testimony. He clearly declares being liberated from judgmental thinking and exclusionary actions. He testified that he had come to understand people from Christ's point of view and not according to human categories that are demeaning and marginalizing. The result was that Paul's ministry and all of ours as well are to be welcoming and reconciling. (See Romans 15:7; 2 Corinthians 5:14-21; Galatians 3:26-28).

To live faithfully today in a Christ-like manner, we need to consider how The Spirit was moving people into more Christ-like living in the early days of the Christian faith and then to ask ourselves: "How is The Spirit trying to move us—to move me—forward now to live more like Jesus and His loving inclusion of all people?"

Third, The Spirit encouraged me to think again about the very few specific passages which speak of same-sex activity. "Rand, to live more Christ-like, you have sought to understand the Bible in its original context. I want you to carefully apply this same principle to those few passages on same-sex activity. I have spoken to you, giving you living truth in three couples; their lives do *not* contradict My Word."

As I sought to follow the Spirit's leading, I discovered that the few passages that do speak of same-sex activity were *not* addressing what we know as sexual orientation or committed, monogamous loving relationships. Rather, they were addressing activities related to religious cults, dominance of one person over another, and possibly war crimes.

The Spirit pointed me yet again to the core of Jesus' teaching as Jesus Himself clearly declared: loving God with all our heart, soul, mind, and strength and loving our neighbors and, yes, also, ourselves, in caring compassion—to love as Jesus loves.

So, I have come to embrace the Spirit-filled lives and relationships of couples like Tim and Scott, Paige and Rebecca, Marta and Patty. Their lives and relationships have ministered to and encouraged Phyllis and me in our marital commitment and growth. Same-sex relationships and marriage are *not* a threat to our marriage. Rather, we discovered that the relational dynamics of same-sex couples are very similar to that of all couples.

In The Spirit's guiding me into more truth, I have come to realize that God's gifting and calling people to be ordained ministers includes those whose sexual orientation I may not understand. It has been a process to come to this conclusion. It has not been easy for me, and the process continues.

I do not understand same-sex attraction and orientation; I cannot explain it, but based on what I have come to know and realize, I am not going to condemn the precious people who find that they are attracted to the same sex. I am not going to deny these precious brothers and sisters in the Lord the gift of intimate relationship, including sexual, because of my lack of comprehension.

With the help of The Spirit and as best as I can, I will continue my effort to accurately understand scripture in its original context and hopefully not to dishonor it by superimposing my own prior unrecognized prejudices and (mis) understandings. My ambition is to ever more faithfully and consistently live what Jesus Himself Embodied toward and with all people.

Because of my own surprising journey, I ask my Nazarene brothers and sisters to be open to the Spirit's leading you into more truth as well.

I ask the Church of the Nazarene to support same-sex marriage.

I ask the Nazarene Church to ordain people who are gifted for, called to, and mature enough for ordination, whatever their sexual orientation or marital status may be.

I think if the all-inclusive Jesus were physically with us now, He would support the foregoing. However, as we all know, He is not physically with us, but He is with us in and by The Spirit. In His final words before His ascension, He underscored, "I am with you always" (Matthew 28:20).

It is ours to remember that by His Spirit, we are His Body and thus we are to be the embodiment of His all-inclusiveness. While my experience of The Spirit's leading me has not always been easy, I am thankful for the process which has been yielding in my life what Peter admonished at the close of his second letter: "Grow in the grace and knowledge of our Lord and Savior Jesus Christ. To Him be glory both now and forever! Amen." (2 Peter 3:18 NIV).

Rand Michael, DMin, LMFT, a licensed mental health professional and a retired Nazarene elder, taught for 30 years as a seminary professor and a graduate level counselor educator. He pastored churches in California, Colorado, and Kansas as well as having trained Christian leaders and mental health workers in over two dozen countries. He remains active in a multi-faceted ministry.

Knocking Down Doors

REBECCA DAZET MILNE & PAUL DAZET

How reflecting on our own experiences can prompt us to fearlessly advocate for others.

Rebecca: I was a curious two-year-old, or so I am told. When I was young, we lived in an old house that, for some strange reason, had a deadbolt lock on the bathroom door. 'Curious me' decided it would be really neat to play with that lock. What was not so neat was that the lock was heavy, and I found myself stuck in the bathroom. Cue, my mother sliding me animal crackers under the door and frantically calling my father, who was 45 minutes away at work.

Paul: I received a phone call from my panicked wife saying that Rebecca was locked in the bathroom, and that all attempts to unlock that door had failed. On the drive home, my heart was overwhelmed with the thought of my daughter, frightened and locked behind the door. As I ran into the house, I found my wife on the floor touching fingers with Rebecca from under the door. "Daddy's here".

Rebecca: I remember being confused and scared, and then finally relieved as I heard my dad's voice. I knew that he would save the day. I was instructed to get as far away from the door as I could, because he was going to knock the door down.

Paul: I wasn't going to let anything keep me from my daughter. As I braced to kick the door, I told Rebecca to get in the bathtub and pull the curtain shut, not wanting any debris to hurt her. I remember it took two kicks to knock down the barrier that was separating me from my baby girl. My wife and I rushed into the bathroom to rescue our daughter. As we pulled the shower curtain back, we found her not just in the bathtub, but ready to take a bath. We hugged, celebrating the reunion of our small loving family, together again.

Rebecca: My call to ministry felt very out of the blue. I was a pastor's kid, and I was not looking to join the family business. But alas, during one of my morning bible reading times, I felt an undeniable tug from God: you are going to be a pastor. As I shared this news with those closest to me, I was met with tears, nods of approval, and encouragement, as they all seemed to know this would happen. It was then that I realized that God was on the move in my life, working on this calling for a long time. I changed my major from Business to Youth Ministry at Mount Vernon Nazarene University and charged forward. My college years were eye-opening and empowering. I was poured into by professors and friends and which helped to refine my calling. During my senior year, however, I was warned that the "real world" was different: that not all places, even within the church, were as accepting of women pastors. I never actually thought I would have to heed this warning. Once the job search began, I contacted all the right people, several times, with my excitement: I'm freshly graduated and ready to put my degree to use, let's do ministry! I was met with a one-sentence email suggesting a preschool director position at a church 90 minutes from me. After I suggested we meet and get to know one another and discuss my calling, I heard no response. I sent more emails, made more phone calls, and was met with radio silence. I felt deep discouragement for quite some time. I followed all the right steps, but got the door shut in my face.

Now what? I found myself contacting a local pastor that I did not know at a church I was unfamiliar with. This turned into a helpful conversation and an open door. Within a few months I was empowered by new mentors, and placed into a new ministry setting where my calling was taken seriously. I felt included again, like I mattered. I have thought about this more in the past several years. I recognize my privilege as a straight, white, woman. If I had doors shut in my face, what does that say for my BIPOC[1] or LGBTQ+ siblings in Christ that are called by God? If the door was opened just a crack for me, then it is currently all locked up for others. It's our job to be the key. All callings matter.

Paul: As a white male coming from the business world, my call was affirmed and celebrated within my home church. I remember feeling the same tug that Rebecca felt, and countless others have felt and continue feeling. It was a pull towards what I didn't want to do, but knew I must do. Once I said, "yes", the ladder of ministerial success was made apparent by my pastor and those around me: Receive your local minister's license, preach your first sermon, start taking district ministry classes, become a youth pastor, lead Bible Studies, go to ministerial lunches to meet

---

1. Black, Indigenous, and people of color

the guys, etc. Step by step, I received a warm welcome into the ministry. Looking back on it, it truly was a rather easy path, with the only obstacles being ones I created for myself, never ones given to me by the system. As a white male, I received phone call after phone call from pastors and district superintendents wanting me to consider bigger positions, giving me the opportunity to climb the ladder of ministerial success. Doors opened for me, they always opened for me. Too bad it took me so long to realize that the doors don't open that easily for everyone.

When Rebecca shared with me the obstacles she faced as she sought a ministry position, I was surprised. My assumption was that the doors would open for her the way they opened for me. At first, I blamed the individuals that didn't respond to my daughter, but eventually I realized there were systemic issues at play that I had never seen before. Why didn't I see that not everyone is affirmed in their calling the way I was? Was it my privilege? Did I not want to see the discrepancies? The truth is, I can't knock down doors if I don't see that they exist. I can't knock down doors that I pretend don't exist. I knocked down the bathroom door all those years ago, but I haven't knocked down doors that are keeping people from being affirmed as valued disciples of Jesus. By being oblivious to the lack of affirmation of those who don't fit the mold of ministerial success, I have participated in the quiet shutting of doors to those different from me. How much trauma has the church induced by not affirming people in their calling to serve in our "loving" churches.

Rebecca & Paul: Try to step into the shoes of someone who is knocking on the door for a moment.

Imagine the discouragement of having the doors shut, the emails not being returned, and the judgmental looks because you are different.

Imagine listening to sermons that say you are not accepted, that you must change who you are to be fully welcomed, accepted, and embraced.

Imagine watching the social media blasts that say you are an abomination.

Imagine searching through websites looking for a church that will affirm your calling, and then having to find the courage to show up.

Imagine the trauma that occurs at every shut door.

How do you feel? Would you give up? Or would you keep knocking? Once we come to know an LGBTQ+ sibling, it is amazing how our views on affirmation change. It is almost as if empathy opens up love.

God is calling everyone into the life of the kingdom. God calls *everyone*! All are needed, but not all are affirmed. Our LGBTQ+ siblings are needed in the church, but the doors are not open. As long as we keep those who are called out of the life of the church, we are missing something significant. It leaves our churches incomplete, missing a spiritual limb. Until we see that all are beloved children of God and gifted by God to participate in the life and mission of the church, we will continue to misrepresent Jesus to the world.

What if by excluding people from the life of the church, we have alienated Christ? What if Jesus has joined those who are excluded and is now outside our churches, knocking on the very doors that bear his name? *"Here I am! I stand at the door and knock"* (Rev. 3:20). There is a knock at our door. Who is going to answer it?

What would it be like if we would knock down every door to get to the beloved children of God who are kept out of church and of ministry? As Rachel Held Evans said, *"The people you are shutting out of the church will be leading it tomorrow. That's how the Spirit works. The future is in the margins."* Let's knock down the doors.

Rebecca Dazet Milne *has a BA from Mount Vernon Nazarene University and an MDiv from Methodist Theological School in Ohio. She serves as a pastor in the United Methodist Church in Columbus, Indiana.*

Paul Dazet *is an ordained Elder in the Church of the Nazarene and has served as a pastor in several churches in Ohio and Indiana. He currently serves as senior pastor in the United Methodist Church in Columbus, Indiana.*

Between a Bad Monologue and a Hard Place

BRIAN NIECE

Quality dialogue with LGTBQ+ friends is what we need in place of all these poor monologues.

PROLOGUE

Dialogue is a tricky thing. It's also a wonderful thing. It's beautiful and intimidating, thrilling and terrifying, messy and comforting. But it's also amazingly tricky. Dialogue assumes that someone has been speaking before I speak; and that I've actually been listening to that person speak; and that when I speak the other person will be listening to me as well. I wonder if those assumptions actually make their way into the practice of dialogue. Probably not as often as we think. And consequently, dialogue is a tricky thing.

ACT 1

Even now, this essay is part of a dialogue. I wish I could peek out from behind the pages and see how you—the reader, the listener—absorb and consider my little snippet of dialogue. And then, I wish I could sit quietly—be a listener myself—to hear your response. I'm like an actor peeking out from behind the curtain during intermission, trying to get a sense of the room that might inform the interpretation of the second act.

But, let me remind us, dialogue is tricky. The circumstances and settings are not always optimal for a conversation to take place. We don't always listen well. We very often respond, not to what is said, but to what we thought we heard or how we heard it. We don't engage in dialogue in a vacuum, severed from our backgrounds and experiences. And we are extremely practiced at crafting our own monologues which likely don't give dialogue even a fighting chance of happening in the first place. In fact, some of us haven't even fashioned our own monologues, because we are so adept at parroting the monologues of others.

My admiration and apprehension toward this tricky thing called dialogue comes from my years in professional theatre. As an actor, director, and writer I've never been able to grasp all the nuances of quality dialogue. Which means I'm never able to control dialogue. What I mean by quality dialogue in the theatre is dialogue that both reveals and conceals the inner workings of characters' minds and hearts. Quality dialogue leaves a lot out. Quality dialogue requires actors to be capable listeners who play into the silences and spaces in order to find or make meaning. Quality dialogue draws in the imagination of the audience, inviting them to do some of the work to fill in the gaps. And finally, quality dialogue always, eventually, inevitably, leads to revelation.

Dialogue is the foundational requirement for a piece of theatre. Unless, of course, it's a one-actor show. In that case there is no obvious dialogue. Instead, it's a monologue: one person, on stage for 90 minutes or more, talking without rejoinder. Yet, if it is well-written, well-directed, and well-performed theatre, listening still happens. The actor who is doing all the speaking must constantly be listening to the mood and energy of the audience. Even if the piece is not a direct address, the actor must be aware of the facial expressions, the body movements, and the general receptivity (or lack thereof) of those listening. And in this sense it's dialogue, because there is so much listening going on.

INTERMISSION

At the intermission point of this essay, you may be a little intrigued (or entirely put off) by all this theatre talk. You may be wondering what this has to do with including LGTBQ+ friends in the faith community. If I may be allowed to step out from behind the curtain, we might have a bit of imagined dialogue right here in this essay, as a means of connecting some dots. It will assist us to have character names for the dialogue. I'll be WILL (in homage to William Shakespeare). You'll be TOBY (in homage to Toby Belch, a Shakespearean character; and also because "Toby" can be any gender, etc., so you can feel at ease as yourself).

Let's go!

ACT 2

TOBY: Why are you talking so much about dialogue?

WILL: Cut to the chase, eh? Ok. Fair enough. I'll answer your question with a question. Do you think we have much dialogue going on in the church today concerning all the "hot button" issues? *(pause)* Take inclusion of LGBTQ+ people in the full life of the church. What do you think?

TOBY: *(plainly, not defensively)* Well, I hear people talking about it all the time. I even hear some pastors preach about it on occasion, though I can't ever figure out exactly what some of them believe about it.

WILL: *(with a wry smile)* Is that really dialogue?

TOBY: I mean, even I talk about it with my church friends. We all seem to agree that those kinds of things are sins and so we can't really have those people as members in the church, can we?

WILL: *(facetiously)* So we'll just judge people, based on what we perceive to be sin, and not really focus on loving people, caring for people, reconciling people to Christ?

TOBY: *(honestly, with no malice)* I guess we actually love them, we just don't love their sin. That's at least the sense I get from our church leaders.

WILL: I see. Then how do we deal with other *perceived* sins? Let's just take gluttony and lust for starters. Do we make the distinction between person and thing there? How do you see that playing out?

TOBY: *(with a huge sigh, as if staring over the edge of a high cliff)* Uh … Well … we might be getting too far into people's private lives.

WILL: *(a bit aggravated)* I think we may need to restart this conversation and you need … No, we both need to … *(pause; closes eyes, leans head back)* This is gonna take a while.

TOBY: *(curtly)* I have to go in about 5 minutes.

WILL takes a deep breath, and looks with compassion and exasperation at TOBY, not sure how to proceed; then decides to speak his mind.

End of Act

ACT 3

Mercifully, the previous act has ended at the point of the dialogue where we're about to go off the rails. Have you ever been in a conversation like this one? Do you see a bit of yourself in either Will or Toby? How easy it is for us to start with good intentions and quickly devolve into getting our point across, or not really listening, or just wanting to stop talking about the issue entirely.

I'm going to suggest something: the institutional church—we, us, those who are attempting to follow Jesus and are connected in some way to a systematized church structure—have far too long spent our time on poorly crafted monologues instead of doing the difficult, long, sacrificial work of seeking out and practicing quality dialogue. And even our dialogue sounds strangely familiar to long, poor monologues chopped up into segments. Poor monologues have no element of listening in them. There is no self-examination, no humility, no asking "What if?" Instead, poor monologues exude certainty and finality.

When we look at how Jesus interacted with people and the nature and character of who Jesus is, we don't find poor monologues; we rarely find monologues at all. Jesus overwhelmingly and in almost all interactions engages in dialogue. In fact, the only times he borders on the kinds of monologues that shut down conversation and don't invite others to respond are when he tells the religious authorities exactly who and what they are. That's very telling.

There's a story in the Gospels of Jesus visiting his hometown. He's teaching, having conversation in the synagogue, listening to the needs of those around him. His conversation partners are family, insiders, those who are well-respected in the religious system. They don't seem interested in dialogue. Instead, they've got poor monologues: posing questions in a rhetorical way, not wanting to hear the answers. "Who is this dude, really? Isn't he just a carpenter? Isn't he Mary's son? We see his family right over there! How does he think he can teach us anything?" They were offended by Jesus (Mark 6:3). The story ends with Jesus unable to do anything there except heal a few sick people. And we can surmise from the context that those few people were not the ones spewing poor monologues at him. Let that sink in: Jesus couldn't do anything there! Not he "chose not to," nor he "waited until they came around." Jesus, the divine, God of the Universe couldn't do anything because of their poor monologues. It's tragic.

I get a bit of what Jesus was dealing with in that story. He was focused on the needs of the few who would be his dialogue partners. He wasn't concerned with the willpower of the religious elite, nor the obstinacy of his supposed friends, nor the offendedness of those who'd known him so long. He wasn't interested in predetermined monologues.

As a college professor at a state school, I'm mostly focused on the needs of my students. They are my dialogue partners. I'm not overly concerned with the health of the institutional rigging, nor the demands of administration, nor the tinkering of state legislators. They all have their monologues on a loop. But listening to and dialoguing with my students is the main practice that yields something worthwhile.

Also as an artistic director of a professional theatre company, I'm focused on the needs of actors and artists. I'm not overly concerned with the high opinions of theatre critics, nor the ebb and flow of audience preference, nor the influence of deep-pocketed donors and businesses. Cultivating a focus on artists' needs is the main thing that helps put something meaningfully creative into the world.

As an ally of LGBTQ+ friends, many who are following the way of Jesus in beautiful and creative ways, my interest is focusing on their needs. I'm not overly concerned with the stance of the system, nor the monologues of supposed authoritative insiders.

And there it is. That's where this thing is landing.

We must end our prepared poor monologues and start to really dialogue with our LGTBQ+ brothers and sisters. And in these dialogues, we need to talk a whole lot less. We need to become better, more sustained, listeners. That means setting aside all our preconceived beliefs and ideas to make space for receiving what we're hearing. When we do that, we might find that we haven't been focused on the needs of the right people.

EPILOGUE

I'll leave you, my reading conversation partner, with this. The Christian story isn't finished. Things are not anywhere near as settled as we think they are and want them to be. We come from a long line—beginning with the Jews who were the first Followers of the Way—in which we debate and discuss and dialogue about the substance of our faith. In fact, to be Orthodox, Anglican, and Wesleyan means a theological trajectory of figuring it out as we go. It means that though all of God's character and nature were revealed in Christ, the risen Christ is still very much alive today and through the Spirit is making known to us—little by little, often by our trial and error, in response to our questions—the Way. Sounds a lot like quality dialogue. If that kind of uncertainty, adventure, and open-endedness doesn't suit us, then a Wesleyan tribe may not be the tribe we're looking for. There are other tribes who happen to think all is more solid and unchanging.

Which leads me to the final thing. We might be wrong. Any one of us; or all of us. Yet, the dynamic of love is something I'm willing to be wrong about. Whatever the end looks like, I don't mind having a dialogue with Jesus that goes like this:

BRIAN: How did I do?

JESUS: Brian, you loved too big, you were too inclusive, your understanding of universality was flawed, and you listened too much.

END OF PLAY (BUT NOT THE END OF THE STORY)

Brian Niece is Professor of Humanities and Theatre at St. Johns River State College and adjuncts in theology, philosophy, and acting at several other universities. He serves as Artistic Director for Lumen Rep Theatre, is a member of Actors' Equity Association, and is an Ordained Elder in the Church of the Nazarene.

A Voice in the Wilderness

CHARLES R. OVANDO

The Nazarene church should be a leading voice that channels the norm-shattering acceptance that Christ taught by fully affirming LGBTQ+ individuals.

The silence has been deafening. As our country has spiraled into a split-screen world where anger, hatred, fearmongering and shock are the fuel of public discourse, I have sat in my church hoping for a third voice to break through. But due to the (possibly) well-intentioned desire to stay out of politics, many churches have been left mute and increasingly irrelevant as they try to stay above the fray with the relentless intrusion of politics into every aspect of our lives.

Even once safe topics like helping the poor and loving one's neighbor have been threaded through a narrow needle to avoid triggering hot button issues. The result is a weakened moral voice that speaks in generalities, allowing those of us in the pews to project our existing biases onto them. We are told to love our neighbor: *My neighbor is white and straight. I'm good. Great message. Should I get the soup and salad at Olive Garden after church?*

One reason this vanilla messaging works for many churches is because it offers the illusion of inclusivity and allows churches to appear as an oasis surrounded by the nastiness of a divided world outside their doors. But we don't live in churches. We ride subways, scroll social media, eat dinner with family members, sit in classrooms, and have jobs that all involve interactions with people whose realities confront us with the very things our churches are reluctant to address. Those realities include ever more brazen and dehumanizing rhetoric about groups of people like our LGBTQ+ family (aren't we all sons and daughters of God?) as well as systematic political attempts to restrict their rights. Churches that remain silent under the guise of not taking political sides need to be reminded that before this was a political issue, it was a human one. And Christ has a thing or two to say about how we should treat one another.

To be clear, yes, the Church of the Nazarene should categorically affirm our LGBTQ+ family. It should speak with an unambiguous voice that is above the political white noise and that is rooted in the two greatest of all commandments: Love the Lord your God, and love your neighbor as yourself. It is a message that we hunger for, both inside and outside of the church. Those inside need to hear explicitly who our neighbors are (hint: not the homogeneous flock that makes up too many of our churches) as well as hear an unequivocal affirmation of human dignity from what may seem like an unlikely source. We ALL need to see that the message of Christ is still relevant and countercultural when it matters most.

I have recently entertained a silly fantasy, imagining Jesus as a special guest in a gathering of church leaders and laypeople for a Q&A session. A respected pastor of an influential church has a turn at the mic: "Teacher, should the church officially make a statement of affirmation for people in the LGTBQ community?" Gasps and murmurs erupt around the hall. Some are giddy with excitement, others nervous with dread, and still others arrogant in knowing exactly what he will say. Jesus takes a few seconds to let the question sink in and then leans into his microphone, creating high-pitched feedback that silences the room and makes the anticipation almost unbearable. His answer? A parable.

The details of the parable itself are unimportant. We all know what the point is: Something unexpected, something that challenges our biases, is counterintuitive, rocks our worldview, and makes us feel slightly uneasy if we initially think we know what it means. It resolves nothing for the people gathered in that room. But it says everything we need to know. Did not all of Christ's parables do this? The prodigal son was undeservedly embraced and celebrated. Ninety-nine sheep were left behind and unattended while the shepherd searched for the one who was lost. The good Samaritan, of all people, helped the injured man and paid for his care. Labels, traditions, expectations, even the law—they are all upended by the Teacher.

The narrative of where evangelical churches stand in the current culture wars is mostly predictable. They have become havens from the "real" world for those who want to live in a bubble of cultural sameness, not the sanctuaries they should be that are welcoming to all. There is an exceptional opportunity before us for that narrative to be shattered, for a voice in the wilderness to rise up and speak with the authority of love, acceptance, and the timeless teachings of the Rabbi.

This is the prophetic voice I have eagerly been waiting for. One that fosters humility, casts doubt on assumptions, and guides us into an open posture of Christlike acceptance of all. One that cuts through our divisions and self-righteousness and holds us to a higher standard. One that allows churches to be nonpartisan without being wallflowers. One that channels His words, "You have heard that it was said … but I tell you…."

Affirming our LGBTQ+ family should not be a singular statement by the Church of the Nazarene that can be construed as one more salvo in the culture wars. It should be a call for inclusivity that goes beyond the legal notion of equal treatment under the law that is the civic affirmation of all people. It should emerge from the most basic tenets of God's love for all humankind and Christ's command to not judge others. It should speak to the spirit of the law. It should be about grace. It should cultivate a community of people who strive to see others through the eyes of Christ and who as a result find themselves less and less concerned about who does and does not belong—we all do.

Charles Ovando is a public-school educator whose professional interests include equity in education, closing the achievement gap, and advocating for English Learners. Raised as a missionary kid in Latin America, he later earned degrees from Point Loma Nazarene University, Olivet Nazarene University, and Concordia University Chicago.

Testimony of a Mother

LISA PERRY

How can a religion based on love allow hate to destroy its children?

He finally said no.

I had asked my son many times if he was straight. He always said "Yes, Mom" and I would release a dramatic sigh of relief and say "Oh good". Today the thought of my words is like a punch to the gut. I wish I could take them back. They must have hurt so much each time we went through this dance. However, in the summer of his 17th year, I asked if he was straight. He said "No." My world turned upside down.

I was raised Nazarene. I married a very religious man, attended church faithfully, and brought my 2 boys up with the "homosexuality is a choice and a sin" doctrine which I had never questioned. In my day, we were taught that being gay was all about hedonistic sex and perversion. A lifestyle choice. Love was never even considered. I remember being shocked when I heard that Jim Neighbors was in a long-term relationship. Love? It was all about orgies, wasn't it? Those terrible gay sinners, who tried to recruit children, were doomed to Hell and they deserved it. They had no right being in church.

Now it was MY son. My baby. My easy, non-rebellious child who had dedicated himself to God. The boy who wanted Greek and Latin language lessons for Christmas so he could study the Bible better. He would argue theology with any missionaries who come to the door. He used to wake me up to pray for a friend who was hurting. Faithfully he would attend church and youth group, even on days when I skipped. He stood up for the hurting and oppressed and always defended the faith. He was an ideal Christian youth, adored by the church leadership and all who knew him.

Obviously I suspected something, or I wouldn't have kept asking. At three, he announced that he was a girl on the inside. I just laughed it off. His best friends were always girls. Unlike his older brother, he totally refused to discuss sex and love and relationships with me. Still, I had no idea that in middle school he was attracted to the football player in his class and not the cheerleader. He tried to have crushes on girls. They never advanced. He staunchly held to evangelical theology and believed that God hates queers and that you couldn't enter heaven if you were gay. For that reason, he spent many nights, in secret, crying and praying for God to change him. He read books on conversion therapy and tried to work it out on his own. He threw himself into Bible and theological study—hoping that God would cure him if he just did more, tried harder, and prayed. He fell into depression and began having suicidal ideations. He once started driving to a nearby cliff to jump, but he turned the car around when he got there. I was completely unaware.

Once he was out, his legalistic dad abandoned him. That was expected. His older brother loves him, and had trouble coming to terms with this. He is very involved in the church the boys grew up in, which is not affirming or even accepting of LGBTQ people. I worry that he might abandon his brother someday too. I cried. Often. He knew my heart was broken. I wanted another daughter-in-law. I wanted to see babies with his curly brown hair. I didn't want him to get AIDS or be beaten up or murdered by a zealot. Most of all, I feared Hell for my baby. The church, while not cruel, tried to get him to attend seminars from people who became "straight" again. We know that doesn't work, just look at Exodus International. People who loved him looked at him with pity in their eyes. I was asked over and over if he was "still" gay. He just couldn't attend anymore.

He couldn't live with the thought that the God he loved had created him this way, hated him for being gay, refused to change him, and was going to send him to Hell. He saw his choices as: 1. Remain celibate, which isn't his calling. He wants love. 2. Become more progressive in theology—but we had successfully raised him to believe in only the American evangelical doctrine and everything else is apostasy. 3. Kill himself before he acted on his desire, or 4. Turn his back on God and the church all together.

So, I spent two years dealing with him wanting to die. Counseling, in patient care, and medications. I cried so much and was always afraid of leaving him alone. His college sent him home early one Christmas because he had made a plan for his death and was steadfast in his determination to do it. He went into treatment. I was frantic. He was angry.

He saw how the church he loved spewed hateful speech about anyone LGBTQ. They were called pedophiles and groomers. That meant him too. So, he made his choice. He chose to live. He turned and walked away from all things Christian. You know what happened? He has thrived. He is on track to receive his master's degree soon and he volunteers on the suicide hotline. He has a large support group of friends and I am proud to be his #1 fan. I don't know if he will ever accept Jesus or

God again. That is his path to walk, not mine. I would love to have a gay Christian son, but I love my boy just as he is. I would not make him straight, even if I could, or he might cease to be the wonderful, loving person he is.

As for me, I am reevaluating and deconstructing. After a lifetime—over 50 years—of blindly accepting what I was spoon-fed about LGBTQ people, my eyes are open to the hate and harm and judgment the traditional church is guilty of. How many of our own babies have we sacrificed, via rejection and suicide, in the name of righteousness? And we dare to say we are "pro-life". When did Jesus say that you must be sinless and conform to the rest of the congregation in order to belong and be saved? God loves my son, as he is. He never says I will only love you if you change. My own faith took the largest shift when I realized how the church makes those who are gay hide or change before they can be part of the congregation. I mean, most churches have addicts, ex-convicts, adulterers, abusive congregants and even leaders. How many churches can say they have gay congregants and if they did, would allow them to even take up the offering?

With that realization, I listened to scripture and sermons differently. They really aren't meant for everyone. Not for gays. I began adding "except the gays" at the end of sentences and realized how far we are from the love taught by Jesus.

"For God so loved the world (except the gays) that He gave His only begotten son. That whosoever believes in Him (except the gays) will not perish but have everlasting life (unless you're gay. Then you will go to Hell.)

Ridiculous, isn't it?

We need to love like Jesus.

Lisa Perry *lives in Idaho with her wonderful husband of three years. She is mother to her two boys and Mimi to two beautiful grandbabies. She is an accounting specialist by day and a community theatre participant by night.*

Be Like Jesus

LISA PONCZOCH

*If the Church of the Nazarene would look into a mirror, would it
see the face of Christ or the face of a Pharisee?*

Labels. We all love labels. It is easy to have them, to apply them, and to use
them. It is an easy form of identification in good ways or in bad ways. Our
youngest son, Caleb had a favorite shirt that he used to wear in high school. It was
a red t-shirt with three statements with three stick figures reading vertically. The
three statements were: Satan is bad, Jesus is good, be like Jesus. Simple statements,
strong message. Over time, many classmates coined him as a Jesus freak. Some
used it as a derogatory label; others used it to refer to his character. "Be like Jesus".
Sound familiar? In the first century, Jesus' disciples were called Christians or "little
Christ" as a derogatory label. It soon became a reflection of their character. Today
we wear that label with so much pride. Do others see it as a reflection of Christ's
character, or has it become more reflective of the Pharisees who plotted against
Jesus? It is a question we need to ask of ourselves and of our church.

I love the Church of the Nazarene. She is in my blood, so to speak, she is a
part of who I am. I am a fourth generation Nazarene on my maternal side, and
was dedicated in the church after I was born. My parents were dedicated lay members who lived out a life of service to Christ, the church and modeled Christlike
character. My love for Christ and the church began at home. Along with that came
traditions, expectations, codes of conduct and the like. However, the love for God
and people was always center. I began serving in the church in various ministries at
a young age, but my call to vocational ministry came later in my life. During the
process of becoming a leader, leaning deeper into the heart of God, on my knees
scared to death of this call before me, the Spirit revealed my true reflection. I did
not anticipate what I saw. I saw myself as one without prejudice or judgmental
biases. I loved people. Yet my reflection resembled more that of a Pharisee than
that of Christ. I had a religious arrogance that was disguised behind the mask of
Christianity.

My heart and my intentions have always meant well. I did not desire to hurt or exclude individuals in my area of influence. I love the diversity of people, cultures, experiences, and stories that create the beauty of humanity. What the Holy Spirit revealed in me was my definition of "us and thems", "saved and sinners", the "insiders and the outsiders". It was obvious that I did not have a problem with racial or cultural differences. I had an issue with "sinners". It did not come in the form of the brow beating, finger pointing. It came in the form of "love the sinner but hate the sin" or "they must not be a Christian because they…" or "you are welcome, but you cannot become a member because…". My heart broke when I saw my reflection. Then Jesus began a new work in me.

In 2008, we moved to Colorado Springs, CO. Todd and I enrolled in Nazarene Bible College. During our time there, the Spirit moved deeply in me. Jesus opened my eyes to see people the way he saw people. My heart fell in love with those who the church has marginalized. People that I did not see before through my church eyes. I began to see all the walls the church has built, the walls I have built. He taught me how to serve and to love the unlovable. To look deeply into the eyes of another and see the image of God in them. Rev. Zell Woodworth, my pastor in Colorado, said in a sermon, "People will either come to know Christ or will reject Christ because of you." Those words have guided and haunted me ever since. My resolve was to provide a space for people to meet Jesus and to allow the work of the Holy Spirit to transform lives the way He saw fit. How would I do that? Be quiet, hear, look, listen, tear down or cut out anything that stands in the way of relationship. Respect, bring dignity and value to an individual, do not judge or condemn but love, love unconditionally.

The Pharisees loved their system more than they loved the individual. The rules that were meant for good, became cumbersome. It became a trap for judgement and condemnation. They desired for the Messiah's return based on their expectations and interpretations of the law and the prophets. Many times, we see them as the bad guys. The reality is, they were trying to do what was right by the law. In their blindness, they missed seeing the Messiah and what the Messiah was trying to show them. I pray that we, the people of God, do not fall into the same trap. I believe that the Church of the Nazarene has great leaders, ordained by God, and have a heart for people. I strongly believe the Church of the Nazarene is made up of many great churches with pastors who lead with a heart of Christ. But we still need to ask ourselves, who do we see when we look in the mirror? Do we like what we see?

As a pastor I am to lead by example. We asked the question, "If our church would cease to exist, what hole would we leave in our community? Who would miss us?" God answered that question for us: the youth in our community, the ones that didn't fit into the church molds. They were kids that had colorful language, smelled of marijuana, and wrestled with their sexual identity. These kids stretched our comfortable congregation, our church folk. We loved them. We became their church. They invited their friends. We became known as the church that was "not all about God," a phrase coined by one of our teens. By this she meant that we did not "cram God down their throats" with condemnation. We loved and accepted them just as they were. They felt safe. They felt safe enough to ask the hard questions. Safe enough to break down in my office asking me if they were condemned to hell because they were attracted to the same sex. Safe enough to ask if homosexuality is a sin because they were gay. Safe enough for the same two girls to cry in my arms as we grieved the loss of one of our own to suicide and another to an overdose. They felt safe enough to be who they were, with no condemnation. Can we say that about our denomination? As the Church of the Nazarene? Have we provided a place for anyone and everyone to feel safe to be who they are? To feel safe enough to call us their church? To invite their friends?

We need to take time to look in the mirror and ask, what do we see? It begins with me. As a pastor, I am responsible for tending to the care of those entrusted to me. Do we see the face of Christ or of a Pharisee? What do others see in us? As a denomination, we need to do the same and ask, what do we see? Jesus is good. Be like Jesus.

*Rev. **Lisa Ponczoch** is an ordained elder in the Church of the Nazarene and co-pastors with her husband Todd. She is a long-time member of the Church of the Nazarene, attended Mid-America Nazarene University, earned an AA degree from North Carolina Community College and received her BA in Bible and Theology at Nazarene Bible College.*

Fair to my Chair

TODD A. PONCZOCH

*In our society today the LGBTQ community exists, and that
community is composed of people—people who are no less valuable
to God than you or me. Jesus said the two most important things
were to love God and Love others.*

I often wonder about how we as people assign value to things, how we say what is
good and what is bad. I wonder because I fear that I myself might get it wrong
way too often. For example, the other day as I sat at my desk, I was overcome with
thoughts of anger toward my chair. You see, I do not like my chair; you could say
it offends me. It does not fit within my body's comfort parameters. It rubs me the
wrong way, the sight of it is unnatural, it is in a word an *abomination* among chairs.
The truth is though there is nothing wrong with my chair, it is not broken, it does
not fail in doing its job of holding me off the floor and in front of my desk. I just
don't like the way it looks or how it functions. I can find textbook reasons and state
medical facts to prove that it is a less then valuable chair. But I wonder if chairs
could talk, what would it say in response to my assessment of its value—would it
find me fair?

I am humbly ashamed to admit I've been even less fair to my fellow human
beings than I was to my chair. I have judged them to be less than valuable based
on my own personal views of what is right and what is wrong with them. Because
someone made me feel uncomfortable, I have felt they didn't belong. Because I
didn't understand them, I have felt they were misguided. I have become angry
because they expected to be treated fairly. I became defensive because they would
not tolerate my assessment of their value. I felt justified because I had scripture
to back up my opinions. I was okay not living in peace with them because I had
scripture on my side. I professed to have faith in the Prince of Peace but I was
okay not being at peace with ALL people. I delivered a message one Sunday from
1 Corinthians chapter 13 where Paul is telling the Corinthians, in a nut shell, "It

doesn't matter what you know, what you say, or what you can do. If it's not known, said, or done in love, it's worthless." In preparing that sermon, I felt my heart break as I considered my own value.

I committed on that day to make Love my guiding principle, to affirm a person's value based solely on their being a child of God created equally with me and every other man and woman on the planet. I decided to stop using scripture to judge a person's value, and instead I use the scriptures to elevate people's value, to make them feel that the most important thing about them is them. I affirm them because they exist. I believe The Church of the Nazarene should fully affirm our LGBTQ brothers and sisters. I think it's time we find a way to move forward and let the love of God move through us—heal the wounds and renew the relationships damaged by our need to be right. I in no way want to condemn a person's conviction, that would make me such a hypocrite. What I am asking is that we align our convictions behind our Love. We claim to seek Holiness and I agree that is right. But who is Holy but God? I have never in my life done a holy thing apart from God. In fact, when I call the shots they are way off target. Holiness has to be defined by something more than personal piety. It has to be more than what we don't do. It must be balanced by what we do. To be filled with God is to be filled with love. To be filled with Love is to love God's creation as God does. A Holy people must learn to wholly Love others.

I acknowledge it will not be easy to change our narrative on what is right and what is wrong. I know that getting beyond our personal biases can be very disruptive to our identity. For some, a lifetime of teaching will be hard to overcome. But if our identities are truly in Christ, it should be an easier transition. I feel strongly that to affirm the LGBTQ community is a witness to our belief that God Loves them. It is a statement that we are open to dialogue and fellowship, that we don't have it all figured out, and that we trust God to lead us through to understanding. It is no secret that the Church in America is struggling to be relevant to a society that sees us as elitist and close-minded. Many within the church—and without— read the Bible and see a disconnect between the message of the Gospel and the actions of the people. This inconsistency is not attractive, and we are losing our ability to influence people for Christ. It is difficult to influence anyone if they will not talk to you. People will not talk to you if they don't trust you. Trust cannot be earned in an atmosphere of condemnation. Therefore, we as the people of God need to find a way, build a bridge, offer an olive branch, and open our hearts to a segment of society that we have not always been to kind to. Remember we are to go throughout the world sharing God's love and we have nothing to fear, because perfect love drives out fear.

As for my old chair, well I'm going to quit complaining. I'm going to appreciate its existence. I'm going to adjust how I engage my seated position. I'm going to consider that my chair might have just as much of an issue with me as I have with it. I'm going to learn to be fair to my chair.

Todd Ponczoch is an ordained elder in the Church of the Nazarene and co-pastors with his wife Lisa. Todd earned his bachelor's degree in Christian Counseling from Nazarene Bible College. He is the father of four and the grandfather of ten.

The Unknown Bundle

JANEL APPS RAMSEY

*When we commit all to God, it includes the
Spirit's guidance in how we care for others.
What is in your unknown bundle?*

You walk into the sanctuary on the last night of the revival, and all across the altar are little white bundles held together with twine. They are non-descript to say the least, but awaken curiosity.

You've sat through the sermons about sin, salvation, and entire sanctification. But tonight is about the future. Where do we go from here?

You've visited or revisited the mountaintop over the last few days. You sang the hymns of your parents and grandparents. Connected deeply into the heritage of circuit-riding preachers calling us to live new lives.

But this next part is the hardest. How do we go back into the world with this new perspective? Will it stick around? Will it wear off? Will I be tempted? Will I stray from the true path? What will happen after this sacred time of encountering the Spirit and refilling my soul?

It's all so unknown.

You are sanctified and ready to do whatever God would ask—no conditions. Having already committed your life to God, and given everything you know to give, you wonder; what's tonight about? As you listen to the sermon, you hear the call to do one more thing: give everything that will come in the future.

What will you do with the unknown?

Will you really walk into the new light he offers?

Will you commit to something, even though you don't know what it is?

Of course, the only answer is yes.

The preacher calls for a response. You stand and slowly work your way to the front. You don't want to be first, that's stressful. You don't want to be last, because that shows a lack of commitment. So you saunter up, tears brimming, waiting to see what God might ask you to do.

You kneel at the altar, on the left, a third of the way from the center aisle. You bow your head.

The preacher instructs you to pick up a bundle and unwrap it. You expect a blank piece of paper in the middle that you'll either write on or offer up to God in some way.

In your dream, as you are unwrapping it, you see a flash of bright color. You refocus on your bundle, you see a rainbow. A beautiful, bright rainbow flag. What does it mean?

Bitterness seeps into your mouth. This can't be what you think it is. How could someone propose such a thing? What does this mean?!

The preacher goes on to share about how God's promise was that he would never destroy us again. He would never destroy humanity from the face of the earth. God made a covenant to love us. That is what God is calling us to do to-day. God is calling us to join him in not destroying the other, not destroying our neighbors, our family members, and our friends. God invites us to step away from violent action and words, and to join in the covenant to love.

And yes, that thought you had, that it couldn't possibly be…

The preacher says, that's part of the unknown bundle.

- LGB young adults who report high levels of parental rejection are eight times more likely to report attempting suicide and six times more likely to report high levels of depression

To this, God says, I will not destroy you.

- More than 1.8 million LGBTQ youth (13-24) seriously consider suicide each year in the U.S.—and at least one attempts suicide *every 45 seconds.*

To this, God says, I will not destroy you.

- Transgender and nonbinary youth who reported having pronouns re-spected by all or most people in their lives attempted suicide at half the rate of those who did not have their pronouns respected.

To this, God says, I will not destroy you.

- Having at least one accepting adult can reduce the risk of a suicide attempt among LGBTQ young people by 40 percent.

To this, God says, I will not destroy you.

- Youth who reported undergoing conversion therapy [a dangerous pseudo-scientific practice that tries to change someone's sexual identity] were more than twice as likely to report having attempted suicide and more than 2.5 times as likely to report multiple suicide attempts in the past year.

To this, God says, I will not destroy you.

Will you join God in saying, I will not destroy you?

That's the question in this *Unknown Bundle.*

He does not say, will you join me to a point? He does not say, will you join me a little? He says to our hearts, will you say "I will not destroy you?"

Will you say, to the college student sitting in a dimly lit, once off-white waiting room, waiting for a life-changing medical test, alone—I will not destroy you?

Will you say, to the rejected and tossed aside young man, freezing on an urban street corner in the middle of winter, alone and without family—I will not destroy you?

Will you say to the woman who is blossoming out of the wrong body, who needs help learning to dress her new shape—I will not destroy you?

Will you say to the young person hanging out with friends at a club in Colorado Springs or in Orlando or in Kansas City or in San Diego—I will not destroy you?

I will not destroy you in person or online.

I will not destroy you with gossip or direct abuse.

I will not destroy you by sharing hateful messages.

I will not destroy you with my thoughts, words, or deeds.

I will not destroy you with things I do or things I have left undone.

I will stand in solidarity with life. I will stand in God's covenant not to harm.

I will not destroy you.

This was the question I had to answer when this bundle was placed in front of me. I always thought I knew this answer. I never expected to change my answer. I never knew how completely transformative it could be to hold the unknown bundle, stare deeply into its colors, and learn to move from black and white, to living in color.

I, like many others writing these essays, was deeply dedicated, entirely (entirely) sanctified, and never ever expecting to leave the Church of the Nazarene. I knew who was in and who was out. I knew the rules. I knew the theology. I helped people find Jesus and find entire sanctification. The only thing I didn't have was more than 3 generations of Nazarenes in my family line. I was all the way in.

The thing was, I was wrong. I was just wrong. But I've learned that the great thing about being wrong is that we get the chance to change. That's what the unknown bundle is all about. God brings to light the things we can handle now, that we couldn't handle before. God sets the spotlight on something, and we get to choose to walk into that new light or ignore the Spirit's prompting.

When that light was put before me, in the form of a friend, I was completely unprepared. But, as I would do for anyone seeking truth and light, when asked to explore the Bible and the texts that are the cornerstones of this battle, I said yes. That's what you do when someone wants to go deeper. I reached out to a trusted mentor to figure out what resources to use, and I started to read.

For me, as a woman minister, this journey took on extra weight. As I saw the way these texts were used against my gay friend, I also saw the parallel to how a few verses are used against women in ministry. And once you understand the role of cultural and historical context, the limits of when and where something was written, and the fact that the Spirit moves in expansive ways through history, I knew that my view was changing, and I found out that I wasn't alone in seeing this.

So, I'm asking you right now, will you ask the question? I committed my unknown bundle to God at 18 when I was sanctified at Indian Lake Nazarene Camp in the Michigan District. As I have been willing to ebb and flow with the movement of the Spirit in response to my bundle, I have found a spacious and loving space with God. A spacious place that includes my LGBTQIA+ siblings of all genders or none.

I have met people that worked even harder than I did at being the best Christian they could be who simply needed to be loved for who they were and told that they were worthy of love. They needed people to walk with them through difficult things, to love them unconditionally, and to accept them as the beautiful bearers of the image of God that they already were.

When we cherish the transformation that comes with salvation and sanctification, but demonize an equally beautiful transformation as a person becomes who they truly are, we let hatred, power, and fear override the redemptive narrative of Christ. When we cling to judgment, we feel in control. But Christ calls us to hold our assessments loosely. When we refuse to open our bundle because we fear we might be changed, we self-limit our access to the grace that God freely offers us.

Just because we can't understand something, or don't want to, doesn't absolve us from the harm we cause; especially when it's brought into the light. Our tradition holds us responsible for things left undone. We can carry this bundle around, bury it, even try to destroy it. But until we're willing to face it and let it change us, we will continue to fall short of the grace God wants us to experience.

When I looked at this bundle, it became clear—I would much rather be excluded for who I include, than included for who I exclude. Jesus had nothing to say about LGBTQIA+ folks in the gospels and a lot to say about religious people that excluded "others."

So today, I'm asking you, as you stare at the unknown bundle: Will you allow the Spirit to influence you? Will you engage honestly, deeply, and authentically with the call of this unknown bundle to embrace your LGBTQIA+ siblings?

I know it's scary. I know it is so unknown. But you're not alone. There are a great cloud of witnesses surrounding you and we will take this journey with you.

You said yes to the unknown bundle before you knew what was in it.

Now what will you do?

———

To get started on your journey, I highly recommend the book *Changing Our Minds* by David Gushee. Dr. Gushee is a theologian and ethicist who has wrestled deeply with this topic. His work is thorough, biblical, theological, and compassionate. I believe this is one of the best ways you can start this journey. If you would like help going through this book, please feel free to contact me at janel@brewtheology.org.

I would also recommend you check out The Trevor Project, www.thetrevor-project.org, an organization dedicated to keeping LGBTQ kids alive. The included statistics can be found there.

———

Rev. Janel Apps Ramsey is the co-director of Brew Theology and co-host of the Brew Theology Podcast (brewtheology.org), co-editor of the book Women Experiencing Faith, *Chair of the Together Colorado Climate Justice Committee, Editor at Faith Mending (mending.substack.com), and member of the Multifaith Leadership Forum. She loves living in Denver with her husband and two cats.*

An Invitation to Be Transformed

PIPER RAMSEY-SUMNER

Sometimes inclusion is not enough.

When I look at the lives of my queer friends and family who have been hurt so deeply by the Church of the Nazarene and those like it—the churches that shaped and formed them from their earliest days—my heart breaks for what could have been. What if my family had *fully* welcomed my aunt and her girlfriend? What if my friend at Southern Nazarene University had been allowed to hold hands and show affection to his partner on campus without fear of punishment? What if the members of my childhood church had celebrated my sister's engagement to a woman instead of withdrawing from her life?

Growing up I was proud that the Church of the Nazarene, since its beginning, affirmed and celebrated women in ministry despite my peers from other Christian traditions insisting that women in church leadership was "unbiblical" by citing verse and chapter. Yet, I knew that the Church of the Nazarene, understanding that greater biblical evidence exists that celebrates women in spiritual leadership and originating in the Wesleyan-Holiness movement, stood apart from other traditions because of the vital leadership and contributions of women preachers, evangelists, and church planters.

Looking back now as a person who strives to be fully affirming of people of all sexualities and genders, I wonder why the Church of the Nazarene, like so many other denominations in the Wesleyan tradition, struggles to see that the same Spirit that empowers men and women of all races, nationalities, and social classes can and does also empower our queer siblings in Christ. Those before us have transformed and resisted exclusionary beliefs in the past, and they can do it again.

The Church has so much to learn from the queer people it has rejected, and I do not believe that simply "creating room for them at the table" is a solution that will create full inclusion and affirmation of their identity, their humanity, their nature as *imago Dei*. In the face of rejection and in pursuit of finding their identity, queer Christians and their allies have found and formed communities that exemplify Christ's invitational nature that calls us to transformation, love, and belonging. We see that in online spaces like TikTok, Twitter, and Facebook, and in-person spaces like gay bars, drag shows, and house churches. The Holy Spirit never needed a church building.

The Church of the Nazarene doesn't need to make room to include queer people, it needs to be completely transformed from the root to the branches. It must catch on to what the Spirit is already doing outside the doors of the church buildings among those that have been locked out, metaphorically and literally, so as not to miss the invitation to participate in what God is doing. The Church of the Nazarene needs to repent and ask permission to join queer Christians and their friends in the work they are doing among the margins—where Jesus called us to go. Perhaps, then, they will make room in their spaces for Nazarenes.

John Wesley, the spiritual predecessor of the Church of the Nazarene, defied the religious structures of his day and created a transformative movement of the Holy Spirit that is still alive today. His theology was shaped by his experience with Christians from the Moravian Church. He first met a group of Moravian missionaries on a ship traveling to America. At sea, the ship experienced such violent storms that everyone was terrified for their life except for the Moravians who calmly sang together. When he returned to London, Wesley was encouraged to attend a Moravian gathering. It was there, while reading Martin Luther's preface to Romans and influenced by the Moravians' deep assurance in God's grace to save, that Wesley's theology was forever transformed. It generated a drive within him to preach a practical divinity rooted in individual and communal holiness.

In his day, as the rise of industrialization and the Enlightenment brought skepticism and a lack of interest in religion, a growing number of common people were disconnected from the church. His desire to minister to the working class led him to leave behind some of the strict practices of his religious training in the Church of England to "become more vile." Learning from and being transformed by their stories and contributions as fellow leaders in the early Methodist movement, Wesley did not simply invite people into the traditional spaces they were averse to. He created new ways of being church *with* them.

Sometimes inclusion is not enough. Inclusion is a term that means a space that was once exclusive of a group is made accessible to that group. If the expectation or result of inviting is that the newly included group must live into the ideals and lifestyle of the dominant group, then there is less room for justice, love, and equity to exist. No one should be asked to diminish themselves—who God made them to be—to be accepted into a community.

If power is expected to stay in the hands of the same people and system when queer people are invited into the Church of the Nazarene, we can anticipate there will be shortsightedness and important considerations missed. Of course the intention of inclusion is to create a diverse, safe space for all, but without centering those who have historically been pushed to the edges, the efforts of inclusion will fall short. It is too simple to invite queer Christians to the table without deep self-reflection and a willingness to learn from and be shaped by queer Christians and their allies who are forging new paths.

What if the Church looked beyond itself to learn from queer Christians, and specifically queer Nazarenes, who have invaluable contributions to make to the life of the Church? What if the Church of the Nazarene looked around at the communities built by those who were rejected and who chose to create their own inviting spaces rooted in Christ's transformative message of love? The Church has acted as host for far too long. Maybe it's time for it to become a guest—to be open to being welcomed in to learn from and be transformed by others.

Inclusion can lead to absorption into the larger community's ideals, while transformation creates the possibility for the larger group to be renewed and changed for good. If Nazarenes open themselves to be transformed by the queer Christians who are willing to walk alongside them, they will rediscover their theological and traditional roots as they find new ways to experience God's love, grace, and holiness. Transformation leaves space for something new—new life, new creation, new ways of being.

The Apostle Paul calls us to resist being conformed to this world and to "be transformed by the renewing of your mind" (Romans 12:2 NRSV). In our world, heterosexuality and gender and sexual binaries restrict human flourishing, because they create a narrow definition of what is normal and even what is human. One cannot break from these norms without being subject to disdain, criticism, or worse. (Even I, growing up a tomboy, experienced negativity and extreme pressure to act and dress like little girls "should.") These norms are created by our culture and reinforced by our actions, yet cultures change as does our definition of normal through the generations.

The founders of the Wesleyan-Holiness movement asked the question: Is there another way to view holiness? They birthed a movement that brought a beauty and depth to Christian theology and practice that would not have existed otherwise. The willingness of the mothers and fathers of our tradition to break the mold is a legacy that queer Christians live out every day. Queer people remind us that it is possible to break out of the patterns of this world that simplify and flatten what it means to be human or Christian or holy or good.

When I was in seminary at Iliff School of Theology in Denver, CO, I met fellow ex-Nazarenes who planted a house church. The church was small, open, and affirming. I felt comfortable inviting my queer and trans roommates who attended with me and felt welcomed and cared for. The pastors were humble, kind, inquisitive, and willing to be challenged and changed by our stories and insights. We talked about how painful it was to leave the church traditions that we loved, but each of us had a reason to leave whether it was our choice or not. Queer exclusion was a factor in each case. I'll always be grateful for that house church and others like it that listen and grow alongside those whose voices are rarely heard. These kinds of churches seem to be catching on to what the Spirit is doing a bit quicker than the Church of the Nazarene.

Christ calls us to repentance—to reorient the way we think, act, and live. That requires a willingness to step out of our comfort zone and the spaces where we hold power and influence, to walk alongside those who challenge us to question what we think we know, and to expand our understanding of what is loving, holy, good, and just. The Church of the Nazarene has contributed to American Christianity's rejection and marginalization of queer people and as a result queer people and their allies are steadily leaving and discovering new spiritual paths and communities to find the belonging they deserve. There is another path the Church of the Nazarene can walk—one that is rooted in that same Spirit that moved in the lives of John Wesley, Phoebe Palmer, Phineas Bresee, and so many more. Repent, and be transformed!

Piper Ramsey-Sumner *grew up a pastor's kid in the Church of the Nazarene. She received her BA in Theology from Southern Nazarene University and her MDiv from Iliff School of Theology. She is the Cultivator of Fresh Expressions for the Florida United Methodist Church and hosts the podcast, Pastor's Kid.*

We're Harming People In Jesus' Name

KADEE WIRICK SMEDLEY

Non-affirming doctrines and policies harm queer folks—Nazarene or otherwise. Affirmation is the path to the love of God and neighbor to which we by the Spirit have been called.

As a teenager in my Nazarene youth group, I thought LGBTQ people were somewhere *out there*. I had good reason for thinking so. It was 1992 and my family had just moved to Oregon, where a group of conservative Christians were trying to legislate against what they called "special rights" for queer folks. I understood from the way most Christian people around me talked that LGBTQ folks were a particularly sinful group of people trying to get special advantages for their particularly sinful lifestyle.

What I know now is that queer folks weren't all "out there" outside of the church. Some were sitting next to me at church absorbing the good news of God's love with the message that their sexuality made them an abomination. Even though we were friends, they didn't confide their struggles in me for the same reason I assumed they couldn't be queer—because queerness was taught to be a choice, a sinful lifestyle one could opt out of with God's help. My queer siblings in the faith endured shame wrapped in Jesus and demanded by the community that was supposed to love them most. It kept them quiet and kids like me ignorant that we were perpetuating harm.

It's been 30 years of life and study and ministry since that year in youth group, and a lot of listening to queer folks and the Holy Spirit. LGBTQ people have been in every religious community I've been part of—at Northwest Nazarene University, at Regent College, and in the Nazarene church I was privileged to serve as a pastor for ten years. It often wasn't until these folks were disconnected from church and discovered I was affirming that they felt comfortable sharing with me who they were.

When Nazarenes speak today of queer folks and the doctrines we insist on about them, it often sounds like we are still speaking of some external group. This is an indictment of our denomination. Queer folks *are* in our midst, if not openly because it is unsafe for them to be honest about who they are. We can lay the blame for our exclusionary teachings at the feet of scripture but the responsibility for the harm is on we who insist upon perpetuating it.

Today I don't believe Jesus' blood holds saving power only for heterosexuals and I don't believe the Spirit, who blows where She will, becomes cowardly in the face of God's children who were born queer. I believe God intends life and welcome for our queer siblings and that he expects the rest of His church to do right by them. As Wesleyans who reflect theologically through the lenses of scripture, tradition, reason and experience, the Church of the Nazarene should repent of our current doctrinal teaching and polity because of the harm it has led us to perpetuate.

And what is that harm? For millennia the Church has inflicted violence upon LGBTQ folks, whether collaborating with authorities to criminalize their relationships, or through ministries like Exodus International premised on the destructive belief that queerness is something from which one can be forcibly converted. Many countries have moved towards decriminalizing queer relationships in the last few decades. Some faith communities have moved towards full inclusion of their queer members. Exodus International eventually acknowledged their work as destructive, shuttered their doors, and repented with a public apology for the harm they caused to the queer folks who came to them to reconcile their faith with their sexuality.

In my work as a spiritual care practitioner with homeless youth, I bear witness to queer teens and young adults who are homeless because they are not affirmed by their families or communities. While queer youth make up 4% of the overall population, they are anywhere from 25-40% of the youth homeless population in Canada. I'd like to say that none of these rejected kids are Christian, but of course they are; and it's not in spite of our beliefs but because of them.

The exclusionary beliefs and practices we link to holiness and righteousness as Nazarenes are found in other religious communities too, as well as the deadly fruits of such exclusion. Catholic, Muslim, Sikh, Jewish and Hindu queer kids end up in shelters or leave the faith the same as Protestant Christian kids do. While spirituality or religious belief serve as protective barriers against suicidality for many people, it does not do so when a person is queer and their spiritual community rejects them because of it. Their communities and beliefs become, instead, a means of increasing their chance of early death.

There are arguments within the Church of the Nazarene that the possibility of becoming LGBTQ-affirming is a moral compromise or act of surrender to secular culture. It is neither. If the Church of the Nazarene were to become LGBTQ-affirming, it would be an act of repentance—a turning from a path of death to one of life.

I believe this is possible because I still worship with Nazarenes, and because I trust in the work of the Spirit. When I am discouraged, I remember a Pentecost Sunday a decade ago, when I preached a sermon about the power of the Holy Spirit and opened the mic afterward for testimonies. To my surprise, a father took that opportunity to share about his queer son and how the church needed to figure out how to respond to people like him. His pleading, punctuated by tears, was followed by another father whose son was queer but for whom that was not a point of pain but acceptance. Third to the mic: a queer person, a beloved member of our community who testified to the love of God at work in their life and His faithfulness to them.

Not one word in my sermon had touched on sexuality or gender identity; I was much younger then and lacked the courage to name publicly what I had just witnessed. But it was clear to me then as it is now: those testimonies of pain and power came in obedience to the Holy Spirit working to birth life in the place of sorrow and death.

This, I believe, is the path the Church of the Nazarene must choose. A path forged by the Spirit that gives a place for all God's children to serve and build families according to how He has made them. A path of life and healing, a turning from harm and hopelessness. I am no longer a Nazarene elder, because I filed my credentials to be licensed with a group that fully affirms queer folks. That decision came out of a desire to no longer do harm, but I remain a member of the Church of the Nazarene with the hope that the denomination in which I came to faith and was first ordained might turn to the path of life the Spirit offers.

May it be so, amen and amen.

Kadee Wirick Smedley *is the lead spiritual care practitioner at Covenant House Vancouver, an organization supporting youth experiencing homelessness. She earned her BA in Religious Studies from Northwest Nazarene University and her MDiv from Regent College. Kadee and her family are members of Vancouver First Church of the Nazarene in Vancouver, BC, Canada.*

The Stakes are High

PHIL STOUT

Can we change? The future of the Church of the Nazarene,
and the lives of countless individuals, depend on it.

Oddly enough, my journey to full LGBTQ inclusion began with a sermon by a fundamentalist preacher. Hearing him over the radio, I did not catch his name, but he said something that did grab my attention. He was railing against the evils of women in ministry. He insisted that only men could preach, teach, and lead in the church, and that a church that ordained women was a church that had rejected the Bible. And then he issued a grave warning—the slippery slope. He said that if a church embraced women in ministry, it would eventually open ministry to gay pastors.

I have always taken great pride in our Nazarene tradition of ordaining women to ministry. Even though our practice has not kept pace with our theology on this issue, we have a vision for full participation of God-called, Spirit-gifted women taking their leadership roles in our churches and our denomination. Many have worked tirelessly to see this vision fully embraced and embodied.

While I disagree with my unnamed fundamentalist brother on his opposition to women in ministry, he had made an important point about consistency of hermeneutics. How do we interpret the Bible? When it comes to controversial topics, do we adjust our approach based on our fears of where careful study may take us?

Our passion for women in ministry is grounded in a theology that, I believe, shows honor and humility in handling scripture. We have not treated the Bible as though it was a twentieth century American document, or as if it was originally written in King James English. Rather, we have explored the original languages, the context in which scripture was written, the authors' understandings, and other issues within the overall context of what we believe about God. And yet, when it comes to passages that we link to homosexuality as we perceive it, that humility seems to evaporate. We adhere to "the Bible is clear" fundamentalist literalism, which we have completely rejected for the rest of scripture.

And so, we find ourselves to be selective fundamentalists. Paul wrote that *"women should remain silent in the churches"* and are *"not allowed to speak"* (1 Corinthians 14:34). While we are confident that this is not a law for all cultures for all time, we take his words in passages like 1 Corinthians 6:9-10 (which we have assumed to align to our current definition of homosexuality), and say they are timeless with no context needed. In so doing we are teaching our congregations how to be fundamentalists. We are teaching them that our form of Wesleyanism works well with the dominant conservative evangelicalism of our day.

Our clear voice is needed. But a Wesleyanism that is compromised by fundamentalism is a convoluted message, rather than a message of hope which springs from a theology of love. Theologically, the stakes are high.

But that is not the worst of it. Toxic fundamentalism that puts doctrine over love, and certainty over acceptance, has done untold damage and destroyed many, many lives. Research from the Trevor Project in 2022 reveals some startling realities. It found that 45% of LGBTQ youth have seriously considered taking their own lives, while nearly 1 in 5 transgender and nonbinary youth have actually attempted suicide. (Rates are higher for LGBTQ youth of color than for their white peers.)

Think about the young people in the youth groups of our local churches. What would we do if we discovered that nearly half of them wanted to die and many of them had attempted to kill themselves? Our panicked hearts would realize that something terrible is happening. We wouldn't wait for the next board meeting to assemble a committee to discuss it. We would run to those precious children and do everything we could to preserve their lives. We would tell them about their worth, their dignity, and their calling. We would open our homes to them. We would do everything in our power to nurture their souls and save their lives.

LGBTQ children are just as precious as our children. In truth, they are our children. They sit in our pews and attend our youth activities. And even those we have never met, those who have never been in a church, those who have been forced to live on the streets because of who they are—they are our children.

Several years ago, I was in a pre-General Assembly meeting in which we were previewing the work ahead of us. When we turned to the documents pertaining to human sexuality, someone said they were against deleting the word "perversion" from the discussion of homosexuality. They boldly proclaimed that same-sex attraction is perverted. Holding back my anger and frustration, I cited statistics about LGBTQ youth and suicide, then simply said, "I don't think they need to hear the church call them perverts."

You see, we were discussing our LGBTQ children as an issue. However, these sisters and brothers are not an "issue" to God. They are God's image-bearers who need and deserve love, acceptance, and—yes—inclusion in the Church of the Nazarene. The stakes are high.

Our inability to fully include our LGBTQ brothers and sisters brings a very practical problem to the forefront—a deficiency in our capacity to fulfill our mission. Again, there is a parallel to the approaches of women in ministry and LGBTQ inclusion that must be addressed.

Fundamentalism has made the monumental mistake of despising the gifts of women. We will never know what has been lost because of this tragedy. Women who are gifted and called to empower the Body of Christ have been disqualified by men—not by the Holy Spirit—and the loss has been incalculable. The same is true of the Christian LGBTQ community. Beautiful people, whose gifts are given by the Spirit and valued by God, have been told that those gifts are not legitimate. I know many of them who are using their gifts for the work of Christ, but they have been forced to use their gifts while being cut off from the broader Body of Christ. This was never intended to be how the Body functions. Imagine how their gifts would flourish if we affirmed what God has already affirmed—*"Now you are the body of Christ, and each one of you is a part of it"* (1 Corinthians 12:27).

God's gifts should not be squandered. The stakes are high.

My wife and I have had the privilege of worshiping in LGBTQ inclusive settings on many occasions. The joy is palpable as people worship in safe spaces. While they know that God accepts their praise and adoration, that truth is enhanced as other believers affirm their hearts for God. But what is also present is a deep sense of pain and woundedness. For many, the simple support of straight people worshiping with them is part of their reprieve from constant rejection and fear. In our spirits, Carol and I are always reminded that in those moments we are standing with the marginalized. Those are very humbling experiences. We always feel honored to be in the presence of this part of Christ's family.

Planting ourselves among the marginalized is what the Church of the Nazarene envisioned in its infancy. We wanted to stand with the poor, the outcast, and the oppressed. Times have changed and needs have changed. For example, unwed mothers are no longer shunned, but people are targeting and murdering black trans women. We never hear about this because, to the media, to politicians, and to the culture at large, these people just don't seem to count. But they matter to Jesus, and they should matter to us.

Needs change, but our calling must never change. We should be the people we were called to be. But we cannot be true to our calling by excluding sisters and brothers who are dangerously ostracized—by culture, by families, and by the church.

God called us to see Jesus in the marginalized. The stakes are high.

In the words above, I have referred to the Church of the Nazarene as "we" and have spoken of my relationship to the church in the present tense. But it's time for full disclosure. While an overwhelming majority of my deep friendships are in the Nazarene orbit, and my love for them has not diminished, there came a time when I chose to resign my ministerial credentials and my church membership. I should not have been surprised at how difficult this step was to take after spending my entire life in the church that I love. But it was—and continues to be—more difficult than I had imagined. But after much prayer over a four-year span, I realized that the ministry and life my wife and I have been given with our wonderful LGBTQ family and friends could not align with a church that did not fully embrace them. While the Church of the Nazarene rejected me for this stance, I also needed to reject my denomination's inability to fully see Christ in these dear friends, and to be Christ to them.

The Church of the Nazarene is not diminished by my departure. But there are many young, gifted, promising leaders who are feeling early in their ministry what I began to feel at a later point in my journey. These women and men are the lifeblood of the future. They are passionate for the way of Christ, and they love the church. But many are coming to the same conclusion to which I came, while many others are simply being told that they don't belong and that they need to leave.

A church that is unwilling to change—even when the way is dangerous and demanding—is a church whose best days are behind it. Please understand: the stakes are so high.

Phil Stout *pastored First Church of the Nazarene in Jackson, Michigan for thirty years. He received his undergraduate and MDiv degrees from Nazarene institutions and earned a DMin degree from Garrett-Evangelical Theological Seminary. Phil currently serves as Spiritual Care Director for David's Promise, a ministry to adults with special needs. He is also a Teaching Pastor at Westwinds Church.*

Without Humility, the Church Will Implode

BRAD STOVER

I have gained a whole new perspective on how to love and accept the gay community and on how our Heavenly Father loves us.

I am writing today as a lifetime member of the Church of the Nazarene—and more importantly as the father of two amazing daughters who are gay and father-in-law to two wonderful daughters-in-law. I am a Nazarene pastor's son and spent approximately 8 years as a youth and worship pastor in the church. I chose to write this essay because of what I have seen as an extreme failure of the Church as a whole in their response and relationship (or lack thereof) to the LGBTQ community.

Our daughters both came out to us in April of 2009. My first response was one of extreme anger, disappointment, and embarrassment. I grew up and went well into adulthood believing that being gay was a one way ticket into Hell. Fortunately, very early into my angry response to my daughter, the Holy Spirit stopped me and told me to just love her and listen to her. Thus began a sometimes very difficult but also very rewarding journey over the last 14 years. I have gained a whole new perspective on how to love and accept the gay community and on how my Heavenly Father loves us.

I feel I need to state my beliefs early on here in regards to full acceptance and full affirmation by the Church of the Nazarene of the LBGTQ community, since that is in the title of this book. As I interpret what the Bible says to us on the subject, I cannot be fully affirming of the practice of homosexuality. That being said, I do believe that we as followers of Christ can be fully accepting of the LGBTQ community, and include them in our communities of faith as brothers and sisters in Christ. I have full confidence that my four daughters and countless others in the gay community are committed followers of Christ.

When I think of the relationship between the LGBTQ community and the church I am often drawn to the book *Us vs. Us* by Andrew Marin. His book is based on over 2700 responses from the LGBTQ community in a survey he conducted. Of the respondents, 84% claimed that they were raised in some type of Church community. Nearly all of them were no longer involved in any type of church at all. Also, most of them stated that they would love to return to a community of faith, but did not feel that they would be welcomed. This grieves my heart!

In the church we have made the terrible mistake of categorizing sins and have made homosexuality out to be the worst of them all. While we do this, we knowingly allow people who are practicing all kinds of other sins (gossip, pornography, gluttony, the list goes on) to hold positions of leadership in our churches. This must stop. We must practice Kingdom living as taught by our Lord and Savior, Jesus Christ who taught us to love and accept all, especially the "least of these". He called out sinners. He told would-be followers to stop sinning. And He warned all of us to refrain from judging others. We must humbly acknowledge our sins and live a lifestyle of repentance. Christ opposes the proud, for good reason. He must be the King of His Kingdom.

Early in our journey with our daughters, we learned that it was not our job to be the Holy Spirit. That brought us an incredible sense of freedom and relief. Let God be God and love our kids. For a long time I prayed that God would change my daughters and make them not gay. Then, the Holy Spirit changed my prayer to "Father, just help me to live in such a way that they see Jesus in me". This approach has allowed me to have beautiful and loving relationships with all of my daughters.

When it comes to the Church and LGBT community, I believe our response must be based in Christ-like humility. We can and must accept them as equal brothers and sisters in the kingdom. Thankfully, I am seeing many churches getting better at this. My own Church of the Nazarene has accepted my daughters with love even though they no longer attend regularly. They have also welcomed into our fellowship a beautiful gay woman who has become one of my dearest friends in our church fellowship. She sits on the front row every Sunday and is in my opinion, the most vibrant worshiper of Jesus in the congregation. As one of the worship leaders up on the platform, she truly blesses me every Sunday. I look forward to the day when she feels comfortable enough to be a part of the worship team at our church.

I believe that God has been and is calling us to do a much better job of discipling one another. And I honestly believe that this discipling can work in both directions between the Church and the LGBTQ community. We can and must grow and build one another up in the Kingdom of Christ here on earth. We all must realize that our identity comes not from our sexual preferences, careers, families, favorite entertainments, etc. but from Christ alone and his teachings about Kingdom living.

Obviously I do not have all of the answers for exactly how to accomplish a right relationship between the Church of the Nazarene and the LGBTQ community. But these things I do know, I love all four of my daughters intensely, God loves them infinitely more and that He accepts them right where they are, and that He is helping them grow in their faith on a daily basis.

I have done my best here to share my heart. My prayer is that it helps in some small way as we all navigate our way in relationship with Christ and with each other in our communities of Faith.

Brad Stover is married to Cindy Stover and father to 4 daughters. He graduated from NNC in 1986. He served as a youth and worship pastor from 1986 to 1992. He currently owns Brad Stover Construction LLC and B&D Siding Inc. He resides in Nampa Idaho.

Hear My Heart

SHARON STUECKLE

God's love does not exclude the LGBTQIA+ community.
Church of the Nazarene, is your love limited?

I began to write this essay like a grade school student charged with writing a persuasive book report: "Reasons Why You Should Read *All About Rainbows*." I'm not sure any student has ever convinced a peer to read a book with an essay. They convince fellow students to read a book by telling them how it made them feel or what really cool information they learned. They tell how the book speaks to them. Why should you be interested in my opinion and reasons? I am unlikely to convince you of anything by stating facts. Instead, I have decided to share my heart. Maybe your heart will hear what mine is saying.

I love people. I believe that God has created all of us in God's image. ALL of us. Regardless of our race, gender, beliefs, or idiosyncrasies, we are made to reflect God to the world. Because of this incredible status we humans have with God, we don't get to judge each other or decide who is worthy enough to carry God's love to others. James 2:8-9 NIRV says, "The royal law is found in scripture. It says, 'Love your neighbor as you love yourself.' [Leviticus 19:18] If you really keep this law, you are doing what is right. But you sin if you don't treat everyone the same. The law judges you because you have broken it." Love your neighbor; judging them and treating them differently is sin. I don't decide who God will use for God's purposes. That is up to God! Isn't it wonderful to be relieved of the pressure of determining who is "in" and who is "out?"

You know what is not wonderful, though? Being rejected by family and church because of who you are. Crying out for God to change you because you are attracted to the "wrong" person and feeling like God is distant because your prayers go unanswered. Falsely claiming that you were wrong about being gay due to pressure from your parents and church—and having to live a lie. Believing that you are "less than" and sinful because of who you love. Giving up on your call to Christian ministry because your church tells you that you will never be a pastor if you are queer. Having to stop serving in a ministry position in the church because you came out as gay and are in a homosexual relationship. These are not made-up examples. They have happened in real life to people I love. It breaks my heart. These dear ones have been treated as though they are unworthy. The pain and trauma that has been imposed on these individuals is unnecessary. I'd go as far as saying that it is cruel.

"Beloved, let us love one another, because love is from God; everyone who loves is born of God and loves God. Whoever does not love does not know God, for God is love." (1 John 4:7-8 NRSV) There isn't anyone God does not love. Created in God's image, we also should be love. We are not loving our LGBTQIA+ neighbors by treating them as "less than." The church is not a place LGBTQIA+ people have found acceptance. They cannot be authentic within the church. In fact, the church is responsible for trauma that some LGBTQIA+ youth have experienced. They have lived with the guilt of being a so-called "sinner." Some can no longer step into a church without experiencing real physical symptoms, which can include elevated heart rate, shaking, and shortness of breath. A good number have turned from Christianity altogether. Again, these examples are not from an overactive imagination. They are confessions of real people whom I know and love. The "hate the sin, love the sinner" mentality and the damage it has caused makes me cry. It is not love. It is hurtful.

The Church of the Nazarene's stance on LGBTQIA+ people and their relationships can affect their mental health. The Trevor Project references two recent studies by Johns et al that show LGBTQ young people are more than four times as likely as their peers to attempt suicide. In the same time frame, The Trevor Project surveyed LGBTQ youth and found that youth who report having at least one accepting adult were 40% less likely to report a suicide attempt in the last year. Death by suicide. A life lost—possibly preventable by the presence of accepting adults. I know LGBTQIA+ young adults who have experienced suicidal ideations. I can't imagine the pain of losing them. I don't want anyone to lose a family member or friend because that individual felt more welcome in death than in life. If the church can take steps to prevent pain, why doesn't it? "Love does no harm to a neighbor." (Romans 13:10 NIV) The church's part in the hopelessness felt in the LGBTQIA+ community makes me angry.

So, what can the Church of the Nazarene do? It can become fully affirming. Fully. Accept members of the LGBTQIA+ community as people made in the image of God who have gifts to share and love to give. Who are we to say who God can or cannot use, anyway? Do we dare to limit God by not allowing members of the LGBTQIA+ community to serve in leadership positions in church? Invite

LGBTQIA+ laypeople to serve as Sunday School teachers, sing in the choir, and become members of the church board. Welcome LGBTQIA+ pastors and their families as God's leaders of local churches. Just as the early church eliminated the requirement for circumcision (see Acts 15), eliminate the stigma placed on our LGBTQIA+ neighbors. Save a teen from contemplating the value of their life as a gay person. Accept them! Give hope to those in the LGBTQIA+ community who feel a call to Christian ministry. Encourage them! Acknowledge that a faithful homosexual relationship can be as much of a marriage as a heterosexual one. Celebrate with them! "Dear children, don't just talk about love. Put your love into action. Then it will truly be love." (1 John 3:18 NIRV)

I have a call on my life to love the marginalized. This includes those marginalized by their race, religion, gender, and immigration status. However, my main focus—one that has been confirmed over and over as a call of God—is the LGBTQIA+ community. Just as the sower in Jesus's parable recklessly sowed the seed, I am to recklessly love. I am not to judge the worthiness of the ground on which the seed of love lands. I am not to sow only on the good soil. I am to follow God's command to love. It is freeing! Ask yourself, "How can I love with the love of God? What must I do to show God's love to others?" God's love is boundless. My heart hopes that you will open yourself to loving everyone as beings created in the image of God. I pray that there will be more heart mending and less heartbreaking. I desire peace and hope for all of us.

"A new command I give you: Love one another. As I have loved you, so you must love one another." (John 13:34 NIV)

Sharon Stueckle is a wife, mom, friend, and teacher with a big heart for the marginalized. Her goal in life is to spread love recklessly and to be a part of God's kingdom business here on Earth. She is a member of Trevecca Community Church of the Nazarene in Nashville, Tennessee.

An Embrace of Love

TRACY TUCKER

The loving embrace of a parent is critical to the journey of their child whose identity is on the other side.

My story as a father who raised his two daughters in a Nazarene parsonage rewinds back to just over 30 years ago. My wife and I were married nearly a decade before the first one arrived. I'll never forget the moment I first held my infant daughter, having to reach for the nearby stool as my knees gave way to weakness. I was elated, intimidated and wildly in love with the new lady in my life. My little girl! And a daddy's girl Allison genuinely became. Almost 6 years later we added the second. "She's an old soul," her grandmother would later declare. Ani was less demonstrative but made up for it with her wit and powers of observation. Both girls are keen artists in their own right and respective fields, a trait inherited from their mother.

I have often said, I was outnumbered—even our kitty was female. But in the truest sense I never stood a chance to begin with. My girls have owned my heart from the day we learned my wife was pregnant the first time. I have always considered fatherhood to be the greatest privilege imaginable. But as likely every parent has experienced, parenting is also filled with pain. My experience has been that I am usually the author of my own pain, especially pain associated with my parenting practices. In a recent late-night conversation with Ani, I confessed that if I could reverse history, I would be silent more often, and more encouraging at other times. I would also likely reconsider some of the expectations which I had felt were of ultimate value. In short, were I given the opportunity for a redo, I would have been a nurturing guide rather than an authoritative guardian.[1]

But don't all compassionate parents tend to look back and observe countless points in their past where they wish they had responded to their progeny at least a little differently than they did? Since the focus of this essay is intended to reinforce

---

1. Sanders, J. (2019). *Embracing Prodigals.* Cascade Books. (1-15).

the conviction that the Church of the Nazarene needs to rethink her official position on the role of the LGBTQ+ community within the church, I will look at factors which affect the relationships most precious within Nazarene homes. I have two daughters and one of them, Allison, is queer. Married for about four years, Allison has faced much opposition in her journey from conservative beginnings to the present. Most, if not all, of that opposition finds its source within the Christian community, followers of Jesus who believe it is their responsibility to fix her (a cloaked form of judgementalism). Ani, on the other hand, is heterosexual and in a loving relationship of her own. While not gay, she has experienced the power of judgmentalism vicariously as Allison's sister and best friend. It has been heartbreaking for Ani to see her sister laid upon the altar of indignant "rightness" under the guise of godliness and holiness.

It is not my job or my intention in this essay to right someone else's wrongs. Neither is it my job nor intent to determine someone else's ethics. To do so would put me at risk of being judgmental. I simply intend to put forth the following faith-related thoughts for consideration that are born out of reasoned rethinking in my own heart as I have been able to make sense of my own family dynamics. The relationship I have always shared with my girls was at risk because I was resistant early on to serious dialog about these ideas. In these matters I have been "the chief of sinners."

I begin with the idea that God is always and at all times loving. Tom Oord develops this thought quite well in his work "The Uncontrolling Love of God".[2] With love as the essential and primary quality of God—God's essence—that starting point becomes the pivot on which we balance and measure everything else we say about God. Thus to be godly is necessarily to be loving. Everything else we do in pursuit of holiness must be shaped by our commitment to love. A fellow student of mine, Pastor Steve Watson had earlier served as an English teacher in the Boston Public School system. In his excellent essay "Learning to Save My Students Instead of Judging Them," Steve described in detail how he transitioned his teaching style from forcing students into a predetermined series of assignments that would ultimately be judged with a clear pass (along a sliding scale of excellence) or fail outcome. This approach simply didn't line up with how Steve felt God engages with humanity. Steve discovered that when he viewed his students as individuals with freedom and varying gifts, and his own role as encourager and guide, then he found himself more in line with the way he understood that God sees him. This

---

2. Oord, T. J. (2015). *The Uncontrolling Love of God.* InterVarsity Press.

thinking was brought home in Steve's reading of John 12:47 "I came not to judge the world but to save the world."[3]

My approach to parenting had much in common with how Steve had been schooled to teach, as an authoritarian whose job it was to critique and correct with the outcome of judgment. Of course I did that under the banner of love, "I push and correct you because I love you." But John 12:47 continues to jump back up. Judgmentalism (or if you prefer to say judgment) has no place in the church nor in Nazarene homes. Yet the understanding of love that I preached and lived was at best dismissive and at worst intolerant of those whose lifestyle in any way smacked of an LGBTQ+ orientation.

When my daughter came out to me, I was crushed. Mostly my pain rested on the fact that she considered the possibility that we might put her out of the house. "Wait, what?" But I now understand her fear. I had never expressed absolute acceptance in all circumstances. The only way for Allison to anticipate my response to her announcing her gayness was by observing my reaction to others within the gay community. I have known gay people, and I have tried to be tolerant and even accepting of them as people. But I had never embraced with loving arms gay people who, like myself, are trying to find their place within the broader kingdom of God. Where is the commitment to unity and universal brotherhood of believers and non-believers alike? I can enthusiastically support and celebrate the missionary effort of the church reaching out to pagans across the ocean, but limit my affection and embrace of the gay couple next door.

It seems as though Jesus' prayer for unity in John 17 is limited in its scope to just those of like mind and not really for those whose life style doesn't line up with the Bible as it is so often preached and taught. And now we are back to judgmentalism. I will let those more skilled in biblical interpretation provide a clearer reading of the half dozen passages within the Bible that are used to condemn homosexuality. My point is that our dogmatic rejection of our LGBTQ+ sisters and brothers, and especially our children, runs crosscurrent to everything within Jesus' teaching about unity and it is contrary to love.

In my first assignment as a Nazarene Pastor (around 1987), a gay couple began attending our small church in southwest Florida. Jerry was a gifted keyboardist, and his spiritual sensitivity was a rare and heartfelt addition to worship whenever he played. I never found out what was said or perhaps what expression was felt, but one week they simply disappeared from our congregation. No complaint was

---

3. Oord, T. J., Rambob, B., Reddish, T., & Stedman, F. (Eds.). (2021). *Partnering with God: Exploring Collaboration in Open and Relational Theology*. SacraSage Press. (333-36).

ever expressed to me, but Jerry and Lawrence simply indicated that they did not want to create further disruption. Jerry and Lawrence had taken in an elderly lady, Fern, who had found herself homeless and in need of care. Lawrence was Fern's hairdresser and had learned of her unfortunate circumstances. Without much discussion, Jerry simply agreed that it was the right and Christian thing to do, so they became "Aunt Fern's" surrogate family. She never had to worry again about how or when she might get her next meal or who was going to care for her. Jerry and Lawrence even purchased a home that would allow Aunt Fern the freedom of her own space within the loving environment of her caregivers. I missed my new friends and Christian brothers.

In a world packed full of beauty and variety where each species of bird has its unique song and each family of flowers has its own look of beauty, what a shame it is to consider that people with varying expressions of love are marginalized by those who claim to have the secret to living well. "This is my commandment, that you love one another as I have loved you." John 15:12 Bruce G. Epperly writes, "God's quest for a world that promotes beauty and complexity of experience always points to the contrast between the church as it is and the church as it is called to be in light of God's vision of beauty and Shalom."[4]

I love sitting with Ani, my younger daughter. She reads me like a short story book. After we have sat together for a while talking about stuff that may or may not be of substance, she always leaves me (notwithstanding my "dad humor") feeling as though I'm important to her. Recently Ani affirmed me for what she observed to be real growth in my faith journey. This is especially significant to me because she has admittedly turned away from the Christian faith that she was raised with. I won't attempt to go into her faith journey, it isn't my story to tell. Ani's exposure to "truth" within the context of the Christian community has been stifling. I get that. Some of what I was willing to die for as a young seminarian makes little sense to me today. My truth has changed. I read the Bible today with a very different understanding from when I first entered the pulpit. I watch as the Bible is raised in a social media pulpit with the preacher declaring "This is truth." Then I remember Jesus' words "I am the truth." I fall in favor of Jesus, rather than the sacred writings, and that is the result of my own growth dynamic. What I was once willing to die for, I no longer subscribe to. I am grateful for the inspired written word of God, and I believe those writings are a primary source of revelation, but I don't assign the characteristic of eternal truth to those writings. I reserve the title of truth for God in Christ.

---

4. Epperly, B. J. (2011). *Process Theology*. T&T Clark International. (122).

Jesus' words about loving enemies and the helpless and the rejected and the poor and the oppressed and the youngest and the oldest and the least of these are compelling examples of the truth as Jesus taught. If this is a more compelling and clearer picture of love and truth, then how can I refuse to embrace my spiritual sister and brother who are trying to find their place in the presence of God? And dare I risk taking a stance which limits grace? A stance on a principle that further along in my journey I very well may determine is a non-issue?

My final statement has to do with legacy. Within my legacy storage locker I have squirreled away my passion for coffee, the fancier the better. I also have a propensity for dad humor. There is space for collecting strange things, like the bobblehead Allison once had made of me, the size 13 wooden shoes a friend brought back to me from the Netherlands, and even the mink fur Cossack hat that another friend brought from an undisclosed location in Europe.

We all leave something behind, our legacy. That legacy is the piece of us that represents our past and potentially inspires the next generation. A legacy of grace and love inspires the next generation to serve as models of grace and love. It promises to promote general well-being and foster healthy relationships. That legacy speaks well of our personal journey, and those who traveled the journey with us.

On the other side, a legacy of adherence to a system of belief can leave a shallow imprint for the next generation to inherit. Systems are by definition not a loving community, but a structure for control and static reproduction. Systems do not breathe or express freedom in the sense of empowerment to grow in love and grace. We need systems for many things, and many systems are essential for maintaining order. But systems are not usually helpful when they are the veil behind which we hide on issues such as embracing alternative loving lifestyles.

The legacy I hope to leave behind has less to do with bobbleheads and wooden shoes or even a fine cup-o-joe. Rather, I want those who follow after me to inherit a spirit of love and acceptance that promotes general well-being and encourages those who have been marginalized. Could today's "Samaritans" be the LGBTQ+ community? Can we as a significant expression of Christ's body, the Church of the Nazarene, laity and leadership, risk our legacy potential on the platform of a rigid dogma? Or will we enter into a healthy and loving dialog for the purpose of promoting the Kingdom of God?

While I have always preached love as the primary theme of the Christian faith, I have not always lived that love when reflecting on or interacting with LGBTQ+ brothers and sisters. But when it arrived at my own home, I was forced to confront it, and I still do. I want Allison to see that I embrace her fully, and that I embrace her wife fully as my daughter-in-law whom I dearly love. I also want Ani to have a much better picture of what it looks like for a Christian to be essentially loving and to demonstrate that as a lived expression without judgment. Maybe if I can get this right, perhaps maybe someone else's son or daughter might not have to endure the loneliness Allison experienced and the rejection Ani felt and feels.

Tracy L. Tucker is a Senior Chaplain for Community Hospice and Palliative Care in Jacksonville Florida, following 30 years in fulltime parish ministry. He earned his MDiv from Nazarene Theological Seminary and is currently working on his DTM through Northwind Theological Seminary. Tracy is a Board Certified Chaplain through APC and has a Certification in Thanatology through ADEC.

I'm Younger Than That Now

DAVID VAN BEVEREN

How I went from "Gay is sin" to "LGBTQ+ needs affirmation,"
and how the Church of the Nazarene was instrumental
in the process.

> Yes, my guard stood hard
> when abstract threats too noble to neglect
> Deceived me into thinking
> I had something to protect
> Good and bad, I define these terms
> quite clear, no doubt, somehow
> Ah, but I was so much older then
> I'm younger than that now.
> —Bob Dylan, "My Back Pages"

Before I tell my story, I need to share what my secular background is. I was born and raised in the Netherlands, which, on April 1st 2001, was the very first country to legalize same-sex marriage:

"Four couples were married that day and soon, more couples followed. Discrimination is unlawful and same-sex couples have been able to adopt children in the Netherlands since 2001. The Netherlands was a pioneer and is standing strong in supporting equal rights for LGBTIQ+. Although equal rights are still not at the point we want them to be, with our human rights policy, the Netherlands is trying to establish justice and respect for all."[1]

---

1. www.netherlandsandyou.nl

That does not mean that everything is fun and games. There are still reports of discrimination, assaults and harassments. This group still needs protection.

I grew up in the mainline Dutch Reformed Church. My faith consisted of what I would call "church beliefs". I was a churchgoer, doing my stuff in church, repeating the Apostolic Confession of Faith in the weekly worship service and praying the Lord's Prayer on a daily basis, but there was no awareness of an authentic unity with a loving God. God was very far away. Sitting on a throne. Judging right from wrong.

When homosexuality became an issue in talk shows, I already had an idea about it. It was wrong. In the words of Bob Dylan, "Yes, my guard stood hard when abstract threats too noble to neglect. Deceived me into thinking I had something to protect."

Later my church beliefs changed into faith in a personal God. And it was easy to change my own opinion about gay people into God's opinion. God thought homosexuality was wrong. No doubt about that. But I was not informed. I just parroted the group of evangelical people of which I became a part. I did not inform myself, and did not listen to people that had really done research on the issue. And further, as long as you don't know individual gay people it's easy to hold this opinion.

In 1977 I became a part of the Church of the Nazarene in the Netherlands. Here I learned that God is love, and not a romantic kind of warm fuzzy loveliness. No, God's love is vast and trustworthy. It is real and active and relational. And the whole of creation is included in that divine love. But I had no idea about the implications of that view.

So, to state that I believe God is total and inclusive love did not practically mean for me that it should become part of my *life*, because the implications had not yet become part of my system.

Thinking about the love of God was especially thinking about God's love *for me*. His acceptance of me. My old opinions were still alive and kicking. But love was seeping into my consciousness. God loved more people than I thought possible. God really was accepting *all* people, even his enemies.

And as a consequence the God in my mind changed too. First I read all the dogmatics into the gospel. But my image of Jesus was peeled like an onion, dogmatic layer after layer was taken away, and I discovered a love so pure, so vulnerable, that it disarmed me. Literally.

That didn't mean that my opinion changed. Confronted with situations about human sexuality I found that my opinions were still alive and hard to silence.

Maybe I didn't want to, because these opinions functioned for me as some kind of security.

However I was confronted with stories of a Jesus who was including *all* people. Because that is what it meant when He said that crooks and whores will precede us into the Kingdom of God (Matthew 21:31). *"And the outcome of that is that crooks and whores also should be welcome as part of the church and as a result as part of your life, David."* I could almost hear Jesus saying this to me.

The story of Simon the Pharisee, who had invited Jesus as a guest at his table, helped me to see the practical implications. Simon was thinking in rigid judgments. There were sinners and saints, and he himself saw himself as a saint, he had the saintly labels all over him. And that woman who had entered his house… she was definitely a sinner. She was certainly not a part of *us*, she belonged to *them*. And then we have Jesus, who looks to people with the mindset that everyone, no one exempted, is in a process of development. In this story, looking through the eyes of Jesus we discover that Simon is in that process as well as this woman. There is no difference (Luke 7,36-50).

For me it meant that it's not up to me to make distinctions. In fact it meant that it's not up to me to judge. So when people had earlier asked me about the command of Jesus not to judge I would have said "amen" to that, and from there I would have continued to place people groups in categories. Not feeling that I was doing something that I was not supposed to do as a follower of Jesus.

But then it dawned on me that I needed to assess my whole life, and all my opinions, and all my beliefs in the light of the down-to-earth love of God for His creation. And I had to acknowledge that there was a time that not all LGBTIQA+ people have felt fully welcome and safe with me.

At the same time I became a pastor in a church of our denomination that had no problem with welcoming LGBTQ+ individuals into their midst. And although I was always aware that I lived in a country where a gay or lesbian couple with three adopted children could knock on the church door asking if they might join your church, this didn't happen. But individuals were accepted. and they found a safe place in our church.

Never did I have to deal with the question if I would officiate a same-sex wedding ceremony. So I didn't need to make decisions about such a request. And, honestly, I was glad that nobody asked me, because I really didn't know what to do next. Not that I was against it, but I was also loyal to the church that had brought me an image of a loving God that influenced me enormously, and brought me a development and practical redemption of all sorts.

Now I am retired—*I'm younger now*—and still growing in the awareness of an always loving and an all-inclusive God. The last six years' latent dogmas that I did not have to deal with in the years I was pastoring, slipped out of my system. And I knew something had to change. I needed to stop trying to save the cabbage and the goat. And needed to align my opinions about LGBTQ+ people.

Because the issue about affirming LGBTQ+ people was not about me anymore, about how I think and what I need to do. But it had become about what the position of my church should be. So looking from a distance to my church I have grown into the person that really longs for the day it will step off of the place where it has to judge, whatever that will be, but that it will take a position of total love and acceptance, and doing so reflecting the God that looks like Jesus.

People in all their colorfulness need to be accepted, need to be safe, need to be trusted, need to be valued, need to be loved. Because that is the way of the cross. Never judging, always serving. Never abandoning, always encouraging. Never afraid, always loving. Not because we are pushed into it by public opinion, and not because the LGBTQ+ community is demanding their rights, but because we have discovered that the love of God is bigger than we thought it was, and that this love urges us to take a new and unthought road.

So my conclusion is that the Church of the Nazarene needs to take the road to become an LGBTIQ+ affirming church, leaving behind the need to protect itself by certain borders, because it has learned to know that it don't need to be *worried and troubled about many things,* because only *one thing is needed. (Luke 10:41-42)* And that one thing is: to love the world as God in Jesus has loved the world.

So yes, I thought I had something to protect, but I'm much younger than that now.

David van Beveren *is retired. He was a pastor of the Church of the Nazarene in The Netherlands and he has worked as an Emotional Focused Couples Therapist.*

Transformation through Friendship

JOHN WAKEFIELD

Friendship with LGBTQ+ Christians can help skeptical Nazarenes draw closer to an understanding of the matchless grace of Jesus and to a faith formed and evidenced by the fruits of the Spirit.

I'd like to begin this brief essay by asking you to pause for a moment and bring to mind the face of a friend. This could be someone you knew as a child, a group of people even, or someone you're in close contact with today. It could be a spouse, a coworker, or a family member. Close your eyes if you need to, and then when you have that friend in mind, open your eyes, and keep them in mind as you read on.

The first face that pops into my head when I do this exercise is that of my childhood best friend, Ryan. Today, Ryan is married, the father of three children, 38 years old, and serving as a pastor in the Church of the Nazarene in Michigan. I live in North Carolina now, but we still stay in touch. We first met when we were just three years old at a Church of the Nazarene in southern Illinois. My parents had just moved our family to town, and when we walked in the door on our first Sunday, the family legend goes that Ryan saw me in the foyer and fainted, somehow overwhelmed by the knowledge that he had just found a lifelong friend. Looking back on that story as a parent today, I sincerely hope that the fainting part was not literally true. (Did they call a doctor?) But I can affirm, thirty-five years later, that the lifelong friendship part of the story definitely has been.

Our friendship has formed me significantly through the years, and I assume it has formed Ryan too. Friendships do that. They can give joy, light, and happiness to your daily life. They can provide a place of refuge and support in difficult times. They can push you out of an endless number of comfort zones. Friendships can influence decisions and opinions; they can send you off in different directions and change how you see the world around you. And often, they can be an overwhelming example of Christ's love breaking into the world.

The Bible is full of such friendships. Jonathan and David are probably the most often-cited biblical example of friendship, as they loved each other as they loved themselves (*1 Samuel 18:1-5*). Naomi and Ruth are another good Old Testament example: Ruth promises to stick by Naomi's side when she is most in need, and they both are made better for it (*Ruth 1:14-18*). Jesus himself had close friendships during his ministry on earth, especially with John the Apostle, "the one whom Jesus loved" (*John 13:23*). This friendship was so transformational for John that he was never the same, writing and preaching about God's love for the rest of his life. And Paul had Timothy and Titus, beloved friends and co-laborers in spreading the good news about Christ throughout the first century world (*1 Corinthians 4:17, Titus 1:4*).

Do you still have your friend in mind? Good, hold on to them. The theme of John the Apostle's transformation through friendship is one I will revisit, so taking a minute to consider how your friend has transformed your life might be a good idea right now. I'm guessing you would not be the same without that friend's influence. Without Ryan, I would never have gone to as many local church or District events in my teenage years, I never would have attended Olivet Nazarene University for college, and I would definitely have laughed a lot less over the last three decades.

Other friendships have shaped me over the years too, and in ways I would never have expected. Remember, friendships can do that.

Ryan and I attended summer camp at the Illinois District's Nazarene Acres, and a mutual friend from those years has since left the church. He was always hilarious, kind, devoted, and Christ-like, but once he began publicly dating another man, there was no room for him in the Church of the Nazarene. His story is sad, and it is not unique.

We also attended Olivet together, where I sang in the Testament Men's Choir and went on a mission trip to Argentina with a great group of singers. Though quiet about their sexual orientation while at ONU, a few from that group had their gifts for ministry rejected as unworthy and unclean (along with the rest of them) after graduation, and many no longer call themselves Nazarenes. Their story is sad, and they are not alone.

Personally, though, I watched those friendships fade away once those young men found the courage to admit to themselves, to their friends, and to their churches that they loved others in a way that the 20th century church in America deemed abhorrent. I let them go because I could see no other way forward.

How could these friends of mine not love the same way that I love; why could they not just be *normal?* Their romantic decisions were inconceivable to me twenty years ago, and I wished they could simply see the error of their ways. Wasn't it clear in the Bible that we all professed to believe that this way of loving was fundamentally *wrong?*

I am hopeful and confident that you will find good answers to those two sociological and theological questions in the other essays included in this book, or elsewhere, if you go looking with an open heart. I have found good answers myself over the years. But well-supported biblical arguments were not what transformed my opinion from silently regretting and judging the orientation and decisions of my friends to actively affirming them and their full participation in the Church.

You might have already guessed this, but friendships did that.

I graduated from Olivet, served with Nazarene Compassionate Ministries in Africa, and then returned to the States to serve as a youth pastor at Seattle First Church of the Nazarene. While there, I enrolled in graduate school to be a counseling psychologist, hoping to listen and care for others as my lifelong vocation and calling. Several of my classmates were pursuing their own vocation through the church and answering their calls to the pastorate and the priesthood. And several of them, alarmingly to me at the time, were gay.

Admittedly, the ivory towers of liberal, west coast academia might not be an admirable place for many, nor a surprising place to find my opinion evolving, but remember that my personal transformation did not come through well-supported biblical arguments or "woke" classwork. My own stance on LGBTQ+ issues in the church and culture at large was transformed through friendship and personal relationships, through listening to my classmates trying to pursue the call of Christ in their lives and through caring for them as they expressed pain, rejection, and heartbreak in the churches and families of their youth. These were young people, like me, hoping to be of use to the Body of Christ, like me, willing to give their lives in service, answering God's call.

And perhaps most importantly for the context of this particular essay, these young people thoroughly and consistently exhibited the fruits of the Spirit. My LGBTQ+ friends were serving one another humbly, in love. They were loving their neighbors as themselves. Their lives were marked by love, joy, peace, forbearance, kindness, goodness, faithfulness, gentleness, and self-control. They had faults and flaws, much like we all do, but they were faithfully trying to keep in step with the Spirit, and they wanted wholeheartedly to devote their lives to the church.

These friendships opened my eyes to a world where sexual orientation was not a dealbreaker nor a litmus test to being a follower of Christ. In much the same way, Paul wrote about these familiar fruits of the Spirit in a time when circumcision and other Jewish laws and customs were being used by the churches in Galatia to keep people out, to treat Gentiles as second-class citizens who needed to conform before they could be accepted into the Body of Christ. As he wrote to them then, "You who are trying to be justified by the law have been alienated from Christ; you have fallen away from grace… the only thing that counts is faith expressing itself through love" (*Galatians 5:4-6*). Paul was calling the Galatians back to the wonderful, matchless grace of Jesus—deeper than the mighty rolling sea—and to a faith formed and evidenced by the fruits of the Spirit.

I continued over the following decade, as maybe you have over the last few years, to find LGBTQ+ Christians exhibiting those fruits of the Spirit in different contexts. My wife and I moved our family to Charlotte in 2014 and eventually found a church home, one where I still serve today. I chose our previous assistant priest, whose sexual orientation would preclude her from serving in the Church of the Nazarene, to be my spiritual director for a class at Nazarene Theological Seminary because of her wisdom, temperament, and gifts for preaching and pastoral care. Our church's Director of Music has been in a committed gay relationship for 40+ years, as has our church administrator. The former knows more about church music than anyone I've ever known, is immensely talented, and can (and often does) quote John or Charles Wesley on a whim. The latter has an enormous heart for God's people, especially the homeless people in the neighborhood around our downtown location, and exhibits more patience and self-control than I could ever hope to demonstrate. Their friendships have shaped me, transformed me into being a better Christian than I would have been without them in my life, and I am eternally thankful for their willingness to continue to serve the Church, even with—no, especially with—their scars of rejection and judgment.

These are the friendships that all of us need, those that turn us toward Christ.

Before I conclude, we need to return to the exercise at the beginning, of bringing to mind a friend. If you took the time in the middle of this brief essay to think about how this friend has transformed your life, fantastic. If not, please do so now. The stories of friendship in the Bible give ample examples of love, comfort, faithfulness, and companionship through persecution and difficulty, and hopefully these friendships you've thought of have done the same in your life. The story of Jesus's friendship with John is particularly instructive, as an encounter with the love of Christ shaped everything about John for the rest of his days. It is nearly impossible to encounter Christ and not be changed. May all of our friendships shape us as John was shaped.

Friendships transform us; it's what they do. My friendship with Ryan has been transforming me for over 35 years, and I would not be who I am today without him. Thankfully, friendships with LGBTQ+ Christians have transformed me too, especially over the last decade: here in Charlotte, Marion, Budd, and Nancy have all helped me fully recognize the need for the Church—the entire Church—to be a place of welcome and grace, affirming the fruits of the Spirit when we see them, and inviting more and more people to a life of faith expressing itself through love.

It is my hope and prayer today for Nazarenes and other Christians across the world to pursue meaningful, open, and loving friendships with their LGBTQ+ brothers and sisters, to lament for the way we have treated our fellow image bearers in the past, and to allow those friendships to transform our lives, through Jesus Christ our Lord, who lives and reigns with the Father and the Holy Spirit, one God, for ever and ever. Amen.

John Wakefield is a 2006 graduate of Olivet Nazarene University and earned his MDiv from Nazarene Theological Seminary in 2023. He is currently a Postulant for Holy Orders in the Episcopal Diocese of North Carolina and serves at St. Martin's Episcopal Church in Charlotte as Director of Youth Ministries and Parish Communications. Find him online at jhnwkfld.com.

Let Anyone Accept This Who Can

ADAM WALLIS

The Church of the Nazarene is ready for LGBTQ+ acceptance, and we should rejoice and be glad in it.

I once shared on a discussion board with other Nazarene academics and clergy that if I had to rank my obligations as a theologian, I would say my first priority is to be a faithful Christian, secondly a thoughtful Wesleyan, and third, at best, a good Nazarene. While the Church of the Nazarene is a home full of extended family for me, the kingdom of God is far greater than can be fully realized anywhere, let alone by our young denomination, without God inhabiting our conversations and actions. If I were convinced that the call of God to pursue justice and love mercy necessarily drew me away from our brand of evangelicalism, then so be it. But I do not think that is necessarily the case.

The decision of the Church of the Nazarene to become fully inclusive of LGBTQ+ people is, in my view, an inevitable one. I say this not out of a sense of impending revolution, but in a sense of hopefulness. The clearest reasons I have for this come out of my experience as a Nazarene and Nazarene pastor's son, who has also attended welcoming and affirming congregations for over 10 years. More concretely, these reasons are also rooted in several realizations. First, Nazarenes are already inclusive of queer[1] people in a variety of ways in many places, inside and outside of our churches. Consequently, many of us already have love for members of our church family who are also part of the queer community, and are not asking them to leave anytime soon. Furthermore, I have come to realize that acknowledging and affirming queer lives can show us far more about God and ourselves than practicing exclusion will ever allow. Finally, I have come to see that it makes sense of the ways we already read the Bible.

---

1. Here I use *queer* inclusively to refer to the whole of the whole LGBTQIA+ community. This is practiced by many in the queer community, often as a way of reclaiming that label and erasing its power as a slur.

The reason the Church of the Nazarene has not already moved toward acceptance of queer people is, as I see it, not as much theological as it is practical and dispositional. I believe we have not moved toward full acceptance largely because many are unwilling to unlearn our assumptions and re-examine our own lives. In what follows, I will offer observations and experiences that many readers will share, and explore how these have led to my own change of belief and practice.

We Already Do

Currently, most Nazarene churches would allow, at least in principle and as a matter of polity, queer people to become members of the church, although usually with limited leadership capacities. After all, even if queerness *were* irreducibly sinful, the church is still for sinners. Sadly, it is very much the norm for queer people in our churches to hide aspects of themselves from an atmosphere of condemnation, often feeling unable to talk about their personal lives without risking judgment or altering friendships within the church. For just one relevant point of research, a 2018 release from Reuters reported findings from the *American Journal of Preventative Medicine* of a connection between religious faith and self-harm among LGBT adults.[2] There, the author reports that

> Religiosity has also been linked to a lower risk of suicidal behaviors, but there is some evidence to suggest that the impact of religion may be different for lesbian, gay, bisexual and questioning (LGBQ) individuals.
>
> Among lesbians and gays who said religion was not important to them, there was no association between sexual orientation and recent suicide attempts. But being homosexual did significantly increase the likelihood of recent suicide attempts in people who said that religion was very important to them.[3]

There is a great psychological harm perpetrated on queer people when the church refuses to accept them *as they are*. Even worse, many churches have fostered a kind of self-loathing among queer individuals that leads to self-harm. But while religious trauma in the lives of queer people is real, and deserves far more words and attention than I can give it here, a growing number of Nazarene churches are actively demonstrating a welcoming and affirming posture, while also conscientiously

2. Anne Harding, *Reuters Health*. https://www.reuters.com/article/us-health-lgbq-religion-suicide/religious-faith-linked-to-suicidal-behavior-in-lgbq-adults-idUSKBN1HK2MA, accessed Feb 10, 2023.
3. Harding, Reuters Health.

navigating denominational commitments and polity. However, it may be more of-ten the case that members and leaders leave the denomination for church bodies that have moved past these hurdles in favor of loving their queer neighbors. It is in-creasingly the case that other denominations and churches are opening their doors to queer people, and working to seek out the Kingdom of God alongside them.

Outside of our local churches, members already work with and have friend-ships with queer people and understand, implicitly if not explicitly, that queer people also bear the image of God. Many no doubt recognize that the politicized tropes about queer lives posing a threat to Christian families, even as simply as existing with and having the same rights as anyone else, is a bit of nonsense rooted in ignorance and bigotry.

We Learn More About God and Ourselves

It would be unfaithful not to mention that queer lives have been a means of grace to me, communicating forgiveness and love in unexpected ways. Countless first-hand experiences compel me to testify that accepting queer lives into full commu-nion in our church will show us more about God and about ourselves. In my time attending a fully welcoming and affirming congregation in Boston—Church of the Covenant—I was greeted, hugged, and shown more love by just one member of that church than I had ever experienced any home church up to that point in my late 20s. This is how I met Kate, a lesbian who had experienced more hate from non-affirming Christians than she would probably care to tell. In our very first conversation over church potluck, she asked about my church background and whether Nazarenes would be open to people like her.

I was not ready for that question. After a few moments of self-evaluation and re-gret, I told her that while there *are* indeed some Nazarene churches who are welcom-ing, the denomination as a whole is still growing and learning, that we still have the marks of bigotry and ignorance that need to heal, and that I am confident we will.

I cannot recall how or when I learned what I did about sexuality before I grew to become welcoming and affirming. Evangelical culture is awash in messaging about "defending marriage", "the moral majority", the "gay agenda", and other turns of phrase for reducing queer lives to sexual deviance. I can recall it being normal to have a visceral reaction when encountering anyone who was gay. After all, I knew everything I needed to know, *right*? But coming to know queer peo-ple, coming to love and be loved by them, you are forced to reconcile what you thought you knew with the faces and lives you *actually* begin to know. How can it ever make sense to tell someone that the church that nurtured you would not also accept them as they are, would not let them teach Sunday School, or preach, or lead music, or work with their children without resounding objections? How do you tell someone whose life is just as loving and hard-fought as yours, that they cannot fully participate in your church because your church does not exercise the same flexibility in biblical interpretation that we extend to the role of women in church, people who are divorced, or people who eat shellfish?

This was not "the gay agenda" looking me in the eyes at the church potluck, it was Kate—a woman so delighted to see me volunteer to do dishes that she would go on to hug me every time she saw me on Sunday mornings. In (almost) the words of Fanny Crosby, *I love my friend Kate because she*, knowing how I had spent the formative years of my life principally opposed to people like her, *first loved me*.

Here is a confession: I am a Nazarene whose past, most regrettably, included speaking and acting as though queer people's lives were, by their nature, sinful and sickening. I was physically uncomfortable around them and have used "queer" and other terms as slurs. After meeting many queer people, befriending them (or being befriended by them), hearing them preach the Gospel of a risen crucified Christ, working and studying alongside them, I had perhaps the clearest realization I can remember: I had sinned against them. What had made me uncomfortable was a trope of 'queerness' that wasn't any more true of actual queer people than it was for many of fellow self-described Christians. I had taken on the impression that queer living brought down society in some vague way, and that, for example, two men marrying each other would have some impact on heterosexual marriages. The only responsible Christian response to this revelation is for me to praise God for queer lives and for exposing my own bigotry, and support queer acceptance in the church.

We Already Read the Bible in Accepting Ways

It did not feel like hate when I accepted, in my youthful Christian wisdom, that queer folk, by definition, were sinners. I was reading the Bible as it had been taught to me in churches, revivals, camp meetings, and youth rallies. The apparent straightforwardness of passages like 1 Timothy 1 and 1 Corinthians 6 helped to keep my conscience clear: it wasn't my *opinion* that their lives were sinful, it was the plain text as it had been interpreted for me by clergy, lay leaders, denominational leaders, and other public Christian figures, so I felt no responsibility for how it affected others. That supposed *clarity* also allowed me, just as easily, to accept that queer folk were not just sinful, but also a threat to my way of life. It did not occur to me that the way I read the Bible could defame and cause harm. After all, I was living by faith as a faithful Nazarene Christian.

To my mind, defending the full inclusion of queer people in the church is akin to arguing that we should not understand creation to have happened in seven

24-hour days, or that we should not actually stone women for having affairs. Most of us are already in the practice of reading these other parts of the Bible in non-literal ways. There is hardly any interest in taking the Bible literally about rich people selling their possessions and giving their money to the poor. Christians are very happy not to read many parts of the Bible literally. But it is a sad tendency to read the Bible literally, or at least without regard to context, *only when* we want to decide who is in and who is out.

The Bible is full of surprises, if we will read it with eyes open. For example, who would have thought that, in an apparent direct reference to forced abortion, God gives instruction to Moses in Numbers 5 for how prepare a concoction that would "cause bitter pain, and [a woman's] womb shall discharge, her uterus drop" in the event that she were unfaithful to her husband?[4] Or what exactly does it mean that Jonathan's love for David was so great as to be "passing the love of women"?[5] Or who would have thought that in Matthew 19 readers could find a recognition of people who are born neither fully male nor female using the most accessible language available at the time?[6] Certainly, these passages beg for closer reading and interpretation than I can possibly give here, and there are far better scholars capable of providing it. But it is also important to see that these passages were not written for *us*, and so they are also not open for us to take at face value for our own facile generalizations. For these and many other reasons, the door is open for us to re-engage things we might have thought were settled. With the eventual move toward inclusion, whether during this General Assembly or some other one, it is time we begin this work now to confess our sins against the LGBTQ community and seek to read the Bible in ways that reflect their dignity within God's family.

Adam Wallis, PhD is the son of a Nazarene minister, a graduate of Southern Nazarene University (BA Theology and Ministry), Nazarene Theological Seminary (MA, Theological Studies), Northern Illinois University (MA, Philosophy), and Boston University School of Theology (PhD, Theology). As one might expect, he is now a software developer and product manager and lives in the Chicago area.

---

4. Numbers 5:11-31. NRSV. "When he has made her drink the water, then, if she has defiled herself and has been unfaithful to her husband, the water that brings the curse shall enter into her and *cause bitter pain, and her womb shall discharge, her uterus drop*, and the woman shall become an execration among her people.

5. 2 Samuel 1:26. NRSV "I am distressed for you, my brother Jonathan; greatly beloved were you to me; your love to me was wonderful, passing the love of women."

6. Matthew 19:12. NRSV. "For *there are eunuchs who have been so from birth,* and there are eunuchs who have been made eunuchs by others, and there are eunuchs who have made themselves eunuchs for the sake of the kingdom of heaven. Let anyone accept this who can."

PART III

Scholarly Perspectives

The Case For Marriage Equality

BRUCE BALCOM

*The convergence of legal and biblical interpretation in the
area of divorce and remarriage provides a compelling case for
marriage equality.*

In 2015, the Supreme Court decided Obergefell v. Hodges, a case which held that
states must issue licenses for same-sex marriages and recognize licenses issued by
other states. The ruling was based upon both the Due Process and Equal Protection
clauses of the constitution and represented a logical extension of the prior case,
United States v. Windsor, which was decided on the same date two years prior.

Windsor held that the Defense of Marriage Act was unconstitutional because
it violated the rights of same-sex couples who were denied federal benefits such as
preferential tax treatment due to their marriage, legally recognized in their home
state, not meeting the federal definition of marriage found in Section 3 of the Act.
Windsor was denied the spousal estate tax exemption for her deceased spouse's
estate, resulting in a hefty tax bill. The Court found that since the marriage was
legally recognized by the state of New York, the federal government was obligated
to recognize the marriage and provide the tax exemption.

Obergefell found that because marriage licensing is a government activity, denying it to a couple based upon the sex of the two people involved was a violation
of due process and equal protection as guaranteed in the constitution. Marriage is
so significant legally, given the many legal benefits and protections it affords, that
this arbitrary denial was seen as constitutionally impermissible.

As a lawyer I find the outcome of these cases unremarkable. It should seem
obvious that when a state recognizes a marriage, as New York did in the Windsor
case, legally speaking that should be the end of the analysis. To permit another
state to refuse to recognize the validity of that state's action is no different than
refusing to recognize the validity of a driver's license. This is a clear violation of the
Full Faith and Credit clause of the constitution.

The same thing is true when the federal government seeks to invalidate a state's action. The federal government has used state licensing to determine marital status for a very long time. The only reason for the Defense of Marriage Act to define marriage for federal purposes was to discriminate against duly recognized marriages due to the sex of those who were married.

Many churches decried these decisions at the time as an assault on the "sanctity of marriage." The reason for their objection is purely religious in nature. Conversely, the law is not permitted to take religious objections into account when providing public benefits. That is a foundational principle of the First Amendment's Establishment Clause.

I find interesting parallels in the law between the very recent issues surrounding marriage equality and the problem of divorce and remarriage. Originally, divorce in the United States was permitted only when someone could prove fault. Generally speaking, to be granted a legal divorce, one had to establish that the other spouse was guilty of something the law recognized as justifying divorce. This generally meant proving infidelity, cruelty, abandonment, criminal conviction, inability to procreate, or permanent serious mental illness. Additionally, the spouse suing for divorce had to have "clean hands," meaning the suing spouse could not have engaged in wrongful conduct in the relationship, or have known about the bad acts and not relatively immediately taken steps to end the marriage.

This resulted in divorce being expensive, difficult to obtain, and contentious. Often the accused spouse would strike back with counter claims of bad acts. Sometimes those claims were valid, but all too often they were false claims made to prevent the granting of a divorce. As a result, divorces were rare, and typically reserved for the very wealthy.

In the middle of the 20th century, as the civil rights movement began to take form, it was becoming clear that there were plenty of marriages that would legally qualify for a divorce, but due to financial constraints, the innocent spouse would never be able to successfully sue for divorce. As a result, states began to look at ways to make divorce easier to attain.

In 1969 California enacted the first no-fault divorce statute. Over the course of the next two decades, virtually every other state followed suit in some fashion. I recall sermons preached during that time that emphasized the sanctity of marriage, and that any divorce which was not based upon "biblical principles" was not truly a divorce. In reality the objections had less to do with divorce as with the behaviors of those who received a divorce after they were in fact legally divorced. Nothing in the law precluded a legally divorced person from subsequently getting remarried, and for those who viewed divorce through a particular interpretation of scripture, this presented a moral challenge.

For those who received a no-fault divorce, their new found freedom allowed them to be removed from a bad situation, sometimes abusive or cruel, other times simply unpleasant and devoid of love. As they recovered from the trauma of divorce, they naturally found themselves making new connections and sometimes, falling in love again. For certain segments of the church, this was simply impermissible.

Regardless of how the church viewed these new relationships, those newly married people, whether from church families, or the public at large, began having children resulting from those marriages. When they came to church, as new converts, or long time members, they brought their new families, complete with children. The church faced a choice: hold firm to the long-held interpretation that these divorces were invalid and any subsequent marriage ongoing sin, or revisit the interpretation of scripture.

Obviously how the church responded was critically important for the families coming into the church. Would they and their children find a welcoming, loving community or a place that condemned them? Churches like the Church of the Nazarene chose wisely. While refusing to trivialize the covenant of marriage, holding firm to the notion that it was a sacred relationship deserving of commitment and worth doing everything reasonably possible to maintain, Nazarene's made space for these divorces. The Church of the Nazarene recognized that sometimes relationships simply don't work out, and despite the best efforts of those involved, going their separate ways is simply the right thing to do.

This isn't to say Nazarenes simply turned a blind eye toward divorce and remarriage, but we accepted the reality that marriage and culture have changed over time, and the church's interpretation of scripture must take seriously the whole task of interpretation. That is to say, we must understand what the scripture says, how it says it, and what it meant within the context of its time, and also apply the underlying meaning to today's context.

There are several instances where the Bible indicates that remarriage while one's first spouse still lives is sin. (See, e.g. Matthew 19:3-11) Despite the clear scriptural references to the contrary, many churches, including Nazarenes, have refused to impose such a draconian interpretation. There are good theological and biblical interpretation reasons for holding to a more permissive position. Today you would be hard pressed to find a community that does not include divorced and remarried people raising blended families.

Earlier I indicated that I saw divorce and remarriage and marriage equality as parallel examples of how the church interprets scripture in our culture and society.

They share much in common. Both involve relationships that are among the most foundational and intimate we have. Both involve biblical interpretation issues where there are scriptural references that seem on the surface to condemn the underlying behavior. Both have arisen in the context of our society determining they are legally protected. Both result in the formation of families with innocent children.

At the end of the day we have a choice. We can choose to refuse to deeply examine our position, choose to decide for God where grace might abound, or we can choose to do the hard work that faces every generation. To take the tradition, scripture and experience of the past and make them new. It isn't a repudiation of our faith to enter into this work, it is the consummation of that faith. It is offering to this present age the good news of the gospel, where grace goes before us, drawing us toward the love of God.

Bruce Balcom *is a third generation Nazarene and practicing lawyer since 1996. He holds a BA in History and MA in Theology from Trevecca Nazarene University, and a JD from Vanderbilt University.*

Some Scriptural Reflections on Same-Sex Relations

LAURIE J. BRAATEN

What some Old Testament passages really say about same-sex relations will surprise most readers.

When I joined the Church of the Nazarene in 1973, I already had clearly formed opinions regarding what the Bible taught about same-sex sexual relationships.[1] I knew two young men (one a neighbor) who were gay and claimed to follow Jesus. I was certain that the Bible taught that they were living outside of God's will and faced eternal punishment. After all, that's what the Bible says, doesn't it? Later, as I prepared for a teaching ministry through graduate studies, my views didn't change much. But I was more careful not to make same-sex relations into a special category of "sin," and viewed it as wrong to discriminate against them in private or public life. Then as a father I had to ask myself what I would do and say if one of my daughters told me she was gay? What would be the proper Christian response? I decided I would accept and love her, but pray that God would show her the truth (as I understood it *then*).

Slowly, however, my views on the biblical teaching on same-sex unions were challenged. They were transformed over nearly thirty years of pastoring and teaching Bible in two Christian colleges. A careful reading of some key proof texts didn't seem as cut and dried as I once thought. Let's take a look at some of these passages.

Sodom and Gomorrah

We'll begin with the text that is probably most often cited by those who claim God disapproves of same-sex unions, the story of Sodom and Gomorrah (Gen 17-19). Judgment is announced against the cities, and the demand of the men of

---

1. From now on I will simply use the phrase "same-sex relations" instead of "same-sex *sexual* relations."

Sodom to have sex with Lot's male guests proves that *the sin* is same-sex relations (Gen 19:4-5), right? As obvious as this claim seems, the Bible doesn't make this connection! True, these men were threatening rape, but that is a wrongful act of violence whether heterosexual or homosexual (compare Judg 19:22-26). But it is a leap to assume that same-sex relations is *the* sin of Sodom. When later prophets speak of the sins of Sodom and Gomorrah, same-sex relations are not mentioned! Instead, they focus on various acts of rebellion against God and violence and injustices against one another. For example, when Isa 1:10-17 compares Jerusalem to Sodom and Gomorrah, he mentions injustice, bloodshed, and not seeking the welfare of the marginalized. Jeremiah compared false prophets to the sinners of these cities because they commit adultery, walk in lies, and enable evil doers (Jer 23:14). Ezekiel described Sodom's sins as people having an abundance of goods and not sharing with the poor and needy. The prophet also says the people were haughty and did abominable things (Ezek 16:49-50). When Ezekiel speaks of abominations elsewhere, he includes bloodshed, oppression of the marginalized, financial exploitation, robbery, and incest.

Did the prophets miss the obvious? Let's look at the story itself. To our surprise, it doesn't name a sin, it simply states that "a cry for help of Sodom and Gomorrah" for "great and weighty sin" has reached the Lord (Gen 18:20, translations are mine unless otherwise stated). The key is the "cry for help" word group (noun and verb forms) which usually indicates a cry for help to God. When victims of violence, injustices, and marginalization need rescue they cry out to God (Exod 2:23; Judg 6:6; Prov 21:13). The term does not mean an outcry or accusation against a neighbor because they were breaking a moral law that did not directly harm someone. Unfortunately, most Bible translations hide this fact by making it appear that Sodom and Gomorrah's neighbors are complaining against them. The "cry for help *of* Sodom and Gomorrah" (v. 20a) is mistranslated as "the outcry *against* Sodom and Gomorrah" (see NIV and NRSVue). Likewise, verse 21 reads, "*Its* cry for help that has come to me" (that is, the cry of the victims in the cities). It is similarly mistranslated as "*the* outcry that has come to me" (see NIV and NRSVue,). Genesis 19:13 reads "… great is *their* cry for help before the Lord," meaning many people from the cities are crying for help. Yet some popular Bible versions change the meaning by mistranslating it as, "The outcry to the Lord *against its people* is so great" (NRSVue, NIV italics in all quotations).

Before we go further, it is important to consider why the entire cities of Sodom and Gomorrah are called wicked and great sinners (Gen 13:13), and how there can be a great cry for help *within the cities*, and then the same verse say "*their sin*" is "so great" (Gen 18:20)? Doesn't this support the traditional view? No, because in the

Bible the character of an *entire community* is often determined by the actions and policies of those in charge. For example, we noted how Isaiah denounced *all Israel* as wicked, likening Jerusalem to Sodom and Gomorrah. The powerful abused the marginalized and there were innocent people crying for help (Isa 5:7). Although the innocent certainly outnumbered the wicked, Isaiah still declared that the *whole country was wicked* and deserved God's judgment. We find a similar idea in the Sodom and Gomorrah story. The character of the city was determined by the unjust leaders, there were not *even ten powerful righteous people* (Gen 18:32) that would stand up for the marginalized.

The mistranslations in the story make it appear that outsiders are making an accusation to God against (the sexual moral depravity of) Sodom and Gomorrah. In reality, the texts say that a group of victims of oppression from the cities are crying for God's help. In other words, there are no outsiders here offended by others' behavior, only victims of evil doers crying for help. So we are back to where we started. This "cry for help" suggests exactly what the prophets later said: some of the people of Sodom and Gomorrah were guilty of various types of violence against others, and these victims were crying to God for help. Unfortunately, one consequence of these mistranslations is that over the years many well-meaning Christians have considered them a mandate to do likewise. They see it as their duty to be God's moral police and call out, condemn and discriminate against people within and outside of the faith if they don't agree with their sexual orientation.

The Mosaic Law

Leviticus seems to be the clincher for Old Testament teaching about same-sex relations. For many people, the prohibition against same-sex relations is clear and decisive. But a closer look and a little reflection might lead to another conclusion. First, a central teaching of this part of Leviticus is that God is holy, and that people are holy by separating *from* unholy influences, and being separated *to* God. A central principle that guides this holiness is the call for Israel to love their neighbors and outsiders as they love themselves (Lev 19:18, 34). This shows others the holy love that God has shown them.

In many of its specific details, how Leviticus pictures holiness and love in action are much different from today's standards. For example, there are directions about how men should trim their hair and beards, and prohibitions against tattoos (Lev 19:27-28). Holiness means not eating certain "unclean animals (Lev 11:1-47). Also, Leviticus often assumes that to be holy, things have to be one or the other; it's either/or, and categories can't be mixed. For example, people aren't supposed to plant a field with two kinds of seed (it has to be wheat or barley), nor make clothes out of two types of cloth (it has to be wool or linen, Lev 19:19). This binary thinking is probably behind the prohibitions of same-sex relations; a man must behave like (most) men, which means his sexual partner must be a woman and not another man (Lev 18:22).

The section on sexual ethics in Leviticus 18:1-30 is introduced by a warning not to follow the practices of the Canaanites (vv. 1-5). The last three prohibitions (vv. 21-23) are against sacrificing children, male same-sex relations,[2] and bestiality (sex with animals). In the conclusion (vv. 24-30), the entire list of sexual prohibitions are called Canaanite abominations. So it appears that Israel considered same-sex relations as wrong because they were practiced by the Canaanites, whom they regarded as sinners.

Matters of Law and Love

Our look at Leviticus raises the question about what we as Christians can accept as still binding. One suggestion is that an Old Testament law is binding on Christians if the New Testament repeats it. But this is only partially helpful. For example, Christians would agree that the incest and bestiality prohibitions still stand. Yet the New Testament does not have general rulings on these issues.

There are some who assert that if we disagree with Leviticus and say same-sex relations should no longer be considered wrong, then what's to stop anyone from claiming that incest or bestiality aren't wrong either? This all or nothing approach is a nonstarter. I have a hunch that no one who argues this keeps all the laws of Leviticus. In fact, they probably wear some clothing made of a cotton polyester blend, contrary to Lev 19:19. And I doubt this person would agree that if someone says it's okay to wear blended clothing, plant tomatoes and cucumbers in the same garden, or get a tattoo, then what's to stop anyone from claiming that incest or bestiality are also okay? This is inconsistent thinking. When it comes to these other laws in Leviticus, they decide their relevance on their own merit. I would add that each ethical command has to be evaluated in light of God's love. There are good reasons today for saying that God's love for the other compels us to love, accept, include, and affirm those with nontraditional (non-binary) sexual orientations.

Where Do We Go from Here?

It took much study of scripture, reflection, prayer, and time for me to change my views. I met some Christians who identified as gay or lesbian who evidence the grace and gifts of God as they proclaimed God's Word and radiated a Christ-like

---

2. Leviticus doesn't mention same-sex female relations.

spirit. How could I say that God doesn't accept them just like he accepts me and others, with all our brokenness, faults, and, yes, sinfulness? Why should a same-sex monogamous relationship be considered wrong? But it is not up to me alone to open the doors of acceptance, it is up to all who take upon themselves the name of Jesus.

The Church is accountable to the Holy Spirit for leading them along the paths of grace for all of God's creatures. Has that leading taken them on new paths? Yes!, most notably in the Church's understanding concerning the injustices and immorality of enslaving other humans, and the sexism inherent in excluding women from ordained ministry and an equal role in the family and workforce. For centuries these biases continued unchecked, and largely unchallenged by the Church. When they were challenged, people accused them of disobeying God, rejecting scripture, and not being true followers of Christ. Now there are some in the Church who are asking us to reconsider our teachings and policies regarding LGBTQIA+ people, including those who proclaim Jesus as Lord. It is time to recognize that what the Bible says about this community communicates more about ancient cultural biases than it does regarding the love of God revealed in Christ. The people of God must now ask ourselves if God's grace, love and acceptance is limited because of who one shares the marital bed with.

Laurie J. Braaten *earned an MDiv from Nazarene Theological Seminary (1979) and a PhD from Boston University (1987). He taught Biblical Studies at Eastern Nazarene College (Quincy, MA) and Judson University (Elgin, IL). He has also served in various pastoral roles. Laurie is currently active in the Society of Biblical Literature. For more information see judsonu.academia.edu/LaurieBraaten.*

In the Image of Perfectly Cis-Het Rule Followers

MICHAEL JOSEPH BRENNAN

The Nazarene Church is harming people with homophobic rhetoric and exclusionary practices. The world does not know us by our love, but by our bigotry and hatred.

There are too many stories I could tell of students, colleagues, friends, and family members of people who want nothing to do with Christianity because of the destruction it caused. They were rejected while trying to talk a Christian about their identity or their experiences. This is not a weeding-out of bad eggs, it's a crisis. And *representative figures* and *peace-makers* are not representing Christ or making peace. They are wreaking havoc on those who are trying to survive.

Of the cross and pride flag, one of these symbols represents nationalism, bigotry, and hate against marginalized communities, and the other represents belonging, inclusion, and acceptance. Churches that fly the rainbow flag encourage safety, belonging, and decision-making. Christians are losing a battle they shouldn't be fighting. Nazarenes should be listeners, defenders, affirmers, and encouragers.

Christians should be working to make sure the cross represents love. My church in Florida made bumper stickers that shows the cross equals a heart, because on its own, it's difficult to know which cross is being represented: the cross where Jesus sacrificed his life for the world, or the cross on fire in someone's front yard. I do not want to be misunderstood: the cross is a powerful symbol, and if we wear it or display it, it should mean that we are good representatives of *agape* and *shalom*.

Nazarene doctrine emphasizes the importance of Christian living, holiness, and social justice. Historically, Nazarenes have defended and served the oppressed and marginalized people in their communities and sought global opportunities to show compassion through service missions. John Wesley said, "Do all the good you can, in all the ways in all the places you can, at all the times you can, to all the people you can, as long as ever you can." With this in mind, we should be making sure our churches and congregations are safe, and they can only be safe when they are affirming.

When Evelynn, who loved being part of the worship team, hasn't been able to tell anyone what she has been experiencing because of her fear of being rejected or attacked, we need to take inventory. We need to decide that churches should not be less safe than therapist offices, schools, and police stations. There are people who are hurting that need a place to turn for safety.

Why would I want to be part of a denomination that doesn't want me? Nazarene theology can be loving and logical. This is the denomination of my closest friends. I admit that I don't like a lot of arbitrary rules, and Nazarenes have been capitalizing on arbitrariness for a long time. (For more on this I encourage you to read *Our Watchword and Song*.) If being a Nazarene means following arbitrary rules like not dancing, then I can't be a Nazarene. But where else could I go to find similar doctrines about God, love, and humanity? I don't want to shop around for other churches and denominations. I love this one. I'm invested.

I became a Nazarene because I admired and respected my professors and pastors while attending ENC. They were brilliant people that loved God with their hands and their brains. While it seemed that initially my mission field would be elementary schools, it eventually became the adults that were "too smart for Christianity." I didn't want to be written off by people that thought I didn't believe in vaccines or dinosaurs.

I am a Nazarene because we believe in sanctification. We believe that we have been chosen to represent God's love and creativity in the world.

I am a Nazarene because I believe in holiness. I believe that we are to mature as peace-makers and bring *shalom* to places of chaos, broken places where people need help and healing.

Queer people are not the enemy, and even if they were, Jesus commands us to love our enemies. In Matthew 5:44, Jesus says "love your enemies and pray for those who persecute you." But queer people are the ones being persecuted. They do not persecute us for our faith, they respond to our rejection with fear and hiding. Churches that fly pride flags are trying to make clear that queer people do not need to be afraid at that church. John Wesley says "though we cannot think alike, may we love alike." He goes on to say "herein all the Children of God unite, notwithstanding these smaller differences." These may not seem like small differences, but in the brevity of life, we should be remembered for how we loved each other rather than harmed each other. How we treat people impacts our witness in the world. At present, queer people know us by our harshness, hatred, and rejection; and not by our love.

"Loving the sinner" is a phrase used to justify discrimination and mistreatment toward queer people. A more loving and compassionate approach is to understand that people are complex and multifaceted, and that their actions are often rooted in a variety of factors, such as systemic oppression, mental health issues, and personal experience. By focusing on the sin rather than the person, it is easier to dehumanize them and miss the opportunity to understand them and offer compassion. This is especially true when harmful remarks are made from the pulpit.

The traditional language of sovereignty often causes a judgment-based response from Christians in relation to queer people. But the language of open and relational theology offers a foundation more conducive to truly understanding the individual person—by loving them, hearing their stories, and affirming their identities. Phoebe Palmer claims that "the love of God is impartial and universal…it embraces all [humanity] without distinction."

The process of sanctification must also acknowledge the process of emerging sexuality and the fluidity of identity. Personality, orientation, and gender are not fixed constructs. They exist in the realm of possibilities.

Nazarenes have been demonstrating that they are more concerned with the teachings of scripture rather than the relationship with God. Phineas Bresee relied on the work of the Holy Spirit to convict people of sin, rather than rules. Rules create a line where people feel that it is easier to leave than to suffer under the weight of shame—and sometimes people would rather die than experience the suffering of shame.

The Holy Spirit calls us *in* rather than calls us *out*. The Holy Spirit changes our desires from within to create shalom for the community and the individual, so that both can experience peace, joy, wholeness, and well-being. The church must speak out against all forms of oppression. For me, this means being patient with non-affirming Nazarenes and helping them to find a posture that allows them to listen to the stories from queer people.

Holiness detached from love is not holy. If holiness defines how we love, then we are neither loving or holy. Paul writes in 1 Corinthians 1:30 that "it is because of him that you are in Christ Jesus, who has become for us wisdom from God— that is, our righteousness, holiness, and redemption." We cannot be holy or righteous on our own. We need to be reliant on God's love and grace. Wynkoop says "love takes the harshness out of holiness."

In 1 Corinthians 1:11, Paul writes, "be imitators of me as I am of Christ." As evidence of this discussion, the Nazarene church, like many denominations, are hung up on the superficiality of the Christian life. Jesus healed on the Sabbath because the person was more important than the rule. God makes accommodations for us. This is grace. We need to be vessels of love and grace.

Nazarenes believe in *prevenient grace*, which means that God provides opportunities for humans to respond to love, and God also enables us to respond. The implication for queer people is that if God desired to change a person's orientation or desires, then God would provide a means for that change. Instead, cishet people are enabled to show *agape* to everyone; therefore, Christians should be demonstrating love in every situation to every person.

The Holy Spirit is at work in each of us, so there is no reason to be judgmental about that process in other people unless it is dangerous or hateful—which leads me to my most important point. The judgment, attitudes, sly remarks, exclusions, and rejections harm people. It causes emotional damage for those people longing to be loved. Queer people should not be mistreated because of whom they love or how they express their love.

I saw two posts recently, both from Nazarenes. One read: "I think the tragedy of modern Christianity is this: that we're more afraid of holiness than we are of sinfulness. We can tolerate sin, but boy, we get our hackles up when we talk about holiness."

We get our hackles up because the word "holiness" is too often misused. Rather than loving God and others more and better every day, we try to manage sin. Now while love might make us want to change behaviors, the behavior we should be looking at is blessing others. Queer identity and sexual orientation is not sinful.

This leads to the second post I saw, which stated, "The question is not, 'Do I approve of your lifestyle, your choices, your relationships?' The question is, 'How can I be a blessing in your life?'"

We need a doctrine that affirms queerness and challenges traditional and antiquated beliefs about gender and sexuality. Queer and affirming Christians look to scripture to support a more inclusive understanding of God's love for humanity.

Behavior management is a poor use of time, and you will fail. You'll feel a weight that eventually you won't be able to bear because of shame. Jesus says His burden is light and His yoke is easy. But it's only light and easy when we rest in who He is, and not on our own power to stop people from sinning. People over thousands of years have tried to figure out how to define sin. I think sin is the antagonist to love. Sin means that we intentionally cause harm. It keeps people from flourishing. From the upside-down translation of 1 Corinthians 13: Sin is impatient, sin is mean. It is envious, it boasts, it is proud. 5 It does dishonors others, it is self-seeking, it is easily angered, it keeps a record of wrongs. 6 Sin delights in evil but fails to rejoice with the truth. 7 It never protects, never trusts, never hopes, never perseveres.

Nazarenes can love in a way that helps others to thrive, with love that frees the spirit, and love that protects others.

The days of thinking God is holding us like spiders over a pit of fire to make us behave better is a strange kind of manipulation and coercion. Should we go on sinning? "By no means." But how do we stop sinning?

If the Nazarene manual discussed doctrine and polity, then being a Nazarene would make logical sense for those people that believe in a loving God. But it also addresses orthopraxy in a way that excludes membership and goes so far as to cause shame. The foreword of the Nazarene Manual states, "Because it is the official statement of the faith and practice of the church and is consistent with the teachings of the scriptures, we expect our people everywhere to accept the tenets of doctrine and the guides and helps to holy living contained in it." Then in the next sentence it states that "to fail to do so, after formally taking the membership vows of the Church of the Nazarene, injures the witness of the church, violates her conscience, and dissipates the fellowship of the people called Nazarenes." Nazarenes seem to believe that conviction of undesired arbitrary behavior like dancing and certain movies is the role of the denomination, and therefore people can and should be excluded from voting, ministry, and teaching. Orthopraxy should not be defined in a way that shames people for their behavior rather than helps people to love God and others more fully.

Every day love the Lord your God, love others, love yourself. Some of your behaviors and attitudes will change. It will take time. The Holy Spirit will convict you of sins if you want.

Stop making up rules against people who are trying their best. Get to know the people you're opposing. Listen to their stories. Learn their language and eat with them before you criticize them. Stop calling out and start calling in. Invite people and be a good host.

Queer people have been mistreated by religious conservatives that insist on forcing those they perceive to be outsiders to follow the letter of a law which is ambiguous and mistranslated. Queer people are the victims of institutional and ecclesiastical homophobia. Accommodation does not reduce scripture or sovereignty, but Christians are better *peace-makers* when they view both through *agape*.

Michael Brennan is the Dean of Students at Oxbridge Academy in West Palm Beach and an editor for The Weight Journal. He received his BA from Eastern Nazarene College. He has earned a Master of English from the National University in LA Jolla CA. He was working toward Nazarene ordination in the Eastern Michigan District before his divorce derailed his goals. Brennan is currently working toward earning a Doctor of Ministry and Theology at Northwind Theological Seminary.

An LGBTQIA+ Proposal to Fix the Nazarene Church Manual

PATTI L. DIKES

The Nazarene church has lost members over its LGBTQIA+ stance. This LGBTQIA+ proposal to fix the church manual could start bringing them back.

The decline in membership of the Church of the Nazarene in the United States and Canada has been attributed in part to its stance on LGBTQIA+ issues. For the church to reconsider its stance, it is important to understand the stance and how and when it came about. A review of church manuals was undertaken to determine whether and how the church can respond to LGBTQIA+ believers with love and justice. This article provides a broad overview of these topics, finds answers in the church's Manual and its preceding manuals, and offers a proposal.

The Church of the Nazarene was founded in 1908 under the influence of John Wesley and the American Holiness movement of the 19th Century. There are 2.6 million members worldwide; fewer than 600,000 are in USA/Canada. The organizing document for the denomination is the Manual of the Church of the Nazarene, which includes its doctrine, history, constitution, governmental structure, policy and procedures, and stances on moral and social issues. The Manual is published approximately every four years when the church meets for its General Assembly. The oldest manual available on the church's website was published in 1919; the most recent is dated 2017-2021. The first one has 137 pages. The current one has 426. Every one of the 24 manuals is different. Some of the revisions can be attributed to the church's growth and institutionalization over its 115-year history. A few adjustments reflect a maturing of Nazarene theology. The most dynamic activity has occurred on moral and social issues and ethical standards and guides to holy living in a section now entitled the Covenant of Christian Conduct (Covenant). Amendments to the Covenant require a 2/3 vote of the members present and voting at a given General Assembly.

337

The Nazarene Church believes the Holy Spirit is "ever present and efficiently active in and with" the church, sanctifying believers, and "guiding into all truth." Great emphasis is placed on biblical holiness. The church sees its role as relating "timeless biblical principles to contemporary society." Older manuals included general membership "rules" on faithful practices of holy living, evils to avoid, and participation in the church, and included special "advice" on matters such as financial stewardship, temperance and prohibition, marriage, and divorce. In later manuals, the rules, special advice, and certain positions expressed in the appendices on a variety of subjects, eventually all became part of the Covenant. The succession of church manuals illustrates how church perspectives on society and holy living shift and change. You might have difficulty guessing how many years rules or positions on each of the following remained in the Manual, and which ones are still there: communism, school drama programs, college athletic intramurals, comic magazines, dancing, using church buildings for recreation or entertainment, movies, vaudeville shows, intoxicating liquors, women wearing jewelry and braided hair, and the circus.

There may be Nazarene church members who are under the impression that the church has always held a stance against the LGBTQIA+ community and fear reconsideration would mean a paradigm shift so heretical as to permanently alter the fundamental character of the church. Those members should know that neither of these things is true. There has never been an official position taken by the Church of the Nazarene on the "LGBTQIA+ community," or transgender, queer or questioning, intersex, asexual, and other people. As its manuals reveal, relative to its history, the church only recently adopted stances directed toward LGBTQIA+ believers.

The topic of homosexuality first made its way into a church manual as a position asserted in a short paragraph of an appendix in 1972. Understanding the historical context for this entry is crucial. Countless sermons may have been preached about homosexuality as a mortal sin in the history of Christianity, but the Church of the Nazarene had existed for almost 65 years without ever creating a rule, offering advice or guidance, or taking a stance against it in any of the 13 previously-published manuals.

The 1960s and 1970s were a tumultuous time in the United States. Those two decades represented the civil rights movement, antiwar demonstrations, and the anti-gay movement. In June 1969, a three-day riot broke out at the Stonewall Inn in Greenwich Village after police officers attempted to raid the popular gay bar. A 1969 Harris poll showed the public believed only communists and atheists were more harmful to America than "homosexuals." In June 1970, on the one-year anniversary of the Stonewall riots, thousands of LGBT community members marched through New York City into Central Park in what is now considered America's first gay pride parade. A cultural rebellion was underway. "Hippies" defied parental authority and college officials. "In 'dropping out' of conventional society, they grew long hair, wore eccentric clothes, gathered in urban or rural communes, used mind-altering drugs, relished "hard" rock music, and engaged in casual sex." (W.W.Norton) All of this civil unrest felt threatening to many Christian families, who looked to church leaders to save their traditional values.

Back then, anyone who today would identify as a part of the LGBTQIA+ community likely had nothing to do with a church or, if they did, hid that part of themselves in the "closet." LGBTQIA+ believers had no place as whole persons within the church. Most church leaders did not truly know any LGBTQIA+ believers well enough to discern the holiness of their lives or the ethics by which they lived. All they had were the caricatures and stereotypes portrayed in books, magazines, movies, and television, and by the news media, televangelists and religious leaders raising money or seeking political power and influence, and others with self-interested agendas.

It was under these circumstances that the church issued a brief statement in 1972 asserting that the "depth of the perversion" leading to homosexual acts affirms the "biblical position" that such acts are "sinful and subject to the wrath of God." The church urged clear preaching and teaching concerning "Bible standards of sex morality." It deplored any action or statement that implied "compatibility between Christian morality and the practice of homosexuality." In 1976, the church's stance moved out of the Appendix and into the rules.

In 1973, Pew Research Study found 73% of the public said same-sex sexual relations were "always wrong" and only 11% said it was "not wrong at all." For more than a decade, the United States and the World faced the HIV/AIDS crisis with fear and anxiety. Many within the church believed the epidemic was a sign of God's wrath against gay men and the victims somehow "brought this upon themselves." We learned later that was not true but public opposition to homosexual behavior remained strong until the early 1990s.

In 1989, the church renamed its rule on homosexuality, "Human Sexuality," which it described as "one expression of the holiness and beauty" that God intended for Creation and "one of the ways by which the covenant between a husband and a wife is sealed and expressed." Instructing further, "husbands and wives should view sexuality as a part of their much larger commitment to one another and to Christ" and marital sexuality "ought to be sanctified by God." The manual explains that, "Sexuality misses its purpose" when treated as an end in itself or by using another person to satisfy "perverted sexual interests." Homosexuality, the church affirmed, was "one means" by which human sexuality was perverted. The only other means mentioned was pornographic images.

In the 2017-2021 Manual, this section expands exponentially and incorporates within it the church's positions on marriage and divorce. The view that marriage is between "one man and one woman," which had entered the Manual in 1928, is moved into this section to complement a prohibition on same-sex marriage. A new stance valuing singleness is expressed without comment on asexuality or masturbation. The Manual adds seven paragraphs discussing at least 24 deep philosophical, theological, ecclesiastical, and practical concepts ranging from beauty to the nature of God and the fracturing and twisting of desire by sin in the Fall. For members to "resist adding to the brokenness of sin," the church provides a comprehensive list of "areas of sexuality" to avoid. The descriptions include unmarried sexual intercourse and other forms of "inappropriate sexual bonding," and sexual activity between people of the same sex, which specifically call out homosexual and bisexual attraction and the practice of intimacy, as contrary to God's will. In addition, the Manual lists at least 15 other sexual practices to avoid, including hate speech and bestiality, with narratives explaining why these are problematic. This section then adds three more paragraphs affirming holiness themes already throughout the Manual on God's healing grace, conformance to God's will, and congregational obligations to act with care, humility, and discernment.

More than 50 years have passed since that little paragraph launched what has become 1/3 of the Covenant. Yet today, according to a 2022 Gallup Poll, roughly 21% of Generation Z Americans who have reached adulthood—those born between 1997 and 2003—self-identify as LGBTQIA+ or something other than heterosexual, as do 7.1%, of all adults in the U.S. According to Pew, about six in ten adults (61%) express a positive view of the impact of same-sex marriage being legal, including 36% who say it is very good for society.

Today, LGBTQIA+ believers are no longer hiding. Some of them may be wounded or scarred by how the church and its members have treated them. But they know God loves them and Jesus lives within their hearts. They live holy lives. Sadly, not because of the Nazarene Church, but in spite of it. As I Corinthians 12:21 teaches, the church body does not consist of one member but of many parts and each part has something to contribute: "The eye cannot say to the hand, I have no need of you, nor again the head to the foot, I have no need of you." All believers in Christ are indispensable members of the church body. In the words of Reuben Welch, "We really do need each other." LGBTQIA+ believers are boldly petitioning for full affirmation as worthy members because they desire the fellowship of the church and the church needs them.

For purposes of this article, I am assuming the Holy Spirit has been at work in the hearts and minds of church members on this issue. They know and love enough LGBTQIA+ believers to evaluate the holiness in their lives and recognize their relationships are just as healthy, loving, and committed as their own. Their hearts ache for the LGBTQIA+ believers who have been alienated, abused, or rejected by the church. They want to be inclusive and affirming despite challenging scriptural passages and the latest church manual more than doubling down on its condemnations. I am assuming those hearts and minds are open to possible solutions.

To change official policy in the Manual, the Holy Spirit will have to move at the next General Assembly to obtain the 2/3 vote necessary to amend the Covenant, but church members should be ready with a proposal. Preceding manuals show stances have been changed, even in the face of problematic biblical passages not unlike the ones commonly asserted to condemn homosexuality. Two helpful examples are divorce and women's ordination.

With divorce, the Bible is very clear: God "hates divorce." (Malachi 2:16) Certain of its obligation, the Nazarene Church maintained a harsh stance against divorce for more than 50 years. The 1919 Manual declares that anyone who obtains a divorce for any reason other than adultery, and subsequently remarries, is "unworthy of membership" and ministers are "positively forbidden to solemnize the marriage of persons not having the scriptural right to marry." In 1964, the church's position softened slightly to state that divorced persons were "ineligible" for membership. Then, in 1972, the church recognized that "many in our society fall short of the divine ideal" and decided previously-divorced marriage partners could become members after giving evidence of their "regeneration" and an "understanding of the sanctity of Christian marriage." However, failure to prayerfully attempt to save an unhappy marriage and seek guidance from their pastor would make "one or both parties subject to discipline."

Thirty-five years later, the 2017-2021 Manual includes no consequences to membership; it merely says that divorce "falls short of God's best intentions" and the church should offer "counsel and grace to those wounded by divorce." In this example, the church never sought to engage the Bible as its position softened, and it took almost 100 years to develop a compassionate response to believers today. The urgency of this moment for LBGTQIA+ believers does not allow the church the luxury of wasting even an extra quadrennium; it must act at the next General Assembly.

The second example is women's ordination. The Bible contains strong opposition to women preaching: "Women should be silent in the churches. For they are not permitted to speak but should be subordinate [to men]…For it is shameful for a woman to speak in church." (1 Cor. 14:34-35). Many conservative evangelical churches point to these passages to prohibit women from preaching and becoming ordained.

In the most recent manuals, the Nazarene Church directly confronts scriptural passages opposing women's ordination in a section entitled, "Theology of Women in Ministry." The church explains that the purpose of Christ's redemptive work is to "set God's creation free from the curse of the Fall." Those who are "in Christ" are new creations. In this redemptive community, "no human being is to be regarded as inferior on the basis of social status, race, or gender." The church acknowledges what it calls the "apparent paradox" created by certain Pauline epistles. However, interpreting these passages as limiting the role of women in ministry presents "serious conflicts" with passages of scripture that "commend female participation in spiritual leadership roles," and "violates the spirit and practice of the Wesleyan-holiness tradition." Finally, the Manual declares, "it is incompatible with the character of God presented throughout Scripture, especially as revealed in the person of Jesus Christ." In this example, the Manual boldly challenges biblical passages antithetical to what has been reclaimed as a central tenet of Nazarene faith. This approach has had a profound impact not only upon the lives of the women called by God into ministry but upon all the lives touched by the love of God through their ministry.

The dramatic shift in society, not only in public opinion but in the spiritual confidence of LGBTQIA+ believers in bringing their petitions for change before the church, portends a head-on collision with the judgmental stances taken in the Covenant. The dynamism of the Manual and preceding manuals is providential for the Church of the Nazarene to become inclusive and affirmative toward LGBTQIA+ believers in the following ways:

1. Preceding manuals show the church's views on what it means to live a life of holiness shifts and changes over time as society changes, and as our knowledge and understanding of ourselves, one another, and the world we live in, grows and changes under the guidance and correction of the Holy Spirit.
2. The examples of divorce and women's ordination offer precedence for movement of the church toward stances in the Manual supportive of believers pursuing holiness even in the face of difficult biblical passages used to condemn them.

3. Relabeling the section on homosexuality as Human Sexuality and inserting ideas about marital sexuality in 1989 deescalates the incendiary nature of the former title and the focus that had been exclusively limited to a segment of the LGBTQIA+ community.

4. Reorganizing the Covenant in 2017 to incorporate previously-independent sections on marriage and divorce into the Human Sexuality section further reorients this section to focus on the role sexuality plays in more than one type of human relationship.

5. The movement to expand and itemize areas and practices covered by this section affords the church the option of either simply removing stances condemning LGBTQIA+ believers as it had with divorce or directly confronting scriptures used to condemn them as it did with women's ordination.

Therefore, church members at the next General Assembly are positioned to propose:

1. Condensing the discursive narrative within the Human Sexuality section to a plain account of holiness and sexuality in all human relationships, including one's self, hospitality toward strangers, friendship, familial, and covenantal marriage, and the importance of seeking guidance "transcending the mere letter of the law" from the Holy Spirit, developing critical thinking skills and discernment, and participating meaningfully in the body of Christ.

2. Removing the laundry list of "areas of sexuality," including but especially areas condemning the lives and relationships of LGBTQIA+ believers.

   a. Avoiding the laundry list does not mean a person is living a sexually healthy, holy life. As acknowledged in another section of the Covenant, "no catalog, however inclusive, can hope to encompass all forms of evil throughout the world."

   b. With or without confronting difficult scriptures, removing the list affirms the church's trust in the Holy Spirit and restores a relationship of mutual love and respect, rather than judgment and condemnation, between the church and its members, although it only begins to restore relationship with LGBTQIA+ believers.

3. Affirming the participation of LGBTQIA+ and heterosexual believers in the Sacrament of Marriage.

   a. The church may choose to remove the "one woman and one man" language and simplify the biblical principles on marriage to focus on the blessing and covenant between two people before God without mentioning gender. Similar moves were used not only with divorce but with the mysterious removal of the marital prohibition against being "unequally yoked" with unbelievers in 1928.

b. Alternatively, the church may decide to directly confront passages confining marriages to heterosexual couples.

Given the damage its LGBTQIA+ stance has inflicted, the Nazarene Church must ask forgiveness and seek reconciliation with LGBTQIA+ believers. More will be required, but this proposal is a start.

Patti L. Dikes, JD is a child welfare policy attorney whose work impacts LGBTQIA+ foster youth. She was raised a 3rd-generation Nazarene. Her nieces and their cousins have no relationship with the Nazarene Church and a few identify as LGBTQIA+. An ally, she supports same-sex marriage and loving, healthy, sexual relationships outside of marriage.

Negotiating a Positive Interpretation

FOREST FISK

Historically, Nazarenes have proved to interpret the Bible in loving ways. They can do it again for the LGBT+ community.

Nazarenes have proudly read between the lines of certain biblical texts and extracted an interpretation of God that, at times, goes against the plain reading of the text. And this practice is done with reverence, care, and love for all involved. It's a skill that, once honed, can be used for good or for ill, but I believe Nazarenes need to put this interpretive faculty to work again to fully love and support the LGBT+ community.

Let's begin with some commonly agreed-upon examples of this work. The Bible doesn't say anything about overthrowing one's own king and setting up a constitutional democracy. At the founding of the United States, the concept of defying the king was quite a difficult decision for many Christians at the time. John Wesley's mother and father maritally separated for a time over their differences of opinion on the matter. Yet Christians found a way to sidestep clearly marked portions of Old and New Testament passages demanding fealty to monarchs and governmental rulers and found a different way. The Bible also says nothing *against* owning slaves, in the Old or New Testament. Yet many Christians in the early 1800s found a way to see the humanity in others, and out of love, reshaped society as a whole to end the practice, despite the many Christians who still read scriptures in a relationally hurtful way. And portions of the Bible clearly say women shouldn't teach or hold leadership above a man in a church, yet Nazarenes proudly present plenty of positive biblical examples of how God equally loves and supports the work of ministry in both men and women. And so, the Nazarenes forged a new and better path in opposition to her peer denominations, and support the ordination of women. I am in full support of this interpretive work, and I believe these practices of negotiating with the text are exactly what work theologians in the church need to do to more closely align with the loving God we see in the life and ministry of Jesus. Let us not balk at the term "negotiating with the text" or shy away from it. We have done the work of negotiation with the biblical text a few times, and it is precisely this negotiation with the text in particular ways that makes Nazarenes distinct from other denominations. And I say, if we've done it for love's sake before, we can do it for love's sake again. I propose we negotiate with the Bible again, because as a culture we have learned a different perspective on how God made people, and in loving God's creation in the newly evident ways we have discovered in the last few decades, we can learn how to accept and integrate our differences in the church, for the benefit of the world. But we must first negotiate with the text, and I will endeavor to give a few examples of how to do that.

The first step in negotiating a biblical text for the sake of love is to allow God to speak to us about the disconnects between God's *intent* of love in every person, and the negative *actions* which prevent such love from occurring. For example, it seems reasonable that God's intent in creating humanity is that we find fulfillment and love with Godself, and with others. The disconnect happens when we realize that within the theology handed to us, some people are asked to *not* be in a relationship with others with whom they find the greatest fulfillment. The arrangement between God and Adam did not suffice for Adam, as God said it was "not good" for Adam to be alone, even when Adam was walking face to face with an (at times) incarnated God in the garden. Read into that story what you may, but it doesn't seem rational to say to the LGBT+ person in our church, "God made you like Adam in every respect, except you may not have, nor do you need a partner like yourself. God is enough for you." No. That theology seems to go against the grain altogether of a relationally loving God. A theology that elevates the necessity of human-to-human relational companionship needs to be consistent for *all* people. What God made right for "Adam and Eve" must be made right for "Adam and Steve" in the same way. We have relational needs that God cannot (or would not) fulfill via the incarnation it explicitly mentions in Genesis. And as the body of Christ, we need to do better than to simultaneously tell LGBT+ people they may not have a partner, and then have as little to do with them to support their social needs as we have done. Yet we are handed this outdated theology, both in the Old and New Testament, that doesn't recognize the new understanding of humans we've discovered in the last few decades. This concept of *orientation* wasn't even a consideration in the ancient Near Eastern world.

We find the next step in negotiating with the text when we see how differently the biblical authors deal with the concept of same-sex attraction. The word *homosexual* was coined as recently as 1886 in Germany and referred to sexual *acts* as well as *orientations*. And that makes sense as those who perform the acts are more likely to be attracted to the idea of sexual interactions. However, this intuitive sense

needs to be reevaluated with a more in-depth, logical analysis. As a biblical example, the townsfolk in Sodom wanted to *rape* the angels as a power play and a show
of dominance against them, not to softly and romantically make love to them. Lot
himself was an immigrant outsider to Sodom, and his presence was barely tolerated, just as many immigrants are barely tolerated in many modern societies today.
Then add to the fact that Lot was being hospitable to *more* outsiders, and allowing
them into town without being vetted by the community was anathema to the
nationalistic and selfish peoples of Sodom (see Ezekiel 16:49-50). The theological
trajectory of the story of Lot is not that penetration itself is bad (just look at Lot's
horrible response to the townsfolk to see that). But it is a story of how the Hebrew
people were to be marked by radical hospitality in comparison to their neighbors.
So not only do we need to decouple the idea that God detests same-sex acts, but
we need to cleave apart the idea that same-sex attractions are somehow evil as well.

Because the word *homosexual* was coined as late as 1886, it wasn't added to
English scripture until 1946 in the RSV version of the Bible. So what word choice
was used before that? The German translation had traditionally inserted (the
German word equivalent to) "boy molester" in verses such as Leviticus 20:13 and
1 Timothy 1:10. And the German translations updated their Bibles as late as 1983
to change the word to *homosexual* for those same verses in direct response to the
homophobic influence of the English-speaking Churches. Some have speculated
that this older interpretation of the "boy molester" concept is due to an ancient
Greek and Roman common custom of pederasty, where men used young boys as
sex slaves. The concept of pederasty comes with a host of ethical problems on its
own which we will not get into. Fortunately, pederasty was *not* a Hebrew custom.
Pederasty might have been known about by a few of the biblical authors because of
surrounding Greek cultural influence. However, the aversion to gay/lesbian sexual
acts was most likely a cultural taboo for the biblical authors regardless, because
most Near Eastern cultures consider it more "natural" for men to be the dominant/
penetrative person in sexual intercourse, and any other position for a man was
simply taboo and therefore sinful. This notion of sexual impropriety includes condemning even *married straight* couples if a man's sexual position was "on the bot-
tom" or in any submissive position. I believe cultural influences shaped the biblical
author's morality rather than a dictated, prescribed morality written straight from
God which formed our biblical text, inspired by God though it may be. Because
we do not share this hierarchical view of marital relations in Western culture, we
do not share the same morals which concerned the biblical authors to view equality
in sexual relations as sinful, and our theological views need to be adjusted on all
sides to form a more loving narrative of equality among God's creation.

If we can look in the Bible and *not* see a God who allows for slavery, or the subjugation of women as the "property" of men, then we have already negotiated with the text in a way to extract a better version of God than what is a common or plain reading of the scripture. And if we have done that work once, then we have all the tools necessary for negotiating a more positive interpretation of God in ways that respect all forms of humanity. Let us again take upon ourselves the idea that all people are created equal in God's sight, and all people deserve to feel they may stand before God and humanity without shame for the ways they exist. To be accepted and not excluded from the community is a good first step, but a better and more loving step would be to allow full acceptance of marriage of LGBT+ people in the church, and even the ordination of LGBT+ people into ministry to match the current Nazarene understanding that God calls all men and women (and everyone between those sides of the spectrum) equally to ministry. So let our theology match up with that reality, and let the Nazarene church fully endorse marriage and ordination within the LGBT+ community.

Forest Fisk *is a straight, fourth-generation Nazarene, NNU and NTS graduate with honors, and lives in the Kansas City area. Forest is in the process of deconstructing his Nazarene theology and is on his way out of the Nazarene Church for various reasons.*

My Interpretative History of Romans 1

ROBERT GRIDER[1]

For Nazarenes, the most important source of theological insight and guidance is scripture. This essay examines the issue of homoeroticism in light of scripture, particularly Paul's words in Romans 1.

W hile a student at a Nazarene college in the 1980s, I had a friend named Terry. Terry was a few years older than me. He was divorced. Before becoming a Christian, he had been a heroin addict. While in a drug-addled state, he and a young women had married. They divorced six weeks later. When I met Terry about 10 years later, he was a dynamic Christian and he wanted to remarry.

Terry asked me what I thought. We looked at the scripture and read where men are clearly prohibited from remarrying after divorce (with one exception): "I tell you that anyone who divorces his wife, except for sexual immorality, and marries another woman commits adultery" (Matt. 16:9). There had been no infidelity in Terry's brief six-week marriage. Would he be committing adultery if he remarried?

What was I to say? I was married and enjoyed all that comes with a healthy marriage, not just sexual relations but the intimacy and joys of building a life together. Was scripture to be applied in a way that imposed a lifelong sentence of

---

1. I have chosen to withhold my name from this publication, not because I am ashamed of my convictions, but because of my concern for colleagues. I work with a large number of Nazarenes in many different arenas (speaking, publishing, etc.). I fear that the release of my name in this context may confront those treasured friends with the painful choice of either denouncing me and our decades of friendship or jeopardizing their career and ministry. I write in the name of two of my theological mentors, J. Kenneth Grider and Robert Staples, both of whom came to espouse positions like the one which I espouse in this essay. Ken made this opinions public. Rob revealed his opinions to me in private conversations. Both were persons of tremendous faith, deep conviction and unbounded love.

forced singleness and celibacy on Terry? Was Terry never to be blessed by a loving and nurturing marital relationship?

I told Terry that I believed in the sanctity of marriage, and that I still believed that the prophet Malachi was speaking for God when he said, "I hate divorce" (Mal. 2:16, NASB). However, I also believed both that Terry hated divorce and that God was a God of infinite love. I told Terry that I believed he could remarry without engaging in sin. Terry got remarried.

Several years later, I was teaching New Testament at a Nazarene college. One of my students named Brent had a brother who was gay. Brent asked me what I thought about his brother being in a relationship with a man. Brent and I went to the scripture.

I told Brent that the Old Testament passages were easily reviewed. There are three real pieces of evidence. First, there are the passages in Leviticus which clearly prohibit homoeroticism, even calling for the death penalty for homosexual activity between men (Lev. 20:13; 18:22). Second, there is the story of the destruction of Sodom and Gomorrah, a story in which the men of the town wanted to rape the angels who were visiting Lot's family. The story ends with God destroying the cities of Sodom and Gomorrah for the depth of their sin (Gen. 19:1-29). Although each of these passages is often used to condemn same-sex marriage, neither can really be applied to the modern situation of two men having a sexual relationship within the confines of marriage.

Rape is wrong regardless of the sexual orientation of the attacker, so the Genesis story about the intended rape of Lot's guests in Sodom is irrelevant to the current conversation about gay marriage. Likewise, the passage from Leviticus falls squarely within the legislation related to ritual purity under the Old Testament Law. The church should be no more concerned with this prohibition about homosexual relations than it should be concerned with how men clean themselves up after an involuntary nocturnal emission (Lev. 15: 1-15), or whether or not a married heterosexual couple has sex during a woman's period (Lev. 18:19), or even if a person eats pork (Lev. 11:7) or wears blended fabrics (Deut. 22:11).

The third passage is set later in Israel's history than the prohibition in Leviticus, but it was actually written significantly earlier than the prohibition in Leviticus. In 2 Samuel, David offered a eulogy for his best friend, Jonathan, and described Jonathan as a "gazelle" (2 Sam. 1:19), a term often used with sexual undertones in the Song of Solomon (2:7, 9, 17; 3:5; 4:5; 7:3; 8:14). Then David spoke to the recently deceased Jonathan and lamented: "Your love for me was wonderful, more wonderful than that of women" (2 Sam. 1:26).

I explained to Brent that the Davidic allusion to a sexual relationship with Jonathan probably indicates that the ancient Israelites had a rather permissive attitude toward same-sexual relationships in the sixth century BC (when David's eulogy was added to Israel's scriptures) than it did a hundred years later in the fifth century BC (when the Levitical prohibitions were added to Israel's scripture).

Moving to the New Testament, there are again three relevant passages. The first two passages (1 Tim. 1:10; 1 Cor. 6:9-10) includes words that are sometimes translated as "homosexuality" (1 Tim.) or "homosexuals" (1 Cor.). However, such translations are clearly incorrect. The ancient Greek and Jewish worlds had no conception of sexual orientation (gay, straight or otherwise). The cultures from which the New Testament arose did not think of people as heterosexual or homosexual. No such categories existed. Instead, they thought of people being sexual and of people engaging in sexual activity with various appropriate and inappropriate partners. Ancient writers were clearly aware of people who had sex with partners of the same sex, but they never thought of such people as "homosexual." In fact, there was no word for homosexuality or homosexuals.

Even though there was no Greek (or Hebrew) word for homosexuality, there were a lot of words for homosexual behaviors. Both 1 Timothy and 1 Corinthians use one of these words, *apsenokoitas*, a rare word formed by joining the Greek words for "man" and "bed." Although the connotations are clearly sexual, the precise activity and relationships are unclear. 1 Timothy also uses another related word, *malakos*, a word which literally means "soft." It was typically used for a man who submitted himself to anal penetration by another man.

Since same-sex marriage did not exist in antiquity, neither of these passages can be easily applied to a contemporary sex marital relationship. All same-sex activity in antiquity took place outside the bonds of marriage. These passages are difficult to apply to same-sex activity within the confines of marriage. Associating the vices listed in 1 Tim. 1:10 and 1 Cor. 6:9-10 to a married same-sex couple would make about as much sense as applying the Bible's prohibitions against heterosexual activity outside of marriage to the sexual activity of a heterosexual couple in the confines of marriage. The sexual vices described in 1 Corinthians and 1 Timothy were viewed as vices in antiquity because they took place outside of marriage (like heterosexual pre-marital sex and adultery).

This brings us to the most important passage for understanding and applying biblical teachings about same-sex unions to the contemporary world: Romans 1. In the context of Paul's discussion about the universality of sin, the Apostle said that sin had become so rampant among humans that God "gave up" people to their sin. As one example of how God gave people up, Paul said, "God gave them over to shameful lusts. Even their women exchanged natural sexual relations for unnatural ones. In the same way the men also abandoned natural relations with women and were inflamed with lust for one another" (Rom. 1:26-27).

I pointed out to Brent that Romans does not actually say that same-sex relations are sinful. Romans 1 only says that the same-sex relations occur "unnaturally" *as a result of sin*. As Brent and I then understood Romans 1 in light of our close reading of the text, we concluded that Paul understood same-sex desire to be a result of sin. We concluded that same-sex attractions were the result of sin and not acts of sin *per se*. Homosexuality, as we understood it at the time, was a result of sin just like the subordination of women, pain in child birth and the necessity of earning one's living through hard work (Gen. 3:14-15). It was not sinful in itself, but it would not exist in a perfect world. We wondered if Brent's brother was in some sense a victim of a sinful world.

I told Brent that he should probably see his brother's homosexuality as a result of living in a fallen, sinful world and that Brent should probably encourage his brother to do two things. First, find a monogamous partner to share his life with, and second, find a church—not the Church of the Nazarene—that would bless his same-sex union (this advice was given long before the legalization of same-sex marriages).

About 15 years later, Todd approached me in tears. He had just broken off his engagement to a beautiful young lady. He had told her that he could not marry her because he was gay. I commended him for his compassion and courage—his compassion for not subjecting his fiancée to a marriage that would not be healthy for either of them and his courage for telling her the truth about why he was breaking the engagement. Then, Todd and I turned to scripture.

My understanding of the Old Testament passages and the words in the New Testament's vice lists had not changed. Those biblical texts had no legitimate application to the contemporary issue of a homosexual couple living in a marriage relationship (same-sex marriage had been legalized in the intervening years).

However, my understanding of Romans 1 had changed. I asked Todd, "Would it be 'natural' for you to have sex with a woman?" He laughed and said, "no." Then I asked, "Would it be 'natural' for you to have sex with a man?" He smiled and said, "yes."

I no longer understood homosexual love to be a result of sin. In the intervening years, I had studied the ancient meanings of the Greek words which are normally translated as "natural" and "unnatural" in Romans (*physikos* and *aphysikos*). The terms are not primarily biological; they are sociological. They convey a sense like "based on the way the [fallen] world works." Paul was essentially saying, "don't the generally accepted structures of society teach you…" Indeed, in Paul's world—and in most social constructions until very recently, "the nature of things" did teach that men marry women and women marry men. However, the world is fallen and sinful.

Just because a social structure—like male dominance, the enslavement of one's fellow humans or the oppression of healthy same-sex love—exists does not mean that it should continue to exist. This, by the way, is why the Church of the Nazarene has wisely ordained women throughout its entire history in spite of clear scriptural teaching condemning the practice (1 Tim. 2:12). Some of presumed social structures of antiquity—like the subordination of women, the enslavement of human beings, and suppression of homosexual love—were oppressive and should be cast aside.

In the time between my conversations with Brent and Todd, my mind had changed. By the time that I talked to Todd, I had come to understand the suppression of healthy homosexual love—and not the homosexual love itself—to be a result of sin. Just as male dominance and slavery became "naturalized" by those in power in a sinful world, heterosexuals (by far the domain cultural group) had "naturalized" heterosexual normativity.

I told Todd that I was okay with him and that I would happily bless his eventual gay marriage. Todd did not need to be "fixed;" he was not "broken." The world needed "fixed;" the world was "broken."

*"**Robert Grider**" holds a BA (in Biblical Literature), MA (in Religion) and MDiv (an honors degree in the history of Christianity) from Nazarene institutions. Rob also has a PhD in New Testament. He is the only New Testament professor who was elected into membership of the Studiorum Novi Testamenti Societas (the most selective scholarly society for scholars of the New Testament) while teaching at a Nazarene institution. Rob is now a "Nazbeen," a former Nazarene. Rob left the Church of the Nazarene because, as he tells it, he felt like he was participating in the institutionalized victimization of gays and lesbians by remaining within the Church of the Nazarene.*

Engaging a Changing Culture:
A Sociological Analysis

JOHN W. HAWTHORNE

The dramatic changes in attitudes toward LGBTQ people require the Church of the Nazarene to reconsider the denominational stance in order to reach young people, connect to the broader faith community, increase its ministry outreach, and support its young clergy.

One of the largest and most rapid changes in America society can be seen in attitudes toward same-sex marriage. In 2010, the Public Religion Research Institute (PRRI) reported than 29% of Americans supported same-sex marriage. As of 2021, that figure stood at 79%: a 50% increase in just over a decade. This change reflects a number of shifts in state level legislation or court action, culminating in the 2015 *Obergefell* decision declaring "traditional marriage only" legislation unconstitutional.

While only 35% of white evangelical protestants supported same-sex marriage in 2021, the same figure for mainline and Catholic populations was right around 75%, fairly close to the population overall. This is important in that not all Christian populations are of one voice on the topic.

That has certainly been true in my own United Methodist denomination, which has seen one-sixth of congregations leave for a more conservative body over this very issue. Within the Catholic tradition, it is notable that Pope Francis announced in early 2023 that being gay shouldn't be a crime. He did say it was a sin, but he also said that mistreating gay and lesbian people was no less a sin.

The diversity of viewpoints is also likely within the Church of the Nazarene. Variability by generation or location or education is very likely. Those 40 and under are much more likely to reflect an affirming view than those of earlier generations. PRRI reported that 2017 was the first year when a majority of millennial evangelicals supported same-sex marriage. Based on early reporting, the percentage of support from GenZ (those born after 1996) is likely even higher. Location matters as well. The more cosmopolitan a location, the more likely to have regular interaction with LGBTQ individuals. Christian universities across the country have seen increased support and activism for their queer colleagues, even at Nazarene institutions. And many straight students have very little tolerance for anti-LGBTQ bias.

This is not hard to understand given the massive changes described above. I regularly tell an anecdote about a conversation I had with two young then-20-something women in 2011. Both were products of Christian universities. I asked them how they thought about the question of LGBTQ affirmation. One turned to me and said, "I had to decide what I thought about homosexuality when my friend Jake came out in seventh grade show choir." My only response was, "Of course you did."

This young woman is not unique. The same is true for those young people sitting in the pews in our churches or in classes in our colleges or around the table at the local coffee shop. They have known their Jakes for years, and the ubiquity of social media means that they may have regularly kept in touch with Jake as well. When a pastor or denominational leader calls out the gay population to demonstrate resistance to the world, they hear that critique primarily directed at their friend Jake.

More than that, the Jakes we are talking about are the children, grandchildren, or siblings of our current congregants. And that is not even considering the Jakes currently sitting in the pew seeking to follow Christ as best they know how.

There has been an assumption in too much of the Christian church that LGBTQ people aren't people of faith. A 2020 Gallup survey found that nearly half of queer people surveyed reported moderate to high levels of religiosity. That means that there is a significant opportunity for ministry to and ministry with the LGBTQ population in our congregations if we would but recognize the potential.

The same is true for those in a congregation's orbit. Five years ago, I conducted a survey of 819 clergy in the Church of the Nazarene, divided between those under 40 and those in their 50s. I had assumed that knowing LGBTQ people would have an influence on clergy attitudes. To my surprise, nearly everyone knew someone who was gay. The margin was 797 to 22. The same question asking about transgender individuals showed 643 knew a trans person while 176 did not. While these patterns did not predict attitudes toward issues of contemporary sexual ethics (in part due to the lack of statistical variability in the responses), they are still important. There is also a question of how much those queer folks within the sphere of influence might know of the denomination's stance and keep their distance accordingly.

It makes me ask what kinds of ministry outreach those clergy were able to do with the gay and transgender acquaintances they had. Could the clergy members feel comfortable engaging with them knowing the denominational stance on LGBTQ issues? Did their district leadership provide them with space to explore such outreach, or would doing so put credentials at risk? I know stories of individuals who have had space and those who were pushed out because of their openness.

The survey asked the younger clergy group how important it was for them to stay in the Church of the Nazarene. The good news is that only 12 people said it wasn't important at all, with another 90 respondents saying it was not particularly important. So Nazarene belonging was important or very important to remain in the denomination—78% of the millennial respondents. They were also asked a question about what might cause them to think about leaving. Over 45% identified "*the denomination's difficulty in dealing with contemporary issues*" as a potential future trigger.

In summary, then, the Church of the Nazarene's current stance of LGBTQ affirmation has several negative consequences for the central mission of the denomination. It makes it difficult to reach queer people in the congregation and their families. It complicates dialogue with other Christians whose views tend toward affirmation. It makes it difficult to reach out to those in the broader community. It runs a real risk of alienating talented young clergy and causing them to conclude that they have no long-term place within the Church of the Nazarene.

There is one more dynamic within the broader social context that is worth attention: the role of jurisprudence around LGBTQ issues. When former Justice Kennedy drafted the *Obergefell* decision, he closed with an appeal to the first amendment protections of religious freedom. It was his hope that religious bodies would not be forced into LGBTQ affirming positions by federal authorities. Subsequent Supreme Court decisions, like *Masterpiece Cake Shop*, have only reaffirmed that position and the current Court shows no inclination to change soon. Even the 2022 Respect for Marriage Law contains provisions protecting religious organizations from any attempts to force changes in their stances.

Paradoxically, laws like Respect for Marriage create opportunities for groups like the Church of the Nazarene. By removing the threat of coercive moves against religious bodies, the LGBTQ issues can be moved outside the culture war dynamic. A change in the denomination position would no longer be seen as the powers that be making the church do something.

Such an opportunity might just be seen as similar to the decision of a young 18th century Anglican minister to take his ministry out to where the people were.

Or an early 20th century Methodist minister who took his work to inner-city Los Angeles.

John Hawthorne is a retired sociology professor with nearly 40 years of experience in Christian universities in both faculty and administrative roles. He served in five different Christian institutions, including two Nazarene schools. He earned his PhD in sociology from Purdue University. He regularly writes a SubStack newsletter at johnhawthorne. substack.com and is working on a book reimagining Christian universities in a post-Christian society.

The Sin of Sodom

DANA ROBERT HICKS

In an ironic twist, the sin of Sodom is wildly different than what most people think it is.

The five of us arrived in Bujumbura, Burundi during a hot and sticky July night. Only one of us had ever been to this east African country before, but a brief look at the US State Department's website suggested that, for our safety's sake, it would be best to rethink our plans. We were there at the encouragement of a Nazarene District Superintendent whom we call Luke. We call him Luke because we Americans find it too difficult to say or remember his complex African name. Luke wanted to partner with us in developing some new ministries in Burundi and invited us to join him for dinner, in his home, in the center of the capital city of Bujumbura.

Crammed into an old and barely road-worthy Toyota Corolla, we bounced through the rutted streets of Bujumbura to Luke's apartment. The lack of a moon or streetlights was foreboding and reminded us that we were a world away from home. The smell of the open fires in barrels greeted us and provided most of the light for the five strange and mysterious *muzungus* (the Swahili word for "white people"). One of us mumbled something about heeding the State Department's suggestions as we took a deep breath and moved toward Luke's humble home.

Luke and his wife provided us with a wonderful meal of tilapia, rice, and beans that we guessed cost him about two weeks' salary. We later learned that he had borrowed furniture from his neighbors to ensure that everyone had a place to sit. We ate and laughed and despite being half-way around the world in a mysterious and dangerous country, we felt safe, welcomed, and loved.

We were all Americans, and so this was the first time in our lives that we were in a situation in which our safety and well-being were completely dependent on the good graces of people we did not know well. But for our African brothers and sisters, this is not an unfamiliar position to find oneself. Luckily for us, Burundian attitudes about hospitality have remained intact for centuries. The ethos of hospitality today in Burundi is very similar to what life would have been like in the Ancient Near East.

In the Ancient Near East, hospitality toward strangers was considered a sacred duty. Because people were so nomadic in the ancient world, travel was almost always out of necessity, not for vacations. As a result, as people would travel from one region to another, often they would encounter hostile environments and would find themselves in vulnerable and dangerous situations. Hospitality was literally a matter of life and death for many people.

So deeply rooted was this ethic of hospitality that a stranger had the right to *expect* hospitable treatment. In fact, a stranger did not need to thank their host because the host was only doing what they were obligated to do. No expense or labor was too great for the traveler, who was treated as the master of the house.

The Hebrew scriptures reinforced this ethic in part through the commands given to them (such as Leviticus 19:33ff and Deuteronomy 10:13ff) but also through the recurring theme of remembering what it was like to be strangers in Egypt and Babylon (Exodus 22:21). Over and over the Hebrew scriptures admonish groups of people for their lack of hospitality: the Ammonites, the Moabites, the Benjaminites, and, most famously, the Sodomites.

The Sodomites were the worst. From some extra-biblical literature, we know that the ancient city of Sodom was famous for its cruelty and unwillingness to care for strangers: the vulnerable, marginalized, and people that were different from them.[1] While following the journeys of Abraham's nephew, Lot, the Hebrew scriptures provide a cautionary tale in Genesis 19.

Two strangers arrive in the city of Sodom and meet one of the city's newest residents: Lot. Unbeknownst to everyone, the two strangers are God's angels. As a person of good character, Lot shows gracious hospitality to the two men and prepares a feast. But as word spreads of the men's presence, people become fearful of the individuals Lot is hosting. A mob surrounds Lot's house and demands that Lot turn over the men to them so that they may "yada" (עָדְיַ) them (Gen 19:5).

Yada is a common word in the Hebrew scriptures, and 99% of the time the word is translated in English, "to know." So, some English versions of the Bible (KJV, ESV, and NRSV) translate the motives of the men of Sodom to "get to know" the angels. But sometimes the Hebrew scriptures use *yada* as a euphemism for sexual intercourse. (Like in Genesis 4:1 when it says, "The man knew his wife Eve, and she conceived and bore Cain"). As a result, some English translations

---

1. Extra-biblical stories included the Sodomites' physical torture of travelers as well as their burning of a young woman who had dared to share food with a family that was starving of hunger.

(NIV and NASB) interpret the motives of the men of Sodom to rape or molest the angels.

The story continues with Lot offering up his daughters to appease the mob. Our modern sensibilities (understandably) have a very difficult time wrapping our heads around this response. However, this is a good example of the degree to which people would go to in the ancient world to practice hospitality. Nevertheless, the Sodomite mob decline Lot's offer and storm the house. The angels blind the mob and the next morning Lot, his family, and the angels all flee Sodom as God destroys the city along with the neighboring city, Gomorrah.

It is a hair-raising story, and everyone would agree that the city of Sodom was an evil mess and we would do well to pay attention to this cautionary tale and avoid being "Sodomites." In the last few centuries, some people have understood that the story was a warning about men having consensual sex with each other. This is, of course, where we get the modern expression, "sodomy." The use of this term is very misleading, however, because the mob was trying to rape the angels as an act of terrorism (something that was neither uncommon in the ancient world nor in our world), not attempting to have consensual sex with them.

Years later, the prophet Ezekiel, speaking on behalf of God, would highlight the story of Sodom by saying: "This was the guilt of your sister Sodom: she and her daughters had pride, excess of food, and prosperous ease but did not aid the poor and needy. They were haughty and did abominable things before me; therefore I removed them when I saw it." (Ezekiel 16:49-50)

According to the Ezekiel, what made Sodom such a dumpster fire was not consensual gay sex; rather, it was those who turned their backs on the "poor and needy", the vulnerable, and those who were different. In other words, the sin of Sodom was their inability to practice hospitality.

In the New Testament, the writer to the Hebrews reinforces the urgency of practicing hospitality by alluding to the Sodom story—"Do not neglect to show hospitality to strangers, for by doing that some have entertained angels without knowing it." (Hebrews 13:2)[2]

---

2. Some thoughtful readers may recognize the Jude 7 reference to Sodom and Gomorrah as a seemingly different interpretation of Genesis 19. However, the phrase σαρκὸς ἑτέρας in Jude 7 literally translates as "strange" or "other" flesh. In this context, I would argue that the phrase refers to the divine, or other-worldly, nature of the angelic visitors to Sodom. As a result, the Sodomite mob's desire to rape God's angels is likened to the sins of the mysterious "sons of God" in Genesis 6 who had sex with human females and led to the Great Flood in Genesis 7.

In Jesus' teachings, the practice of hospitality towards the stranger among us is, in reality, the reception of Jesus himself (Matthew 25:43). And conversely, the lack of hospitality is a rejection of Jesus himself.

In Paul's letters to Timothy and Titus, he takes it one step further by declaring that one of the requirements of church leaders is people who practice hospitality (1 Timothy 3:2 and Titus 1:8). When we hear this with our American ears, we might assume that it means we should occasionally throw dinner parties or have a spare room for visiting friends. But Paul is thinking and writing with more of an ancient mindset, similar to what my church leader friend Luke in Burundi modeled for us. The practice of hospitality means to welcome, embrace, and love people that we may not understand, that we may not agree with, and that we may even find repulsive for one reason or another. And even to protect them from others who may mean to do them harm.

The whole concept of hospitality is hard for me to wrap my head around. I am a white, straight, middle-aged man who lives in the most prosperous country in the world. As a result, I literally had to travel 8,944 miles to Bujumbura, Burundi in order to get far enough out of my element to be regarded as a strange and mysterious *muzungu*. I had to travel 8,944 miles in order to appreciate what it means to be the beneficiary of true, authentic, God-inspired hospitality—to feel the vulnerability and to experience the effort, the sacrifice, and the love of my friend Luke.

The point is this—to call our LGBTQ brothers and sisters "sodomites" is to completely miss the point of this ancient story. Instead, perhaps the deepest irony of the modern church is that the Sodomites in our midst are those of us who refuse to practice hospitality with the poor, the needy, and the vulnerable—those who we may not understand, that we may not agree with, and that we may even find repulsive for one reason or another. *The LGBTQ are the strangers among us*, the forgotten ones of impoverished opportunity. The Sodomites among us, therefore, are those who refuse to welcome them.

Pride is at the root of the sin of Sodom as we close the door to those God is sending to stand in our midst. We are guilty of wanting sanctification on its own terms while condescendingly refusing to extend hospitality to these strangers. If we have the spiritual integrity to reject the sin of Sodom, we entertain angels while embracing all that God is doing among those whose sexuality is different than ours.

This is not a fashionable position to take. Lot and his family had to flee Sodom because of their fundamental commitment to practice hospitality. The question remains for all of us—will you be among those who are willing to entertain the angels among us?

The Reverend Dr. Dana Robert Hicks *is a third generation Nazarene. He received a Master of Divinity from Nazarene Theological Seminary, and a Doctor of Ministry degree from the Besson Pastor Doctoral Fellowship at Asbury Theological Seminary. He is author of* The Knot *(SacraSage Press, 2022) and blogs at DanaHicks.blog. He currently resides in Phoenix, Arizona.*

The Church Need Not Survive

CRAIG KEEN

The only condition for human sanctity is faithfulness to the gospel of the glorified mutilated body of Jesus.

It is important to distinguish between the Church of the Nazarene as a *self-protective institution* (with a headquarters) and the Church of the Nazarene as a *history of local churches entangled in each other's memories and hopes*. The institution will always resist the work of churches that might weaken its likelihood of survival. A faithful little local church—and a communion of faithful little local churches— will pray to go gladly into each new day "the Lord has made," knowing *it doesn't have to survive*. Remembering the faithfulness of God, it will expect to be as surprised as was Peter when God called him to the household of Cornelius (Acts 10). The *institution* will always respond as it did to Peter. "The circumcised believers who had come with Peter were astounded that the gift of the Holy Spirit had been poured out even on the Gentiles" (Acts 10:45).

It is similarly important to distinguish a little local church—and a communion of little local churches—from a group defined by a system of ideals used to manage lived life. Life is hard. We are understandably anxious. We lean hard on customs to moderate the trauma of the unexpected. Thus we may meet shockingly new events with an immediate "No!" As long as we are vulnerable to being wounded or killed, we will continue to do so. And that is okay. It is just that the gospel has taught little local churches that there is something more important, something that is unthreatened by wounds or death, something for which every little local church is to strive, even if doing so leads to the loss of its property rights: "Indeed your heavenly Father knows that you need all these things. But strive first for the kingdom of God and his righteousness, and all these things will be given to you as well. So do not worry about tomorrow, for tomorrow will bring worries of its own. Today's trouble is enough for today" (Matthew 6:32—34).

It was a shock to the churches in and near first-century Palestine to realize that God was calling them to embrace those the law of Moses had cast out. The ideas, customs, habits, and especially the holy texts that the young church loved made clear that contact with the unclean will always separate us from fellowship with the holy God. The temple was closed to those with bleeding cuts or tears in the skin, who had touched a corpse, who were strangers to Israel's covenant with God, or who had been emasculated by accident or design. Isaiah 56 imagines a new covenant. There the prophet declares that the day is coming when the temple will be opened to the Gentile and eunuch, people declared by the law of Moses to be unfit to enter the temple. Isaiah announces that the day is coming when the only condition for sanctifying entry into fellowship with God is that—even though unclean, even though strangers and eunuchs—they "join themselves to the Lord, to minister to him, to love the name of the Lord, and to be his servants… to hold fast [God's] covenant." If they do that, they will be welcomed into God's sanctifying embrace: "for my house shall be called a house of prayer for all peoples" (Isaiah 56:6—7).

It is this passage from Isaiah that Jesus quotes during Holy Week as he drives out "those who were selling and those who were buying in the temple" (Mark 11:15—17). That same week his body, too, was to be made unclean, according to the law of Moses, by the blows of the barbed leather thongs of the whip that tore his skin, by the spikes, the spear, and the other cruelties that mutilated his body as he was hanged on the cross.

It is ironic that sexual activity has become so highly exalted in the well-meaning ecclesiastical discourse in the modern age. Of course, this is not without precedent. Indeed, sexual activity is often carefully policed by societies of all kinds and sizes. It is by sexual activity that children are born and it is by means of children that a household, a village, a tribe, and a nation survives. Sex is the way by which one generation follows another. Especially in times of very high rates of mortality among mothers and newborns *during* childbirth and of infants and adults *subsequent to* childbirth, survival required sexual practices to be policed. What is especially strange about the gospel is that it so severely reins in this anxiety over childbirth and the survival not only of the particular human being, but also of the household, the village, the tribe, and the nation. What we call "singleness" and the early church called "virginity"—for the sake of devotion to the God of the gospel—was *an abandonment of the prospect of childbirth*. The clearest text in support of such a thing is perhaps 1 Corinthians 7, where Paul strongly advises those who are unmarried, to remain unmarried. This is not a new abstraction, a new commandment, that "real Christians must remain single!" Not at all. It is just that sexual activity is so very demoted in importance in the gospel that it is no longer necessary. Because God raised the unclean, mutilated body of Jesus from the dead, it is clear to all who have been embraced by the gospel that *we do not have to survive.*

Because of the very real possibility of a faithful childless lifetime, whether that be the lifetime of an unmarried person or eunuch, there is no longer a reason to exclude from full participation in the life of the local church any couple whose union will never yield children, so long as they "join themselves to the Lord, to minister to him, to love the name of the Lord, and to be his servants…to hold fast [God's new] covenant."

Craig Keen is an ordained deacon in the Church of the Nazarene and Professor Emeritus of Systematic Theology at Azusa Pacific University. He is a graduate of Southern Nazarene University, Nazarene Theological Seminary, and Claremont Graduate University. He is the author of After Crucifixion: The Promise of Theology *and* The Transgression of the Integrity of God *(both published by Cascade Press). He taught theology and philosophy for 24 years at three universities of the Church of the Nazarene. He lives with his wife of 53 years in San Diego, California.*

A Hope For Change

SELDEN DEE KELLEY III

For the sake of the Kingdom and the survival of our church,
we need better ways to converse on LGBTQIA+ matters.

In 1978, a publication of the Church of the Nazarene, whose target audience
was youth workers, published an article addressing the topic of homosexuality.
The article offered explanations for same-sex attraction and suggested pathways for
overcoming such attractions. I was a youth pastor in Kentucky and felt the need
to respond to the editor, suggesting that the article used numerous stereotypes,
contained biased opinions, and offered one-sided arguments. I never heard back
from the editor.

In the years since then, the public discussion has expanded to include a much
broader range of human sexuality and sexual identity issues. There has been more
research, books and articles on these topics than one could ever hope to read. And
instead of this increase in information bringing us closer together, it has instead
divided the faith community even further. And for many this division has led to
a fear of public discourse. In the current climate, public discourse seems to be less
about learning and more about winning. I hope our church might continue to be
a place where discourse is welcome. I hope we chart a course where disagreements
are viewed as opportunities for learning and growth. We certainly disagree on how
to embody the Gospel message when it comes to the LGBTQIA+ community.
May this become a time for learning and growth.

Like many others, the conflict between what I was taught as a child and the
complexity of life as an adult led me to read, study, and learn. (Maybe the most important revelation in learning was realizing how little I actually know.) The reading
of scripture and the practice of prayer were the anchor points on this exploration
of faith and life. Also significant to my journey was the privilege of meeting people
whose history and experiences were different than my own. I am forever grateful
to the people—-teens, parishioners, fellow pastors, professors—who have been
patient with me as they have taught me through their words, through their actions,

369

and through their grace. There was the father who taught me the power of alliance, the teen who taught me the importance of pronouns, the professor who taught me the value of friendship, the military man who taught me the horror of unintended consequences, and the colleague who taught me the urgency of speaking up. One such "teacher," reflecting on a letter I had written about the church and same-sex marriage, penned these words:

> The only thing I would add is something about how queer identifying people are able to serve the church in many capacities, but are prohibited to participate in one of the most meaningful experiences of what it means to be in a committed relationship. We seem to say "yes, yes, yes" (volunteering, attending, serving, etc.) up until a certain point, when there is a very clear, "no" (marriage).

In May of 2019 the Board of General Superintendents approved a new ruling regarding legislation on human sexuality and marriage. The ruling stated that a person with same-sex attraction who feels called to ministry must commit to a life of celibacy. That same document includes the ruling that "Nazarene clergy shall not bless, or perform same-sex marriage ceremonies." I disagree. (1) A person with same-sex attraction *should* be allowed to marry. (2) Nazarene clergy should be allowed to perform same-sex marriage ceremonies if they desire to do so. (3) Nazarene clergy should feel free to bless same-sex ceremonies.

When two people love one another and want to make the world a better place by living out that love in lifetime union with one another, want to provide a loving environment for children, ask for godly counsel from a pastor, and seek a place which can help form their spiritual journey, I find it irrational and unscriptural to turn them away. There are certainly many same-sex couples who are doing more to create a just and loving world than I am. And I welcome their counsel on how I could do it better. I am unable to justify telling a couple, who are in love with Christ and each other, seeking godly counsel, and participating in the life of the church, that I must refuse them blessing and participation in the sacrament of marriage.

My calling as a pastor, and as a Christian, is fundamentally to love God and love others. One of the privileges in life, and one of the ways to express love, is to bless others. I believe this means conveying to another person, "I love you, I care for you, and I pray God's best for you." I then trust God with leading that person in the life of faith. As long as I am on the journey with the person, I hope we can learn from one another, but I never intend to withhold blessing. Blessing is so woven into my calling that I don't imagine them as two separate things. Though I am currently prohibited from *joining* two people in same-sex matrimony, I can't imagine withholding *blessing*, encouragement, counsel or love.

I am not asking that everyone (or anyone) within the church agree with me on my understanding of scripture, just that there be room in the church for those of us who are passionate about the sacredness of scripture but land in a different place in our conclusions.

One of my primary reasons for writing this brief essay is to encourage further dialogue among the clergy concerning LGBTQIA+ issues; and I'm not referring to select committees or an isolated task force. We need open dialogue among the rank and file, and we need the dialogue to be encouraged by leadership. I believe that our viewpoints are spread across the spectrum. I fear that we are headed for a crisis confrontation just like other denominations before us. Why not have more constructive dialogue now before we get to that point? We have some wonderful facilitators in our ranks who could help us do this well.

The Church of the Nazarene has a rich history of theological teaching and biblical interpretation that has led our church to its current position. However, there are many Nazarene pastors and theologians who have spent years wrestling with these issues and don't align with the church's current stance. I can't speak for any of them, but I believe they might agree with me when I state that I love the church and I long for it to make room for differing theological and interpretive approaches—as long as those approaches exhibit Jesus' proclamation of love, holiness and justice.

I hope, for the sake of the Kingdom and for the survival of our church, we will find better ways to converse on this very important issue. I am afraid we will be forever stuck, metaphorically standing by the tree of knowledge of good and evil. We eat its fruit every time we insist on being the authority on what is good and what is evil, who is in and who is out, what is right and what is wrong, who is privileged and who is not. Hopefully we can move the dialogue, and consequent actions, to what is loving, what is kind, what is hospitable and what is just.

Selden Dee Kelley III has been a Senior Pastor in the Church of the Nazarene since 2006. Prior to that he served on the administrative cabinets of three Nazarene universities. He is married with two grown daughters. He loves learning (which has led to five academic degrees), and has particular interests in scripture, dreams, prayer, spiritual imagination, croquet, sailing, and hiking.

Grider's Gridlock: Shall We Honor His Life and Legacy?

MICHAEL LODAHL

If we were to follow Kenneth Grider's counsel, we would be running to help, to hear, and love LGBTQ+ people.

Anyone with even a little familiarity with the history and lore of Nazarene Theological Seminary knows the name of a rather colorful theologian who taught many hundreds of students there for nearly four decades. That theologian was J. Kenneth Grider (1921-2006), and the stories of his quirky "absent-minded professor" ways have been spread widely, primarily by oral traditions, throughout the Nazarene tribe.

I was his student for a two-semester, yearlong sequence called History of Christian Thought in 1978-79. I have my own Grider stories. He was delightfully odd and unpredictably unusual. He had a reputation for being the champion of a more conservative tone in Wesleyan theology, such that it was not difficult for seminary students (nor for him!) to pit his convictions—always kindly—against the likes of Mildred Bangs Wynkoop and Rob Staples, his theological colleagues at NTS during my time there as a student. Being thoroughly captivated by the relational commitments of Wynkoop and Staples, my default position was to be respectfully leery of Dr. Grider. Nonetheless, over that year of study I came to love this gruff yet gentle man.

It is precisely in the light of his decades-long role as a kind of guardian of holiness teaching, particularly of the American holiness movement variety, that we ought not and cannot let his final years be conveniently swept under the rug. To do so is to dishonor the man and his thinking. Yet those last years provide a great deal of discomfort for many in the Wesleyan-holiness traditions. For in the dusk of his life, J. Kenneth Grider became a tireless advocate for the Church of the Nazarene's full welcome and inclusion of gay people. I daresay our leaders would find it far more convenient to erase this chapter from Grider's legacy.

Sometime early in this century I became aware of a monograph Grider had written, entitled "Wesleyans and Homosexuality." He had written it for presentation at the 1999 meeting of the Wesleyan Theological Society; however, he informs his readers that he was prevailed upon by leadership at Olivet Nazarene University, where he was by this time serving as Distinguished Visiting Professor of Religion, not to publish his views. A year later he plunged ahead. Here is his paper's opening line: "We Wesleyans, with warmed hearts made about three sizes too big, have enjoyed a long history of running to help when almost any group has not been getting a fair shake."[1] It was time, he continued, for us to run to help gay Christians who certainly were not (and are not) "getting a fair shake."

To be honest, I was not terribly impressed with Grider's essay despite my strong inclination to be in his corner on this issue. My regret then was that his monograph took what I thought to be an overly simplistic approach to the matter; my regret now is that I stayed conveniently silent while he was sticking out his neck in ways that he knew would tarnish his name and reputation in Wesleyan-holiness circles. But there he was, coming running to help, to lend his voice, for Christian people who experienced (and yes, interpreted) themselves to be attracted to people of their same-sex.

What I propose to do in what follows is to highlight some of the strongest passages in Grider's monograph, and lend my voice to his. It's the least one can do for one's teacher. "He being dead yet speaketh" (Heb. 11:4).

Grider was often blunt in expression. "Born as gays? Yes. We used to suspect it. Now we know it most especially from a study of DNA strips" (3). Grider cites the research of the widely-known, sometimes controversial, geneticist Dean Hamer (1951-), who was an independent researcher at the National Institutes of Health from 1976 till his retirement in 2011. Of the study to which Grider refers, Hamer had written in 1993, "This study provided the first concrete evidence that 'gay genes' really do exist and narrowed the location of one of them to a few million out of several billion bits of information that make us human" (cited by Grider, 4).

Grider understood well that homosexual attraction is deep and enduring. "Cures, failed so-called ones, have been as varied as have the theories of its origin—hypnosis, exorcism, injections with male hormones, prayer and support groups, you name it" (8). Nothing has changed in this regard over the past two decades-plus since Grider wrote these words. Indeed, the evidence continues to

---

1. J. Kenneth Grider, "Wesleyans and Homosexuality," unpublished manscript (n.d.), 1. Further citations from Grider's essay will be parenthetical in-text.

mount: same-sex attraction is a fundamental aspect of existence for a small but significant percentage of human beings.[2]

Grider also cited numerous studies of same-sex behaviors among non-human animals such as rats, primates, and sheep. In the light of this evidence he suggested, "One matter…is most clear, as it relates to homosexuality in animals as it might relate to human same-sex proclivity: that perhaps same-sex attraction is not unnatural. If it obtains in animals, who make no moral decisions, but simply act according to their nature, perhaps acting on such interests, in humans, is natural, based on an orientation, and is not unnatural"(13). This suggestion flies in the face of arguments based on Romans 1 that same-sex relations are contrary to nature (vv. 26-27). If the natural sciences offer strong evidence that in fact the world of nature includes creatures (human and otherwise) whose "natural" sexual attractions are toward partners of the same sex, then we might seem to be at an impasse.

But are we really? For decades now leading biblical scholars and theologians, both from within the Wesleyan tradition and without, have insisted that we do not read the Bible for scientific information. It would be an exceedingly rare Nazarene scholar, for instance, who would argue against evolutionary theory on the grounds that Genesis 1 gives us differing scientific information. (Never mind Genesis 2, which offers a whole different array of "information"!) We don't expect the Bible to provide us with scientific data regarding the world's age or details about its long distant past; rather, in the words of Article IV of the Church of the Nazarene Manual's Articles of Faith, we hold that the scriptures are "inerrantly revealing the will of God concerning us in all things necessary to our salvation." For further treatment of this matter, see my *All Things Necessary to Our Salvation* (San Diego: Point Loma Press, 2004), available free online: https://tinyurl.com/Lodahl-All-Things. That salvation, ultimately, is bound up in the dual command / promise that we shall love God with all of our being and energies, and love all neighbors as our very selves (Matt. 22:34-40; Lk. 10:25-28). If the Bible's function is to lead us toward, and to nourish us in, such love as this, then we need not assume that its function is to provide us scientific information—including, of course, scientific information regarding human sexual attractions.

And this indeed seems to have been Grider's assumption (as it is mine). In his words, "Do the Bible's authors know that the world is round, or that the earth spins one round each day, or that it circles the sun every year? Did they need to

---

2. See Julie Rodgers, *Outlove: A Queer Christian Survival Story* (Broadleaf Books, 2021); see also https://www.christianitytoday.com/ct/2021/october/lgbt-homosexual-identity-what-comes-after-ex-gay-movement.html

know such facts of science in order to direct us, as Wesley says they do, on how to make it to the celestial city?" (26). Of course, there were those theological luminaries who resisted these "facts of science" precisely because they were convinced that the Bible told them so. Martin Luther comes immediately to mind. Today, such facts of our solar system tend not to bother many Bible readers at all. Similarly, we are now generally dismayed that apparently well-meaning Christians once believed that the Bible gave them permission, even encouragement, to enslave other people (indeed, other Christians!) largely on the basis of a divine curse involving skin color. This was a horridly damaging theological anthropology based on particular (and peculiar) interpretations of biblical passages. Might we not suspect that a similar process is in play nowadays with regard to prejudice against people who experience and interpret themselves as queer?

This is not an insignificant point. Biblical interpretation must be undertaken within the contexts provided by reason and experience—meaning, in this case, all the evidence that the natural sciences may provide us. For the fact is, if we do assume that God's creative activity is expressed in what we have learned to call evolution, then we also should assume that all manner of genetic variabilities find expression across a wide range of human proclivities, attractions, and behaviors. Sexual attraction (and even perhaps to some extent, at least, sexual identity) would be quite *naturally* located across this very wide spectrum. Granted, there are surely many other factors (personal history, family dynamics, social constructs, the wide variety of human relations) that contribute to sexual desire and attraction. One of my reservations regarding Grider's monograph is that he appears at times to have adopted a far too simplistic, unnuanced, approach to these matters. Nonetheless, if genetics play a (not insignificant) role in human sexual attraction and behavior, we cannot and should not simply brush this aside.

The official position of the Church of the Nazarene is not to deny that there are people—indeed, good Christian people—who experience same-sex attraction. Rather, the official position is that such people ought to refrain from sexual activity and pursue a life of chastity. The problem with this position is that it is formulated and enforced by people who enjoy the privilege of heterosexuality. We all should be suspicious of our positions of privilege and power when it comes to biblical interpretation and application. It is one thing for a homosexual person voluntarily to undertake a life of chastity (just as it would be for a heterosexual person); it is another thing for people in authority to enforce upon others what ought to be considered a vocational decision.

In 1978 Letha Dawson Scanzoni and Virginia Ramey Mollenkott authored a book entitled *Is the Homosexual My Neighbor?*[3] This is a profoundly misleading title. We should immediately add that their reply to this question was a hearty Yes. So why is the question misleading? Certainly it was a play on the question asked of Jesus in Luke 10:29, "Who is my neighbor?" According to the logic of this question, if I am given a working definition of "neighbor," I may proceed to identify what people are situated outside the "neighbor" category. But Jesus answered this question with the well-known parable about the compassionate Samaritan, at the end of which Jesus utterly transformed the question: "Who proved to *be the neighbor* to the person in need?" No longer is "neighbor" a term to be defined in such a way that some person or people might be considered outside the category; rather, Jesus challenges his questioner to "go and do likewise" (10:37)—that is, to go forth and be a neighbor to the ones in need. So the question would no longer be "Is the LGBTQ+ person my neighbor?"—but instead, "Am I becoming a neighbor to LGBTQ+ people?"

To become the neighbor literally means to draw nigh, to draw near, to the other. My fear is that far too often we who experience ourselves in the privileged position of heteronormativity have not been willing to draw near, to listen carefully and compassionately, to *become the neighbor to those in need.* And if we were to follow J. Kenneth Grider's counsel, we would be running to help, to hear, to love.

Michael Lodahl *is Professor of Theology & World Religions at Point Loma Nazarene University. He is the author of many books including* The Story of God *and* Matthew Matters.

---

3. The book has since undergone a second edition in 1994.

See No One As "Other"

K. STEVE MCCORMICK

It is time to soften our gaze; we must stop seeing LGBTQIA+ people as "Other."

We See as We Breathe

For nearly 40 years, I have been teaching in our Nazarene schools. I have been gazing into the faces of my students and listening to their hearts. They are the freshest faces from the future, and I have had a front row seat watching the God of our future arrive in them. Our future from God depends on them, and we are for them the signposts of God's faithfulness in years past. As I would glance into their faces, I would see the promises of the promise keeper made surprisingly present in the most novel ways. New Creation keeps coming in them and through them, and because of them my hope of future glory is strangely renewed. What I have seen in them I cannot unsee, and what I have heard from them I cannot unhear. So, pay close attention to the Spirit, the God of our future that keeps coming through these new faces. Through the Spirit's respiration, they will touch you deeply. And I promise they will take your breath away and give back to you your future.

What does this mean for the Church of the Nazarene? When the future hope of glory breaks in, the present moment of glory passes away. We must breathe deeply from our future hope, or we will die! We must change or we will die! Faith without hope from the future is not a faith that can see what God has promised: "future glory already begun." (Wesley)

Our past faith with all its moments of glory *and* failure is not permanently fixed, because our promised future hope of glory is not yet finished. We must breathe out our past and breathe in with our future. It is that simple. Breathe deeply with the inbreaking of New Creation by breathing out passing moments of glory. The Spirit that came from the future to raise Jesus from the dead is the same Spirit that breathes future hope into Christ's living Body—the Church catholic.

We live and move and breathe from creation to New Creation. With every breath we take a new way of seeing from the future emerges.

If our Nazarene doctrine and faith does not see as it breathes, it will not evolve and change in the ebb and flow of life to see the next 100 years of holy life together. If we do not grow and change in our faith along life's way, our tradition will become the kind of traditionalism that Jaroslav Pelikan called the "dead faith of the living." When Love, Almighty Love determines the content of the Church's Faith, then of course our faithful doctrines will change over time. Our doctrines must change, or our love together as a community of faith will die.

From our inception, the founders of the Church of the Nazarene never expected Nazarene doctrine and faith to remain permanently fixed. How could faithful consensus for the sake of unity in our ecclesial body be reached without the necessary space for faithful tension between our growing convictions of faithful seeing and breathing to live *alongside* our past formulations of doctrine, episcopacy, and yes, our thorny codes of conduct? How could our faith not change if the heart of our faith and life and its doctrinal language is derived from the love of God?

A careful reading of Phineas Bresee and John Wesley's sermons will bear this out. In practice, the wisdom of our founders expected the denomination to hold in the Body, the faith of the tradition as it is expressed through the Manual with the growing convictions of faithful love. They expected us to hold the tensions of faith *and* doubt, until the Church reaches faithful consensus at the General Assembly to change the Church's Articles of Faith, episcopal forms of governance, and various codes of conduct, etc. If there is no space in the denomination for faith *and* doubt, there will be no room for a faith filled with the energy of love to grow and expand.

What is contradictory to the nature of living faith and illogical to sound reason is our blatant refusal to engage in discussion and exploration over the sexual equality and identity of LGBTQIA+ people. At this juncture of our history, we have become so fearful of losing our ecclesial identity that we have defiantly censored or removed ordination credentials from anyone expressing a desire to hold the tension in holy conversation for the sake of ecclesial consensus. The inconsistencies at all levels of denominational leadership are glaring and revealing! Stubborn blind "dead faith of the living" persists.

In the past, we have managed to hold the tension until consensus could be reached to change or add to Articles of Faith, our position on divorce, and numerous other historical and social positions written in our codes of conduct. May we hold faithful tension to let the Spirit, the God of our future make some "good trouble" for us by disrupting our long-held assumptions.

At this place in our short history, we presume to stand on the side of God's holiness with a particular understanding of righteous sexual purity that exists between a man *and* a woman, because we have found seven little texts in Holy Scripture (Genesis 19:5,13; Lev. 18:22; Lev. 20:13; Judges 19; Romans 1:26-27; 1Cor. 6:9; 1Tim 1:10) to justify our Nazarene position on the sexual equality and identity of LGBTQIA+ people in the Church.

Gender is a social, religious, political and cultural construct of our making. And now, the Church of the Nazarene is "certain" that gender is absolutely and universally fixed as consisting of men and women, and that holiness is sexually pure when it is between a man and woman in marriage. This is the criteria that is used to faithfully exegete those seven little "wounded texts" of Holy Scripture that groan for God's redemption.

We should have learned by now that we cannot restrict or prescribe authentic human experience of the Spirit's deeper work in us. We forced everyone to fit their experience into a particular narrative and doctrine that was reduced into a formula for how one will experience the second work of grace subsequent to regeneration through the baptism of the Holy Spirit. That narrowing of human experience has effectively killed what was good and right about biblical holiness. Once again, that pattern of control and certainty regarding the absoluteness of what constitutes gender is once again gutting the very essence of biblical holiness.

There are some who think that gender exists on a spectrum with multiple variations. And there are some who oppose such thinking. According to emerging neuroscience, gender identity is as complex and mysterious as our individual experience. No definitive answer to gender can be given. Not even the mapping of the genome can make definitive claims about gender. It is possible to generalize and make approximations about gender on the basis of genetic markers associated with sex chromosomes, but ultimately, gender is a social and cultural construct attempting to determine male *and* female binary bodies. Moreover, 1.9% of the world's population has been identified as having non-binary bodies that do not fit the typical male (XY) or female (XX) chromosomes. And if this is not stunning enough to take in, think about this: the number of non-binary bodies in the world far exceeds the membership count in the global Church of the Nazarene. To stubbornly ignore the mystery and complexity of neuroscience will be to our own peril.

At best, neuroscience *and* faith are merely stammering as pointers to the mystery and wonder of being made in God's image. Binary (both/and) and non-binary (either/or) bodies are mere constructs of our own making that could never capture the full mystery of original, unique and most definitely unrepeatable persons made in God's image. Our faith cannot grow unless it lets go of old patterns of consciousness for new patterns of conscious knowing.

The seven "gotcha" texts of scripture regarding homosexuality must be reconsidered in light of both their ancient historical context and in the wake of modern-day science. If there are more non-binary bodies in the world than there are Nazarenes, we should at least begin to see these seven texts of scripture as no longer holding absolute universal claim. Groaning for redemption, these seven "wounded texts" have been weaponized as "texts of terror" to "close the loop" (those are your words used in District Advisory Board meetings) and keep out of our Nazarene tribe those that we fear will compromise our denominational identity. We will not solve ancient views of human sexuality that live on in the present by refusing to see in the evolution of time and science what the Spirit, the God of our future is trying to tell us about the sexual equality and identity of LGBTQIA+ people.

Oh, the irony of our blind stubbornness when we fail to see the future hope of God's promises contained in our scriptures. Not only do we fail to see that all of scripture is a "means of God's grace" that speaks to us and through us from our historical, religious, political, cultural and circumstantial contexts, but we fail to see the Spirit, the future of God coming to us in and through these Holy Scriptures. Not one aspect of scripture is untouched by these perspectives. Ignore them and you deny the nature of Holy Scripture as the Incarnate Word. That is to say, scripture is not only a divine Word, but it is also a human Word. God is truly and definitively revealed in scripture. The fullness of God has been spoken and revealed in Christ and the most definitive and explicit revelation of God has been recorded in Holy Scripture.

What we fail to see from scripture, however, is that the Almighty Vulnerable Loving Creator is not completely contained nor exhaustively revealed in Holy Scripture. There is more, much more to the infinite love of God and God's promise of New Creation than scripture could ever contain. The future coming of God for us, and our salvation remains open while God awaits our responsive participation in the future glory that has already begun. Jesus taught us as much. Scripture was never meant to be an end of our faith, just a means of grace for its journey.

The greatest pushback to the Nazarene interpretation of these seven "wounded texts" has come from my female students seeking ordination in the Church of the Nazarene. Their reasoning is as follows: If the Church of the Nazarene applies an unchanging, strict, literal and universal application of these seven "wounded texts," groaning for redemption regarding the sexual identity and equality of LGBTQIA+ people, what is to stop the Church from applying the same hermeneutic on the "wounded texts" of scripture that speak against women holding such authority as ordained ministers in the Church? After all, the full embrace of women in or-dained pastoral ministry has not been practiced in full step with its doctrine on women in ordained ministry.

This inconsistency has not been lost on my female students. Many are fearful that it is just a matter of time before a male-dominated Church sees the incon-sistency of their own hermeneutic and corrects their glaring inconsistencies. My female students seeking ordination in the Church of the Nazarene have expressed concern that the Church may weaponize those "wounded texts" that speak of women keeping silence and not teaching with authority in the Church in the same way they have weaponized the seven "wounded texts" to control and protect a denominational identity that is pure and holy. Dead faith lives from fear to protect a Nazarene identity that has ignorantly reduced holiness to a particular under-standing of sexual purity. Fear of the "Other" weaponizes scripture as a message of holy terror!

Dead faith of the living no longer lives faithfully into the future of New Creation. It presumes that there is nothing new to learn from the Spirit who brings an open future that awaits our participation for its fulfillment. Dead faith is dead on arrival because it has long stopped seeing and breathing from the Spirit who brings God's promise of future glory.

Hard Words of Love in Truth-Telling

Allow me to tell you with a heart of deep compassion for the sexuality and equality of LGBTQIA+ people what I have been seeing and hearing from these young icons of "future glory already begun." From this place of deep compassion and growing theological conviction, I have some hard and even unfamiliar words of truth that I am compelled to voice in love to our Nazarene episcopal leadership. Board of General Superintendents, District Superintendents, Regional Directors, ordained deacons and elders, I pray that my earnest and unswerving convictions of faith will be received with my sincerest respect, humility and most certainly with my unwavering love that seeks Christ's Peace not only for the Church of the Nazarene but for the life of the world. After all, I am convinced that the energy of God's love that lives in me also lives in you. May we all breathe deeply from the Spirit who is the Lord and giver of Life, and may we see and hear what the Spirit who is the God of our future is bringing to us.

As a "son of the Church of the Nazarene" who was educated in two of your academic institutions (SNU and NTS) and taught for nearly 40 years in 4 of them (EUNC, ENC, MVNU and NTS), I must ask some hard questions of you: When did you start cleansing the Temple with your authoritative whip of episcopacy by "closing the loop" to keep out those that you have deemed to be "Other" than us? Do you see LGBTQIA+ people as "Other" because they do not fit your strange way of defining holiness as "sexual purity?" "Either we see Christ in everyone, or we hardly see Christ in anyone," says Richard Rohr.

When we Nazarenes identify ourselves as the pure and the righteous and see our holiness mostly in terms of sexual purity, we begin to see everyone that is not like us, as simply "Other" than us. Purity of any kind without love is never holy because the essence of holiness that is derived from God is perfect love and the purity that is derived from God's holiness is always perfect love.

To be clear, I am not advocating for sexual promiscuity; I am advocating for lifelong, covenantally faithful and monogamous relationships between two people. No, I am pushing back against a view of holiness that is so embedded in a purity culture of sexuality that it has morphed into an impenetrable shell of indifferent love that seeks to protect the Church and its "elusive identity" by excluding the unholy and impure, the sexually impure. And to be clear, to welcome LGBTQIA+ people without affirming them is to push them out the door. Remember, the Church catholic is only holy because Christ is holy. The Gospel that Christ declares, and the Church serves is the Good News that all belong to God and are made holy by God's love. The unity of God's perfect holy love desires to unite everyone into God's family.

Simply put, no one made in God's image is "Other." No one! When we see humankind as "Other" because we see them as unholy and sexually impure, we become the exact opposite of God's declared justice and righteousness and redemption in Christ's Good News for the whole world. We no longer see as God sees! We no longer love as God loves! Blindness and callous indifference to those we deem as "Other" have made us idolatrously certain of our holiness and purity and woefully deficient in love for one another.

When we "close the loop," we cordon off ourselves into an ecclesial tribe that works from the top down towards the removal of those "Other" than us. As we see ourselves as holy and pure, especially sexually pure, and then use that tribal criteria to deem LGBTQIA+ people as "Other" than us because they do not fit our Nazarene defined criteria of holiness, we will begin to grow idolatrously unaware of the ways that we begin to "exclude" the "Other."

Once we are comfortable excluding the "Other" we will not have trouble "killing" the "Other." A long sordid history of institutional Church and Christianity will bear this out. A doctrine of holiness that is defined by a particular understanding of sexual purity and is driven by cold indifference will burn hot with righteous anger and idolatrous certainty to justify the exclusion of the LGBTQIA+ community because they are deemed "Other."

A Proposal for Hopeful Change

It is time to soften our gaze. We must stop seeing LGBTQIA+ people as "Other."

Can we grant enough space and time to listen to one another in close proximity to hear and see what the Spirit is bringing to us from the future through LGBTQIA+ people?

The Quaker practice of holding faith *and* doubt in tension offers a way to faithfully "correct and fulfill" what the Spirit, is bringing for our future. To wait on the Spirit for consensus echoes the same wisdom and condition of the human heart and predicament that was expressed by John Wesley. The best way to navigate our convictions that threaten to "breach our love" and divide the Church is through the faithful practice of the Great Physician: "*Do No Harm.*"

How do we hold theological convictions that go against the grain of the Church of the Nazarene's teachings? How do we make space for honest conversation about such matters if they are not in that space of holy conversation? As long as we see them as "Other" we fail to fulfill what God has entrusted to us with the Gospel and the promise of New Creation.

We live by faith to see from our future hope with every breath we take. God is infinite love and that means God's love is everywhere. God is not "exclusively" present anywhere. This means that no religion, tribe or cult, nation, political party, denomination, etc. can claim "exclusively" that their rendering of God is the "only" true one. God cannot be named, and God certainly cannot be tamed to fit our narrative. And our denominational holiness narrative is not our ecclesial identity.

Our ecclesial identity is found in God's infinite love. Let God's Story be God's Story that "includes" all of creation into God's Story. God is no respecter of persons or religion, but a God who loves all. Christianity cannot claim a monopoly on truth because God is not a Christian. God is infinite love making infinite space for all things of creation to share and participate in the promise and mission of New Creation.

The convictions and contradictions of our Nazarene tradition run deep and now they threaten to "breach our love" and divide our family. May God's perfect holy love pierce our impenetrable hearts of indifference, so we stop seeing with fearful hearts LGBTQIA+ people as "Other." Let us keep looking over the horizon to the Spirit who is the God of the future making good on God's promises in all of creation. For such a time as this, the best practice and habit that I can offer the

Church of the Nazarene is to: ***See No One As "Other."*** I am convinced that the love of God that lives in me is the love of God that lives in you!

Rev. K. Steve McCormick, PhD: *NTS Faculty Emeritus Professor of Historical Theology. William M. Greathouse Chair for Wesleyan-Holiness Theology. Professor of Systematic and Historical Theology at Eastern Nazarene College. Professor of Systematic and Historical Theology at Mount Vernon Nazarene University. Professor of Systematic and Historical Theology at European Nazarene College. Ordained Elder in the Church of Nazarene.*

Dialog

SAMUEL M. POWELL

An account of an overheard dialog

Many years ago—decades, in fact—I attended my first Nazarene Theology Conference, giddy with the prospect of rubbing shoulders with denominational luminaries both academic and administrative. I anticipated three days of stimulating ideas, with penetrating analysis of challenging issues. The event did not exactly live up to my youthful and overblown expectations. There was, however, one moment that remains with me. During one session, after an interesting afternoon presentation on the Socratic dialog as a model for theological conversation, I felt myself falling asleep as the next speaker droned on, searching for a thesis. I went for a walk and, on the way, I heard voices emerging from a room, engaged in a spirited conversation. Since I had come to the conference in search of such conversation, I stopped and shamelessly listened in.

I recognized the voices as two veteran Nazarene academics of blessed memory, one a biblical scholar, the other a theologian. Both are now as dead as their conversation was lively. The biblical scholar (whom I will call "W") was relating his experience at a recent meeting of the Society of Biblical Literature. He had heard a presentation that he found both forceful and troubling.

"What was the topic?" the theologian (whom I will call "R") asked.

W: "The passages in the Bible about homosexuality. The scholar was very thorough—he covered them all, I think. Wrong, of course, dreadfully wrong in his interpretation."

R: "You corrected him, I assume?"

W: "That's just the thing. Each point seemed plausible and each led logically to the next, so that by the time he was done, I felt as confused as a freshman theology student."

R: "Hopefully you're not still confused—are you?"

W: "Oh, absolutely not. While he was talking, I felt that I was under a spell of some sort, but as soon as the presentation was over, my orthodox convictions returned."

R: "As strong as ever, I trust."

W hesitated.

R: "What were these points that shook your assurance?"

W: "He started by asking why, if we accept the authority of Leviticus' condemnation of homosexuality, we don't also accept its condemnation of another abomination—having intercourse with a woman during her menstrual period."

R: "That's in Leviticus?" R seemed, from the tone of his voice, incredulous.

W: "It is, and just a verse or two away from the passage about homosexuality."

R: "Well, but that's Leviticus. As you know, we are not under law, but under grace."

W: "Yes, but it's not just the law of Moses—the prophet Ezekiel insists that such intercourse is completely inconsistent with righteousness."

R: "Well, we know that the Old Testament contains much that is irrelevant to us today. All those food laws and such."

W: "But that's just it—his next point was about the New Testament. You know how Paul says, in Romans 1, that homosexuals have given up the 'natural function?' Well, the scholar asked why, if we accept the argument from nature in Romans 1, we ignore Paul's argument from nature in 1 Corinthians 11."

Though widely regarded in Nazarene circles as a theological genius and polymath, R must not have known the reference, for W went on to explain: "It's where Paul says that nature teaches that long hair on men is a disgrace. The scholar, I think, may have had a good point, don't you think? I does seem wrong to arbitrarily pick and choose which biblical passages we accept and which we don't."

R: "Of course it's wrong. But no one could possibly accuse us of that. Everyone knows the church operates by sound and consistent hermeneutical principles when it formulates its ethics. Everyone except the poor fools who've been indoctrinated by liberal theology." He said this last part in a somewhat accusatory tone.

W was silent. I wish that I had been in the room so that I could determine whether this silence stemmed from thoughtful agreement or from something else.

R: "What did he have to say about the New Testament's other unassailable foundations of the truth about homosexuality?"

Apparently, W was not sure which unassailable truths R was referring to, for R went on: "1 Corinthians 6:9 and 1 Timothy 1:10. I mean, no one can doubt that here Paul condemned homosexuality expressly and categorically."

W: "In fact he did have a question about these verses. Why, he asked, did the church place so much weight on passages where the meaning of the key terms is uncertain."

R: "Uncertain! Where did this impudent clod get his education? Any student of first year Greek knows the meaning of those words—'effeminate,' 'men who have sex with men,' 'those practicing homosexuality.' It's as plain as day.'

W: "Um, perhaps we should be a bit more hesitant on this point."

R: "What? This infidel hasn't persuaded you, has he?"

W: "No, of course not."

There seemed to be a note of caution in his voice. I knew him to be a man of impeccable orthodoxy as well as being an accomplished biblical scholar, sensitive to the occasional bumps in the road as he practiced his scholarship in service to the church. Although he would never criticize orthodox dogma or ecclesiastical edicts publicly, on at least one occasion I had heard him gently and tentatively question whether some official doctrine (I forget now which it was) was as securely biblical as the leaders of the church proclaimed. At the same time, I knew that R simply did not understand how a biblical scholar could question church doctrine, assuming that the scholar was a Bible-believing Christian. He was not, of course, trained in biblical scholarship, but no one could doubt his adamant rejection of its results.

"It's just that," W continued, "well, I did some study of the matter after the conference and, well, let's just say that this issue deserves further consideration. Scholars don't seem to agree on exactly how to translate those key terms."

R: "Well, there's no lack of agreement among *Evangelical* scholars. Maybe you should stop associating with liberal scholars—there's a danger that their ideas will rub off on you. 'Bad company corrupts good character,' you know."

W: "Yes—sound advice. Of course, that's one reason I'm here at this Nazarene conference—no possibility of dangerous ideas being touted here."

R: "Indeed. We're perfectly safe here, inoculated against error. Everyone can go home secure in the truth, with new and even stronger reasons for believing what the church teaches. Still, we have to be careful—you were wise to share all this in private. We don't want to get our people worried."

W: "I agree. I do, however, wish that we could find a way to discuss these things."

R: "I don't see what there is to discuss, but perhaps something could be arranged—a small gathering of responsible people. Of course, we would need to include church leaders. General Superintendents, possibly a few of the more, um, significant DSs, college presidents, heads of departments. Someone would have to be in charge to make sure that the conversation moved in the right direction. I mean, theology is not a rushing river that creates its own channels. We must carefully guide it. Well, back to this liberal scholar's questions. Were there more?"

W: "Oh, I'm afraid so. He questioned whether the focus of the story of Sodom and Gomorrah was really homosexuality?"

R: "What? He's obviously delusional."

W: "Oh, no doubt. Still, he scored points with the audience—mostly fellow liberals, I'm sure—by suggesting that the story was actually about rape or an attempt to dishonor Lot. I must admit I had never considered these possibilities. He provided references to studies that, he claimed, supported his questioning. Would you like me to send them to you?"

R: "Absolutely not. What are the ramblings of a few liberal scholars compared to the unanimous voice of the church? Why contaminate my thoughts with such poison? I'm surprised you gave it a moment's consideration."

W: "Oh, I assure you, it was much less than a moment. But then he also asked why Ezekiel's comments about Sodom are routinely ignored?"

R: "What comments?"

W: "You know, the place where Ezekiel identifies Sodom's sin as being lack of hospitality. The scholar put great emphasis on this point."

R: "Well, there's no conflict with orthodoxy here. The Sodomites could very well have been both perverted and inhospitable, couldn't they?"

W: "Of course you are right, although the scholar thought it important that Ezekiel does not mention their homosexuality."

R: "He was obviously reading something into the biblical text that was not there. Typical of liberal scholars. What else did he have to say?"

W: "Oh, there was a long rant about Evangelical hypocrisy."

R: "What did he mean?"

W: "It was about the way we focus on certain biblical texts but then ignore others. Why are we obsessed with a few passages about homosexuality while ignoring explicit commands in the New Testament?"

R: "And which are they?"

W: "Foot-washing, the holy kiss, compelling women to have a head covering when they pray, forbidding the braiding of hair."

R: "Doesn't the dolt know that these commands are dependent on the particulars of ancient cultures? That they don't apply to us today in a different culture?"

W: "In fact, he brought that up, wondering if perhaps the Bible's view of homosexuality is itself an example of a culturally-conditioned belief."

R: "Heresy! Any fool can plainly see the difference between condemning homosexuality on one hand and commanding foot-washing on the other. Culture's got nothing to do with the first and everything to do with the second."

W: "If only you had been there to set the man straight. At any rate, the last set of questions pertained to science. He mentioned studies in neurology and genetics suggesting that homosexuality may be a natural phenomenon."

R: "Natural? Impossible! The Bible states clearly that it is unnatural."

W: "That's just the point I wanted to make in the Q&A. But he went on to ask why Evangelicals accept the authority of science until it challenges their beliefs. I think he was accusing us once again of hypocrisy—selectively using the results of science when it supports us and rejecting science when it contradicts us."

R: "But it's not us that science contradicts, it's God. Are we going to let scientists teach us about nature? When we have God's own word to teach us?"

W: "That's a good point. Still, even Evangelicals have begun to accept that science may help us get rid of false interpretations of Genesis 1. The presenter obviously thought that science may have something to say about homosexuality."

R: "Well it doesn't. Science can help with facts but not with values."

W: "Homosexuality isn't a fact?"

R: "Of course it's a fact, but…but, it's a different sort of fact, it's… Now you're getting me confused like that scholar made you confused."

W: "I guess I am a little confused. Of course, my orthodoxy's intact, but I'm no longer sure that its biblical basis is as strong as I once thought."

R: "That's very disappointing, especially for someone in your position. You know that the church requires us to have clear views on important matters."

W: "Maybe you can help me and others like me. Write a book that refutes this scholar, point by point—the biblical arguments, psychology, neurology, genetics, everything."

R: "Yes—I will. But first, you know, I've got to respond to an article just published that insists that entire sanctification is about extirpation, not eradication. Can you imagine? This sort of error cannot go unchallenged."

W: "That's a worthy task, but when you can help me? I can't stay in this state of confusion forever. Can I at least send you the book this scholar wrote on homo-sexuality and the Bible?"

R: "I'm afraid I won't have time to read it. There's a new book about carnality that demands my attention."

W: "But—"

R: "Sorry, but I must run—Oh, look, I'm late for a meeting."

With that R left the room and rushed past me. W left a few seconds later.

R never published that refutation of the liberal scholar, although he did, in his remaining years, churn out 17 books on the subtleties of eradication. To the end of his life, W was a model of orthodoxy and of faithful submission to the church. I never had a chance to talk with him, so I do not know whether he ever emerged from his confusion. But I always wondered.

Samuel M. Powell *taught philosophy and religion for many years in Nazarene institutions and is an ordained deacon in the Church of the Nazarene.*

The Bible Changes What
The Bible Accepts

MATTHEW A. RUNDIO

My journey to being fully open and inclusive runs straight through the scriptures, realizing that the Bible itself changes its own rules over time and always moves toward greater inclusion.

I am no longer a Nazarene. I found it unacceptable for me to remain in a denomination that is, in many ways, actively hurting LGBTQIA+ people—so I resigned my ordination credentials. That was a difficult decision because I love my (former) denomination. The Church of the Nazarene has a marvelous history and theology and contains many excellent and admirable people. If this good denomination would become open and affirming, she would become even more beautiful. This paper tells some of how I became convinced that God accepts people who identify as a part of the LGBTQIA+ community and that the church should, too.

For many years, while lead pastor at Scottsdale First Church of the Nazarene, I was a lectionary preacher. The lectionary (a standardized set of readings) assigns four scriptures each Sunday of the year—we would read each of them and preach from one (or several) of them. The readings from Easter, week 5, year C[1] stand out as my favorite because they helped me embrace God's inclusion more fully. Together, these readings draw us all toward greater and greater love.

One year, as I was reading the passage from John 13, verse 34 struck me: "I give you a new commandment: Love each other…" (CEB). I thought, "New? What is *new* about the commandment to love? Isn't that already part of the Bible?" Indeed, Leviticus 19:17-18 already reads, "You must not hate your fellow Israelite in your heart….you must love your neighbor as yourself; I am the Lord."

---

1. The readings are Acts 11:1-18; Psalm 148; Revelation 21:1-6; and John 13:31-35. Each of these will be mentioned in this essay.

Eventually I came to realize that what makes Jesus' command "new" is in defining one seemingly simple phrase, "each other." In the Leviticus passage, "each other" or "neighbor" was understood to mean "fellow Israelite." So with Jesus, the new thing is that "each other" means "everyone," not just people who are already like me.

As I thought more about this, I realized that Matthew 5:43-48 makes this same point. Matthew's Jesus knows that people interpreted the "love your neighbor" instruction as "love your neighbor and hate your enemy" (v. 43). So Jesus states his version of "love your neighbor" explicitly as "love your enemy." In fact, that Matthew 5 passage defines "perfection" as loving in the same way God does: God who shows love indiscriminately to everyone and everything, demonstrated when God "makes the sun rise on both the evil and the good and sends rain on both the righteous and the unrighteous" (v. 45).

This point of loving everyone, even (especially) those considered enemies and outsiders (or evil or unrighteous), is made in these lectionary passages. Jesus' "new" command to "love each other" in John 13 is coupled with the story contained in Acts 10 and 11. I find this pairing particularly potent.

Acts 10 and 11 is the culmination of a series of stories that depict ever expanding circles of inclusion. Here is a brief overview: In Acts 1-5, all of the first Christians are strictly Jewish (Peter calls them "fellow Israelites" in Acts 2:22, echoing Lev. 19) but this quickly expands to include "Hellenistic" or "Greek-speaking Jews" in Acts 6. You can begin to see the circle expanding—not just the people that look, sound, and smell like us, also the ones who are culturally different. Then, in Acts 8, Philip's ministry in Samaria continues the expansion. Philip's baptism of the Ethiopian eunuch expands inclusion to people previously excluded by biblical law (Deuteronomy 23:1 reads, "no eunuchs can belong to the Lord's assembly."). The baptism of a foreigner and a eunuch (but still "Jewish" in a way) would have been controversial because circumcision is demanded in biblical law, yet a eunuch cannot be circumcised. Finally comes the inclusion of uncircumcised Gentiles in Acts 10 and 11. It is hard to overemphasize the importance of these moves, especially the last one.

In Acts 10, Peter has a vision in which the Lord asks him to eat food forbidden by the Bible; Peter refuses (because the Bible says "NO"!) but the voice insists (three times) saying, "never consider unclean what God has made pure" (v. 15); Peter then receives an invitation to visit some Gentiles; Peter would normally refuse to associate with such people (who don't follow the Bible), but because he just had that vision, he goes (v. 28); these Gentiles—who do not follow Sabbath, food laws, or circumcision, *all things commanded in the Bible*—hear, believe, and receive the Holy Spirit (without changing their old ways); this surprises Peter who says,

"These people have received the Holy Spirit just as we have. Surely no one can stop them from being baptized with water, can they?" (Acts 10:47).

Then Acts 11 records a trial—Peter was called before a council to investigate his actions which *clearly contradict* scripture. Everyone knows how central Sabbath laws are—it is right there in the Ten Commandments! The food laws are clearly stated in the Bible. And circumcision! God makes this part of the covenant with Abraham, told in Genesis 17, to be practiced "in every generation" (v. 9) and calls this custom an "enduring covenant" (v. 13) and that, if someone doesn't follow this covenant, that person "will be cut off" from God's people (v. 14, and yes, I assume the pun is intended). This is a big deal. This is all clear teaching in the Bible. And here is Peter, breaking all these rules in the Bible by visiting, eating with, accepting, and baptizing people who do not keep Sabbath, who break the food laws, and who are outside God's enduring covenant of circumcision.

So in Acts 11, Peter tells his story. (By the way, when the Bible was written— and for many centuries after, when it was copied—writing materials were costly resources. That means if a story is repeated, thus taking up valuable resources, it must be important. The same story is written twice, in Acts 10 and Acts 11, help- ing to highlight how important it is.) After recounting the story to the apostles, Peter concludes by saying, "When I began to speak, the Holy Spirit fell on them, just as the Spirit fell on us in the beginning. I remembered the Lord's words: 'John baptized with water, but you will be baptized with the Holy Spirit.' If God gave them the same gift he gave us who believed in the Lord Jesus Christ, then who am I? Could I stand in God's way?" (Acts 11:15-17).

We can probably guess how the council ruled: Peter was clearly out of bounds and going rogue. These people are clearly not following the explicit teachings of the Bible, things that are self-evident and have been upheld for thousands of years. Peter must be expelled, his ordination revoked. These sinners who are not follow- ing the scriptures should be kept safely away from true believers until they repent and follow God's clear standards. And surely we should warn people about Peter and his progressive, woke, teachings. Right?

Of course not. Instead, what the Bible records is this: "Once the apostles and other believers heard this, they calmed down. They praised God and concluded, 'So then God has enabled Gentiles to change their hearts and lives so that they might have new life'" (Acts 11:18). The church recognized that this is the story of God's love, a love that expands in ever increasing circles of inclusion, and they changed to match God's love. To this day the church does not require Sabbath keeping (not as it is commanded in the Bible), Christians do not eat kosher, and (praise be) are not required to practice circumcision.

When the leadership and concerned believers heard Peter's story and, especially, the part that the Holy Spirit fell on the uncircumcised Gentiles, the church decided to agree with God, rather than the Bible.

When the Bible and God seem to be going different directions, we are to follow God not the Bible.

The God of the Bible, in the Bible itself, changes the rules of the Bible, even "enduring" covenants for "every generation." The Bible changes what the Bible accepts.

The Revelation passage (from the Lectionary texts of Easter 5, year C) includes this line: "Then the one seated on the throne said, 'Look! I'm making all things new'" (Rev. 21:4-5). Part of what God is making new is the Bible's own expectations and rules. Part of what God is making new is our perception of "in" and "out" and who belongs in which categories. The more we know of God, the more we move to include what God has already included.

In thinking about why the Church of the Nazarene should change its position and becoming fully open and inclusive of LGBTQIA+ people, here's the point that convinces me most: many people who identify as somewhere on the LGBTQIA+ spectrum *already believe and are already Christians* which means, to quote Peter, "These people have received the Holy Spirit just as we have. Surely no one can stop them from being baptized with water, can they?" And because God has already accepted LGBTQIA+ people as part of God's church (again to quote Peter) "then who am I? Could I stand in God's way?" (Acts 11:17). I hope the Church of the Nazarene will say, "Who are we? Could we stand in God's way? Of course not!"

I'm not convinced that the Bible even addresses LGBTQIA+ issues in ways we intend today. I think passages in the Bible that we take as "anti-gay" are actually speaking against sexual violence and come from a place of patriarchy in the authors. But even if the Bible is against aspects of LGBTQIA+ people and their lives, the story of the inclusion of the Gentiles in Acts 10 and 11 would convince me to get out of God's way.[2] Because God already includes people thought to be outside of God's perfect plan, so should we. We should learn Peter's lesson: "God has shown me that I should never call a person impure or unclean" (Acts 10:28).

The lectionary readings for Easter, week 5, year C help make the point that God's love and inclusion push beyond our boundaries (and even beyond boundaries we thought God erected). But it is not alone in the scriptures in this regard. The Good Samaritan story pushes us in the same direction. And the Magi's inclusion in

---

2. I am grateful to New Testament scholar J.R. Daniel Kirk for helping me realize many of these insights from Acts 10 and 11.

the Christmas narrative is another good example of people, clearly outside biblical laws, norms, and expectations, being included by God when others would have cast them aside as sinners. God's boundary-breaking love becomes a theme. One we need to hear. We must know and believe that God's love "goes beyond the highest star and reaches to the lowest hell."

Jesus gives us a new command: love each other. So we are to love and include everyone whom God has included, even if they are people who live lives that break biblical standards as we understand them. For the Church of the Nazarene, the new-ness of this command would be to stop harming LGBTQIA+ people and instead love everyone, fully.

I can hear God saying to us: Love each other, everyone. Yes, people who look and sound and smell like you already. But also those who don't. And those you don't like. And those you call enemies. And those you can't categorize on a gender binary. Those who eat, worship, and rest differently than you. Those who don't follow the rules in the Bible you think are important. Love and include all of them. I get it, this is *new*, so it's hard. But this new command is *the* command: Love each other.

I have stepped away from the denomination that helped raise and loved my children, me, and three generations of family before me. But that denomination was harming people in the name of God and holiness. So I left. I hope that the denomination will change and follow God's love into greater inclusion. The type of inclusion that is expressed in this song of praise, Psalm 148—another reading from Easter 5, year C. Someday the church will realize. Someday God's love will soften hard hearts so that we will no longer call people impure or unclean. Someday we, a body made up of *all* people, along with *all* things and *all* beings in *all* the universe, will together sing praise to the God of love, whose love has no boundary. Let us pray:

Hallelujah!
Praise the Lord from the heavens!
Praise God in the heights!
Praise God, all you angels!
Praise God, all you heavenly host!
Praise God, sun and moon!
Praise God, all you shining stars!
Praise the Lord from the land,
and even from the deep, even sea monsters!
Lightning and hail, snow and clouds;
stormy wind, fulfilling God's word;

mountains and all hills;
fruit trees and all cedars;
wild animals and all livestock;
small creatures and flying birds;
kings of the earth and all peoples;
princes and all judges of the earth;
All people, any gender, single and married,
the aged and children:
let them praise the Lord's name,
for God's name alone is exalted.
Hallelujah!
(Psalm 148:1-3, 7-13, my translation)

Matt Rundio *served in pastoral and adjunct professor roles in the Church of the Nazarene for over 20 years. He holds an MDiv and an MSMFT from Fuller Theological Seminary and a DMin from NTS. He currently works as a Licensed Associate Marriage and Family Therapist in Arizona.*

Who Would Jesus Exclude?

WM. ANDREW SCHWARTZ

Jesus never excluded or condemned LGBTQ+ individuals.
The Church of the Nazarene should be like Jesus."

This book is a collection of essays arguing why the Church of the Nazarene should be fully affirming of LGBTQ+ individuals. To be honest, I find this task somewhat difficult because it first requires me to understand the mindset of those who still need convincing—that is, those who believe the Church of the Nazarene should be "closed" and "rejecting." It's as perverse a task as trying to argue to a group of fish why they should live under water…Because it's what fish do? Because not doing so will result in death? Perhaps you, dear reader, are offended by my tone. If so, fair enough. I guess I'm just tired of being polite toward bigotry in the name of Jesus. But before I lose you, allow me to walk things back a bit.

What is the Church of the Nazarene? It is a Christian denomination in the tradition of the Holiness Movement, Methodism, and Protestantism. "The Nazarene" for whom this Christian community takes its name, refers to Jesus (a.k.a. the OG Nazarene). It stands to reason, then, that in asking whether or not the Church of the Nazarene should accept LGBTQ+ people we should take a closer look at Jesus. As my childhood bracelet said, What Would Jesus Do?

As a philosopher and theologian, I can attest to how easy it is to get lost in the weeds when answering such a fundamental question. Fortunately, we find in scripture very clear guidance from Jesus himself. When asked which is the greatest commandment, Jesus showed his Jewish cards and cited the Great Shema: "You shall love the Lord your God with all your heart, and with all your soul, and with all your mind" (Deut. 6:5, Matt 22:38, Mark 12:30, Luke 10:27). Then he adds that the second great commandment is, "You shall love your neighbor as yourself," going on to explain that everything else—all the other scriptures, all the other religious practices, all the other rules and regulations, everything that we would consider fundamental to Christianity today, all follows from these two commands.

Given the absolutely central and comprehensive nature of this call to love, this seems like a good place for us to start. One of my favorite theological bumper stickers is the one that says, "When Jesus said 'Love your enemies,' I think he probably meant don't kill them." And now that we've identified the low bar of love, the natural thing to do would be to seek clarity on what love looks like in practice. Unfortunately, many theologians go the opposite route, wasting countless pages on figuring out who our neighbors are. In the words of the great Homer Simpson, "D'oh!" Rather than embracing the call to love as a distinctive mark of Christianity by exploring in greater detail how we can love better, these theologians resist the call to love and seek to clarify who is worthy of such benevolence. It reminds me of that clip from the Adam Sandler film *Big Daddy*, when in a fit of utter despair Leslie Mann's character declares, "We wasted the good surprise on you." It's as if Christians are, for some reason, concerned about wasting the good love on undeserving people. By asking "who" we should love, rather than "how" we should love, the Church of the Nazarene has been acting like a bunch of velociraptors testing the fence for weaknesses to see if we can escape the confines of Jesus' command to love. Yet I can't imagine Jesus calling us a "clever girl."

I can hear the conversation now: "Okay Phineas, I figured out how to work the system...If we only have to love our 'neighbors', then all we need to do is figure out who doesn't qualify as our neighbors, so we don't have to love them!" "Great thinking Hiram. Let's ask Jesus to clarify. Um, Jesus, are poor people my neighbor?" Jesus rolls his eyes and replies in an exhausted tone, "Yes, Hiram, poor people are your neighbors." Phineas pipes in, "But what about people who look different, or speak a different language, or have a different religion?" Jesus nods his head, "Yeah, them too." Hiram tries again, "But what if they murdered my friend? Or stole something valuable from me? Our gossiped behind my back?" Jesus explains, "Yeah, that's tough, but you should love those people too." Hiram and Phineas exchange looks, and the lightbulb goes on. "But what if they're gay?" Phineas yells. They finally found the weak spot in the fence of love. Of course, this is where we get that famous quote in the Gospel of Todd, where Jesus confesses, "Ew gross. No, not those people. You definitely don't have to love homosexuals."

Christians are supposed to be followers of Jesus. We won't always get it right. But trying to prioritize the thing that Jesus said unequivocally is the most important seems like a good place to start. This is the same Jesus that spent all his time hanging out with people who were marginalized by the rest of society and persecuted by mainstream religious institutions. The same Jesus that warns crowds, "Beware of the yeast of the Pharisees and Sadducees!" (Matthew 16:12). It's natural to read ourselves into the story as the protagonist, but who is the Church of the Nazarene in this passage? The crowd of marginalized folks listening to Jesus? Jesus himself teaching about love? Or the group of self-righteous Pharisees and Sadducees watching from the wings? Perhaps it depends on what the church does next.

There are many different ways I could have written this essay, and I'm sure some of the other contributors will fill the gaps I leave. I could have provided biblical exegesis on Genesis 9:20—27, 19:1—11, Leviticus 18:22, 20:13, 1 Corinthians 6:9—10; 1 Timothy 1:10, or Romans 1:26—27. However, many biblical scholars far smarter than I have already shown that passages such as these, which are commonly used to justify Christian homophobia, don't actually refer to loving relationships between two consenting adults, but describe rape, prostitution, etc.[1] I hate bickering over biblical interpretation. Let's not forget that Christians once used the Bible to justify slavery. We now look back on that history in shameful confusion. How could "they" have called themselves Christian? Is the current use of scripture to exclude and condemn LGBTQ+ folks so different? I believe that in the not-so-distant future, historians will look upon our current situation—the failure of the Church of the Nazarene to be open and affirming toward our LGBTQ+ neighbors—and ask, "How could they call themselves Christian?" When it's a choice between using the Bible to condemn and exclude or using the Bible to nurture and embrace, it seems pretty clear what Jesus would do.

I also considered appealing to the self-interest of Nazarene leaders, or anyone with a vested interest in the future of the Church of the Nazarene. The message is simple: adapt or die. The hard truth is, if the Church of the Nazarene wants to avoid dying out, it needs to reach new generations. How do you do that? Interestingly, the trend remains consistent across generations—young people are more progressive than old people; that's how progress works. What that means in this historical moment, among other things, is that an increasing number of young people are fully affirming of LGBTQ+ neighbors. If the Church of the Nazarene wants to attract young people, it needs to start listening to young people and adapting accordingly. If the Church of the Nazarene fails to adapt, it will literally die out in a few generations. But this isn't the argument I wish to make in these pages.

I finally settled on the most basic and (hopefully) most compelling argument I could think of—be like Jesus. Afterall, what else should a Christian do? If you still aren't convinced that Jesus would be fully affirming of our LGBTQ+ neighbors, then perhaps the best I can do now is turn the tables. I invite anyone that remains

---

1. See Robert Gnuse, "Seven Gay Texts: Biblical Passages Used to Condemn Homosexuality" in *Biblical Theology Bulletin*, Vol 45, No 2 (2015).

unconvinced by my essay to write a response titled "Why the Church of the Nazarene Should NOT Be Open and Affirming." Good luck! I think you'll have a difficult time writing that essay while sounding like Jesus, the OG Nazarene. Afterall, who would Jesus exclude?

Wm. Andrew Schwartz, PhD *is an author, scholar, and activist who serves as Assistant Professor at Claremont School of Theology, Executive Director of the Center for Process Studies, and Co-Founder of the Institute for Ecological Civilization.*

The Gospel Changed Marriage, Not the Gays

RYAN SCOTT

*Surprisingly, the most compelling scriptural argument for
Christians to affirm marriage between two men is our
understanding of women.*

During my time in seminary, I dove deeply into the scriptures for support of
our denomination's stance on gay marriage. If I was going to be a pastor in
the Church of the Nazarene, I wanted to be prepared not only with a statement,
but with a solid explanation for our beliefs. I found, though, the more I studied,
scripture gave me fewer and fewer reasons to oppose same-sex couples and more
and more reasons to affirm them.

At the core of everything is our understanding of marriage itself.

When it comes to a theological argument about LGBTQ+ inclusion, you can
throw out the issues of sex and biology—the Church of the Nazarene already
affirms that the most appropriate context for sex is within a committed, Christ-
centered marriage. The answer to who should be sleeping with whom is simple:
spouses.

From there, the only remaining questions are 'Who should be in a marriage
and why?'

If you look at the history of marriage and the evolution of theology both in
scripture and after it was written, you'll see a stark difference in how God's people
have answered those questions. There's an obvious movement from marriage as a
social institution to marriage as a fully religious commitment, and it mirrors the
movement of women as property to the recognition of women as full equals (at
least in theory).

While our wedding liturgy talks about Genesis 2:24 as the foundation of
Christian marriage, citing Adam and Eve becoming one flesh, it's an interpretive
leap that may not be wholly appropriate.

There's no mention of marriage at all in Genesis 2 (there's no separate word for 'wife' in Greek or Hebrew, it's the word for 'woman' that becomes the English 'wife' when translators think it's appropriate). In this passage we find only the kind of holy commitment to one another we now associate with marriage. But it took human society, as well as the Church, a long time to get from one to the other.

Early human marriage was a simple transfer of property. Women were objects to be owned—first by their fathers and then by their husbands. In fact, this social arrangement was so unseemly to God's people that priests wanted nothing to do with performing or solemnizing marriages until the late Middle Ages, when the power of the Church was waning and requiring clerical approval of a marriage proved a particularly effective means of social control.

The religious rules around marriage all had to do with property rights. Fornication was a violation of a father by 'defiling' his property (daughter) and adultery was a violation of a husband by 'defiling' his wife—again, a property crime.

There's no scriptural prohibition of extra-marital sex by men, so long as these other rules are observed. There was no written recrimination for, say, a man sleeping with a prostitute or his own servant girl, until Paul started calling it out by name in 1 Corinthians.

Modern conservative Christian sexual ethics essentially took the scriptural chastity rules for women and applied them to men, where it just as easily could've gone the other way (which is essentially what modern liberal Christian sexual ethics look like). In either event, things changed because we went from viewing women as property to viewing them as people.

Galatians says there is "neither Jew nor Greek, slave nor free, male nor female." It's not saying that these distinctions don't matter, that men and women are the same; it's saying these distinctions are not of degree. Jews are not better than Gentiles. Slaves do not have a different status from free people. Men and women are not fundamentally different in value.

Many use this verse to support LGBTQ+ inclusion. I do not. I don't believe inclusion can be proof-texted, just as exclusion cannot be derived from any one or series of verses. Affirmation of gay marriage arises as the necessary theological conclusion of broader arguments made in scripture. Our understanding of marriage has changed because of the massive theological shifts made in the process of God's people better understanding how God has called us to live.

We see, even in the Hebrew scriptures, the beginning of the marriage analogy for the relationship between God and God's people that continues through the New Testament. The Church is the bride of Christ and God's faithfulness to us becomes the template for our marriage relationships with one another.

Paul introduces the notion of mutuality in marriage that was earth-shattering for the time. 1 Corinthians 7 teaches that women share ownership, not only of their own bodies, but of their husbands' bodies as well, and that sexual practice in marriage should be by mutual consent. He's tearing apart the notion of marriage as property exchange and recognizing the relational aspect, something we take for granted today, but is a relatively recent development.

Up until the last 100 years, almost no one married for love. Sure, spouses might have loved each other and certainly love can grow in any relationship where it's fostered. But love as a primary motivation for marriage wasn't even contemplated at any point in the Bible's writing.

The point of marriage was to solidify or improve social conditions, to secure peace between powerful families, or to enhance the economic status of one or both parties. This was built primarily around having children. The purpose of marriage was to produce heirs, which is why barrenness is seen as such a curse throughout the bible.

For most of human history, if you wanted love, you looked outside your marriage. This is, again, why Paul's words are so ground-breaking: husbands love your wives as Christ loves the Church. For Paul, and subsequently for Christian theology, marriage was not just about meeting your wife's physical needs to enable child-bearing, but to care for her as a person. Your beloved is God's beloved, and you must care for them the way God cares for them.

This modern, thoroughly scriptural, thoroughly Christian understanding of marriage is then read back into Genesis 2. As God declares "the two become one flesh," we understand a far deeper meaning than anyone at the time of its original writing could've comprehended.

Genesis communicates the human need for connection and community. We are not designed to be alone. We need partners. We need each other. Marriage has become our best earthly approximation of the connection we were created to have with each other.

We embrace Jesus' teaching from Matthew that in the Kingdom "people will neither marry nor be given in marriage," because we'll be able to love everyone as God intends. Until that time, we commit to focusing on one relationship above all others.

Thus, our understanding of Christian marriage is about as far from the social regulation of female property transfer as it could possibly be. We have completely transformed the institution into something beautiful and important and good, but also something unrecognizable to the writers and first readers of scripture.

So, no, Paul doesn't talk about gay marriage, likely because he couldn't envision it. It wouldn't make any sense in his social context. He was just beginning to apply Christian principles to what was an entirely secular economic and social system. At the same time, though, gay marriage makes perfect sense in our contemporary context, largely because of the ways in which Paul himself reframed the Christian understanding of marriage.

The final piece of this puzzle is gender. Genesis talks about a man and a woman. Male and female biology fit together for procreation in obvious ways. The analogies in scripture are gendered, referencing husband and wife. But, if Christian marriage, as we understand it, is two people committing to God, and to each other, to love their spouse as God loves God's people, does it matter what gender those two people happen to be?

It can't matter—not unless we're willing to require men and women to inhabit specific and differentiated gender roles. If there is some innate difference (beyond our sex organs) that makes men and women truly unique from each other, then there's some reason to make a gender requirement in marriage.

But scripture doesn't support that differentiation, not anywhere from Genesis to Revelation.

Sure, scripture was written in the midst of a patriarchal society; but much like the theological evolution of marriage, it also challenges the faithful to a broader, more egalitarian understanding of men, women, and humanity in general.

There's insufficient space here to fully explain the equality inherent in Genesis 2, but the literature is voluminous that the spouse God crafted for the first human was an equal and complementary being. For years, we've gendered this complementarity, relying on stereotypes that women are sensitive and men are strong, women are carers and men are conquerors, that women and men possess uniquely different traits that must fit together for marriage to work.

We don't have to deny this complementary picture of marriage to expand its definition beyond a man and a woman. If anything, those gendered stereotypes limit both men and women from being the full, beautiful creation God intends them to be. How much pain and misery have we caused by communicating there are only certain ways to be "real" men and women?

Things are never that simple.

I do most of the cooking in our home. I do the shopping, and I stayed home when our daughter was young. My wife asks for power tools for her birthday, makes most of the money, and enjoys getting her hands dirty far more than I do. Yet she's also the decorator, finely attuned to aesthetics, while I spend much of my free time watching sports.

We don't fit any gendered stereotype or its opposite. We're unique individuals who happen to be male and female. What's more important is that we complement each other in ways that make our marriage stronger than either of us could be on our own. We got married because we were convinced we could do more for God's Kingdom together than we could do separately.

I know plenty of same-sex couples for whom the same is true, whose marriages are a blessing to them, to God, and to the world. I see no reason to deny them an equal place in the Kingdom of God or in the Church of the Nazarene.

Christ calls us to break down barriers, cross lines of division, and embrace that self-giving love of God which is the only hope for the salvation of the world. The Church should be at the forefront of recognizing, affirming, and embracing marriage for all people as it is the natural next step in the Spirit-led transformation of marriage from misogyny and oppression to freedom, equality, and love.

Adam, Isaiah, and Paul may not have understood what they were starting at the time, but God is always at work among the faithful to transmit and transform God's world into what it was created to be. Recognition and affirmation of LGBTQ+ couples is not a capitulation to culture, but a gospel-infused counter-cultural movement to further welcome God's coming Kingdom.

Ryan Scott *is a writer and substitute teacher from Middletown, DE, where he lives with his wife and daughter in The Nest, a 140 year old fixer-upper and hub of hospitality, which also hosts Middletown Church of the Nazarene, where he serves as pastor. Ryan is Lead Columnist for D3hoops.com and can be found online almost anywhere as @RyanAlanScott.*

We Dance the Dance

KRISTI J. ATTWOOD-SEATON

To be made in God's image is to be made to dance with
God and one another.

I was dressed in my best dress with my shoulders and elbows covered to honor the modesty standards of my hosts. My friend Heshy had invited me to his wedding with his beloved bride Olivia. I was experiencing my first Jewish wedding and I was in for a treat. Heshy and I met online over social media. After chatting online for a few years, we met in real life while I spent a weekend in Brooklyn, New York to celebrate Shabbat with Heshy and several other friends. This was a blended wedding of two different Jewish traditions; Hasidic and Modern Orthodox. The traditions and liturgies were completely foreign to me. Heshy's aunt took me under her wing and sat next to me. She helped me understand what was happening during the ceremony and bits and pieces of the Yiddish conversations being shared around me. I felt like I had been picked up and plopped right in the middle of a set for "Fiddler on the Roof."

As the reception began to warm up, there was a wall of cloth panels brought into the reception hall that split the room into two halves. One side designated for the men and one side specifically for the women. The music began to play; lively, loud, and celebratory. The bride grabbed my hand and invited me to dance with her and I soon found myself joining a circle of joyful women dancing around the bride. This dancing went on for hours.

At some point ladders were brought to the women's side of the curtain and young single ladies climbed them to peer over the curtains to the men's side of the reception. I was encouraged to climb a ladder and peek for myself, and the men were doing much of the same dancing on the other side with Heshy the bridegroom at the center of the festivities. I later learned that while the men were not allowed to look at the women from their side, the women were allowed to watch and pick out potential suitors from the single men. There were many hopes for potential match-making opportunities after the wedding. It was all very fascinating and part of a culture that I had never experienced before.

Attending Olivia and Heshy's wedding was the closest thing I had ever experienced to the gospel story of the Wedding at Cana, and I was hooked. The dancing brought energy with the circles growing faster and tighter and wine poured freely brightened cheeks and loosened tongues. It was, and remains, one of the absolute best weddings I have attended.

I grew up in the Nazarene denomination, I am third generation, raised in the 1980s performative holiness tradition where "nice girls don't drink, smoke or chew or go with boys that do". Holiness had been reduced to a moral social conduct code. It would take decades of quiet thinking and a few years of seminary to unlearn this toxic understanding of holiness.

I was given a book by a seminary professor written by Father Richard Rohr called "The Divine Dance." It was a book that explored the trinity and specifically "perichoresis;" a Greek word used for a circular dance also performed at Greek weddings, almost identical to what I witnessed at that special Jewish wedding many years ago. Many early church mothers and fathers witnessed this dance, and it sparked their imaginations that this is what the trinity is like. The three persons of the trinity exist in a divine dance that is giving, receiving, dynamic, loving, serving and interactive. This divine dance is a model for our own human experience.

In the beginning God created them male and female, in God's image the Triune Creator created them. This is a foundational understanding for the human experience in the Christian faith that we are in created in the image of God. I am afraid that we often skip over these words without much deep thought or regard. What does it mean to be created in the image of God? Is it that we are made into old bearded white men peering down from the clouds? Are we an older African American man dressed in white linen with the voice of Morgan Freeman? Are we a raging destructive wind like what Indiana Jones and the Nazis experienced in Raiders of the Lost Ark? Of course not! We are not God; we are not the Holy Spirit, and we are certainly not Jesus. Just as the Father, Son and Holy Spirit are not each other, neither are we made in God's image, God. We are all in relationship with one another and being in relationship is at the core of the image of God (the imago Dei) and what we experience as humankind.

So often though, we cheapen or disregard this part of our human experience, the one experience that is so central to the nature and character of God. Certainly not because of our humanness, but in and through our humanness we sin against God and one another in thought, word, and deed. As John Wesley would say in his signature description, to be made in the image of God is to be made "capable of God." Jesus is the prototype of what it means to be human, not Adam. Jesus points the way and shows us how to be capable of God; trusting in the same Spirit that led him and raised him from the dead. Failing to walk in love, do justice and exercise mercy with one another, we ruin our relationships. Sometimes we ruin our relationships with enormous explosive blow-ups and sometimes they die over years and decades by a thousand little cuts that never fully heal.

Theologian Elmer Collier has observed that a weak understanding of the Trinity colors our understanding or misunderstanding of the gospel. When we neglect the Trinity, we are prone to forget that Christian faith, life, and ministry are participatory. Being a Christian is more than just having a correct "legal" status before God. Christians are prone to hyper focus on forgiveness, usually personal and not collective. The work that God did in Christ through the Holy Spirit on the cross was not just simply an act of forgiveness for the individual but an act of restoration and renewal for the entire universe! What God has declared in Christ was God's justice and shalom for the entire creation. Forgiveness aimed toward the kind of participation that dances with God and one another. We are invited to dance. Thanks be to God!

Our LGBTQIA+ siblings are also invited to dance. There is no guest list that we hold that has any power over the restoration that God also offers them. Our queer brothers, sisters and the gender fluid are also made in the image of God. Their bearing the image of God does not depend on anyone's acceptance or rejection. To deny them fellowship, relationship, and full participation in ministry and gospel work is to second guess God himself and his creative power. To deny them full affirmation of their own relationships is to deny the very core of their bearing the imago Dei.

LGBTQIA+ individuals are also created for relationships. If salvation is indeed full restoration and not a mere "legal" status or simply fire insurance then we must affirm, encourage, and nurture their callings to ministry as they experience them. To deny these individuals their calls to ministry or their marriages is to question the participatory nature of restoration and salvation itself. To deny LGBTQIA+ individuals their calls to ministry or their marriages is to deny the imago Dei that they carry. The stakes are not whether LGBTQIA+ people have the image of God, but whether we will honor the image of God in them.

If our salvation is to be of any use to the world it becomes less personal and a lot more open and embracing of others. One question I have grappled with for several years is what difference does my salvation make in the world? There are some days that I come close to answering it for myself and other days it feels mysterious and unknowable. I think that my salvation, my own restoration, exists to show the world how to dance. To take the hands of those who are marginalized and "othered" and bring them to participate in the love and rhythm of the divine dance with me and the one who knows and loves me more intimately than even my own mother or husband.

Humankind having been created in the very image of God means that we have been created out of the overflow of love that is shared extravagantly between the Father, Son, and Spirit. CS Lewis wrote that "We were made, not primarily that we may love God (though we were made for that too), but that God may love us." That we are so scandalously loved by God frees us to love others without reservation or condition. It is time to throw away the artificial guest list. It is time to tear up the dance cards that limit and exclude others. May we all hold hands and dance the eternal dance of inclusive and expanding love. A giving, receiving, dynamic, loving, serving, participatory and interactive divine dance. Let it be so.

Kristi J. Attwood-Seaton is a wife and mother to a large, blended family. She graduated with honors from Nazarene Theological Seminary and was given "The Heart of a Servant" award by her classmates and professors. Kristi was formerly a foster mother to LGBTQIA+ teens and young adults and hopes to become a Deacon and Chaplain in the Episcopal Church.

The Queerness of the Holy

ERIC R. SEVERSON

The question of inclusion has it backwards: the Church of the Nazarene is being invited to join the Kingdom of God, which resides in the margins, where holiness abides, among the poor, with the oppressed, as queer. Everywhere else is not the church.

Readers of the Bible, and careful students of Christian history, should be worried about the word "normal." There is very little about the message of the Gospel that can settle comfortably into norms, and the apostles, prophets, and leaders of the church historically have been decidedly weird. The weird, the strange, the unusual, and the *queer* are often harbingers of change. The tendency to read modern versions of "normal" back onto biblical characters is a powerful one, but the oddity of Jesus, his followers, his predecessors, and other biblical characters is impossible to ignore. "Blessed are the meek," Jesus tells us, but meek folks win few battles and rarely get rich. Cultural acceptance and success have always required conformation to a broad set of normalized ways of thinking and living. These concepts of normality are entangled with power; they constitute the web of ideas, practices, concepts, and priorities that support structures of power. Paul calls these structures "principalities"—political and social authorities that constitute the "present darkness" of the world (Ephesians 6:12). There is grave danger afoot whenever people attempt to conform to these, to assimilate. The powers and principalities have a deeply vested interest in forcing such an assimilation. Christianity was originally politically dangerous for its refusal to conform. The following article will suggest that if Nazarenes wish to be the church, they should accept the invitation from LGBTQ folks to participate in the Kingdom of God.

That Jesus would reject the normal life of a first century Jewish citizen was foreshadowed by his cousin and predecessor, John the Baptist. John prefigured the coming of Jesus and announced his arrival, dressed in odd clothing, living in the wilderness, subsisting on bugs. Jesus was about 30 years old when the gospels begin to narrate his ministry. In modern times, it is not uncommon for people to wait until their thirties to marry or have children, but in Jesus' day this was highly unusual and a direct rejection of the expectations that would have been laid on him by his family and community. "Normal" people got married in their teenage years, and by the age of 30 were looking for spouses for their own children. The average lifespan of people in first century Palestine was about 30 years, though people who survived the very dangerous years of childhood averaged 48 years. Nobody who knew Jesus, before he began his ministry, would have thought of him as normal. He was a declared bachelor, a rejector of normal life patterns, a weirdo. His ministry sustained this strangeness; he resoundingly and routinely rejected opportunities to join the powers and principalities. He turned with intentionality toward people who had been crushed by these powers. For shorthand, we might call these folks "the poor," though we misunderstand Jesus' blessing on the poor if we think of that term merely economically. The poor are the oppressed, the outsiders, the misfits, the queer.

For various reasons, Christians down through the ages have attempted to make Jesus the standard-bearer of whatever they wanted to normalize. When people want to normalize the nobility of supposedly righteous warfare, Jesus is depicted as a military leader, and people etch lines from the Bible on their weapons. When people want to normalize whiteness, Jesus is depicted as white—though he most certainly was not what people today consider a "white person." Republicans, Democrats, Libertarians, Communists, and countless other political groups create a Jesus who normalizes their ways of operating politically. It is not controversial to point out the tendency of people to make Jesus into their own image, or into their image of normalcy. Surely some of these people are closer than others in their understanding of how Christians should think and live and operate today, but they all miss a crucial and seemingly obvious point about the person of Jesus: he was not normal, and will never conform to anybody's system of normality. The queer, the unusual, the weird, and the abnormal serve an irreplaceable role in the story of the Gospel. Jesus was not a family man. He did not hold down a job. Jesus relates anarchically to both the religious and political legal structures of his time. He did not *go to the poor*—Jesus *was* poor. Every expression of the Kingdom of God that we find in his life and teachings occurs at the margins of contesting philosophies of normalcy. He doesn't go to the margins of the world—these margins are the birthplace of the Kingdom of God.

All four gospels tell an odd and erotic story of a woman who anoints the feet of Jesus with extremely expensive oil. This story is one of the rare incidents to appear in all four of the gospels, though details differ between the four accounts.

Each description of the event is its own version of shocking. The act is stunningly wasteful, with three gospels directly questioning the economics of the gift, and wondering whether such a resource should have been put to better use. Both Luke and John add an extraordinary detail: the woman uses her long hair to dry the mixture of tears and oil on his feet. Luke calls her a "sinful" person, and adds that she used her mouth to kiss his feet (Luke 7:36-50). This scene is a straight-up scandal; Jesus calls it an act of faith. It is an affront to decency, to normalcy, to the expectation for public relationship between men and women, and to the economic metrics by which virtue is measured. This is a very queer exchange, indeed, and yet somehow a holy moment. It culminates, in fact, with salvation: "Your faith has saved you; go in peace" (Luke 7:50). This story is wasteful, extravagant, erotic, scandalous, and queer.

The Kingdom of God is a movement, but it isn't a movement *to the poor*, to the oppressed, to the queer. The site for the events of grace, salvation, forgiveness, is on this margin of the world's normalcy. Holiness is *queer*. The Kingdom of God, Jesus teaches, is like an irresponsible shepherd who risks it all for one lost sheep. Bad shepherding. The Kingdom of God is like a landowner who pays workers the same whether they showed up in the morning or at the end of the shift. Bad leadership. The Kingdom of God is not a powerful empire trying to decide what percentage of its time, energy, and resources move toward the poor. That empire, whose shape the church too often takes, is a power and principality of our age.

My short contribution to this volume is a welcome chance to say this: the chance to include LGBTQIA+ folks in the Church of the Nazarene is not a question of inclusion, at least not of including queer folks. To participate in the Kingdom of God is to release one's grip on the powerful cultural and economic forces that threaten to reshape Jesus, and the church, into something "normal," economical, prosperous, *straight*. The question is whether or not this particular denomination is interested in participation in the Kingdom of God. The invitation goes the other way; queer folks are wondering whether or not people who think of themselves as Nazarene are interested in *being* the church.

Rev. Eric Severson *is a philosopher specializing in the work of Emmanuel Levinas. He is the author of* Before Ethics *(Kendall Hunt, 2021),* Levinas's Philosophy of Time *(Duquesne University Press, 2013) and* Scandalous Obligation *(Beacon Hill Press, 2011), and editor of eight other books. He lives in Kenmore, Washington and teaches philosophy at Seattle University.*

God's Creative Diversity

FOREST FISK

There are far more people in the world who don't fit perfectly into the categories of "male" and "female" than there are members of the Church of the Nazarene.

In the beginning, God created Adam and Steve. I use this wry opening to make us think about whether or not a hypothetical homosexual "Steve" could sit along-side our view of God's perfect creation without needing to "fix" anything. We acknowledge Adam and Eve, and yet many of us fail to validate the spectrum of humanity between the two in any significant or authoritative way. We have other examples of bodily differences we accept without feeling the need to change them, and that is precisely the itch I would like us to scratch in this essay. Why do we accept some differences in humanity, and seemingly not accept others? I believe it is because we still think that LGBT people have a choice in the matter. I will try to dispel this myth, and in so doing, point a way to a better doctrine of humanity and perhaps theology as a whole.

Let us begin with the complicated ways God has created our bodies, and re-alize any theology we create needs to encompass and positively include all forms of humanity God has created. Atypical variations of the body can be observed within nature, and although in the minority, these variations are within a natural spectrum of God's creation. An intersex person, for example, is a person born with a combination of both male and female biological traits (they have one or more sexual characteristics that are atypical for their sex). This differentiation can affect chromosomes, hormones, gonads, or genitalia too. Let's look at some of the num-bers to see why this matters.

There are more intersex people alive than there are Nazarenes worldwide. There are 2,640,200 Nazarene members. And it is estimated that up to 1.7 percent of the entire 8 billion human population has an intersex *trait*. In addition to specifi-cally intersex traits, approximately 0.5 percent of people have clinically identifiable sexual or reproductive *variations* (malformations or deformities of sexual organs). With 8 billion people alive, that's 40,000,000 clinically identifiable intersex people (15 times the global Nazarene membership), with up to 136,000,000 people (51.5 times global Nazarene membership) with various states of sexual traits (malformations of a singular sexual body part). That's just the physical "plumbing" of a person. There are variations in the *code* as well as the hardware. Chromosomes themselves have variance and there are six sexes (biological karyotype sexes) that do not result in death to the fetus:

> X—Roughly 1 in every 2,000 people has Turner's Syndrome, that's 4 million people globally.
>
> XX—Most common form of female.
>
> XXY—Roughly 1 in 500-600 people has Klinefelter Syndrome, globally 13-16 million people.
>
> XY—Most common form of male,
>
> XYY—Roughly 1 in 1,000 boys has XYY Syndrome, that's 8 million people globally.
>
> XXXY—Roughly 1 in 17,000-50,000 has XXXY Syndrome, that's 160,000-470,588 people globally.

And even with males who are fully chromosomally XY, the hormones can misfire completely, such as in the case of people with Androgen Insensitivity Syndrome. These chromosomal males physically develop as female. That's roughly 160,000-400,000 people globally.

So, despite what we *think* the Bible says, God did not make them *only* "male *or* female." To blindly cling to a binary is to discount real chromosomal variations, and to ignore these variations is to deny a deep and actual reality within our humanity. And if you accept the text as written, it says God made them "male *and* female," (Genesis 1:27) which is an inclusive term. In the same way that God is not the Alpha *or* the Omega, but God is Alpha *and* Omega, (Revelation 1:8) and everything between the Alpha and Omega, God made male and female *and* everything in between. Our theology must positively include everything which God has made.

If you can see the rich diversity by which God has made human bodies, we must be willing to accept that God surely has made us as diverse in our psyche, or mental representations, and such diversity in our psyche is no more sinful than the ways God has made us physically. To be clear, I'm not saying chromosomal variations come close to explaining all the variations of LGBT+ people at all. I would argue *most* of the diversity of people's sexuality is precisely in the software running between our ears. But let us shed this idea that our mental orientations are in any way sinful, or somehow more sinful than the ways God has created our physical bodies.

To some in the faith, it seems completely reasonable that the faithful can "pray away the gay." I know. I've tried. While attending Nazarene Theological Seminary I had a friend from my Bible study group come to me and confess I was one of the first to find out he was a "gay Christian." I begged him right then and there at 10 p.m. to go with me to a local 24-hour-praying church where we could go and I could pray for him around others. Reluctantly he obliged, and I prayed with all the emotional energy I could muster to God to change this man in all the ways I know "God wanted". My arms were surging with electrical energy like Emperor Palpatine from Star Wars. I felt like God would certainly zap a crater into the ground beneath us if I had asked for harm instead of healing. But after an hour of laying my hands on him in earnest prayer, pulsating with prayerful energy, there was no release of energy, nor did God "fix" my gay friend. Leaving in defeat, my friend confessed that he had prayed for years to not be gay. It's from this personal story that I believe, as well as from scientific data that supports, being gay is mostly something that cannot be changed. I have heard of very few people in the faith that have somehow changed orientations, but those are very rare outliers among the many Christians who are LGBT+ and, out of pressure from the greater Christian community, do not wish to be LGBT+. Even with the power of prayer and fasting, and laying on of hands, they can't seem to change, or it seems that God *won't* change them. Statistically, the majority who have sought a change in their orientation have been *harmed* in their attempts at change. Yet I was led to believe, in my Nazarene experience, that as a faithful Christian, I can and hence should "pray away the gay." Imagine if all families in our churches were constantly met with such negative expectations to "fix" their children through prayer? And yet we ask the LGBT+ families to stay in church and continually accept the abuse of our hurtful theology.

So what is a better theology? I am unsure I can answer that, let alone in the time we have. But seeing the ways in which we *are* has shown me the faults in our theology, both practically and theoretically. I am personally left to believe that God has created all of us in the way God intends to create us, including a hypothetical Steve, and all those in the LGBT+ community. I personally find *creation via evolution* to be a more comprehensive and compelling foundation for discovering the-God-that-is compared to accepting a systematic theology we were handed which is based upon the creation account(s) found in Genesis. It is apparent to me that God relishes diversity rather than idealistic and static perfection. Even within the whole of the greater Church, we see the splintering of diversity in our belief systems, and I personally see the benefits of these divisions. And although it may pain the Nazarene reader to consider it, I believe God would be happy with a division among the Nazarenes on these points if it comes down to it, not only for diversity's sake but for the sake of fully loving and including our LGBT+ family.

Forest Fisk *is a straight, fourth-generation Nazarene, NNU and NTS graduate with honors, and lives in the Kansas City area. Forest is in the process of deconstructing his Nazarene theology and is on his way out of the Nazarene Church for various reasons.*

Holiness is Queer

BRYAN P. STONE

A holy church is not marked by moral perfection and exclusion but by vulnerability and an openness to God's unpredictable grace.

Should the Church of the Nazarene be fully LGBTQ+ affirming? For me, the answer is unreservedly yes. At the same time, I am keenly aware that an answer to this question entails answers to several other questions with which it is necessarily entangled: should the Church's understanding of scripture be enlivened and broadened such that it takes into account the vast cultural differences between the ancient world and ours—especially in relation to gender and sexuality? Should the Church take a more informed and responsible approach to human sexuality, drawing on rather than disregarding the last century of social scientific research? Should Nazarenes trust and take seriously the witness and experience of LGBTQ+ Christians who—in their words, life, and spirit—testify to the fact that they have already been accepted by Christ and included by the Holy Spirit in Christ's body? Should the Church of the Nazarene find ways to move closer to a Wesleyan understanding of holiness that emphasizes Christlikeness, humility, openness, and welcome to the marginalized other? Should the Church of the Nazarene shift away from an over-reliance on static models of holiness as moral perfection that lead to legalism and exclusivism?

I cannot develop answers to all these questions in this short essay. But they go together, and by viewing them together one can readily see that even if one takes an open and affirming position on the Church fully including queer people, the work that would need to be done to move the Church of the Nazarene toward an affirming and inclusive position is considerable. Large institutions have a hard time changing, and with a question this complex and implicating so much of Nazarene theology, history, and culture, it is difficult to imagine the Church changing its position. It would just take too much. And yet…who knows? After all, holiness is queer. It defies the binaries of in and out, sacred and profane, saint and sinner. It always has. And as much as we try to predict it, calculate it, set up fences around it, or possess it, God's sanctifying grace finds ways to break through our definitions, barriers, and rules. Holiness is queer. So perhaps even if we cannot be optimistic, we can still hope, speak out, and take action.

Almost 30 years ago, I tried to outline a Wesleyan view of scripture that might guide us when it comes to thinking about homosexuality ("Wesleyan Theology, Scriptural Authority, and Homosexuality" in the *Wesleyan Theological Journal* (1995). I continue to believe that re-thinking the nature of biblical authority is among the most crucial tasks related to the question of full inclusion for queer folks. I stand by that article, though I was too reserved and qualified in my conclusions. I will not duplicate here all of what I said there, but for Wesleyans, the relationship of scripture to homosexuality is far more complex than trotting out a few verses from the Bible that appear to condemn homosexuality. Wesleyans also take experience and reason into account when forming theological and ethical conclusions, though putting those sources into play is not a simple and straightforward task. It takes time, patience, study, and a willingness to grow.

I have come to know many, many queer Christians during my life. As a Nazarene, I am asked to discard this knowledge and reinterpret their clear witness as a mistake, a distortion, and a deviance. But the reverse strategy is always possible—and, in our time, necessary. Perhaps by attending more carefully to the witness of queer Christians, we can begin to read scripture in a new light.

John Wesley's distinctive vision of grace can help as we wade into these waters. For Wesley, grace does not reject, negate, or override human experience and reason, but instead appeals to it and poses questions to it. The sovereignty of grace is, thus, not a power "over" us, but a persuasive and loving presence, a lure, a beauty that we know by the name of the Holy Spirit. If, as Wesleyans, we believe what Wesley says about grace when talking about salvation, why should we not extend his view of grace to how we understand God's revelation in scripture? For revelation is indeed an act of God's grace. On this view, the Bible is a faithful guide, companion, and authority, but not one that triumphs over us, repudiating our experience (for example, our experience of queer Nazarenes) and asking us to sacrifice our intellects. And if elements of the ancient worldview contained in scripture are known to be oppressive or inaccurate (household codes, condoning slavery, reliance on patriarchal frameworks, a pre-Copernican view of the cosmos, and obsolete understandings of human gender and sexuality), we do not merely throw out scripture, but we work hard to interpret it for our time. Proof-texting from scripture on matters of human sexuality is about as misguided an enterprise as I can imagine—at least for 21st century Wesleyans.

The more we know about human sexuality, the more we realize how central to who we are as human persons is this important dimension of our lives and how impossible it is to separate out our sexuality (including our sexual "practices") from our very identity as persons. Sexuality is not just a practice reserved for pleasure or procreation, it is also an "orientation"—something the ancient writers of the Bible could never have known. Treating homosexuality as a sin, then, is vastly different from the way the Church considers sins such as murder, gossip, or adultery. Unlike the church's stances on these sins, the church's stance on homosexuality leads children to grow up hating and deceiving themselves—or worse. This is why the often-repeated adage, "love the sinner, hate the sin," not only lands wide of the mark but is deadly dangerous when it comes to homosexuality.

Side by side with biblical prohibitions against homosexuality are prohibitions against inter-breeding cattle, sowing a field with two different kinds of seed, or wearing a garment made of two different kinds of material. Moral purity was bound up with ritual purity, with an emphasis on separation from all that might "stain" us or result in a mixing of the holy and the profane. But Christ dissolved this ironclad connection between moral purity and ritual purity. It is not separation from those deemed "impure" that makes us holy. Holiness is found in engagement with the world and an embrace of those who are dispossessed, marginalized, or rejected. Holiness is queer.

One of the things that makes holiness so queer is that the more we seek to define it, contain it, and stake out the lines of who is in and who is out, the less holy we become. The truth, of course, is that Nazarenes have long picked and chosen their favorite sins and then made those the litmus test of inclusion and fitness for ministry. Not that long ago, visiting a motion picture theatre could get you into big trouble on Nazarene college campuses and in Nazarene churches. But our efforts to identify the kinds of sins that would keep someone from being fully included in the church are inevitably slippery and arbitrary—almost always omitting the ones that are rampant among us. But Christ has shown us a path to holiness that rejects this kind of legalism. Holiness is not a moral achievement or a state of perfection at which we arrive. It is rather a relationship with God, neighbor, and creation characterized by love and respect. It is a disposition of spirit characterized by vulnerability, brokenness, and openness. Rather than being a possession that some of us have while others don't, holiness is a receptivity to God's grace, which often arrives in ways unpredictable and impossible to calculate. If holiness can be thought of in Wesleyan terms as a journey toward Christian perfection, it is thus never a static perfection, but always an openness to growth and to ever-expanding forms of inclusion.

There may well be sins that would exclude one from full participation in the body of Christ, but if Jesus' sparring with the Pharisees is any clue, those have more to do with the way we block others from entering the kingdom. There is a perverse irony in all of this, for clearly the more serious sin is excluding others deemed sinful from the body of Christ. At its best, the church is not to be understood as a community marked by moral perfection or achievement, but rather a community marked by vulnerability, by standing with the marginalized, and by openness to a grace that arrives from outside of ourselves. The more we attempt to control who is in and who is out, the more we will find that control slipping through our fingers like sand. Holiness is queer indeed.

Bryan Stone *is Associate Dean for Academic Affairs and E. Stanley Jones Professor of Evangelism at Boston University School of Theology. He is the author of multiple books and articles on evangelism, ecclesiology, and the intersections of theology and popular culture.*

Sometimes What You Say Gets in the Way of What You Mean

KEVIN M. TALBERT

The cultural message of the Nazarene Church's stance on LGBTQ+ issues undermines God's mandate to love the vulnerable.

The Church is a cultural institution as much as it is a theological one. If this were not true, then Christians would have no part in Culture War politics and there would be little meaning, or little to debate, in the Christian aphorism to be "in the world but not of the world." No doubt those in The Church of the Nazarene who advocate against LGTBQ+ people as full members of the church community do so, at least in part, out of a desire to "protect" their church from outside cultural influence they perceive to be undermining The Church's theological grounding. While understandable, I find this effort misguided and, ultimately, hurtful.

Indeed, it is easy to think of any church as itself "having a culture," whether one thinks of their local congregation or more broadly of "The Church" universal. Ministers and congregants alike often speak of the culture of their church with words like "welcoming," or "contemporary," or "relevant [to the culture]." Yes, even describing the church as "affirming," as the authors in this volume advocate, is a comment about the desired culture of The Church.

Culture is, in large part, formative. It helps educate people about "how to be" and "how to live" in a particular context. In that sense, culture has a pedagogical aspect, that is, it teaches people the symbols and meanings needed to successfully navigate life in a community. Consequently, one may understand the culture of a given community as a sort of "text" that is both written and interpreted by the members of the community, as well as those outside the community. These cultural messages are a form of curriculum that helps people learn whether they belong in a community, and how to belong.

Cultural texts are informed and shaped not just by the local context, but also by broader, more widespread contexts. In this way, then, The Church exists not just *as a* culture but *within* a larger culture that includes its own texts, its own symbols and meanings that shape peoples' understanding of the world. And, the culture of The Church is shaped within/through cultural understandings from the wider society. Thus, when The Church takes a stance about a particular cultural issue, much less a theological one, it is also performing an educational function. That is, we can take The Church's stance on any particular issue as a sort of curriculum that "teaches" both its members and the culture at large about The Church, its priorities, and, especially, its vision of who God is and the work (it contends) he does in the world.

This cultural educational effect of The Church is also implicated with relations of power. That is, The Church as an institution manifests power in the world, at least the power to determine what (and, therefore, *who*) is "acceptable" and "good" in God's sight, and what or who is not. What a weighty role! In a real sense, the cultural messages The Church sends not only communicate messages about a given issue, but communicate that The Church claims power as *the* primary arbiter of God's authority in/over the world. When The Church includes certain people and excludes others from the sacraments, from its rituals and practices, from its leadership, it is exercising power with potentially eternal consequence in peoples' lives! It is also denying people friendship, community, even livelihoods. I daresay these are often felt in peoples' lives in a more real and potent way than they feel any eternal consequence, whether we like that or not.

My wife and I left a Nazarene Church in part because of its refusal to acknowledge its cultural power and, especially, to use its cultural power affirmatively on the side of the vulnerable in its community. It chose, instead, to rest in platitudes about "loving everyone equally" and "staying above the fray," which in effect suggested a curricular message that those who were being harmed were to have no refuge in that church. It taught my wife and I that that congregation was willing to ignore Christ's mandate to protect the vulnerable if it meant not being controversial. Sadly, this means it was willing to use its power to sacrifice on the altar of "unity" those who needed the affirmative, active protection of a loving community willing to risk itself on their behalf.

LGBTQ+ people in the United States continue to be among the most vulnerable to discrimination, harassment, and premature death, whether by suicide, murder, or the cumulative effects of the stress of trying to survive in a society that hates their existence.

I support the full affirmation of LGBTQ+ people within the Church of the Nazarene. I do so because I believe God loves LGBTQ+ people with the same reckless love he has for me, a straight cisgender person and a sinner. I urge the

Nazarene Church to fully and publicly affirm LGTBQ+ people. I believe not doing so communicates a cultural text that undermines The Church's theological
position. That is, the cultural message received by those inside and, especially,
outside The Church, is that they are not welcome in God's kingdom since they are
not fully welcome in God's earthly community. I believe this cultural text subverts
any theological message coming from The Church, such as the common saying
that God loves LGBTQ+ people even as he abhors their sin.

My formation in the Wesleyan tradition leads me to believe God loves people
through their sin, which I take to have a double meaning. God loves people by
looking beyond their sin—not ignoring it, but seeing the person for more than just
their sin. And, perhaps more importantly, God's love is restorative, it is healing, it
moves people beyond their sin into redemption. As a denomination, The Church
of the Nazarene's message of love should be unambiguous. And The Church should
use its cultural power to demonstrate in concrete and material ways to the world
and, especially to all those most vulnerable in our society, that God loves them
first, last, and always.

Dr. Kevin M. Talbert, PhD *is Associate Professor of Education at The College of Idaho
where he teaches courses in curriculum studies and the sociocultural foundations of education. Educated in a United Methodist Church and a UMC-affiliated college, he and his
family now attend a Nazarene church in Nampa, Idaho.*

Created in the Image of God:
A Polemic Against Today's Crusade

LEEROY TOMAS

This current crusade against LGBTQIA+ people is killing our children and it is time to put our bodies on the line.

In this brief essay, I will suggest that the Church of the Nazarene's posture toward LGBTQIA+ people causes unequivocal harm and is at odds with the life, teaching, death, and resurrection of our Lord and Savior, Jesus the Christ. Young adults are leaving the church rapidly. LGBTQIA+ teenagers and young adults are leaving the Church of the Nazarene even more rapidly. There are numerous reasons that this may be the case, but I suspect examining the churches' posture toward these beloved people, created in the image of God, is worth reassessing.

There are numerous passages in the Bible that can help us reassess our posture toward LGBTQIA+ people. In this essay, I will reflect on two: Genesis 1 and John 4.

The sacred creation narrative says, "*So God created humankind in his image, in the image of God he created them; male and female he created them*" (Genesis 1:24, NRSV). First, this suggests that God created all humans in the image of God. This is not just the first humans, but all humans are created in the image of God. In the Statement on Human Sexuality, the Church of the Nazarene affirms this when it says, "*Because all humans are beings created in the image of God, they are of inestimable value and worth.*"

I have heard from Nazarene pulpits that Genesis 1 suggests that God only made two genders, male and female. This myopic view denies the humanness of non-binary, transgender, genderfluid, and agender humans who are created in the image of God. Scientific evidence suggests that many people are born each day with diverse chromosomal makeups. This is not to say that a valid transgender experience is contingent upon an atypical chromosomal makeup. Dehumanizing another human or group of humans because we do not understand their experience is a clear example of bigotry, and utilizing the Bible to do it is evil. I suggest that this is a gross misreading of this text.

Genesis 1 is poetry, a beautiful illustration of who God is and how God creates. Earlier in the creation narrative the biblical writer says, "*And God saw that the light was good; and God separated the light from the darkness. God called the light Day, and the darkness he called Night*" (Genesis 1:4-5, NRSV). Yet, are there not times that the day and night come together, where neither day nor night exist, or both day and night exist? These sunrises and sunsets happen to be some of the loveliest times in each twenty-four hour period. Later on in the creation narrative, God says, "*Let the waters under the sky be gathered together into one place, and let the dry land appear*" (Genesis 1:9, NRSV). Yet, are there not places, where the land and seas run together where neither land nor sea exist, or both land and sea exist? Beaches, swamps, and marshes are some of the most beautiful places in God's creation.

Pastors do not deny the existence of sunrises, sunsets, and beaches from the pulpit. Therefore, neither should we deny the existence of non-binary people. So what is the difference? We see sunrises, sunsets, and beaches, but far too often, the church has chosen not to see LGBTQIA+ people. Not only do we need to see these beloved humans, but we also need to demonstrate a recognition of their humanity, their dignity, their sacredness, and the image of God living in them.

Another text that I believe helps us reassess our posture toward LGBTQIA+ people is John 4. In John 4, Jesus spends some time with the Samaritan woman at the well. Jesus asks her for water and spends time conversing with her. Even this action would have appalled good, religious people. She would have been considered one of 'those people.' Jews do not associate with Samaritans, much less Samaritan women in public. However, Jesus saw her deep worth and value. I would like to bring your attention to verses sixteen to eighteen.

"He told her, 'Go, call your husband and come back.' 'I have no husband,' she replied. Jesus said to her, 'You are right when you say you have no husband. The fact is, you have had five husbands, and the man you now have is not your husband. What you have just said is quite true'" (John 4:16-18).

I have heard from Nazarene pulpits that that Jesus had to go through Samaria to convert this 'sinner among sinners' and that this woman was 'basically a sexworker.' I believe that is an inadequate interpretation of this passage and is rooted in our modern understandings of relationships. To situate this passage in its historical context, we must remember that women were considered property. In the patriarchy of the ancient world, women did not have the right to divorce their husbands. Their culture only allowed men the right to choose to divorce a woman.

In addition, if a women's husband died she would become the possession of his brother whom she would then be forced to marry.

I suggest that this passage is not about Jesus having to go to Samaria to convert a 'sinner among sinners,' but Jesus having to go through Samaria to identify with a hurting woman who had been abandoned at least five times by her husbands, either because they died or decided they were done with her. Our modern interpretation of this passage continues to marginalize her and her story through no fault of her own. Maybe Jesus had to go through Samaria to identify with a person whom was excluded socially and religiously from who God made her to be. Maybe Jesus had to go to Samaria to empower a woman whom the religious community had excluded to invite her as a co-laborer and partner in the mission of God. God then utilizes her to begin evangelizing the Samaritan people.

LGBTQIA+ people have been excluded from the opportunity to serve God and the Church of the Nazarene in leadership and pastoral ministry because of other people's assumptions about them. Jesus did not exclude the woman based on other's assumptions about her. Jesus did not exclude her from ministry because other people thought she did not have an appropriate lifestyle. He simply let her go back to the town as a co-laborer and partner in the mission of God. Jesus positioned himself between the judgments of the religious folk as well as the astonishment of the disciples and this woman-who had done nothing wrong-and I believe that is our task as well. We need to position ourselves between the judgment of the legalistic, religious folk and LGBTQIA+ people.

Theologically, in the incarnation, we affirm that God became a human being as Jesus the Christ. Jesus came to identify with our hurt, offer forgiveness of our sins, and absolve the pain and suffering that he did not cause. God created us and offered us free will. As an indirect result of that gift of free will, pain, death, and suffering entered into the world. God became incarnate as Jesus to be responsible for all of the pain and suffering that God did not cause. It is my position that this should be the role of the church: to be responsible for pain and suffering that we have caused and that which we have not caused. If this is what God did through the incarnation, this is what we must do as well.

LGBTQIA+ people have encountered immense trauma at the hands of Christians. Their pain is our pain. Their hurt is our hurt. Their suffering is our suffering. This is the way of the incarnation, the way of Jesus. Like racism, ableism, and sexism, transphobia and homophobia exist in and through structures of society and community.

Frequent studies reveal that LGBTQIA+ teenagers have higher rates of suicide than straight, cisgender teenagers do. Additional studies expose that LGBTQIA+

teenagers who participate in religious traditions like a local church are at greater risk of suicide.

It is time for the Church of the Nazarene to repent from its participation and complicity in the dehumanizing structures of homophobia and transphobia. I imagine, Nazarenes mean well when they argue passionately to defend their definition of marriage and their specific understanding of human sexuality. However, the time has come for the Church of the Nazarene to realize that this crusade is killing our children. God forgive us, and empower us to see, value, and welcome all people, especially those who identify as LGBTQIA+.

LeeRoy Tomas *(name changed for anonymity) is an ordained elder in the Church of the Nazarene. He holds bachelor's and master's degrees from Nazarene institutions.*

On the Biological Sexual Spectrum

MARK VAUGHAN

*LGBTQ+ people are born, not made. Trying to change them
is hurtful and harmful. Offer charity instead of therapy.
Embrace, don't disgrace.*

Others have addressed the scriptural and doctrinal aspects of homosexuality. As a physician, I can provide some biological context to the conversation. First, we should define some terms. The words sex and gender are often mistakenly used interchangeably. Let me clarify. Sex refers to biological physical forms, while gender refers to behavior. Homosexuality is same-sex attraction. The terms lesbian and gay refer to homosexuality. The term "same-sex attraction" is used in some circles to refer to LGBTQ people who are not acting on their same-sex orientation by engaging in sexual behaviors, but this is incorrect. It is the attraction which defines homosexuality and not outward behavior. Bisexuality is attraction to both men and women. Transgender identity is the distinct personal identification as a different gender than the one which a person was assigned at birth.

How it Starts

The etiology (cause) of homosexuality was explained to my Nazarene church in the 1980s by James Dobson's films. He attributed it to environmental factors, mainly family dynamics, experienced by the individual. While this is still an area of active research, most scientific data point to prenatal hormonal influences on the developing brain. These hormonal influences may sometimes be triggered by environmental factors, but this still implicates a biologic basis for homosexual orientation.

Male and Female

Although "male and female he created them," (Gen. 1:27) we see a more nuanced spectrum clinically than this binary view of sexuality. I say "clinically" because a person who is seen casually in public appearing as either a man or a woman may have surprising secrets about their anatomy known only by them and their doctor. There are two main components which influence sex identification. They are chromosomes and hormones. A basic human biology class usually teaches that humans have 22 pairs of autosomal chromosomes and one pair of sex chromosomes. It also usually teaches that this pair of sex chromosomes determines the sex of the individual. While this is usually the case, it is not always that simple. If the sex chromosomes do not include the usual genes, or if there is another cause of an unusual prenatal hormone environment, the sex organs and outside appearance of the individual may be that of the opposite sex or even an in-between variation of the two (intersex). In some cases, a person with the typically male sex chromosomes (XY) will appear to be female until they reach puberty when a work up is commenced to determine why they never menstruate. It is then discovered that, although they identify as female and can even function sexually as female, they have a Y chromosome and testes inside their body. This is a pattern seen in some patients with a condition called androgen insensitivity. There is a mutation in a gene of the X chromosome which prevents androgen (male sex hormone, mostly testosterone) receptors from working correctly. It doesn't matter how much testosterone they are given because the receptors on their cells don't recognize it. Their brain and sex organs never receive the signal to develop in the typical male pattern, even though the male genes are there waiting for that signal to activate them.

To restate: these individuals are born with a Y (male) sex chromosome and testes, yet they also have a vagina, feel they are female, and may be sexually attracted to men. They are also infertile. I go into detail on this extreme example which is typical of complete androgen insensitivity (CAIS) to illustrate the potential for mismatches between chromosomes and a person's sexual identification. In some aspects, these individuals have it simple compared to those with *partial* androgen insensitivity (PAIS) who may not have such an obviously female appearance, but whose genitals, historically, were made to appear female because it was the easier surgery to perform. As I stated, this was a relatively obvious example. Allow me to go into detail explaining how the other mismatches occur.

We have some understanding of how other variations work to cause someone's brain to function like that of the opposite sex when their body does not look like the opposite sex. This can happen for either an individual's gender identification (transgender identity) or sexual orientation (homosexual). The effects on the brain can be the opposite of effects on the sex organs. The time of the hormonal effect determining the appearance of the sex organs is during the first three months of prenatal development. The hormonal effect on the brain influencing sexual orientation or gender identity occurs during the last half of pregnancy. These are two completely separate periods during fetal development. A different hormonal envi-ronment, for various reasons, between these two critical periods of development results in a mismatch between the sex of the physical body and the sex-associated brain function. Research has mostly described this as a direct cause of homosexu-ality, and it seems transgender identity is caused by a similar mechanism. Despite the expectation that these brain effects would be permanent, some advocate for treatments to reverse the effects.

Conversion Therapy

Homosexuality used to be classified as a mental disorder. It is now considered a normal variant of human sexuality. When it was considered a mental disorder, var-ious "treatments" were tried on patients to eliminate homosexual thoughts and in-clinations, or at least to eliminate homosexual behavior. Little success was achieved by these efforts using a huge range of treatment modalities, including electrocon-vulsive (electric shock) therapy. Once homosexuality was recognized by both the American Psychiatric Association and the American Psychology Association as a normal behavioral variant, most attempts to reverse homosexuality were dis-continued. In recent years conversion therapy has found a home in conservative Christian churches and parachurch organizations, motivated by the teaching that homosexuality is a sin.

The data for the effectiveness of conversion therapy to "cure" homosexuality or transgender identity is both limited and inconsistent. Overall, the more reli-ably conducted studies find poor outcomes for conversion therapy. Most report participants are more likely to describe harmful effects like depression and sui-cidality, rather than decreased homosexual thoughts or inclinations. One of the more well-done studies reported a success rate of less than 4% and a rate of harm of 37%, with improved psychological outcomes found in individuals instead un-dergoing affirming psychotherapy.[1] The successful conversions certainly represent a minority, and it comes at a much much higher rate of participants who feel that the experience harmed them without helping. To evaluate it in the same manner as any medical therapy I am considering for a patient, my recommendation would be to stay clear of it.

Being homosexual or transgender is associated with increased adversity which is worsened when affected individuals are told there is a way to "cure" their

---

1. Kate Bradshaw, et al., (2015) Sexual Orientation Change Efforts Through Psychotherapy for LGBQ Individuals Affiliated With the Church of Jesus Christ of Latter-day Saints, *Journal of Sex & Marital Therapy*, 41:4, 391-412.

sexuality. I strongly urge loving support of affected individuals without applying pressure to change their sexuality.

Mark Vaughan, MD *grew up on the Sacramento District of the Church of the Nazarene and graduated from NNC before completing medical school at Saint Louis University. He is the founder and medical director of the Auburn Medical Group. He is the co-host of the Changing Faith podcast and the Auburn Medical Group YouTube channel.*

True Colors

JAMES TRAVIS YOUNG

Humans are created to love one another through covenantal relationships that defy tradition, legal definitions, and unify all people in Christ Jesus.

We are created to be relational.

This begins even with our physiology: we have skin that feels, eyes that see, mouths that speak, noses that smell, and ears that hear. Our ability to process these billions of signals not only navigates our interpersonal communication, but how we actually understand and interpret the world around us.

We are fearfully and wonderfully made so that our relationships with one another define our relationship with our creator and the world he created.

This isn't a new concept or theology. Starting in the beginning with the Genesis account, although everything God had created was good and humanity was "very good," a world without human relationships was not good enough in God's sight: "It is not good for man to be alone. I will make a helper suitable for him" (Genesis 2:18, NIV).

This had nothing to do with gender roles or physical anatomy—quite simply, no other creature God had made could be a worthy human partner except another human. Indeed, rather than establishing any sexual dynamic whatsoever, Adam identified Eve's qualities in terms of how much she was *like* him, describing her as "bone of my bones and flesh of my flesh" (Genesis 2:23a), truly made of the same substance.

Adam saw her not for what made her different, but what made them the same.

Without basic human relationship, our lives are "not good;" but when we find connection with others, we can become greater than the sum of our parts.

This partnership portrayed by scripture is not exclusively sexual, nor is it limited to marriage as we may understand it today. Although its importance supersedes gender roles and legal definitions, it is remarkably simple yet profound:

Love is the central and supreme theology of the whole of scripture, and functions as the universal core of our connection with one another and our creator. It is the greatest commandment Jesus ever gave, the source from which any other law must flow. Without love, we are nothing.

That doesn't mean that every relationship is loving. There is no love in abuse or suffering, much less degradation, malice, or wrath. And many classical definitions of love seem callow, even narrow and limiting—from Augustine's "desire" to the overemphasized Greek concepts of *agape, eros, philia,* etc. that many modern Christian authors have capitalized upon. However, beyond and including these varied arguments, a singular quality does emerge: that *love is expressed in relationships by seeking to do good.*

Of course, that is deceptively simple. Because we are created to be relational, love is a response to others that, "by seeking to do good," encompasses more than mere intentions, but actions, for the purpose of positive outcomes.

This is reflected in how God expressed his love to humanity through covenants:

- He proved his love for Adam and all humanity through a covenant of grace.
- God loved Abraham, and blessed him and his descendants with covenants including entire nations of people, generations of kings, and the promise that God would use Abraham's people to bless all humanity.
- By covenant, God gave Moses and the Israelites redemption through commandments.
- David was given rest from his enemies, and promised that not only would God's love never be removed from him, but that his kingdom would endure forever through a covenant God ordained.
- Of course, Jesus himself is the fulfillment of the New Covenant: a high priest greater than Aaron, a king greater than Solomon, and the perfect sacrifice once for all.

In the same way God used the commitment of covenants as expressions of loving relationships, according to scripture, humans too used covenants as commitments to express love for one another.

For example, Jonathan loved David so much that scripture literally says that his very soul was joined with David's (1 Samuel 18:1), and Jonathan's response was to commit that his love would last forever. This was a covenant not only to David, but to God as well—a commitment scripture records that each man even affirmed with one another a second time (1 Samuel 20:16-17). Their commitment extended beyond the grave with the promise that their future generations would always remain at peace with one another.

Ruth made a covenant with her mother-in-law Naomi that "where you go, I will go, and where you stay I will stay. Your people will be my people and your God my God" (Ruth 1:16b, NIV). Like Jonathan, Ruth's covenant was not merely to Naomi, but to God too. And also as with Jonathan and David, Ruth promised her commitment even unto death (Ruth 1:16-18).

With each of these examples, just as how Adam saw Eve for how they were the same, these people loved someone else as they loved themselves. According to the synoptic gospels, Jesus paraphrased Leviticus and described loving your neighbor as yourself as like loving God above all else, that no other commandments are greater than these.

How can we "seek to do good" in loving relationships? *We love others as ourselves.*

Loving others as ourselves is the key to Christlike love—everything else depends upon it, and nothing should diminish it. This simple commandment should be the guiding theology behind how the church as a living body with the mind of Christ should interpret all relationships.

Unfortunately, many in the church have charted a different path. Somehow, we have culturally and theologically determined that the standard for loving relationships should be tethered to a *legal* definition—specifically marriage.

To be abundantly clear, nothing in scripture implies that marriage is bad or a faulty institution. But because marriage is intended to serve a legal rather than loving purpose, it remains a limited and ultimately inferior lens that is out of focus with Christ-minded loving relationships.

Historically, marriage was a legal framework to establish rights and responsibilities, and that is consistent with its presentation in scripture. Many biblical passages codify marriage and its purpose in ancient society; these topics range from establishing the legitimacy of children so they may receive an inheritance, or what distinguishes a wife from a concubine, to which household tasks women are obliged to undertake.

It is correct that in most antiquated cultures, marriage was an institution that legitimized ownership. That isn't a quality that should be romanticized in any way, and instead should be understood in terms of how men in those cultures considered wives as property. (Indeed, a Hebrew word we commonly translate in English as "husband" does technically mean "master.")

Of course, times have changed…right?

Laws are still how marriage is advanced in the church and in most cultures worldwide, for better or worse. For example, it was not until 1967 that the Supreme Court of the United States (SCOTUS) ruled that any law banning interracial marriage was unconstitutional. And while some may reason that laws are not truly driven by community standards, consider that Gallup found nationwide public support for interracial marriage rose from only 4% in 1958 to 94% in 2021, while the percentage of people who self-identify as Christian plummeted drastically over the same period.

Then there are many who rightly point out that the doctrine and polity of the Church is not bound by the laws of any nation. Unfortunately, the Church of the Nazarene has always considered marriage the biblical definition of loving relationships. This is backwards. Marriage should not define loving relationships—loving relationships should define marriage.

These words are not intended to dilute the institution of marriage, but to elevate marriage to the biblical standard of relational love: seeking to do good by loving one another as we love ourselves.

Well-intentioned denominational leaders have expressed great fear that society is challenging or redefining marriage, but the more we idolatrize marriage the less we demonstrate covenantal virtues of love.

On June 26, 2015, the SCOTUS ruled that the fundamental right to marry is guaranteed to same-sex couples, and required all states in the union to perform and recognize marriages of same-sex or opposite-sex couples. The very same day, the Board of General Superintendents of the Church of the Nazarene released a statement declaring that "divine truth has not changed" and stated that a life of holiness is "characterized by holy love and expressed through the most rigorous and consistent lifestyle of sexual purity."

By equating the legality of same-sex marriage with sexual impurity, our denomination reinforced the common perception that Christian evangelical denominations condemn homosexuality. To be clear, being heterosexual and married doesn't make your heart pure, the Holy Spirit does: this is the difference between theology and legalism.

It is not marriage that must be defended, but love in the face of human fear. "There is no fear in love, but perfect love drives out fear, because fear has to do with punishment. The one who fears is not made perfect in love" (1 John 4:18, NIV).

As a denomination, we betray our amazing heritage as pioneers in the theology of love when fears dictate doctrine instead of faith. It is time for us to defend relational love for the sake of unity in Christ.

In his letter to the Galatians, Paul wrote:

"Before the coming of this faith, we were held in custody under the law, locked up until the faith that was to come would be revealed. So the law was our guardian until Christ came that we might be justified by faith. Now that this faith has come, we are no longer under a guardian. So in Christ Jesus you are all children of God through faith, for all of you who were baptized into Christ have clothed yourselves with Christ. There is neither Jew nor Gentile, neither slave nor free, nor is there male and female, for you are all one in Christ Jesus." (Galatians 3:23-28, NIV)

If we are truly in Christ, every legalistic barrier must be toppled from the inside out. When we attempt to create any divisions within the church, we are not in Christ. If we are all one in Christ Jesus, there are no exceptions, no identities that may be excluded. In Christ, no one is too old, too young, the wrong race, or class, gender, pronoun, or sexual orientation.

Christ's standard of relational love must be applied consistently to every person and every part of scripture that would inform our doctrine and theology. It's more than understanding that the stories of Sodom and Gomorrah are about sexual violence, not same-sex attraction, and Levitical codes seeming to prohibit same-sex partnerships merely address fears regarding dying lineages and hygiene concerns in ancient times, or that every New Testament reference to what is called "homosexuality" in English translations actually condemns non-consensual acts between adults and children rather than adult same-sex intimacy.

The problem is so many in the church feel the need to determine what is and isn't sinful by codifying sexual immorality, because it is easier to talk and write about laws than it is to love and accept people you do not understand.

Divine truth really *hasn't* changed, but applying a theology of love can and should reorient our perspective of scriptural narratives in ways that challenge and grow us. For example, when held to the standard of "seeking to do good by loving one another as we love ourselves," many Old Testament depictions of sexuality seem abhorrent—such as Moses commanding his soldiers to kill all Midianites but spare female virgins for themselves, strongly implying sexual violence (Numbers 31), or the Israelites avenging the rape of a single woman by sanctioning the rape of six hundred more (Judges 19-21). In contrast, love does not dishonor others, is not easily angered, keeps no record of wrongs, and does not delight in evil.

Love is not self-seeking, but Lot's daughters got him drunk and raped him without his knowledge to preserve their family line (Genesis 19:30-36), and Tamar disguised herself as a prostitute to trade her father-in-law sex in exchange for a goat so she could secretly birth his heir and remain in the family (Genesis 38).

Love is patient, love is kind, it always protects, always trusts, and in "love stories" like Shechem and Dinah (Genesis 34) and Samson and Delilah (Judges 16), consent is utterly absent.

Tomes of laws and codes written before the birth of Christ do not keep us pure, nor do articles, statements, or press releases. The pursuit of such is madness and folly, a chasing of the wind, but *love never fails*. There is no substitute for covenantal love.

This love is not bound by law or tradition, gender, chromosomes, or pronouns. We love because God first loved us. He sees us, knows us, and loves us for who he made us to be: he sees our true colors, his love in us, beginning with the first humans, and what they saw in one another.

To accept relationship with Christ incarnationally is also accepting those he loves, those he calls his own, those who are known by his love. When we come to the table, we are connected to one another and to Christ by taking the bread and the cup, joining with him and one another as disciples in love.

It is the very mission of the Church of the Nazarene: to make Christlike disciples in the nations, to cultivate this loving connection we have with Christ in one another. This includes anyone at the table—even those we may not understand or agree with—seeking to do good by loving one another as we love ourselves. Jesus said this is like loving the Lord your God with all your heart and with all your soul and with all your mind.

This sacred connection of the bread and the cup we were created to share relationally has been forsaken by some. Many have found themselves at tables where their only mutual connections are fear and prejudice, tables that will eventually be overturned.

Every kingdom divided against itself will be destroyed, but Christ is not divided.

To truly all be one in Christ, we must comprehensively affirm the LGBTQ+ community. That is what Christlike relational love requires.

Our true colors are what we will be known by, and this is love.

James Travis Young is an ordained elder in the Church of the Nazarene making Christlike disciples alongside his wife, Mandie, in Galveston, Texas. A lifelong Nazarene, Travis has served in several active ministry roles including pastor, church planter, and teacher, and his writing has been featured in several publications.

Appendix

Glossary of Terms

This list of terms was adapted from The Safe Zone Project. To see the full list of terms, as well as a list of LGBTQ-Inclusive Language Dos and Don'ts, visit TheSafeZoneProject.com.

ally—a (typically straight and/or cisgender) person who supports and respects members of the LGBTQ community. We consider people to be active allies who take action on in support and respect.

asexual—experiencing little or no sexual attraction to others and/or a lack of interest in sexual relationships/behavior. Asexuality exists on a continuum from people who experience no sexual attraction or have any desire for sex, to those who experience low levels, or sexual attraction only under specific conditions. Sometimes abbreviated to "ace."

biological sex—a medical term used to refer to the chromosomal, hormonal and anatomical characteristics that are used to classify an individual as female or male or intersex. Often referred to as simply "sex," "physical sex," "anatomical sex," or specifically as "sex assigned at birth."

biphobia—a range of negative attitudes (e.g., fear, anger, intolerance, invisibility, resentment, erasure, or discomfort) that one may have or express toward bisexual individuals. Biphobia can come from and be seen within the LGBTQ community as well as straight society.

bisexual—a person who experiences attraction to some people of their gender and another gender. Bisexual attraction does not have to be equally split, or indicate a level of interest that is the same across the genders an individual may be attracted to. Often used interchangeably with "pansexual".

cisgender—a gender description for when someone's sex assigned at birth and gender identity correspond in the expected way (e.g., someone who was assigned male at birth, and identifies as a man). A simple way to think about it is if a person is not transgender, they are cisgender. The word cisgender can also be shortened to "cis."

coming out—the process by which one accepts and/or comes to identify one's own sexuality or gender identity (to "come out" to oneself). Also, the process by which one shares one's sexuality or gender identity with others.

gay—experiencing attraction solely (or primarily) to some members of the same gender. Can be used to refer to men who are attracted to other men and women who are attracted to women. Also, an umbrella term used to refer to the queer community as a whole, or as an individual identity label for anyone who is not straight.

gender expression—the external display of one's gender, through a combination of clothing, grooming, demeanor, social behavior, and other factors, generally made sense of on scales of masculinity and femininity. Also referred to as "gender presentation."

gender identity—the internal perception of an one's gender, and how they label themselves, based on how much they align or don't align with what they understand their options for gender to be. Often conflated with biological sex, or sex assigned at birth.

heteronormativity—the assumption, in individuals and/or in institutions, that everyone is heterosexual and that heterosexuality is superior to all other sexualities. Leads to invisibility and stigmatizing of other sexualities: when learning a woman is married, asking her what her *husband's* name is. Heteronormativity also leads us to assume that only masculine men and feminine women are straight.

homophobia—an umbrella term for a range of negative attitudes (e.g., fear, anger, intolerance, resentment, erasure, or discomfort) that one may have toward LGBTQ people. The term can also connote a fear, disgust, or dislike of being perceived as LGBTQ.

homosexual—a person primarily emotionally, physically, and/or sexually attracted to members of the same sex/gender. This [medical] term is considered stigmatizing (particularly as a noun, i.e. "homosexuals") due to its history as a category of mental illness, and is discouraged for common use. Use gay, lesbian, queer, or LGBTQ instead.

intersex—a term for a combination of chromosomes, gonads, hormones, internal sex organs, and genitals that differs from the two expected patterns of male or female. Formerly known as hermaphrodite (or hermaphroditic), but these terms are now outdated and derogatory.

lesbian—women who are primarily attracted romantically, erotically, and/or emotionally to other women.

LGBTQ—shorthand or umbrella term for all folks who have a non-normative (or queer) gender or sexuality. LGBTQ is Lesbian Gay Bisexual Transgender and Queer and/or Questioning. Sometimes I for Intersex and A for Asexual are included, and a plus sign (+) may be added to indicate the broad range of queer identities included in the term.

nonbinary—a gender identity label often used by people who do not identify with the binary of man/woman. An umbrella term for many gender non-conforming identities (e.g., agender, bigender, genderqueer, genderfluid).

pansexual—a person who experiences sexual, romantic, physical, and/or spiritual attraction for members of all gender identities/expressions. Often shortened to "pan."

queer—an umbrella term to describe individuals who don't identify as straight and/or cisgender. Historically a slur used to refer to someone who isn't straight and/or cisgender. Due to its historical use as a derogatory term, and how it is still used as a slur many communities, it is not embraced or used by all LGBTQ people. The term "queer" can often be used interchangeably with LGBTQ (e.g., "queer people" instead of "LGBTQ people").

sexual orientation—the type of sexual, romantic, emotional/spiritual attraction one has the capacity to feel for some others, generally labeled based on the gender relationship between the person and the people they are attracted to. Often confused with sexual preference.

straight—a person primarily emotionally, physically, and/or sexually attracted to some people who are not their same-sex/gender. A more colloquial term for the word heterosexual.

transgender—an umbrella term for anyone whose sex assigned at birth and gender identity do not correspond in the expected way (e.g., someone who was assigned male at birth, but does not identify as a man). Also, a gender description for someone who has transitioned (or is transitioning) from living as one gender to another.

transphobia—the fear of, discrimination against, or hatred of trans people, the trans community, or gender ambiguity. Transphobia can be seen within the queer community, as well as in general society.

Further Resources

Thanks to Kara Hudson for her help in compiling these resources.

Books

Braving the Wilderness: The Quest for True Belonging and the Courage to Stand Alone—Brené Brown
- Penguin Random House, LLC: New York, New York. (2017).

"Thou Shalt Not Love": What Evangelicals Really Say to Gays—Patrick M. Chapman
- Haiduk Press, LLC: New Rochelle, New York. (2001).

Lesbian, Gay, and Bisexual Identities Over the Lifespan—Anthony R. D'Augelli and Charlotte J. Patterson
- Oxford University Press: New York, New York. (1995).

Coming Out: An Act of Love: An Inspiring Call to Action for Gay Men, Lesbians, and Those Who Care—Rob Eichberg
- Penguin Group, Penguin Books, USA, INC: New York, New York. (1991).

Love Does No Harm: Sexual Ethics for the Rest of Us—Marie M. Fortune
- The Continuum Publishing Company: New York, New York. (1995).

What the Bible Really Says About Homosexuality—Daniel Helminiak
- Alamo Square Press: Estancia, New Mexico. (1994).

Beyond the Darkness: Recovery for Adult Victims of Sexual Abuse—Cynthia A. Kubetin and James Mallory
- Rapha Publishing/Word, Inc.: Houston and Dallas, TX. (1992).

Taking a Chance on God: Liberating Theology for Gays, Lesbians, and their Lovers, Families, and Friends—John J. McNeil
- Beacon Press: Boston, Massachusetts. (1988*).*

The Church and The Homosexual,—John J. McNeil
- *Fourth Edition.* Beacon Press: Boston, Massachusetts. (1993).

Jesus, the Bible, and Homosexuality: Explode the Myths, Heal the Church—Jack Rogers
- Westminster John Knox Press: Louisville, Kentucky. (2006*).*

Stranger At the Gate: To Be Gay and Christian in America—Mel White
- Penguin Group, Penguin Books, USA, Inc: New York, New York. (1995).

Articles

"Implementing Trauma-Focused Cognitive Behavior Therapy for LGBTQ Youth and Their Caregivers"—Judith Cohen, Anthony Mannarino, Kelly Wilson, and Arturo Zinny
- Allegheny Health Network: Pittsburgh, Pennsylvania. https://familyproject.sfsu. edu/sites/default/files/documents/TF-CBT%20LGBT%20Implementation%20 Manual_v1.pdf (2018).

"Part 2: Sexual and Gender Minorities: The Trauma-Focused CBT and Family Acceptance Project: An Integrated Framework for children and Youth"—Judith Cohen and Caitlin Ryan
- *Psychiatric Times*, TM. 38 (6). (June 2021).

"Generating a Revolution in Prevention, Wellness and Care for LGBT Children and Youth"—Caitlin Ryan
- *Temple Political and Civil Rights Law Review,* 23(2): 331-344. https://familyproject.sfsu.edu/sites/default/files/documents/Ryanc_Wellness %2CPrevention%20%26%20Care%20for%20LGBT%20Youth-fn.pdf (2014).

"Family Rejection as a Predictor of Negative Health Outcomes in White and Latino Lesbian, Gay, and Bisexual Young Adults."—Caitlin Ryan, David Huebner, Rafael M. Diaz, and Jorge Sanchez
- *Pediatrics* 123 (1): 346-352. https://publications.aap.org/pediatrics/article-abstract/123/1/346/71912/Family-Rejection-as-a-Predictor-of-Negative-Health?redirectedFrom=fulltext?autologincheck=redirected (January 1, 2009)

Digital

Family Video Series from the Family Acceptance Project
- San Francisco State University: San Francisco, CA. https://familyproject.sfsu.edu/ family-videos.

"A Practitioner's Resource Guide: Helping Families to Support Their LGBT Children" from the Substance Abuse and Mental Health Services Administration

- HHS Publication No. PEP14-LGBTKIDS. Rockville, MD: Substance Abuse and Mental Health Services Administration, 2014. https://store.samhsa.gov/sites/default/files/d7/priv/pep14-lgbtkids.pdf

"Renounce and Announce (feat. Jacqui Lewis)" from the podcast *Learning How to See* with Brian McClaren

- https://cac.org/podcasts/renounce-and-announce-feat-jacqui-lewis/ (March 10, 2023).

Thomas Jay Oord's Response to Accusations Brought by Signatories Outside the Intermountain District but Reformulated by an Intermountain District Board

THOMAS JAY OORD

What follows are my responses to questions listed at the conclusion of this document. The questions were formulated by a committee from the Church of the Nazarene's Intermountain District after considering six broad accusations against me made by a group of 10 or so signatories. The people in this accusing group are not members of the Intermountain District but sent their accusations to District Superintendent Scott Shaw. After he talked with General Superintendent Fili Chambo, Shaw moved forward with the proceedings.

Superintendent Shaw met with me in November 2021 to relay the original charges. He explained the process and asked what I wanted to do. I said I would face the accusations and undergo the hearing/trial as laid out in the Manual. Superintendent Shaw said he'd choose the committee to hear my case, evaluate my written response, and receive my verbal defense on a date to be determined. He thereafter assembled a district committee and appointed Assistant District Superintendent Brent Deakins as the chair.

To my mind, the charges against me divide into two parts. One part is theological. The other is about social ethics, specifically the denomination's stance on Lesbian, Gay, Bisexual, Transgender, and Queer (LGBTQ) people outlined in Covenant of Christian Conduct in "Human Sexuality and Marriage."

The committee assigned to my case wisely set aside most theological charges leveled by the accusing group. Those charges revealed a lack of understanding of how the Wesleyan-holiness tradition thinks about salvation, God's love, other religious traditions, and more. The accusing signatories fail to understand the range of acceptable beliefs in the Wesleyan-holiness tradition and the Church of the Nazarene.

Because I consider the theological charges without basis, I'll address them first and rather briefly. I'll deal with questions about LGBTQ people and the denomination's view of Human Sexuality and Marriage later. I regard the latter issues as the primary reasons I am undergoing this hearing/trial. Those issues provide an opportunity to explain the meaning and primacy of love in the Wesleyan-holiness theology that undergirds the Church of the Nazarene.

Theological Concerns

- The Church of the Nazarene's Articles of Faith

I appreciate, embrace, affirm, and endorse the Articles of Faith in the Church of the Nazarene.

Occasionally, I am asked why I chose to be ordained in the Church of the Nazarene and choose to remain thirty years after my ordination ceremony. I respond that I'm compelled by the Wesleyan theology undergirding the denomination's articles of faith. No set of statements can perfectly express all one wants to say about God, of course, and the articles are constantly being revised. I appreciate, embrace, affirm, and endorse the Articles of Faith in the Church of the Nazarene. I have no issues with them and see my views as aligned with the articles.

Part of question three below asks, "How do you deal with any discrepancies between your teaching (in public comments, blog posts, conference speaking engagements, etc.) and your harmonious support of the Church of the Nazarene Articles of Faith?" In my view, there are no discrepancies, so I regard the question as misinformed.

My accusers apparently interpret the articles differently than I do. My beliefs and teachings do not align with their views. But I do not see my teaching as leading to discrepancies about valid interpretations of the articles. And many scholars in the Church of the Nazarene interpret the articles in the way I do, especially those with extensive theological education.

I believe my accusers do not sufficiently understand what it means to embrace the Wesleyan-holiness theology that undergirds the Articles of Faith in the Church of the Nazarene. For example, I make statements about truth in other religious traditions that trouble my accusers. Our Wesleyan theology of prevenient grace, however, supports God's work in religions other than Christianity. The beauty of the Wesleyan tradition is it's understanding that God's love and truth aren't reserved for just a few; they are available to all. I consider the claims of Christianity, however, more true and more winsome than those of other religious traditions.[1] That's the major reason I choose to be a Christian.

Or take my view of the afterlife. My accusers apparently do not understand my stance on this subject and have consequently misrepresented me. They seem not to realize the possibility that no one will be "finally impenitent," to use the statement in the Manual. Wesleyan-holiness people believe God wants to save all. I reject the idea that God *forces everyone* into heaven. I'm not what many call a "classic universalist," because of my view of creaturely freedom, another Wesleyan emphasis. Scripture and the Manual leave open the possibility that God's love will ultimately redeem all creatures through loving persuasion. The Church of the Nazarene is optimistic about the power of God's grace.[2]

- Believing God Exists

I believe God exists. I'm exceedingly surprised by this question.

I'm not certain God exists, however. I doubt anyone can be 100% certain, although I admit some people claim to be. Even if certainty about God's existence is possible, the Manual doesn't require anyone to attain this state of confidence.

Throughout history, Christians have typically steered clear of claiming to be certain about God. We talk instead about having *faith*. Christians are believers, not "certainers," to coin a word.

I don't advocate blind faith, however, and I often argue against it. There are good reasons to believe God exists. The phrases I use to describe my stance are that I "reasonably trust" God exists or think God's existence is "more plausible than not." Those phrases, in my way of thinking, point to good arguments, evidence, and experiences that indicate God exists… requiring no one to be certain.

Incidentally, most people I talk to about this issue find immense encouragement after hearing they can have genuine doubts about God and yet be faithfully Christian. My statement, "I'm not certain," offers them hope. They're relieved to discover Phineas Bresee's words that "Faith isn't the absence of doubt; it's choosing to believe, despite doubt."[3]

---

1. For details on my view of God's loving revelation to all creatures, see Thomas Jay Oord, *The Uncontrolling Love of God* (Downers Grove, Ill: Intervarsity Academic, 2015).
2. For details on my view of the afterlife, see Thomas Jay Oord, *Questions and Answers for God Can't* (SacraSage, 2020).
3. I explain myself on these matters in a book I co-edited called *Postmodern and Wesleyan?* published by the Nazarene Publishing House. Instead of cutting and pasting paragraphs here, see my essay, "Truth and Postmodernism," among others.

• Jesus and God

Christians have throughout the centuries tried to discern how to make sense of Jesus' relation to God. Some scripture passages say Jesus has a unique relationship with the One he calls "Abba." Biblical writers, over and again, say Jesus reveals God, and I strongly affirm this. In this sense, I believe Jesus is divine. I stand with scripture and the Manual.

We Christians have various theories for why Jesus did not have the attributes we think characterize God. One that I've cited in many writings says those attributes were set aside in the incarnation. Often, Philippians 2 is the basis for this theory, and I've written extensively about this. It fits what I and other scholars call a "Spirit Christology:" Jesus responded perfectly to the Spirit and revealed God's nature of love.[4] A Trinitarian model that says God is revealed in Jesus makes the most sense to me.

Nearly all Christians think God is omnipresent and omniscient, by which we mean God is present to all creation and God knows all that's possible to know. But Jesus clearly was not omnipresent. And he lacked complete knowledge, illustrated by the questions he often asked and statements made (e.g., "Who touched me?" "No one knows the day and hour, except the Father"). Simply saying "Jesus is God" can be easily interpreted as meaning Jesus was also omnipresent or omniscient, which, according to the Bible, he was not.

I don't recall the specifics of the conversation with Michael McElyea noted in question 4c below. I suspect my point in the exchange was simply to say that while Jesus reveals God, he did not have *all* the attributes many Christians claim God has. But more importantly, I see no conflict between my views and the Manual's statements on Jesus.

I affirm the Article of Faith on Jesus.

Sexuality Concerns

I have for decades worked for changes in the Church of the Nazarene's statements on LGBTQ people, their identities, and sexual practices. In my view, the denominational statements do not reflect well the love at the heart of Wesleyan-holiness theology. I was happy about the progress made in the recent General Assembly

---

4. For more on this, see my essay, "Essential Kenosis Christology," in *Christology: From the Wesleys to the Twenty-first Century,* Jason Vicker and Jerome Van Kuiken, eds. (Nashville: Wesley's Foundry Books, 2020) and my book, *The Uncontrolling Love of God* (Downers Grove, Ill.: IVP Academic, 2015).

rewriting of the "Marriage and Sexuality" statement. But I believe more changes are needed.

My desire to see changes in the Manual comes from my love for God, for members of the Church of the Nazarene, for LGBTQ people, and for the friends and family of LGBTQ people. I think God is pleased by healthy LGBTQ sexual practices and God affirms nonheteronormative identities. I think the Church of the Nazarene ought to imitate God's love by being pleased in the same way.

I am one among a sizable number of members of the Church of the Nazarene who are LGBTQ affirming. I say a "sizable number" because I don't know the exact total. Most affirming members are reluctant to say so in public, although many divulge their beliefs to me in private. By "LGBTQ affirming," I mean many members of the Church of the Nazarene believe non-heterosexual (e.g., Lesbian, Gay, Bisexual, Transgender, and Queer) orientation, identity, and sexual behavior (expressed in a covenant relationship) are compatible with authentic Christian faith.

As evidence for this claim, I rely upon the Pew Research Center. A 2007 Pew poll showed that 31% of those who identify with the Church of the Nazarene thought society should accept homosexuality. That percentage jumped to 40% by 2014.[5] I suspect the percentage is higher today, but Pew has not released current numbers.

Assuming the USA Church of the Nazarene has around 600,000 members, the Pew polls suggest that 200,000+ US Nazarenes hold views about LGBTQ matters similar to mine. From my conversations with pastors and laity on the Intermountain District, I believe the percentage of affirming people on the district is higher. Even if these polls and estimates are off several percentage points, it remains the case that a sizable number of members of the denomination think society should accept LGBTQ people and their behaviors. Every person I know who thinks society should accept LGBTQ also thinks the denomination should accept it. They have the same standard for love in the church and society.

A Barna Report indicates that 46% of practicing Christians under the age of 40 want more laws to protect Same-Sex Marriage and LGBTQ rights.[6] This is not the same as saying LGBTQ is compatible with Christian faith, of course, but most who want protections and rights are also LGBTQ affirming. In other words, they think about these matters much like I do. The two major takeaways from that Barna report are 1) American Christians are becoming increasingly accepting of

---

5. See https://www.pewresearch.org/fact-tank/2015/12/18/most-u-s-christian-groups-grow-more-accepting-of-homosexuality/

6. See https://www.barna.com/research/americas-change-of-mind-on-same-sex-marriage-and-lgbtq-rights/

LGBTQ people and their sexual behavior, and 2) younger American Christians are more accepting than older Americans.

Based on the Pew and Barna polls and my own interactions, I suspect most US Nazarene youth want the Church of the Nazarene's views on LGBQT issues to change. And from my time speaking in Europe, I believe the percentage of European Nazarene youth who want change is even higher. If the views of the young eventually become the views of the majority, the Church of the Nazarene will undergo change in the coming decades. We have revised many topics in the Covenant of Christian Conduct over the past century; we should expect and welcome changes related to LGBTQ issues.

My experience speaking at nearly every Church of the Nazarene higher educational institution in the US and many Nazarene institutions overseas tells me that most university students and faculty are LGBTQ affirming. Many talk to me about these matters in private, fearing accusations and the treatment I'm currently undergoing. They want a safe forum without fear of reprisal to make their case for full LGBTQ inclusion in the Church of the Nazarene.[7]

Should I Stay Or Should I Go?

Many people—especially young people and including some pastors—leave the Church of the Nazarene because of its current stance on LGBTQ people. A 2008 poll of twenty religions/denominations said the holiness tradition—of which the Church of the Nazarene is the largest denomination—is the *worst* of all religious groups at retaining young people. Only 32% of Nazarene youth remain with the denomination.[8] A similar poll in 2015 showed no change in this rate of exit.[9]

Some members who want changes on LGBTQ issues ask my advice on whether they should stay or leave. I counsel them on a case-by-case basis. Some leave to become Methodists, Lutherans, Episcopalians, or something else. I respect their decisions, and I wish them well.

Some stay. Despite thinking the denomination's view of human sexuality is unloving, unbiblical, or just out of touch, some LGBTQ-affirming youth, pastors,

---

7. The call for safe and irenic discussion of LGBTQ issues is also present among Church of the Nazarene clergy. See the doctoral work of Reg Watson on this matter (R. G. Watson, Nazarene Clergy Responses to Homosexuality and Interactions with LGBT People [Doctoral dissertation, Regent University, 2015], 123, 125, 279, 317).

8. See http://thomasjayoord.com/index.php/blog/archives/atheists_only_slightly_worse_at_retaining_children_than_holiness_folk

9. See https://www.pewforum.org/2015/05/12/chapter-2-religious-switching-and-intermarriage/pr_15-05-12_rls_chapter2-04/

scholars, and leaders remain with the Church of the Nazarene. I respect those decisions too.

Why do some stay, despite disagreeing with the Manual on LGBTQ matters? Here are the reasons I often hear…

1. Family and Friendship

Many LGBTQ-affirming members of the denomination have strong friendship and family ties to people in the Church of the Nazarene. Rather than think beliefs and rules are primary for membership, they think of the denomination as a family or intimate community. As you know, this way of thinking about the church has strong biblical support.

This approach assumes people are more important than rules. Besides, do you leave a family just because other members hold beliefs that you don't… especially when *so many* of your siblings believe as you do? Friendship and family are more important than rules and regulations.

2. Changing Groups

Some who remain are students of denominational history. The Church of the Nazarene has changed its views on many issues, especially issues in the Code of Christian Conduct. Divorce is now considered appropriate in some cases, for instance, although it's still mentioned in the Code alongside same-sex marriage. Jewelry is commonplace today, but was once condemned. Few members today think twice about going to the theater or circus, but these practices were forbidden in the 1928 Manual. The denomination has changed its mind on dancing, movies, and many other topics in the Covenant of Christian Conduct.

Denominational leaders also realize context matters. In some African contexts, we tolerate polygamy among Church of the Nazarene members. In some European contexts, members consume alcohol with no fear of repercussion. Divorce no longer carries the stigma among US Nazarenes it once did.

Groups change, including denominational groups. Why think the Church of the Nazarene will keep its current stance on LGBTQ? We made positive strides at the recent General Assembly to alter the denomination's official view. But we need more changes for the Church of the Nazarene to become fully LGBTQ affirming. Many stay expecting that eventually change will come, hopefully sooner rather than later. The optimism of grace leads me to believe the denomination will eventually see that love calls it to embrace and affirm LGBTQ people.

3. Loving Experience

Others believe the denomination's theology implies that LGBTQ people and their loving practices ought to be affirmed. Like me, some cite love as the core of the holiness message. Others consider religious experience vital for discerning authentic Christian faith. They know LGBTQ people who have vibrant Christian testimonies.

Those who oppose LGBTQ people and activity often reference seven or eight biblical verses to support their view. Biblical scholars, theologians, and Christian ethicists have written massive tomes on this material. Many argue those verses either apply to ancient practices not identical to contemporary LGBTQ issues or those verses reflect cultural biases of their day. The biblical witness to sex and marriage is complex.[10]

Many people in the Church of the Nazarene already endorse this general approach to biblical interpretation when defending the full status of women in ministry. In fact, we could cite more biblical passages that relegate women to sub-servient roles than verses condemning LGBTQ people and behavior. And yet the Church of the Nazarene rightly privileges scriptures that support full status for women in ministry and equality in marriage.[11] Many of the passages cited call for love and equality for *all* people. Love and lived experience matter, and we should use this hermeneutic for LGBTQ concerns.

---

10. Among the helpful books and essays on this subject, see Cheryl B. Anderson, *Ancient Laws and Contemporary Controversies: The Need for Inclusive Biblical Interpretation* (Oxford University Press 2009); John Boswell, *Christianity, Social Tolerance, and Homosexuality* (University of Chicago Press, 1980); James V. Brownson, *Bible, Gender, Sexuality: Reframing the Church's Debate on Same-Sex Relationships* (William B. Eerdmans, 2013); Elizabeth M. Edman, *Queer Virtue: What LGBTQ People Know about Life and Love and How it Can Revitalize Christianity* (Beacon, 2016); Richard Elliott Friedman and Shawna Dolansky, eds. *The Bible Now: Homosexuality, Abortion, Women, Death Penalty, Earth* (Oxford: Oxford University Press, 2011); Victor Paul Furnish, "Homosexuality?" in *The Moral Teaching of Paul: Selected Issues*, 3rd ed. (Nashville: Abingdon, 2009), 55-93; David Gushee, *Changing Our Minds*, 2nd ed. (Spirit Books, 2015); Karen R. Keen, *Scripture, Ethics, and the Possibility of Same-Sex Relationships* (William B. Eerdmans, 2018); Craig S. Keener, *Romans: A New Covenant Commentary* (Cascade, 2009); Colby Martin, *Unclobber: Rethinking Our Misuse of the Bible On Homosexuality* (Westminster John Knox, 2016); Dale B. Martin, *Sex and the Single Savior* (Westminster John Knox, 2006); Russell Pregeant, *Engaging the New Testament* (Minneapolis: Fortress, 1995); Eugene F. Rogers, "Same-sex Complementarity: A Theology of Marriage" (The Christian Century, 2011); Robin Scroggs, *The New Testament and Homosexuality* (Philadelphia: Fortress, 1983); Matthew Vines, *God and The Gay Christian: The Biblical Case in Support of Same-Sex Relationships* (Convergent, 2014).

11. On the role culture plays in discerning LGBTQ matters, see Rev. Bruce Barnard, "Cognitive Dissonance and the Progression of the Church on Major Cultural Norms," (DMin, George Fox University, 2016).

The Theological Difference

Other members of the Church of the Nazarene ask me if they should leave because of theological differences with the denomination. Those differences are not with the Human Sexuality and Marriage statements; they disagree with the Articles of Faith. I tell them the articles were not handed down from heaven, and each allows for a range of interpretation. The articles have also changed over time, at least to some degree. Articles 15 and 16 are currently going through a major overhaul, and the future will bring more changes.

Many say their theological views differ drastically from the articles. Some believe, for instance, the denomination's view on biblical inerrancy is too soft. They want a Manual statement that affirms absolute biblical inerrancy. Others think the Articles are at odds with the sovereignty of God. They believe God is in control and we have no freedom to do other than what God decides. Some think the Articles of Faith are wrong about hell, original sin, women in ministry, sanctification as transformation, or something else.

In these conversations, I realize some members of the denomination actually want a Calvinist or Catholic theology. Or something else. So I lovingly tell them to consider joining another community.

Am I wrong to encourage some to leave but encourage some LGBTQ-affirming members to stay?

I don't think so. As I see it, the essential theology of the Church of the Nazarene is compatible with believing LGBTQ people are welcome in the denomination. Here's what I mean:

The core of our holiness message is love. "Love" doesn't mean, "we accept any behavior or beliefs whatsoever." It means we want the well-being of others. We seek the transformation of ourselves and all creation. Some LGBTQ behavior—including same-sex marriage—can promote well-being. It's good and healthy; it represents the values of the Kingdom of God. The transformation God desires rarely if ever requires LGBTQ people to change their sexual orientation, identity, or loving behavior.

Let me put this another way: LGBTQ people can live Christlike lives. Some of the most loving people I know are not heteronormative. Living Christlike lives is the holiness gospel, and some LGBTQ people act like Christ. They love like Jesus loved. And their identity or behavior as LGBTQ people is not an obstacle to their being Christlike.

Love calls us to be faithful in our partnering commitments. Those who commit to monogamy—whether heterosexual or same-sex marriage—are called to be faithful to God, their partner, and the Kingdom. If the Church of the Nazarene—as people who seek purity—wants to encourage loving faithfulness and discourage promiscuity, it ought to endorse same-sex marriage. The denomination also ought to lead the way in advocating for transgender people. It ought to recognize the variation of attraction experienced by bisexual people. And so on.

As those who care for the marginalized, Nazarenes ought to be allies for LGBTQ people rather than adversaries.

My Role as a Licensed Minister and Thought Leader

Some questions at the conclusion of this document come from the district committee and not from the original charges against me. These questions pertain to how I see my role as an acting minister and thought leader in the Church of the Nazarene.

One set of questions asks about officiating same-sex marriages. Given what I've said above, it will come as no surprise that I look forward to the day the denomination endorses same-sex marriage. If members of the Church of the Nazarene truly believe in sexual purity, they ought to encourage lifelong sexual partnerships in marriage. The holiness message ought to compel members of the denomination to support same-sex marriage.

I have never officiated a same-sex marriage, and I have no plans to do so. But if one of my daughters was a lesbian and wanted me to officiate her marriage to her lesbian partner, I'd do it in a heartbeat. If needed, I'd officiate the ceremony as a layperson and ask the couple to get an official marriage endorsement from a state official. But I love my children and think this love far exceeds any commitment I have to a statement in the Covenant of Christian Conduct I think needs changing. I hope all clergy would privilege love for their children over denominational rules, even if it comes at personal cost. And if they would, they likely understand much of the LGBTQ logic I'm presenting here.

I do *not* think ordained elders should surrender their credentials if they officiate a same-sex wedding. Our allegiance is first to God and the love to which God calls. But because most members in the Church of the Nazarene currently do not think about same-sex weddings the way I do, I'd encourage the Nazarene elder who wants to officiate a same-sex ceremony to do so and subsequently have it endorsed by some other person or agency. Or do so with a minister of another Christian denomination. I give this advice with a sad heart, however, believing that on this issue, those outside the Church of the Nazarene are more in tune with the Spirit's leading.

The final set of questions asks about my personal beliefs and the denomination's. It asks if I support the denomination and whether I'm in "hearty accord" with the statement on human sexuality. I strongly support the denomination; I love the people who comprise this community. I've given much of my time, emotional energy, and resources to help the Church of the Nazarene broadly and to help individual members specifically. To use the language of the Apostle Paul, I have "poured myself out" sacrificially for this body of believers.

I heartily support and believe myself to be in accord with the Articles of Faith. But I think the denomination's statement of human sexuality should evolve. I will continue working to see changes made. That will mean speaking against current denominational practices and ideas I believe are not aligned with our core theology of love. I expect all people associated with the Church of the Nazarene—whether they are ordained or not—to place their allegiance with the God of love and see allegiance to the Church of the Nazarene as secondary. God and denomination are not identical.

I would also expect people who disagree with the Covenant of Christian Conduct to do so respectfully. And to be discerning in how they disagree. I don't claim to have always been wise, but I feel good about most of my speech and activities. I commit myself to working for change in wise and loving ways. I aim to love in word and deed.

The Process of Change in the Church of the Nazarene

In 2007, I gave a plenary paper at Northwest Nazarene University's Wesley Center Conference. The paper was titled, "Revisioning Article X: Fifteen Changes in the Church of the Nazarene's Article on Entire Sanctification." In my presentation and the paper that circulated widely thereafter, I suggested both major and minor changes to the denomination's views on sanctification.

No one brought me up on charges. No one thought I was a heretic or was teaching false doctrine when I suggested *fifteen* changes to the article widely regarded as the denomination's distinctive doctrine. In fact, many fellow scholars applauded my suggestions, while suggesting changes of their own or noting differences in nuance. An official denominational committee formed soon thereafter, and years later, several of my suggested changes occurred.

Before this event, I suggested a change to Article I in the Manual, the article on the doctrine of God. I suggested we should add a statement about God's love. My suggestion made its way through the system and now is part of the official statement. Again, no one brought me up on charges for thinking the Articles of Faith needed changing.

To be clear, I'm not claiming I *alone* orchestrated these changes to the Manual. Others played key roles; it takes a community. But I bring up these examples to note that even with the Articles of Faith—which are widely thought *essential* rather than nonessential like the Covenant of Christian Conduct—differences of opinion can lead to changes in denomination's official views. Someone—or many someones—initiates conversations leading to those changes.

It's also important to note that not *all* of my proposed changes were accepted. But no one said, "the new Manual doesn't reflect *everything* Tom suggested, so he should leave." Nor did I feel compelled to abandon the denomination. Apparently, differences of opinion are acceptable for the Articles of Faith. How much more should a difference of opinion be acceptable to the denomination's Covenant of Christian Conduct? While Covenant issues are important, they are *not* essential.

Far better to follow the advice of Phineas Bresee and many others: "On essentials, we seek unity. On nonessentials, we allow freedom. In all things, we seek to love."

How Does Change Come?

According to the polls I've cited and my experience, a huge number of Church of the Nazarene members agree with me. Probably hundreds of thousands. But the majority do not. Some districts or world regions are more "progressive" on this issue. But the majority currently does not think like me and many, many others.

If the change I want to see is to become a reality, how will that occur? What brings people to change their minds about LGBTQ people and issues to endorse views like mine?

Most people who change their minds do not suddenly realize the few biblical passages that directly pertain to same-sex relations don't apply today. Change rarely comes through biblical argumentation, as important as scripture is.

Change comes when people we know well—our children, best friends, or family members—"come out" as lesbian, gay, bisexual, transgender, queer, or something similar. Close relationships also lead many to realize LGBTQ identity, attractions, and behaviors can be healthy and loving. A growing number of members of the Church of the Nazarene are experiencing these perspective-changing encounters with family and friends.

Others change their minds on issues of human sexuality when they spend time with LGBTQ Christians who love like Jesus. These people may not be family members or friends, but they clearly live lives of love. "The proof of the pudding is in the eating," says the adage, and the proof is that many LGBTQ people live fruitful lives of the Spirit. They are transformed into the image of the invisible God.

When I think of those people in my own life, friends like Alicia, Carol, Cindy, David, Dwayne, Flora, Fraser, Gary, Isaac, John, Jordan, Lisa, Manuel, Matthew,

Michael, Monica, Scott, Susie, Tim, Tyler, and more come to mind. LGBTQ people show evidence of the gifts of ministry, pastoral leadership, and general good works in the world.

Still others change their minds on intellectual grounds. That's how I changed my mind. Through a study of scripture, theology, science, and more, some people come to realize traditional binary views of human sexuality do not apply to all people. It's no minor point that the consensus opinion in psychology and other human sciences is that LGBTQ behavior can be healthy and life-giving.[12] Scientific consensus is on the side of people who think like me about LGBTQ issues. Those who point to examples of LGBTQ misbehavior—e.g., abuse, promiscuity, unsafe sex—often fail to note this misbehavior also occurs among heterosexuals.

What *won't* happen is that every single member of the Church of the Nazarene awakes one morning and simultaneously says, "we should change the statement on human sexuality and marriage today." Instead, change takes time. In the beginning, there are a few dissenters. Momentum builds. And eventually, the majority see the need to alter official statements. It's a process, and if the statistics I offered and my experiences are correct, the Church of the Nazarene is changing its views on LGBTQ issues.

In fact, change is already here. It's just that many members of the Church of the Nazarene are afraid to make the public statements I make. They know negative repercussions will probably come if they speak out or ask for civil conversation. But I predict many will become more vocal in the coming days. The issues at the heart of my case are likely to grow in importance.

Where Should We Go From Here?

I know the decisions this Intermountain District committee makes carry real and widespread consequences. If the committee endorses and wholeheartedly affirms what I say, those who believe traditional views about sexuality and marriage will be angry. Some may leave the denomination.

If the committee rejects what I say and votes to take my license, those who want change will be angry. Pastors and laity will leave the Church of the Nazarene. Others will go into hiding, fearing that speaking out will mean their trial and dismissal. Rejecting the way forward I have proposed—opening up a conversation about accepting people with LGBTQ identity, orientation, and loving sexual behaviors—means more Nazarene youth will leave.

---

12. I could cite numerous sources to support this claim. But here's a link to the American Psychological Association statements on LGBTQ issues https://www.apa.org/topics/lgbtq/

It's not too dramatic to say the denomination's future vitality is at stake.

I trust that those hearing my case will find my theological views within the spectrum of viable interpretations of the Articles of Faith. I certainly think they are, and so do many others.

Ideally, the committee would join me in seeking changes in the statement on Marriage and Human Sexuality. Even if committee members do not take a proactive approach to make changes, I hope they see the Covenant of Christian Conduct as a nonessential document. There is room for those who in good conscience and in the name of love disagree with the denomination's statement on marriage and human sexuality.

I hope the committee will also see the need for open conversations about LGBTQ issues. People want to speak freely and without fear of dismissal from their leadership roles or the denomination. My case could spark healthy discussions.[13]

Above all, I hope this committee will stand for what, in my mind, is the way of love.

Rev. Dr. Thomas Jay Oord (January 2022)

Questions for Dr. Thomas Jay Oord

1. Do you affirm and support the statement in the Nazarene manual on Human Sexuality and Marriage (31)?

   If not, what areas are of concern for you and why?

   If yes, help us understand how your statements in the evidence (Exhibit 1 & 4) and your personal beliefs about human sexuality are in harmony or are not in harmony with the doctrine of the Church of the Nazarene? Specifically, your comments stating:

   a. "I am one among those who thinks it (homosexual activity) is not always sinful" (Exhibit 1)

   b. When asked the question: "Should Ministers of the Church of the Nazarene should be allowed to marry LGBTQ couples?" You responded: "Yes on the first." Do you believe Nazarene ministers should be allowed to perform same-sex ceremonies? If you were asked to do a same-sex ceremony, would

---

13. I am grateful to wise friends who read previous drafts of this document and give helpful advice. Because some could receive criticism for being associated with me or this document, I'll not list their names. But I'm *deeply* grateful for their kindness, encouragement, and suggestions.

you do it? In your view, would performing a same-sex ceremony be a violation of the Church of the Nazarene beliefs and be cause for surrendering of ordination credentials? How are your publicly stated views and opinions concerning same-sex marriages consistent and in accord with the Church of the Nazarene statements on human sexuality?

2. What do you mean by "full inclusion" with your view and stance on same-sex sexuality? (Exhibit 1: "I am in favor of full inclusion of LGBTQ people...") For which of the following roles are you in favor of a same-sex sexually active person being eligible to serve in the Church of the Nazarene? As an Ordinated minister? As a non-ordained minister? As a member? In an elected Leadership position? As a lay teacher? As an attender? Other? Does your position on "full inclusion" also include marriage ceremonies bless and sanctioned by the Church of the Nazarene?

3. Do you affirm and support Articles 1-16 in the Nazarene manual?

   If not, what areas are of concern for you and why?

   If yes, how do you deal with any discrepancies between your teaching (in public comments, blog posts, conference speaking engagements, etc.) and your harmonious support of the Church of the Nazarene Articles of Faith?

4. Help us understand your statements on the certainty in the existence of God and your understanding of Articles 1, 2 and 3.

   a. Specifically you say in a blog "But I'm not 100% sure God exists..." (footnote 9 on pg. 5 of accusation document). Are you now certain in the existence of God as stated in Article 1, 2 and 3?

   b. Exhibit 5 "I know few scholars who think the only people who can rightly self-identify as Christians are those who think Jesus is God." Are you one of those scholars? If so, help us understand how someone can be a Christian without believing that Jesus is God. (Article 2)

   c. Do you remember or have documentation on the conversation in Exhibit 5 with Michael McElyea? His comment states that you told Michael that "you told me that you do not even believe that Jesus is God Himself." Does this comment accurately reflect what you said and what you believe personally? Or what did you mean by that implied statement? Do you believe that Jesus is God as stated in Article 2?

5. How do you differentiate your personal beliefs and role as an ordained minister in the Church of the Nazarene and your role as a teacher in the Church of the Nazarene? What responsibility do you have as a Nazarene minister supporting the Church of the Nazarene and respecting the office of an ordained elder for the public/online statements that you make? How do your public/online statements and teachings demonstrate that you are in hearty accord with the statements of the Church of the Nazarene on human sexuality?

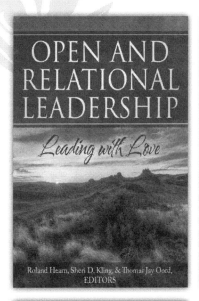
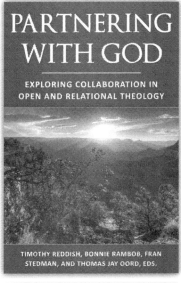
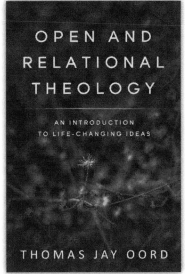
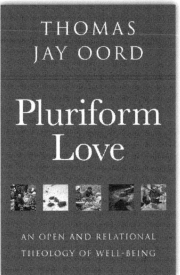

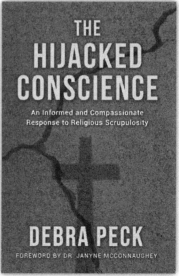

Made in the USA
Columbia, SC
10 February 2024

6b796586-fab8-4e00-b11b-ce27667118e7R01